MW00795763

New Directions in India's Foreign Policy

Since the Cold War, Indian foreign policy has witnessed a dramatic transformation. Though academic study of the subject has shown a degree of maturity, theoretical developments have been underwhelming. Scholars have introduced new concepts and examined Indian foreign policy through new prisms, but a cohesive research agenda has not yet been charted. This volume intends to fill that void. It brings together cutting-edge research at both theoretical and empirical levels with the aim of shaping the foreign policy discourse of one of the most important players in global politics.

The volume focuses on key concepts and issues which are shaping the trajectory of the study of Indian foreign policy. New concepts such as 'constructivism' and 'territoriality' are explored to assess what value they add to the academic study on Indian foreign policy, and discussions on 'Indo-Pacific' and 'Responsibility to Protect' help readers in understanding the broadening horizons of the field.

Issues that have been studied less but have the potential to significantly alter the trajectory of Indian foreign policy studies are the focus of this volume. The first section examines the conceptual and theoretical advancements, and the second section is devoted to emerging themes in the practice of Indian foreign policy. The chapters provide detailed discussions of concepts and themes under consideration and situate them in the wider context of Indian foreign policy studies.

Harsh V. Pant is Director of Research at Observer Research Foundation, New Delhi, and Professor of International Relations at King's College London. He is also a non-resident fellow with the Wadhwani Chair in US–India Policy Studies at the Center for Strategic and International Studies, Washington, DC.

New Directions in India's Foreign Policy
Theory and Praxis

Edited by

Harsh V. Pant

CAMBRIDGE
UNIVERSITY PRESS

CAMBRIDGE
UNIVERSITY PRESS

University Printing House, Cambridge CB2 8BS, United Kingdom

One Liberty Plaza, 20th Floor, New York, NY 10006, USA

477 Williamstown Road, Port Melbourne, vic 3207, Australia

314 to 321, 3rd Floor, Plot No.3, Splendor Forum, Jasola District Centre, New Delhi 110025, India

79 Anson Road, #06–04/06, Singapore 079906

Cambridge University Press is part of the University of Cambridge.

It furthers the University's mission by disseminating knowledge in the pursuit of education, learning and research at the highest international levels of excellence.

www.cambridge.org
Information on this title: www.cambridge.org/9781108473668

© Cambridge University Press 2019

First published 2019

Printed in India by Rajkamal Electric Press

A catalogue record for this publication is available from the British Library

ISBN 978-1-108-47366-8 Hardback
ISBN 978-1-108-46219-8 Paperback

Contents

Preface

The study of Indian foreign policy has been undergoing a significant shift in recent years with new themes and new theoretical approaches emerging and newer voices adding their vibrancy to the field. This project was commissioned by Cambridge University Press (CUP) to specifically examine the impact of the emergence of Narendra Modi as India's Prime Minister in 2014 on the study and practice of Indian foreign policy. As we thought about the project more, we concluded that though the debates about the impact of Modi on the study of Indian foreign policy would continue, the field has been undergoing an evolution of its own. So this volume turned out to be not about Narendra Modi's impact on Indian foreign policy *per se* but about the key debates in Indian foreign policy as they have evolved over the last few years. In some cases, Modi's personality and convictions have had a role to play but in others, underlying institutional, structural and ideational factors beyond Modi have been powerful drivers of Indian foreign policy's trajectory.

I would like to thank CUP for giving me this opportunity, allowing me to relook at the state of the field. The whole team at the CUP – Qudsiya Ahmed, Sohini Ghosh, Aniruddha De – was very encouraging even as the project took much more time than was earlier anticipated. The contributors to this volume have been extremely cooperative and their patience in seeing this volume through to publication is much appreciated. I would also like to thank the two institutions I am associated with – the Observer Research Foundation, New Delhi, and King's College London – for giving me time and space to conclude this project. Finally, thanks are due to my family members who make sure that I remain insulated to concentrate on my projects.

This book is dedicated to the emerging new voices in the study of Indian foreign policy who, slowly but surely, are transforming the subject. More power to them!

Harsh V. Pant

1

Introduction

Harsh V. Pant

Foreign policies of nations do not alter radically with changes in governments, but with the backing of the Indian electorate's decisive mandate, the Narendra Modi government which came to office in May 2014 underlined that it was keen to bring about a realignment of Indian foreign policy priorities and goals. Ever since the end of the Cold War, the changing structural imperatives have been shaping the trajectory of Indian foreign policy.[1] As a rising economic power, India has been gradually moving from the periphery to the centre of global politics, generating new demands on the conduct of Indian diplomacy. Yet, change in Indian foreign policy is also emanating from within: new constituencies with stakes in India's external relations have in the past quarter of a century become important to its foreign policy. Given these constellation of influences on Indian foreign policy, the agency of Narendra Modi's prime ministership adds another dimension to understanding India's external behaviour. On the one hand, Modi seems to exude an understanding of power and interests, thereby appearing ready for a realpolitik approach, while on the other, his emergence also underscores the changing identity of the Indian state itself.[2] There is a vigorous debate in the emerging literature on whether Modi's foreign policy represents a transformation or merely an evolution in Indian foreign policy approach. Yet it is also evident that because of a range of structural and domestic political and unit level factors, new dimensions have emerged in the study and conduct of Indian foreign policy. Modi's prime ministership is just one of them.

The Modi factor

In his first few years, Modi has defied many expectations and confounded his detractors and supporters alike. On the foreign policy front, remarkably for a politician who was considered provincial before elections, Modi hit the ground running from the very first day. On the security front, there has been a new purposeful response against China with a focus on more efficient border management and defence acquisitions. Modi also reached out to the US immediately after his election, despite his personal grievances over visa denial by Washington when he was the Chief Minister of Gujarat, and there has been a focus on immediate neighbours, though not without setbacks.[3]

Modi's 'neighbourhood first' foreign policy is aimed at putting renewed emphasis on revitalizing India's regional profile. India's neighbours, barring Pakistan, are certainly looking at India with a new sense of expectation and New Delhi remains keen to operationalize the aspirations that have been articulated. Recognizing that the implementation of declared projects has always been a problem for India's regional credibility, the Modi government has been focusing on completing projects in its neighbourhood that are already in the pipeline rather than announcing new ones. And a new regional identity is being forged by investing in regional groupings such as the Bay of Bengal Initiative for Multi-Sectoral Technical and Economic Cooperation (BIMSTEC) and sub-regional configurations such as the Bangladesh, Bhutan, India and Nepal (BBIN) initiative.

The biggest strategic challenge for India remains managing China's rise.[4] The Modi government started off with an understanding that the need was to strike a balance between enhancing economic and trade ties with Beijing while building a deterrent military might. But it has been a difficult relationship to manage as China's persistent refusal to acknowledge India's core security concerns underscores, thereby further entrenching anti-China sentiment in India. Modi remains confident of India's ability to emerge as a significant global player, allowing him to leverage ties with China and the US to secure Indian interests. He has followed a dynamic foreign policy, developing closer ties with the US and strengthening military cooperation with Australia, Japan and Vietnam while working to regain strategic space in the Indian Ocean region. After rejecting the US–Japan–Australia–India Quadrilateral arrangement – the Quad – in 2007, India joined this resurrected arrangement in 2017. To counter Chinese presence in the Gwadar port in Pakistan, which many in India view as a potential Chinese naval hub, India is building a port in Iran's Chabahar to gain access to Afghanistan. After years of dithering, India moved to sign the Logistics Exchange Memorandum of Agreement (LEMOA) with the US in 2016 that will enable both countries to use each other's bases for repair and replenishment of defence supplies. For years, Delhi was labelled as the obstacle to normalizing Sino-Indian ties. Modi seems to have turned the tables on

Beijing by signaling that he is willing to go all out in enhancing cultural and economic ties but the onus of reducing strategic distrust rests with Beijing.

Modi seems to be redefining the terms on which India is likely to engage with the world in the coming years. Pragmatism coupled with a more confident assertion of Indian interests has been his hallmark. He has also reached out directly to new constituencies such as the Non-Resident Indian (NRI) and business communities in other states. For India's friends, a new outreach is in the offing. For India's adversaries, new red lines have been drawn.

Most significantly, Modi's ascendance has marginalized even the rhetoric of 'non-alignment' in Indian foreign policy outlook. New Delhi today seems ready to work with anyone and everyone to secure Indian interests, the most important of which is to take India on the path of rapid economic growth. For Modi and his government, however, the biggest challenge remains moving away from an overly personalized foreign policy towards a more institutionalized foreign and national security decision-making, a weakness that previous governments too have failed to tackle. There is much that is a continuation of the previous government's approach in the Modi government's foreign policy outlook but also much that is new. And it is some of these trends that this book intends to examine.

The study of Indian foreign policy and the Modi factor

Though academic study of Indian foreign policy has shown a degree of maturity, theoretical developments have been underwhelming. A number of scholars have introduced new concepts and examined Indian foreign policy through new prisms, but a cohesive research agenda is yet to be charted. Interestingly, studies on Indian foreign policy have not yet laid enough emphasis on individuals and personalities as drivers of change even when foreign policy decision-making has been highly concentrated in the office of Indian Prime Ministers.

However, as was underlined in the previous section, with the coming of the Modi government, Indian foreign policy debates have entered a new phase. Even before Modi came to power in New Delhi, scholars and commentators either exuded great confidence in his ability to usher change or ignored the possibility of change in the fundamentals of India's external behaviour. Over the years, opinions, whether from supporters or critics, have accepted that change has indeed accompanied the conduct of Indian foreign policy. Obviously, Modi's foreign policy has generated a lot of debate in the scholarship and in the media.

Yet, systematic studies of Indian foreign policy under Prime Minister Modi are few and far between. They also hardly situate Modi in the wider context of the established scholarship on India's foreign policy.

Sreeram Chaulia, for example, in his book *Modi Doctrine: The Foreign Policy of India's Prime Minister* argues that Modi has ushered fundamental changes in India's foreign policy.[5] Calling Modi a force of nature, Chaulia finds Modi imbuing India's foreign policy with a doctrinal purpose. As far as Chaulia is concerned, ambiguity and confusion were the default answers before Modi arrived on the scene. Modi is seen as one who is slowly correcting decades-long strategic laziness and putting India's priorities on the right track. In other words, he is changing India's strategic culture and the DNA of India's foreign policy The author goes on to praise Modi for running India like a CEO, for his spirit of competitive federalism and notes how Modi as Prime Minister employs Indian democracy as a tool to spread New Delhi's influence in the global realm.

In a similar vein, C. Raja Mohan's *Modi's World: Expanding India's Sphere of Influence* is an effort to provide a coherent commentary on Indian foreign policy in a contemporary framework.[6] The book takes up different aspects of India's foreign policy, in particular, its relationship with the subcontinental neighbours, and evolution of ties with the USA, China and Pakistan amongst others. He argues that Modi's worldview has been focused on multi-alignment rather than non-alignment. While giving Modi credit for initiating major departures in India's foreign policy, there is also an acknowledgement that the Prime Minister is treading on paths marked out by his predecessors.

In a more sympathetic evaluation of Modi's foreign policy Anirban Ganguly, Vijay Chauthaiwale and Uttam Kumar Sinha's *The Modi Doctrine: New Paradigms in India's Foreign Policy* makes a case for Modi's foreign policy measures, enumerating policies to attract foreign capital, technology and open foreign markets for Indian products, alongside Modi's attempts to establish regional stability, peace and prosperity.[7] The book claims that India under Modi is following 'enlightened self-interest', after a prolonged spell spent following the Nehruvian worldview.

Rajiv Kumar's *Modi and His Challenges* takes a rather measured strategic stance, neither aiming to completely dismiss the worth of Modi's approach nor exalting it excessively.[8] The book provides significant insights into how Modi's past as a member of the Rashtriya Swayamsevak Sangh (RSS) has shaped him as a leader, tangible differences that sets him apart from the RSS, and the impact of personalities such as Vivekananda and Deendayal Upadhyay on his economic thoughts.

Though interesting, the aforementioned literature suffers from a few methodological challenges. First, any change in Indian foreign policy can only be ascertained in the light of its historical behaviour. Most of these accounts are ahistorical in nature. Second, even when most authors agree that Modi has changed Indian foreign policy, no systematic scholarly explanation of how and why Modi has been able to achieve a significant alteration in India's external behaviour is provided. Where should we locate the sources of Modi's influence: in his sheer personal leadership, in his absolute control over the BJP or the mandate of 2014 which vests on him a parliamentary majority?[9] Modi's prime ministership is also a product of the changing context in which India now finds itself. It is the third largest economy and one of the strongest military powers in the world. It has the world's fastest growing population, 65 per cent of which is below the age of thirty-five. This new demography has experienced the fruits of economic liberalization and expects much more than any Indian electorate in the past. It also demands an assertion of India's identity and power as well as aspiring to influence and prestige in India's external relations. The extant literature also lacks in providing a contextual understanding of a changing India which has been a primary factor in ushering Modi to India's political centre-stage.

To fully explore new dimensions in Indian foreign policy, this volume brings to the fore new scholarship on the subject, engaging both the theory and praxis of India's external relations. This will help in contextualizing changes and continuities under Modi in the larger dynamic of political, economic and social change within India as well as contrasting it with Indian foreign policy's historical record. Such scholarly engagement with Modi's foreign policy may not only provide us valuable insights into contemporary Indian foreign policy but also explain the reasons behind it.

Literature on Indian foreign policy

Literature on Indian foreign policy has been growing over the last few decades. Both practitioners and academics have covered Indian foreign policy as it evolved through the decades. The following survey is of major themes addressed in the most recent literature on Indian foreign policy, which include, if not exclusively, India's relations with global players as well as its neighbourhood, nuclear strategy, military and economic issues. This brief review follows a specific pathway by classifying the literature conceptually and derived from a select survey of some of the most recent works on Indian foreign policy.

The post-Cold War phase in Indian foreign policy

While Modi's personality has had a significant impact on the changing contours of Indian foreign policy since 2014, the structural underpinnings of New Delhi's engagement with the rest of the world have been undergoing a shift ever since the end of the Cold War. The government of late P.V. Narasimha Rao initiated far-reaching economic reforms and altered the trajectory of the nation's foreign policy as he grappled with an international order in which the certitudes of the past had disappeared. Since then Indian policymakers have been struggling to redefine Indian foreign policy priorities even as India's material capabilities have been growing significantly.[10]

And slowly, but surely, the process continues to unfold as India has tried to redefine its place in the international system in consonance with its existing and potential power capabilities. The Narendra Modi government wants India to be a 'leading power' in the international system taking a more active approach on global issues.[11] After punching below its weight in key regions and on global issues over the last quarter of a century, policymakers now want to move India away from being a reactive power to one that actively shapes regional and international outcomes.

If the end of the Cold War was a major inflection point in India's approach to global governance, the current turmoil in international politics is another. The post-Second World War global order, to use the words of Henry Kissinger, is now in a state of 'crisis'.[12] The US hegemony, which was primarily responsible for the liberal global order, seems to be in decline. The rise of Chinese power has thrown a challenge to the existing norms, rules and institutions which govern global politics.[13] Global governance, just like global balance of power, is witnessing the rise of a bipolar system.[14] China's influence on structures of global governance is likely to create immense problems for India's rise. Both India and the international system are undergoing profound changes, complicating the interplay between India and the international system. With India's rise, there are new demands on the country to play a larger role in regional and global governance.

At the domestic political level, the rise of the Bharatiya Janata Party (BJP) has seen the emergence of centre-right in India with a distinctly new voice on foreign policy. The shift to the Right has been almost complete in India with the emergence of Narendra Modi as a formidable political force since 2014. The rise of the BJP and its emergence as the central pole of Indian foreign policy has shifted domestic politics as well as foreign policy discourse in new directions.

At an individual level, a new generation of leadership is emerging in India, unconstrained by ideological predilections of the past. The risk aversion of the past is giving way to a new boldness which is not tied down by the hesitations of history. A more confident assertion of Indian interests is being viewed as critical not only for preserving India's growing global equities but also for accelerating India's internal transformation. As discussed above, Modi's own personality is now playing an important role in how Indian foreign policy priorities are being articulated and operationalized.

It has been suggested that while Modi has been pursuing foreign policy with great vigour and enthusiasm, the change is largely of style and not of substance. It is indeed true that foreign policies of major powers do not change dramatically with a change in leadership. Structural factors play a much more formidable role in shaping their contours. But if we look closely, we will find that something substantive is also changing in Indian foreign policy. Whereas in the past, Indian diplomacy was responding to the tectonic shifts in global politics by stealth, the Modi government has been unabashed in changing the foreign policy trajectory of India. Gone is the diffidence of the past in articulating the need for robust Indo-US ties. India's relations with Israel have finally come out of the closet. And, rather than Beijing challenging New Delhi, India is standing up to China and challenging its profile.

Non-alignment has been given a decent burial and major power diplomacy is being conducted on the basis of strict reciprocity. In the name of non-alignment, New Delhi was often seen as pandering to Chinese sensitivities, imaginary or otherwise. Now India is building pressure points around Chinese periphery and is not hesitant to use powers like the US, Japan and Australia to stabilize the Indo-Pacific. While sections of the Indian intellectual establishment still retain reflexive anti-Americanism, Modi has used his decisive mandate to carve a new partnership with the United States to harness its capital and technology for his domestic development agenda. He is not ambivalent about positioning India as a challenger to China's growing regional might and assertiveness.

This has also meant that Indian adversaries are now facing an unpredictable Indian foreign policy. Where in the past there was certain predictability in New Delhi's responses to Chinese and Pakistani postures, the Modi government has introduced some uncertainty in the relationship. This has given India greater strategic space for manoeuvring. India has climbed the escalation ladder, which many in India were scared of climbing for long, and all that Islamabad has been left with is to deny the Indian military's response.[15] For long, it was Pakistan that was testing Indian boundaries by provoking India. Now, New Delhi is trying to retain some initiative. The same goes for China where India's response to the Belt and Road Initiative was a reminder to Beijing that New Delhi too can keep its cards close to its chest till the last minute and has many ways to respond to the challenge being posed by the Beijing–Islamabad collusion with the China–Pakistan Economic Corridor. India was firm in its handling of the Doklam crisis in 2017 – refusing to be drawn into escalation by bellicose rhetoric and not losing its nerve. Tensions continued to rise throughout the 73-day-long crisis which ended when disengagement was announced and an understanding reached on the withdrawal of Indian troops and cessation of Chinese road construction in the area. It was a diplomatic triumph of the Modi government.

There are challenges for sure. The Modi government is willing to take more foreign policy risks than its predecessors but this comes with its own costs. There are also some fundamental changes shaping the domestic political milieu in the West and the great power relationships are undergoing a shift which India will have to navigate with utmost seriousness. Sino-Russia relationship is acquiring connotations which can have long-term consequences for Indian interests and Sino-US ties can also become transactional under the Presidency of Donald Trump.

For a Prime Minister who was being criticized for being provincial when he had assumed office, Modi has underscored his potential to gradually but decisively shift Indian foreign policy in directions which few would have dared try before. This will be one of the most debated terrains in the future, both for academia and policy, for Indian polity's decisive shift to the Right in 2014 is also a structural change which will have foreign policy repercussions.

History and policy

A large set of writings on India's foreign policy underline its historical evolution, through catering to specific analysis of policies India has followed in the past. This set of literature attempts to link the historical with the contemporary conduct of Indian foreign policy.

David Malone, a former Canadian High Commissioner to India, captures the complexities of Indian foreign policy without providing an overarching theoretical argument in *Does the Elephant Dance?*[16] Malone's work is empirically and historically grounded and draws significantly on Indian sources without the 'self-referential' engagement that tends to animate Western analyses of Indian foreign policy. Malone chronicles the evolution of India's relations with regional actors, internal and external challenges, its economy, Sino-Indian relations, US–India relations, India's West and Southeast Asian policies, its diminishing relations with Europe and Russia and eventually Indian multilateralism. Neil Padukone's work, *Beyond South Asia*, traces the evolution of India's strategic worldview.[17] His central claim is that New Delhi's strategic worldview is the by-product of conflicts of interest which are derived from geography, history and culture and additionally from India's conceptions of power and hierarchy. Much like Malone's, if not in its sweep and depth, it is an analysis expressly undertaken to avoid theoretical categorization. Post-independence India, according to Padukone, has pursued its brand of the 'Monroe Doctrine' that sought to limit the autonomy of the region's other states, while simultaneously attempting to prevent the interference of major external powers in the region. This policy redounded to India's disadvantage, because it did not prevent the involvement of either the United States or China and poisoned New Delhi's relations with other regional states.

Taking up some of the major concerns in Indian foreign policy, Chris Ogden's *Indian Foreign Policy* traces its course since India's emergence as a modern state in 1947 to the present day, as he examines the nation's foreign policy process, strategic thinking and search for economic growth.[18] This is an empirically and historically grounded work. The author enunciates four central themes in the book as a means to understand the motivations of the Indian elite. These critical themes include India's great power aspirations, development and modernization, history and memory and finally paradoxes and tension. Ogden's work is primarily an analytical account of the trajectory, capacities, expectations, contradictions and constraints that have inhered in Indian foreign policy since independence.

India's Foreign Policy: A Reader, edited by Kanti Bajpai and me, stresses critical foreign policy issues including India's relations with China, Pakistan, the US and the extended neighbourhood in Asia as well as international trade and climate change issues.[19] *The Oxford Handbook of Indian Foreign Policy* edited by David Malone, C. Raja Mohan and Srinath Raghavan engages with the historical roots of Indian foreign policy from the Raj to the post-Cold War, juxtaposed with India's changing approach towards national security, natural resources, international development and soft power.[20]

Reversing the prism, Kate Sullivan's edited volume *Competing Visions of India in World Politics: India's Rise Beyond the West* is an exploration of a range of non-Western perspectives on India's growing international influence.[21]

Delivering insights into a range of shared global issues, these readings provide a critical evaluation of India's success in reconciling a quest for recognition from established global powers coupled with a desire to sustain friendly relationships with developing countries.

Arijit Mazumdar's *Indian Foreign Policy in Transition* entails an in-depth understanding of India's regional policies.[22] The author is sympathetic to the idea that India should engage Pakistan in cultural, economic and sporting activities. Looking at India's relations with Nepal, Bangladesh and Sri Lanka from a realist standpoint, the book argues that India's desire for regional dominance has shaped its regional policy.

Bharat Karnad's *Why India Is Not a Great Power (Yet)* lists ten specific criteria for a state to become a great power, which include attributes such as a 'driving vision', 'outward thrusting nature' and 'a sense of destiny', among others.[23] Casting a sharp eye on India's national security apparatus to expose its shortcomings and flaws, Karnad points out the price that India is paying for its grossly inadequate nuclear arsenal, a military–industrial complex that has failed to deliver and an inefficient higher defence organization.

Policy-relevant literature from practitioners has also emerged in recent times with some regularity. Former diplomat Rajiv Sikri in *Challenge and Strategy: Rethinking India's Foreign Policy* argues that India's standing in the international system will be determined by whether it lives up to its 'potential' and 'promise'.[24] Critically surveying the global strategic environment, Sikri is convinced of America's decline globally but contests the prospects of China replacing the US and sustaining perpetually high economic growth. For Sikri, the future of world politics and the larger Asian region hinges on the Sino-Indian relationship and he remains suspicious of close Indo-US ties. Former National Security Advisor under Prime Minister Manmohan Singh, Shivshankar Menon, in *Choices: Inside the Making of India's Foreign Policy* engages with some issues that have perennially dogged Indian foreign policy makers.[25] Menon highlights Indo-China border dispute, strategic engagement with the United States, military action against Pakistan, support for the Sri Lankan government in the final stages of the civil war and India's insistence on maintaining a posture of 'no-first use' in its nuclear doctrine. Arguing that India is not a status quo power but wants to modify though not overthrow the existing world order, Menon criticizes the Modi government for being marked 'by much activity and energetic projection' but without a 'conceptual framework'. Shyam Saran, former Indian Foreign Secretary and former Prime Minister Manmohan Singh's Special Envoy for Nuclear Affairs and Climate

Change, discusses the wellsprings of Indian foreign policy drawing on his extensive experience in the government in his *How India Sees the World*.[26]

A group of scholars and practitioners in 2012, in a widely debated policy document, made the case for the revival of non-alignment as the organizing basis of India's foreign policy. Titled *Nonalignment 2.0: A Foreign and Strategic Policy for India in the 21st Century*, this report underlines the primary principles and drivers that would make India a leading player in the world stage while preserving its strategic autonomy and values.[27] It argues that the strategy of non-alignment serves India's need to manage complicated coalitions and creates opportunities in an environment that is not structurally settled. If *Nonalignment 2.0* tries to make a case for non-alignment as the basis for Indian grand strategy, Shashi Tharoor in *Pax Indica* argues for the pursuit of 'multi-alignment' as a grand strategy which would require New Delhi to 'interface with major powers' without constricting its autonomy of choice.[28] Tharoor draws attention to the intricate link between India's foreign policy and domestic transformation and emphasizes leveraging India's enormous strengths in the arena of soft power.

Despite a growing body of work, most of these studies and analyses tend to rely largely on realist frameworks privileging power and interests as the fundamental drivers of Indian foreign policy. Even when these frameworks explain a lot in Indian foreign policy, crucial issues of identities, norms and aspirations as drivers of Indian foreign policy have remained largely outside their purview.

Identity, norms and ideas in Indian foreign policy

If most scholarship on Indian foreign policy has privileged power and interests as the fundamental drivers of India's behaviour, a new genre of foreign policy analysis underlines the role of identity, norms and aspirations in shaping India's global outreach.

Priya Chacko's *Indian Foreign Policy: The Politics of Postcolonial Identity from 1947 to 2004* is an attempt to understand the key drivers of India's foreign policy from a constructivist standpoint that moves beyond the idealist/realist foreign policy framework.[29] The book argues that India's identity as a postcolonial nation-state strongly influences its foreign and security policies. She draws attention to India's post-colonial identity embracing modernity to rid itself of backwardness, yet seeking to repudiate modernity for being subjugative and exploitative because of its colonial experience. This profound ambivalence resulted in an 'ethico-political' project that emphasizes India's 'civilizational exceptionalism', which renders India uniquely equipped to create a distinct ethical modernity. The author emphasizes India's identity taking cognizance of it as a civilization-state that brings to international politics a tradition of morality and ethical conduct.

Arndt Michael in *India's Foreign Policy and Regional Multilateralism* unearths the normative and ideational determinants of India's foreign policy.[30] He traces the evolution of multilateralism in South Asia to unpack the impact of ideas, norms and values of India's foreign policy on the normative structure in the region. Michael concedes that the grand norm influencing India's foreign policy and regional organizations is Nehruvian 'Panchsheel multilateralism' of 1954, which enunciated the notion of peaceful coexistence, mutual respect, non-aggression and respect for sovereignty.

Approaching Indian and Chinese foreign policy through a post-colonial lens, Manjari Chatterjee Miller's *Wronged by Empire: Post-Imperial Ideology and Foreign Policy in India and China* attributes a strong sense of victimhood to their foreign policy conduct.[31] She argues that 'extractive colonialism' has traumatized India and China severely to the point that it each sees the other as victimizer and advancing an imperialist agenda. Perceptions of national elites as shaped by the collective memories of their traumatic experiences of the past ills of their colonizers have shaped their current discourse.

Focusing on India's prospects as a rising power, and its material position in the international system that has received significant attention, is Kate Sullivan Estrada and Rajesh Basrur's *Rising India: Status and Power*.[32] It emphasizes the social dimensions of status from a constructivist perspective, contrasting their central claim with realist arguments that the quest for material power was not a feature of India's foreign policy in the initial years following independence. Despite material weakness and an absence of the accoutrements of power, India enjoyed high international status defying realist expectations. These initial years contrast sharply with the post-1991 period when India's material power has grown. The book challenges traditional meanings and understandings of linear relationship between material power and status focusing instead on India's shifting status concerns and aspirations of being a major power. The authors concede that acquiring material power is but one of the routes Indian leaders have adopted to secure greater status in the global realm.

The aforementioned literature offers an exciting alternative to the traditional realist framework of foreign policy analysis in the Indian case. It has emerged as an important body of literature in its own right. However, it is still at a nascent stage of development and its engagement with the wider body of work on Indian foreign policy still remains limited.

Volume overview

To bring some of the key scholars of Indian foreign policy together as well as to move beyond the debates on paradigms, this volume focuses on key concepts and issues which are shaping the trajectory of the study of contemporary Indian foreign policy. New theoretical concepts such as constructivism and territoriality are explored to see what value they add to the academic discourse on Indian foreign policy. New themes such as the 'Indo-Pacific' and the 'Responsibility to Protect' are examined to give the readers a sense of the broadening of Indian foreign policy horizons. Those issues which have been studied less but have the potential to significantly alter the trajectory of Indian foreign policy studies are the focus of this volume with the first section examining the conceptual and theoretical advancements in the study of Indian foreign policy while the second section is devoted to emerging themes in the practice of Indian foreign policy. All chapters provide detailed discussions of concepts and themes under consideration and situate it in the wider context of the study of Indian foreign policy. The chapters trace their evolution and what roles they are playing in contemporary academic discourse on Indian foreign policy.

Part I of this volume begins with Rohan Mukherjee examining the manner in which the study of Indian foreign policy has engaged with power which, according to him, has been defined largely in terms of capabilities: material (economic and military) as well as normative. According to Mukherjee, 'India is viewed as somewhat exceptional in its ability to synthesize material and normative power resources in order to serve its foreign policy objectives' even as scholars of Indian foreign policy remain divided in their assessment of India's approach to power politics in the realm of international affairs. Mukherjee effectively maps this terrain in his analysis, underlining that 'while some argue that Indian leaders have been opposed to power politics, others argue that they have floated above it, seeking different goals; yet others argue that non-alignment and strategic autonomy are nothing but variants of power politics'. He is optimistic about the future trajectory of the research agenda on power and Indian foreign policy.

Priya Chacko, in the following chapter, takes the discussion to constructivism by examining how scholars have used constructivist approaches in International

Relations to take the study of India's foreign policy forward. She concludes that while constructivist literature on Indian foreign policy remains relatively small, 'scholars of Indian foreign policy were among the earliest to contribute to the development of constructivist theories, they have developed constructivism in distinctive ways through Indian case studies and they have made valuable contributions to the study of Indian foreign policy, by highlighting the broader social relations that produce India's foreign policy interests and behaviour'. Chacko is emphatic in her assessment that 'constructivist frameworks, methodologies and concepts will be essential in elucidating the changing construction of India's foreign policy interests and its ability to achieve its foreign policy goals as its global engagement grows and domestic political contention deepens'.

A related though conceptually distinct approach is taken by Manjari Chatterjee Miller who argues in her chapter that 'despite the demise of colonialism over five decades ago, and despite India having led an influential anti-colonial movement from which it emerged independent, historical memories of colonialism persist'. She suggests that 'the identification of specific historical experiences and memories, the mechanisms of collective memory and their ongoing effects have mostly been very lightly explored in the Indian international relations and foreign policy literature'. She contends that shifts in national identity such as the identity of a 'rising power' can be effectively explored by examining historical memory and its institutionalization. She goes on to conclude that 'as the historical memories recede further it would be interesting to observe how newer identities emerge and whether they exist in parallel with these memories or whether they succeed in replacing them'.

Offering a post-structural and post-colonial analysis of foreign policy in the next chapter, Itty Abraham makes territory and territoriality the conceptual underpinnings for examining the protracted territorial disputes between India and its neighbours. He uses a critical approach that seeks to understand the processes by which territory becomes naturalized as a meaning of state/ state practice – and thus to show how there is nothing 'natural' about it, and how different modes of territorialization emerge in response to changing circumstances. Questioning the assumption of control of land being necessary for and prior to the creation of political identity, Abraham 'traces multiple origins of the spatial category of the national homeland, and explores its intersections with the legacy of imperial political practices on modern state territoriality'. On the one hand, he critically evaluates 'classic Indian geopolitical thought, a land-centred viewpoint that is oriented towards the north by northwest passages to India' while on the other he also manages to examine the 'ongoing transformation of the Indo-Pacific region as a result of the extraordinary growth of Chinese power'. Abraham ends up by offering a genealogy of modern Indian political thinking about the seas by focusing on a few key maritime thinkers of India.

Avinash Paliwal and I underline the need to bring application of Foreign Policy Analysis (FPA) to the study of Indian foreign policy in our chapter and argue that it offers a 'new direction' that holds tremendous merit despite methodological difficulties related to lack of good primary sources of information. We argue that 'it shows how different ideas compete for influence over policy output on different thematic issues and in varying contexts, that is, crisis policymaking and during non-crisis situations'. Moreover, though underlining the Prime Minister's role in shaping policy course in India, analysis of the policymaking process shows that Prime Ministers are not always 'free agents' working towards their vision of India in the world. They are constrained by political and institutional pressures that can play both a limiting and a liberating role in shaping policy output on critical issues. Effective use of FPA also helps in unpacking operational level debates and nuances therein, rather than focus on the grand narrative of Indian strategic practices or the structural determinants of India's foreign policy. By highlighting the complexity of the process and nuances of policy motivation, FPA challenges a long held myth of foreign policy consensus in India, but underscores the continuities in India's strategy formation since 1947.

The focus of Part II of this volume is on some key themes which have been shaping the conduct of Indian foreign policy in recent years. We begin by discussing non-alignment which has remained a central component of Indian identity in global politics. Julie Super and I argue that India has arguably been in pursuit of strategic autonomy since independence, which in practice has led to semi-alliances fashioned under the cover of non-alignment and shaped by regional dynamics. In this setting, the rise of China raises an interesting conundrum for Indian policymakers as New Delhi seeks to balance the benefits and risks of an increasingly assertive neighbour and a network of alliances with like-minded countries. Amid China's growing influence, the success of India's modern-day pursuit of strategic autonomy may well rest on a strong foundation of strategic partnerships that move beyond the limited commitments of non-alignment. The Modi government has signalled a move away from even the rhetoric of non-alignment with significant implications for the future of Indian foreign policy. This approach seems to be predicated on the belief that rather than proclaiming non-alignment as an end in itself, India needs deeper engagement with its friends and partners if it is to develop leverage in its dealings with its adversaries and competitors. India is today well positioned to define its bilateral relationships on its own terms and is likely to continue engaging more closely with those countries that can facilitate its rise to regional and global prominence.

In his chapter, Arndt Michael argues that 'multilateralism at the global and regional level has been an important part of India's foreign policy agenda as well as her international identity and profile, with a drastic increase in activities at both levels in the recent past, albeit with varying degrees of success'. He suggests that 'together with this increase in the praxis of multilateralism, Indian scholarship on multilateralism has also proliferated and introduced new concepts and ideas for analysing multilateralism, challenging "Western" conceptions of multilateralism'. As India's power and influence in global and regional multilateral institutions increased, New Delhi successfully introduced specific normative and ideational concepts into multilateralism even as it preferred global over regional institutions. Michael contends that 'the analysis of India's future behaviour will thus necessitate focusing on select issue-areas in India's dealings with global or regional institutions respectively'. He makes a case for theoretical eclecticism to understand India's different approaches in her multilateral priorities.

The next chapter by Ian Hall outlines the evolution of India's positions on human rights and humanitarian intervention, both in theory and practice. Hall focuses on the Libyan and Syrian crises and observes that those crises 'revealed not just divisions within the Indian elite about R2P itself, but also weaknesses in the institutions and processes of foreign policy-making that will have to be addressed if India is to be a "leading power"'. He suggests that 'the story of India's reaction to R2P opens window on the attitudes that prevail among foreign policy elite in New Delhi, its broader understandings of how international relations do and ought to function, and how these beliefs are changing, as the composition, training, and experience of that elite itself changes'.

India's engagement with the Indo-Pacific narrative is the focus of David Scott's chapter which looks at three overlapping fields, namely India as an Indo-Pacific 'actor', the Indo-Pacific strategic discourse 'around' (that is, on) government, and the Indo-Pacific language and policies used 'inside' (that is, by) government. For Scott, the 'Indo' bit of the term 'Indo-Pacific' points not only to the Indian Ocean but also to India. He observes that 'whereas India is marginal to the term 'Asia-Pacific' (that is, the Pacific basin and the Pacific Rim), it is self-evidently politically and geographically right in the Indo-Pacific'. As such, the adoption of the term Indo-Pacific reflects a shift of focus by India from land to maritime concerns with significant implications for the future of Indian foreign and national security behaviour.

Rajesh Basrur examines the evolution of the deterrence framework in Indian foreign policy study and practice. He argues that there are two central questions that have engaged both policy practitioners and scholars: how much is enough and how best can a stable strategic environment be maintained under the nuclear shadow? Basrur suggests that the answers to both questions continue to be problematic. This is because, according to him, 'the first requires a clear sense of how deterrence actually works, but this is not adequately understood' while 'the second is dependent on the strategic behaviour of adversaries that are not inclined to prioritize stabilizing options'. From the standpoint of theory, these are 'undesirable outcomes arising in the first case from within India, while in the second, they arise from without'. Basrur argues that scholars require separate theoretical frameworks – neoclassical realism and classical realism respectively – to understand them fully.

Latha Varadarajan focuses on the role of the Indian diaspora in Indian foreign policy and argues that 'the valorization of the Indian diaspora by the Indian state can only be understood in the context of changes in the global capitalist economy, manifested in the turn towards neoliberal restructuring'. According to Varadarajan, 'their ability to influence the policy agenda of the Indian state rests not so much on their connections to state actors, but rather their class positions within a global capitalist economy'. Though the Indian diaspora today constitutes the largest migrant population in the world and that its economic ties to the homeland remain unsurpassed in terms of remittances, its role, Varadarajan argues, remains limited in the shaping of Indian foreign policy. And this very limitation, Varadarajan suggests, 'makes the study of the peculiar position of the Indian diaspora a critical subject for scholars and policymakers alike'.

Conclusion

This volume is intended to spark a conversation among the various strands of academic work that is emerging in the realm of Indian foreign policy. As the practice and study of Indian foreign policy goes into new directions, the academic discourse also needs to keep pace with these changes. A new generation of scholars is taking the study of India's external relations in new and interesting dimensions and, as the chapters point out, a new research agenda is needed to map out this new terrain. If this volume manages to take this discussion forward, it would have served its purpose.

Notes

1   For an examination of the role of structural factors in shaping Indian foreign policy priorities, see Harsh V. Pant (ed.), *Indian Foreign Policy in a Unipolar World* (London: Routledge, 2009).

2   Harsh V. Pant, 'Is India Developing a Strategy for Power?' *The Washington Quarterly*, 38, No. 4 (Winter 2016): 99–113.

3   Harsh V. Pant, 'Modi's Unexpected Boost to India–US Relations,' *The Washington Quarterly*, 37, No. 3 (Fall 2014): 93–112.

4   A useful account is in J. Mohan Malik, *China and India: Great Power Rivals* (Boulder, CO: First Forum Press, 2011).

5   Sreeram Chaulia, *Modi Doctrine: The Foreign Policy of India's Prime Minister* (New Delhi: Bloomsbury, 2016).

6   C. Raja Mohan, *Modi's World: Expanding India's Sphere of Influence* (New Delhi: HarperCollins, 2015).

7   Anirban Ganguly, Vijay Chauthaiwale and Uttam Kumar Sinha (eds), *The Modi Doctrine: New Paradigms in India's Foreign Policy* (New Delhi: Wisdom Tree, 2016).

8   Rajiv Kumar, *Modi and His Challenges* (New Delhi: Bloomsbury, 2016).

9   For a discussion of some of these issues, see Harsh V. Pant and Yogesh Joshi, 'Indo-US Relations under Modi: The Strategic Logic Underlying the Embrace,' *International Affairs*, 93, No 1 (January 2017): 133–146.

10 For a discussion on the evolution of Indian foreign policy since the end of the Cold War, see Harsh V. Pant, *Indian Foreign Policy: An Overview* (Manchester: Manchester University Press, 2016; New Delhi: Orient BlackSwan, 2016).

11 S. Jaishankar, 'India, the United States and China,' IISS Fullerton Lecture, 20 July 2015, Singapore.

12 Jeffrey Goldberg, 'World Chaos and World Order: Conversations with Henry Kissinger,' 10 November 2016, *The Atlantic*. Available at https://www.theatlantic.com/international/archive/2016/11/kissinger-order-and-chaos/506876/, accessed on 20 December 2017.

13 Robert Kagan, 'The Twilight of the Liberal World Order,' 24 January 2017, *Brookings Institution*. Available at https://www.brookings.edu/research/the-twilight-of-the-liberal-world-order/, accessed on 20 December 2017.

14 Yan Xuetong, 'From a Unipolar to a Bipolar World System: The Future of the Global Power Dynamic,' *The Global Times*, 30 December 2011.

15 Ellen Barry and Salman Masood, 'India Claims "Surgical Strikes" Across Line of

Control in Kashmir,' *New York Times*, 29 September 2016.

16 David Malone, *Does the Elephant Dance? Contemporary Indian Foreign Policy* (Oxford: Oxford University Press, 2011).

17 Neil Padukone, *Beyond South Asia: India's Strategic Evolution and the Reintegration of the Subcontinent* (NewDelhi: Bloomsbury, 2014).

18 Chris Ogden, *Indian Foreign Policy* (London: Polity Press, 2014).

19 Kanti Bajpai and Harsh V. Pant (eds), *India's Foreign Policy: A Reader* (Oxford: Oxford University Press, 2013).

20 David Malone, C. Raja Mohan and Srinath Raghavan (eds), *The Oxford Handbook of Indian Foreign Policy* (Oxford: Oxford University Press, 2015).

21 Kate Sullivan (ed.), *Competing Visions of India in World Politics* (New York: Palgrave Macmillan, 2015).

22 Arijit Mazumdar, *Indian Foreign Policy in Transition* (London: Routledge, 2014).

23 Bharat Karnad, *Why India Is Not a Great Power (Yet)* (New Delhi: Oxford University Press, 2015).

24 Rajiv Sikri, *Challenge and Strategy: Rethinking India's Foreign Policy* (New Delhi: Sage India, 2013).

25 Shivshankar Menon, *Choices: Inside the Making of India's Foreign Policy* (New Delhi: Penguin Random House, 2016).

26 Shyam Saran, *How India Sees the World: Kautilya to the 21st Century* (New Delhi: Juggernaut Books, 2017).

27 Sunil Khilnani et al., *Nonalignment 2.0: A Foreign and Strategic Policy for India in the 21st Century*. Available at http://www.cprindia.org/research/reports/nonalignment-20-foreign-and-strategic-policy-india-twenty-first-century, accessed on 20 December 2017.

28 Shashi Tharoor, *Pax Indica* (New Delhi: Penguin India, 2013).

29 Priya Chacko, *Indian Foreign Policy: The Politics of Postcolonial Identity from 1947 to 2004* (London: Routledge, 2012).

30 Arndt Michael, *India's Foreign Policy and Regional Multilateralism* (London: Palgrave Macmillan, 2013).

31 Manjari Chatterjee Miller, *Wronged by Empire: Post-Imperial. Ideology and Foreign Policy in India and China* (Stanford, CA: Stanford University, 2013).

32 Kate Sullivan Estrada and Rajesh Basrur, *Rising India: Status and Power* (London: Routledge, 2017).

Part I
Theoretical Evolution

2

Power and Indian Foreign Policy

Rohan Mukherjee

Power is not a new concept in the study of Indian foreign policy. Like Indian policymakers, scholars of Indian foreign policy have long displayed a sophisticated understanding of its role and function in international relations. Moreover, there has been a clear evolution in the way scholars have treated the concept, an evolution that roughly tracks changes in India's capabilities over time and has been sensitive to major developments in India's external relations. In the wider realm of world politics, the nature of power itself has changed over the last seven decades due to technological change, globalization and the shifting distribution of capabilities across states in the international system. Today, the world stands at an unprecedented threshold, not quite unipolar and not quite multipolar, with global power transitions taking place in the shadow of nuclear weapons.

As a rising power with nuclear weapons and multiple security challenges in its neighbourhood, India is likely to play a pivotal role in shaping scholarly understandings of power and its limits in the twenty-first century. Equally, it will be vital for Indian decision-makers to develop the appropriate theoretical tools to address new challenges to state capabilities and the changed landscape of opportunities to most efficiently achieve their external objectives. The foundational instruments of statecraft such as deterrence, balancing, diplomacy and war take on different meanings depending on the underlying conception of power on which they are premised. If the nature of power changes, then states that fail to update their conceptions of these instruments risk significant losses.

The questions this chapter examines therefore pertain to the manner in which the study of Indian foreign policy has dealt with power. Drawing on debates over power in the wider international relations literature, the chapter asks of the Indian context: Is power purely based on capabilities or is it relational? Where does power come from? Is power essentially zero-sum in nature or can it be positive-sum? Is the pursuit of power – or power politics – rational and/ or legitimate? What are the existing gaps and blind spots in the study of power in the context of Indian foreign policy? Answers to these questions provide a coherent picture of the evolution of the study of power and Indian foreign policy, while also charting a course for future research.

The rest of this chapter is accordingly organized as follows. The following section discusses the theoretical underpinnings of power as they have been debated in political science, especially the literature on international relations. The next section studies the manner in which scholars of Indian foreign policy have treated various aspects of power. These include the definition of power (capabilities-based or relational), its sources (economic, military, normative), its nature (zero-sum or positive-sum) and India's approach to power politics. The section after that lays out an agenda for future research on power and Indian foreign policy, focusing on two relatively under-theorized subjects in the literature: the issue-based or geographical contingency of power, and the social purpose of power. The final section provides concluding observations.

Theoretical approaches to power

Perhaps the most widely accepted definition of power in political science comes from Robert Dahl, who put forward a *relational* conception of power such that 'A has power over B to the extent that he can get B to do something that B would not otherwise do'.[1] Under this conception, statements such as 'A is powerful' or 'A's power has increased' are meaningless unless anchored in a specific relation and context that provides information about what it is that A's power can enable it to do. This definition of power is thick – Dahl argued that for a meaningful discussion of power as a relation, in any situation the analyst should seek to determine the *source* of A's power over B, the *means* by which A exerts its power over B, the *extent* of A's power over B, and the *scope* of A's power over B (that is, the set of B's responses).[2] If A and B were states, then the source of A's power would be the size of its economy and military, and the means would be A's grand strategy. The extent and scope of A's power over B would depend on B's capabilities and grand strategy. A's power over B is thus measurable in terms of the probability that A can get B to do something that B would not otherwise do; and probabilities are comparable across different actors, contexts and time periods.

Dahl's relational definition has been challenged for being insufficiently ambitious as well as overly ambitious. Bachrach and Baratz criticized Dahl for ignoring the deeper levels at which power operates. They argued that power is not only exercised in direct causal relations between A and B, but that actors can also manipulate the institutional environment in which they interact in order to keep certain issues from being tabled, in essence possessing agenda-setting powers.[3] In the context of international relations, focusing only on direct power relations at the expense of deeper institutional investigations is likely to result in faulty understandings of how power operates both within and between states in the international system. Scholars have thus studied the manner in which states exercise power through international institutions.[4] A deeper criticism originates in the work of Steven Lukes, who argued that in addition to the so-called second face of power (agenda-setting) there exists a third face whereby A has power over B not by coercing B or manipulating the rules of the game, but by altering B's very preferences over an issue.[5] At this level, A has power over B to the extent that A can get B to *think* something that B would not otherwise think. International relations scholarship focused on norms and the socialization of states takes this type of power seriously and explores its implications for world politics.[6]

Despite their differences in terms of the levels at which power operates, the above conceptions – the three faces, as it were – all rely on a relational definition of power.[7] A number of international relations theorists have followed Kenneth Waltz in rejecting this definition. Waltz argued that Dahl's definition 'ill fits the requirements of politics' because it equates power with control and thus asserts that only power is needed in order to get one's way'.[8] Power, argued Waltz, is but one of the many factors at play in any relation between A and B, and Dahl's definition is too ambitious because it ignores the various unintended consequences and other factors (such as domestic politics) that might distort the final result of any application of power. In other words, by defining power in terms of A getting B to do something that B would not otherwise do, Dahl confuses process with outcome.[9] Moreover, as William C. Wohlforth has argued, Dahl's definition is difficult to apply empirically because it is impossible to know the counterfactual, that is, what B would otherwise have done were it not for A.[10] These criticisms have led theorists of international relations to define power in terms of capabilities and not a causal relationship. Waltz's definition of power is much thinner than Dahl's: 'an agent is powerful to the extent that he affects others more than they affect him'.[11] Power is thus a function of relative capabilities for many scholars.

The capabilities-based definition, while helpful in terms of identifying countries possessing large amounts of 'power resources' – or 'power bases' (Dahl's terms) – does a poor job of explaining actual outcomes. Chief among these outcomes is what David Baldwin has called 'the paradox of unrealized power',[12] or why in fact A is frequently unable to get B to do what B otherwise would not do, even when A's power base vastly exceeds B's power base. Prominent examples of such instances include the Vietnam War, the Soviet occupation of Afghanistan and more recently the US-led wars in Afghanistan and Iraq. Scholars have consequently called for a distinction to be made between 'power as material resources' and 'power as influence', even though much of the literature uses the terms interchangeably.[13] Particularly important in this distinction is the fact that often influence must be bought by sacrificing some amount of material resources. Materially preponderant states frequently enhance their influence when they act within rule-based frameworks that are considered legitimate by less capable states.[14] A purely capabilities-based conception of power misses the political processes by which 'powerful' states actually translate their power into influence, or control over outcomes.

Despite this weakness, the field of international relations has found use for the capabilities-based definition of power, with measures such as the Composite Index of National Capability (CINC) used as a proxy for national power in large-n studies.[15] In other types of studies, however, the relational conception of power allows for more fine-grained analysis and explanation of outcomes. Ultimately, the definition of power one employs has important consequences for the study of a state's foreign policy. If power is viewed as a function of material capabilities alone, then a country with relatively few capabilities will be viewed as less powerful and hence less able to get other countries to do what they otherwise would not do. The set of capabilities that scholars such as Waltz have considered relevant in this regard includes 'size of population and territory, resource endowment, economic capability, military strength, political stability and competence'.[16] Thus a country with relatively low levels of population, per capita income, military expenditure, and so on, is not expected to exert much influence in international politics.

By contrast, a relational view of power suggests that while capabilities (which constitute the power base) matter, the *means* by which capabilities are translated into influence (power over another actor) are just as important, as are the domain and scope of power, that is, the functional area in which the relation is played out, and the set of choices available to the subject of power (state B in Dahl's formulation). In other words, context matters and different contexts may lead to different levels of efficacy with which material capabilities are translated into control over outcomes. Scholars have used the term 'policy-contingency framework' to describe the set of variables that might make up a particular context, basically 'specifying who is trying to get whom to do what'.[17] A relational view of power sets the stage for explaining the gap between capabilities and outcomes, that is, why materially preponderant states often lose or why materially weak states frequently get their way in international politics.

The capabilities versus relational views of power also impact real-world policy decisions. Should a country invest more in building up its military if most of its influence comes from its diplomatic abilities? The capabilities view would suggest that diplomacy in the absence of material strength is ineffective, whereas the relational view would suggest that diplomatic skill can often compensate for material weakness in the context of a reasonably institutionalized global order. Indeed, the central mechanisms of institutionalist theories of international cooperation – the density of issue-linkages and the reputational costs of not cooperating – help produce the kind of influence that weaker countries enjoy in the post-1945 global order where numerous international institutions govern inter-state interactions and the global commons.[18] Globalization, or the growth of complex interdependence between nations, has a similar effect, in that a straightforward tallying of capabilities is less likely to predict whether A has power over B in a globalized world.[19] This would not have been the case a hundred years ago, and even less so 200 years ago, when multilateral international law and institutions were barely existent. In those contexts, power flowed more straightforwardly from the barrel of a gun, as it were. Even in situations of low institutionalization and interdependence, however, differences in the intensity of preferences over outcomes between two states – for example, in the Vietnam War – can explain outcomes that the calculus of capabilities cannot.[20] Ultimately, context matters in the study of power, though scholars have had a difficult time incorporating it into their theories without sacrificing parsimony and generalizability.

Power and Indian foreign policy

Scholarship on India's foreign policy tends to evince a deep awareness of power dynamics while eschewing formal analyses of power, which for better or worse is seen as a particularly Western obsession. This aversion is not solely an artefact of the Cold War and India's foreign policy of non-alignment. As late as 1997, M. S. Rajan, a major figure in the study of Indian foreign policy, wrote of the need for a more India-centric study of international relations, which 'would hopefully reduce the traditional preoccupation of IR specialists with power politics between/among nation states'.[21] This type of formal disavowal is often paired with a pragmatic acquiescence in the realities of world politics where power is understood to be the coin of the realm. As Kanti Bajpai has characterized this belief, 'In a world regulated by power, India, by virtue of its size and economic potential, would constitute one of the major regulating powers.'[22] Contemporary scholars frequently (mistakenly) identify discussions of power exclusively with the Realist school of thought in international relations, and scholarship by Indians in particular tends to categorize itself as Constructivist, focusing on the role of culture, identity and ideas in the study of Indian foreign policy.[23] Again, the theoretical disavowal of power is accompanied by ubiquitous Realist thinking in think tanks, the media and sections of academia as well.[24] Even critics of the so-called Realist agenda of power analysis note that '[a]lmost all writings on Indian foreign policy have essentially been exercises in the presentation of a historical-diplomatic-political narrative in which key military conflicts and political events…provide the points around which the narrative is structured'.[25] Thus, while power has not been central to any single study of Indian foreign policy, it permeates the field in ways that few concepts have done, making it possible to survey the literature to find answers to the questions that motivate this chapter.

The definition of power

Although studies of Indian foreign policy have not centrally addressed power in a theoretical fashion, it is possible to investigate underlying conceptions of power in the literature in order to determine if they hew closer to the capabilities-based definition of power or the relational definition. By and large, academic writing on Indian foreign policy has relied on a capabilities-based definition of power, with hints of an acknowledgement of the relational nature of power. India post-independence in 1947 is portrayed as a weak country unable to muster the economic and military might necessary to be a top-ranking great power.[26] Over time, academic assessments of India's power have changed as a result of India's increasing economic and military capabilities. As noted above, scholars have consistently evinced a keen awareness of India's great-power *potential*. A part of this assessment also reflects the desire of Indian leaders for great-power status, which is a common theme in the study of Indian foreign policy. The general consensus among scholars has been that India's geographical, physical, demographic and other attributes make it a prime candidate for great-power status in the eyes of Indian leaders.[27] In this sense, status at least in part is understood to depend on material capabilities.

Some scholars have paid lip service to a relational conception of power. Appadorai and Rajan, for example, define power as 'the ability of nation A to influence the policy of other nations B and C, in the direction desired by it for securing its national interests'.[28] This is not quite the same as Dahl's definition, which requires B or C to do things they would not otherwise do, but it does define power as inhering in a causal relation between two or more actors. The authors, however, go on to argue that A's ability to influence B and C depends on factors such as 'economic and military resources, technological development, geo-political situation, the number and morale of the people, the strength of the government and its diplomatic maturity'.[29] This formulation accepts power as relational but then privileges only the power base of A and not the means, scope and domain of A's power over B and C. In effect, this is no different from the capabilities-based view.

The capabilities-based definition of power comes through more clearly in the literature on India as a rising power since the early 2000s.[30] As India's economy entered a period of relatively rapid growth in the 1990s and India's military expenditure increased in tandem, the scholarly consensus was that India's power was increasing. A relational model of power would have examined India's grand strategy and its diplomatic skill across a range of issue-areas and geographies to determine whether and where India's influence over other states in the international system was increasing. However, India was either judged not to have a grand strategy or at best it was judged to have multiple competing schools of thought regarding India's place in the world.[31] Although the consensus in the schools-of-thought literature is that all the various strands of Indian strategic thought share the understanding that power is one of the 'staples of international relations',[32] it lacks a discussion of what exactly power has meant to Indian thinkers and if they have viewed it in terms of capabilities or relations. As far as the latter is concerned, the schools-of-thought literature does not focus on outcomes and hence has little to say about India's power except to take a capabilities-based view of India's rising power as motivation for understanding India's strategic thinking.

Scholars of India's state capacity come closest to transcending the pure capabilities-based view of power. They argue that while India may possess abundant latent resources in terms of population, natural resources and economic fundamentals, the key variable in generating power is the state's ability to govern efficiently, extract resources effectively, and allocate them optimally, mostly for the purposes of domestic economic development.[33] A number of scholars extend this analysis to India's standing in the world, arguing that state capacity is the crucial mediator of India's great-power aspirations.[34] However, even in this literature state capacity is conceptualized as an attribute of the state, without any consideration of the relational aspects of the exercise of power in international affairs. On the whole, therefore, the capabilities-based definition of power dominates the study of Indian foreign policy.

Sources of power

Given that scholars have taken a largely capabilities-based view of Indian power, it is worth examining prevailing views of the sources of this power. On this front, there is a clear consensus in the literature that economic and military capabilities – known together as hard power – are the primary ingredients of India's power, and this is also held to be true of all other great powers in the international system. There is, however, a perceptible shift over time in the emphasis scholars have placed on hard power capabilities. In the early years following independence, scholars generally appeared to appreciate the importance of hard power but were unsure of India's willingness to possess and wield it. In the words of one scholar, 'it is unrealistic to expect India to play a leading role in international affairs – she has neither the power nor the money'.[35] This view is likely a function of Jawaharlal Nehru's rhetoric on power politics and the Cold War, which is discussed in a later section of this chapter.

The prevailing consensus is that Nehru's own rhetoric and policies of non-alignment, peaceful diplomacy, and Third World solidarity were proved disastrously wrong in the Sino-Indian border war of 1962 (though more recent accounts have challenged the conventional wisdom, arguing that Nehru was no idealist when it came to China).[36] In any event, the role of hard power in scholarly assessments of India's power was amplified following the defeat of 1962. As the Indian government started ramping up its defence budget and preparedness following the war, scholars began to note that '[m]ilitary power was not at all well-developed in India [prior to the Chinese invasion] and like agriculture it needed modernization'.[37] Commenting on the national security lessons of the war, another noted, 'due recognition has to be given to the fact that diplomacy not backed by requisite amount of force is ineffective and also that the force which does not further the end of diplomacy is useless'.[38] A few years later, an eminent writer echoed this view in the context of the Sino-Indian contest for influence in Southeast Asia: 'Diplomacy and influence are no substitute for real economic and military strength. On the contrary, the strength and influence of diplomacy is largely a reflection of the latter.'[39]

As the superpowers achieved nuclear parity in the 1970s, the diplomat and analyst K. R. Narayanan argued that Asia's (and therefore India's) role in world affairs was even more important because '[t]he struggle for power has...shifted to other [non-nuclear] fields in which large countries, large populations, and large conventional armies play a greater role in determining the international political balance and in shaping regional military balances'.[40] The idea that hard power is the primary basis of national power was reinforced by India's successful use of military power in the Bangladesh War. As noted by A. Appadorai and M. S. Rajan,

> The attention given by the Government of India after 1962 to the strengthening of India's defence forces is ample evidence of the realisation that an adequate foreign and defence policy must be based on greater military power than the Government of India originally thought it necessary. That India was able to inflict a crushing defeat on Pakistan in the fourteen-days war of December 1971 is further proof to the increased weight which the Government of India is now giving to military force in maintaining the territorial integrity of the State.[41]

This type of thinking has been carried forward by a number of writers, who have emphasized the economic and military dimensions of India's power. In perhaps the most widely read text on India's post-Cold War foreign policy, C. Raja Mohan argued that India's nuclear tests of 1998 were a threshold event by which '[f]ifty years after independence, India now wanted to become a normal nation – placing considerations of realpolitik and national security above its until recently dominant focus on liberal internationalism, morality, and normative approaches to international politics'.[42] In this vein, various scholars have viewed India's power through the lens of economic growth, military modernization and nuclear weapons acquisition.

Not all who study Indian foreign policy accord equal weight to economic and military factors as bases of India's power. In Kanti Bajpai's typology of strategic subcultures, for example, 'neoliberals' prioritize economic capabilities over military capabilities while the opposite is true of 'hyperrealists'.[43] In the aftermath of the Sino-Indian War, a handful of scholars argued that increased defence expenditures had harmed India's economic growth.[44] Others since then have highlighted the foundational role of economic development, even for the development of military capabilities.[45] This argument has gained considerable traction especially after the end of the Cold War, as the Indian economy has scaled new heights. India's economic growth has been described as a 'history-making' shift in 'capabilities and potential material power and global influence'.[46] It has even been suggested that 'since today's international balance of power is fundamentally determined by economics, if India became the economic and technological powerhouse it has the potential to be, it would not have to pursue the chimera of nuclear weapons'.[47] There is thus a major strand of scholarship that emphasizes the primacy of India's economic capabilities over all others, both as a source of power and a tool of statecraft.[48]

In addition to hard power, a number of scholars have highlighted the normative bases of Indian power, particularly with regard to India's civilizational greatness, the success of its anti-colonial struggle, and the principled stances that Mohandas Gandhi, Jawaharlal Nehru and other first-generation leaders of the Indian republic took both before and after independence from British colonial rule. In essence, these can be viewed as India's soft-power resources, which are now the subject of a substantial and growing body of literature.[49] As is well established in the international relations literature, soft power is the power of attraction,[50] and India is said to possess great soft-power potential in terms of its culture, political system and external policies. In the words of Pratap Bhanu Mehta, 'India certainly has a sense that the greatest source of its power in the world will be the power of its example.'[51] Indeed, many have argued that India's foreign policy of non-alignment had the effect – intended or otherwise – of allowing India to 'exercise…a considerable moral and political force' in international affairs during the Cold War.[52]

The deeper argument here is one of legitimacy and the third face of power. The naked exercise of power that military and economic capabilities alone permit is likely to be short-lived and met with resistance by other states unless it is couched – sincerely or insincerely – within an acceptable moral framework. An acceptable moral framework carries the required degree of legitimacy or 'oughtness' for the exercise of power – states give in to the influence of this type of powerful state not out of coercion or inducement but because they believe its model is intrinsically valuable and worth emulating. Thus, for example, 'principles of accommodation and mutual adjustment', especially in a thickly institutionalized international system, can produce influence where hard power cannot.[53] As noted by Deepa Ollapally,

> The currency of power is viewed [by Realists] as the distribution of capability which in turn is defined in military-industrial terms. Power as a social variable, quite apart from being a simple reflection of material strength or epiphenomena, with independent standing, is not well accommodated. For example, the notion of political legitimacy…flowing from rather socio-culturally determined rules, is generally not taken seriously by scholars of the realist ilk.[54]

A dichotomy thus appears between hard and soft sources of power as far as Indian foreign policy is concerned. In the words of the former diplomat and writer J. Bandyopadhyaya,

> At one end of the spectrum are the extreme Realists who would equate national interest with national power, and then measure power in terms of material strength, primarily military and economic strength. At the other end are the extreme Idealists or Utopians who would identify national interest with some universal moral aspiration of mankind, such as eternal peace or human brotherhood, and be willing to sacrifice the material power of the nation for the moral uplift of mankind.[55]

However, most scholars do not see this as fatal to the conduct of policy. In fact, many have positively assessed this dualism of so-called Realist and Idealist ways of thinking as a source of great flexibility for India in its external relations. India's foreign policy during the Cold War has been described as 'a negative balance of power policy at once ingenious and high-minded overlaid with idealism, but with hidden sharp edges of realistic power-politics'.[56] Similarly, India is said to both genuinely abhor and protest armaments, alliances, the balance of power, and war, while also appreciating the role of power in maintaining international peace and the territorial integrity of states.[57] Even ancient Indian statecraft and Indian epics such as the *Ramayana* and the *Mahabharata* are studied for their embodiment of the synthesis of Realist and Idealist thinking, balancing 'the calculated acquisition and exercise of power' with the 'ethical dimensions of power such as peace and justice'.[58] According to Pratap Mehta, India is often viewed in international relations scholarship as an example of what Kanti Bajpai, following Stephen Krasner, has called 'modified structuralism', a state that accepts the basic Realist assumptions of an anarchical world of power-maximizing states but maintains that cooperative structures can have a significant impact.[59]

India thus emerges as a nation whose power is defined largely in terms of economic, military and normative capabilities. The last category tends to set India apart from many other middle or rising powers in the international system. It is difficult to argue, for example, that Brazil, Turkey, Indonesia, South Africa or Mexico have possessed the normative resources that India has in the post-1945 world order.

The nature of power

On the whole, the nature of power that emerges from the literature on India is one of power as an attribute of a state in international affairs (as opposed to power as a causal relation). Increases in capabilities of any type thus lead to increases in the state's power. This raises the question of whether scholars of Indian foreign policy view power as a zero-sum attribute of states or a positive-sum one. In the former view, an increase in A's power automatically reduces B's power, whereas in the latter view both A and B can experience increases in power simultaneously. In the international relations literature, the zero-sum view informs measures of national capabilities such as the CINC (discussed earlier), which is a composite index of six indicators aggregated into one relative score, expressed as the share of the world's total capabilities belonging to any one state.

As with the other aspects of power discussed so far, views on the nature of power too have changed over time. Assessments of the Nehru period tend to emphasize the positive-sum nature of power, in that India could bolster the power of other nations without losing any of its own power or influence. According to some scholars, Nehru viewed the Cold War security dilemma – the notion that increases in the security of state A, no matter how defensive, posed a threat to state B – as originating in 'a state of funkiness of mind...a clumsy and enervating game whose participants, with all their brave gestures, are really scared of each other'.[60] It was not surprising, therefore, that Nehru turned down offers from the superpowers of a permanent seat on the UN Security Council for India: although Nehru did not deny India's right to great-power status and the power resources that UNSC membership would have brought India, he did not believe these gains could come at the expense of China's interests and aspirations.[61]

With the Sino-Indian War and Nehru's passing, scholarly assessments of Indian foreign policy began emphasizing the balance of power over cooperative positive-sum notions of power. Writing in early 1962, an analyst warned that 'Chinese aggressiveness' and 'expansionistic tendencies' may force India to 'pursue a more effective policy of balance of forces in Asia because in a system of powerful states (which is bound to come into existence) in Asia and Africa "politics of powerlessness" may not work'.[62] A year after the Sino-Indian War, another observed that '[b]alance of power is…the corner-stone for long-term planning of national security'.[63] The ensuing decades saw a gradual and begrudging acceptance of balancing as the appropriate foreign policy response to increases in Chinese and Pakistani power, thus serving to entrench a zero-sum conception of power. Contemporary work on Indian foreign policy – especially on India's rivalries and strategic competitors – takes this conception of power for granted.[64]

The pursuit of power

Although scholars of Indian foreign policy do not employ concepts of power very differently from those in the wider field of international relations, there is considerable debate over India's perception of power politics, or the pursuit of power as a state's primary foreign policy objective. The answer turns partially on how one defines power politics. India's immediate post-independence aversion to power politics is perhaps most adequately expressed in Hans Morgenthau's view of power politics as 'rooted in the lust for power which is common to all men'.[65] Morgenthau argued that politics was not a science that was amenable to 'the rationality of the engineer' but instead an art that required 'the wisdom and the moral strength of the statesman'.[66] Nehru filled this role aptly for many analysts of his era. Over time, a more pragmatic and systemic view of power politics took hold in the study of international relations, driven by the ascendancy of theorists such as Waltz and culminating in the work of John Mearsheimer, who argued that the relentless pursuit of power was in fact the only rational strategy in an anarchic world of potentially dangerous states.[67] For their part, students of Indian foreign policy embraced the pragmatism of *realpolitik* but not the aggrandizing drive of *machtpolitik*.

This reluctance to embrace an unfiltered power politics is rooted in India's Cold War foreign policy of non-alignment, which has survived in the post-Cold War era as the pursuit of strategic autonomy. What was non-alignment's relationship to power politics? There are broadly three answers to this question in the literature. First, there are those who argue that non-alignment was inherently opposed to power politics. The most common refrain here is that Indian leaders viewed power politics as essentially an imperialist instrument of oppression, part of the 'old World-order'[68] in which 'India lived as an appendage of the

Britishers [*sic*] and was a pawn' in the latter's machinations.[69] India's prolonged
and successful struggle against 'Western imperialism and racialism' had made
it 'rather suspicious of Western Powers and the diplomacy of power-politics'.[70]
Nehru associated power politics 'almost exclusively with empire-building,
and [he] was no empire-builder'.[71] He opposed colonialism, imperialism, and
racialism 'not only because they were unjust and exploitative, but because their
very essence was rivalry and competition for the world's resources which fuelled
wars and conflicts and power politics in general'.[72]

Related to the argument about imperialism is a deeper strand of thinking
which suggests that Indian leaders intrinsically viewed the pursuit of power as
something immoral. In this view, power is equated with war-mongering and
aggrandizement independent of any colonial experience or design. India, it is
argued, was 'not interested in becoming a world power by backdoor methods'.[73]
India's reaction to *machtpolitik* is described as 'puritanical',[74] and one of Nehru's
normative assumptions according to this line of thinking was that 'power politics
are evil and ought to be limited and ultimately eliminated'.[75] There is some
debate over the extent to which this worldview blinded Indian leaders to the
reality of international affairs. In the context of the Panchsheel agreement and
the Sino-Indian War, for example, one view was that '[i]n our well-meaning
zeal to sponsor a morally desirable principle, we neglected in ourselves and
overlooked in others the expedient and the ever-present profane urge of
power politics'.[76] Others claimed that although Indian leaders abhorred power
politics, they were by no means idealists unconcerned with the imperatives of
national security in an anarchic world. On this view, India was wary of Chinese
expansionism and was in the process of building up the economic resources to
support a deterrent capability. 'The Chinese invasion…merely upset the time-
schedule of the Indian strategists'.[77]

The second group of scholars argues that rather than being *against* power
politics, non-alignment was *above* it. In this line of thinking, non-alignment
essentially had goals orthogonal to power politics or was premised on a
conception of power incommensurable with commonly accepted notions. Thus,
there are those who argue that far from being a moral stance against power
politics, non-alignment was premised on a bid for status and prestige on the
world stage, either as ends in themselves or as substitutes for hard power.[78]
As one scholar has put it, 'there are, and were, definite short-term gains to be
obtained by asserting one's independence and making India's voice heard in
the world, thereby acquiring a prestige and status far beyond our actual "power

position'".[79] A separate line of reasoning is premised on India's exceptional status as a democratic developing country with a mixed economy. Consequently, being in part democratic capitalist and in part socialist, 'India could not have categorically rejected or accepted either of the stereotypes represented by the two superpowers'.[80] Ashis Nandy puts forward a similarly exceptionalist argument on the Indian view of power. He traces its roots to the Middle Ages and Hindu society's 'tenuous relationship…with a succession of alien political orders, and…the large-scale Hindu withdrawal from high politics'.[81] This led to the 'privatization of the concept of power', which came to mean 'power over self' (a concept Gandhi embraced and deployed with great success).[82] The end result was the de-legitimization of holding political power and the identification of politics with 'amoral statecraft… [A]lthough political leaders are expected to assume a self-righteous tone, there is also a certain cynicism about their moralism'.[83] Nandy's argument applied to the international realm suggests that this view of power arguably led to a detachment from power politics and the pursuit of 'private' goals in international affairs – a plausible explanation for India's inward economic orientation and grand-strategic aloofness during the Cold War, and to a lesser extent to the present day.

The third group casts non-alignment as simply a *type* of power politics. It did not entail the naked pursuit of power, but rather the measured and cautious pursuit of self-interest. Under this view,

> non-alignment as a doctrine carried within itself a device to protect the security and independence of newly born states because it was based on *realpolitik*. It was receptive and responsive to the nuances of power politics among the major powers. As a broad apparatus to conduct foreign policy, non-alignment offered ample room for individual states to define their long-term as well as short-term interests by remaining within the stream of non-aligned states.[84]

The Non-Aligned Movement (NAM) was therefore less a coalition of like-minded states and more a third bloc of states wishing to protect their autonomy from the superpowers. As a leading member of this bloc, India enjoyed considerable bargaining power in multilateral institutions, particularly on issues of economic development.[85] Even outside of international institutions, in a purely power political sense, non-alignment gave India leverage with regard to both superpowers – in a world of nuclear parity where war as a means of dispute resolution was ruled out for the superpowers, 'a country like India could, by a policy of non-alignment in the Cold War, effectively threaten potential alignment without overtly saying so'.[86] In this manner, non-alignment was 'really another form of balancing in a balance of power system'.[87] Indeed, since the end of the Cold War, India has eschewed the moral overtones of non-alignment and overtly pursued balancing strategies. As C. Raja Mohan argues,

> India has moved from its past emphasis on the power of the argument to a new stress on the argument of power. The conscious rediscovery of power as the crucial dynamic by Indian foreign policymakers does not mean India has become a cynical nation unconcerned with the normative dimension of global politics. Instead India has merely reconfigured the mix between power and principle in the pursuit of its national interest. [88]

So far has India gone down the path of becoming a 'normal' great power that some have criticized it for 'how much like the U.S. [it wants] to become... unilateral, oriented towards hegemony more than stability of the world, and besotted with its own sense of power'.[89] The transition from non-alignment as anti-imperialism to strategic autonomy as balancing has been a long one, and a lively debate exists around India's foreign policy today about the potential and desirability of India forming alliances, projecting power, and acting 'like a great power'.[90]

An agenda for future research

A strictly capabilities-based view of power naturally yields the picture of India as a rising power. However, as discussed earlier, this type of view cannot account for the variable nature of influence, or control over outcomes, that states enjoy in world politics. An important question in measuring India's power trajectory, therefore, is 'whether India gets what it wants from other states and the international system. No state gets all of what it wants all of the time, but does India get much of what it wants much of the time?'[91] Answering this question requires a relational definition of power, which scholars of Indian foreign policy have rarely operationalized. A relational understanding becomes particularly important given the manner in which the world is changing. New technologies and technological innovations have both created new non-state actors and strengthened existing non-state actors in the international system. Terrorists, hackers, transnational activists, private security firms, and the media are among those that have contributed to the fragmentation of power in world politics. Traditional conceptions of power have been state-centric and focused on national economies, military-industrial complexes, production and population. As the control of states over their own territories and populations becomes increasingly uncertain, the locus of power shifts away from states towards other entities. Even at the traditional inter-state level, the relative decline of US power and the rise of China have diminished the utility of capabilities-based notions of power. For example, China's development of anti-ship missiles and an anti-access military strategy means that the US – despite a military budget 2.8 times larger than China's and worth 36 per cent of global military expenditure – can no longer exert the kind of dominance it once did in China's maritime periphery.[92]

These developments have not gone unnoticed in India. A 2012 report by a group of public intellectuals noted that

> power itself is becoming far more diffused and fragmented – less a once-and-for-all achievement, and more a constant wary game to stay a few moves ahead of competitors and opponents...

> While China and the United States will undoubtedly remain superpowers, it is unlikely that they will be able to exercise the kind of consistent, full-spectrum global dominance that superpowers exercised during the mid-twentieth century Cold War. Alongside the U.S. and China, there will be several other centres and hubs of power that will be relevant, particularly in regional contexts.[93]

The report goes on to add that while 'great power competition of a classical kind' will continue in the future, 'we need to devise appropriate responses that address the unpredictable ways in which weak states, terrorist groups and new post-modern media-based and other forms of power, can influence or threaten our interests'.[94]

There can be no clearer statement of a research agenda on power and Indian foreign policy. As Baldwin noted almost four decades ago, any discussion of power must at the very least specify the domain and scope of the exercise of power.[95] Keeping this in mind, a number of avenues for research suggest themselves. First, in the realm of international cooperation, the field is in need of research that examines variation in the exercise of Indian power across multiple issue-areas such as international trade, international financial institutions (IFIs), climate change, nuclear proliferation and maritime security, among others. So far, research on Indian multilateralism has focused on India's strategies and policies.[96] A systematic focus on power and outcomes is likely to yield significant new insights.[97]

Second, as noted above, power is increasingly exercised in regional contexts and there is likely to be great variation in India's ability to exercise power across different geographies. For example, it has been observed that 'India's use of hard power is more evident in domestic politics [that is, internal security] and in its extended domain, in its relations with the smaller states of the [Indian] subcontinent that are within the Indian social and cultural orbit, than in its dealings with the more consequential countries'.[98] An understanding of the instruments available to India across different geographies – including economic diplomacy, alliances and strategic partnerships, among others – and the failures and successes of Indian foreign policy across regions would provide a much fuller picture of India's power and even generate prescriptions for future decision-making.

Third, possible interaction effects between issue-areas and geographical regions remain under-explored. India's weight in the international trading system and in global financial governance, for example, can act as a significant power resource in far-flung areas to which it is traditionally difficult to project power and secure influence. Similarly, it bears examining whether India's growing ties with East and Southeast Asian countries have translated into tangible benefits in multilateral forums such as the UN General Assembly and Security Council, the World Bank, the Asian Development Bank, and so on. These types of interactions are premised on the notion that non-military sources of power might be fungible between international institutions and geographies.

Fourth, the temporal dimension is vital. Is it really the case that India's power has increased over the last seven decades? By all measures of capability, the answer is yes. However, does a different frame of reference focused on the relational conception of power yield a different answer? If one thinks of power in terms of the ratio of a state's control over relevant outcomes in international affairs to its total capabilities (measured in economic terms, say), then arguably India was at least as powerful in the 1950s as it is today. To prove or disprove this claim, one would need to investigate India's power relations (not capabilities) over time, which is also likely to yield important information on the nature of India's rise and its possible future trajectory.

Finally, future research needs to examine how Indian foreign policy has been affected and will be affected by the changing nature of power globally, both due to technological change and due to the emergence of non-state actors as pivotal players. Collaborative research between international relations (or political science more broadly) and the fields of cybersecurity, robotics, genetics, nanotechnology and similar areas will be increasingly valuable in coming years.

Within the realm of international politics itself, research can shed light on viable ways in which India can leverage the growing flux in the nature of power worldwide to engage in the 'skillful management of complicated coalitions and opportunities – in environments that may be inherently unstable and volatile rather than structurally settled'.[99]

In all of the above areas, a relational conception of power will provide significantly more traction than a capabilities-based approach. To this end, scholars of Indian foreign policy would do well to steal a march on their counterparts in the West and other countries, who are yet to fully internalize the lessons that more sophisticated theorists of power have been offering for quite some time. The longer mainstream international relations scholarship remains wedded to capabilities-based notions of power, the greater the opportunity for Indian foreign policy as a domain of inquiry to push ahead with new theoretical insights and empirical investigations.

In addition to the lack of research on the issue-based and geographical contingency of power, there is a dearth of studies on the social purpose of power in the Indian context. What is India's power to be used for in world politics?[100] What kind of 'political project' would India pursue as a great power?[101] What might be the nature of an India-led global order? These are not questions of fiction or fantasy; they are vital to an understanding of how India will shape world politics as it grows more powerful and influential. Answering these questions will require detailed historical investigations – perhaps using the South Asian regional system as a microcosm of Indian hegemony – of the manner in which India has used its power to structure its international environment, address its pressing challenges, and further a particular conception, if any, of world order.[102] A small body of work exists on the global visions of key political figures in colonial and early post-independence India.[103] More research is required to uncover other historical strands of foreign policy thinking and trace their evolution,[104] particularly as they relate to power and its uses.

Conclusion

Power in the study of Indian foreign policy has been defined largely in terms of capabilities. India's capabilities are viewed as both material (economic and military) and normative. In the material realm, scholars have tended to privilege economic over military capabilities, the former being a precondition for the successful development of the latter. India is viewed as somewhat exceptional in its ability to synthesize material and normative power resources in order to serve its foreign policy objectives. As far as the pursuit of power in international affairs is concerned, scholars are divided in their assessment of India's approach to power politics. While some argue that Indian leaders have been opposed to power politics, others argue that they have floated above it, seeking different goals; yet others argue that non-alignment and strategic autonomy are nothing but variants of power politics. On the whole, there remains a rich agenda for future research on power and Indian foreign policy. Two promising areas are the issue-based and geographical contingency of power, and the social purpose of power in the Indian context. There are undoubtedly other aspects of power not considered in this chapter. The field of Indian foreign policy analysis will benefit from periodically revisiting the progress it has made in studying this vital issue in the future.

Notes

1   R. A. Dahl, 'The Concept of Power,' *Systems Research and Behavioral Science*, 2, No. 3 (1957): 202–03.
2   Ibid., 203.
3   P. Bachrach and M. S. Baratz. 'Two Faces of Power,' *The American Political Science Review*, 56, No. 4 (1962): 947–52.
4   See, for example, S. D. Krasner, 'State Power and the Structure of International Trade,' *World Politics*, 28, No. 3 (1976): 317–47; S. D. Krasner, 'Global Communications and National Power: Life on the Pareto Frontier,' *World Politics*, 43, No. 3 (1991): 336–66; T. M. Moe, 'Power and Political Institutions,' *Perspectives on Politics*, 3, No. 2 (2005): 215–33.
5   S. Lukes, *Power: A Radical View* (London: Macmillan, 1974).
6   See G. J. Ikenberry and C. A. Kupchan, 'Socialization and Hegemonic Power,' *International Organization*, 44, No. 3 (1990): 293–315; M. Finnemore, *National Interests in International Society* (Ithaca: Cornell University Press, 1996); A. I. Johnston, *Social States: China in International Institutions, 1980-2000* (Princeton: Princeton University Press, 2008).
7   D. A. Baldwin, 'Power and International Relations', in *Handbook of International Relations*, edited by W. Carlsnaes, T. Risse and B.A. Simmons, 276 (Thousand Oaks, CA: Sage Publications, 2013).
8   K. N. Waltz, *Theory of International Politics*, 191 (Reading, MA: Addison-Wesley, 1979).
9   Ibid.
10   W. C. Wohlforth, *The Elusive Balance: Power and Perceptions during the Cold War* (Ithaca: Cornell University Press, 1993).
11   Waltz, *Theory*, 192.
12   D. A. Baldwin, 'Power Analysis and World Politics,' *World Politics*, 31, No. 2 (1979): 163.

13 G. J. Ikenberry, M. Mastanduno and W. C. Wohlforth, 'Unipolarity, State Behavior, and Systemic Consequences,' *World Politics*, 61, No. 1 (2009): 3.

14 See G. J. Ikenberry, *Liberal Leviathan: The Origins, Crisis, and Transformation of the American World Order* (Princeton: Princeton University Press, 2011); M. Finnemore, 'Legitimacy, Hypocrisy, and the Social Structure of Unipolarity: Why Being a Unipole Isn't All It's Cracked Up to Be,' *World Politics*, 61, No. 1 (2009): 58–85.

15 D. J. Singer, S. Bremer and J. Stuckey, 'Capability Distribution, Uncertainty, and Major Power War, 1820-1965,' in *Peace, War, and Numbers*, edited by B. Russett, 19–48 (Beverly Hills: Sage, 1972).

16 Waltz, *Theory*, 131.

17 Baldwin, 'Power Analysis,' 164. Baldwin borrows the phrase from H. Sprout and M. Sprout, *Man-Milieu Relationship Hypotheses in the Context of International Politics* (Center of International Studies, Princeton University, Research Monograph, 1956).

18 For institutionalist theories, see R. O. Keohane, *After Hegemony: Cooperation and Discord in World Politics* (Princeton: Princeton University Press, 1984); L. M. Martin, 'Interests, Power, and Multilateralism,' *International Organization*, 46, No. 4 (1992): 765–92.

19 R. O. Keohane and J. S. Nye, *Power and Interdependence: World Politics in Transition*. (Boston: Little, Brown, 1977).

20 A. Moravcsik, 'Taking Preferences Seriously: A Liberal Theory of International Politics,' *International Organization*, 51, No. 4 (1997): 524.

21 M. S. Rajan (ed.), *International and Area Studies in India*, 13 (New Delhi: Lancer, 1997). Quoted in S. Mallavarapu, 'Introduction,' in *International Relations in India: Bringing Theory Back Home*, edited by K. Bajpai and S. Mallavarapu (New Delhi: Orient BlackSwan, 2005).

22 K. Bajpai, 'International Studies in India: Bringing Theory (Back) Home', in *Bringing Theory*, edited by K. Bajpai and S. Mallavarapu, 27–28.

23 K. Bajpai, 'Introduction', in *International Relations in India: Theorising the Region and the Nation*, edited by K. Bajpai and S. Mallavarapu, 4 (New Delhi: Orient BlackSwan, 2005).

24 Ibid., 2.

25 A. Vanaik, '1945 to 1989: The Realist Paradigm and Systemic Duality', in *Bringing Theory*, edited by K. Bajpai and S. Mallavarapu, 413.

26 See, for example, Devdutt, 'Non-Alignment and India,' *The Indian Journal of Political Science*, 23, No. 1/4 (1962): 380–97; R. Chakravarti, 'India in World Affairs,' *The Indian Journal of Political Science*, 24, No. 4 (1963): 355–67.

27 B. R. Nayar and T. V. Paul, *India in the World Order: Searching for Major-Power Status*, 3 (Cambridge: Cambridge University Press, 2003).

28 A. Appadorai and M. S. Rajan, *India's Foreign Policy and Relations*, 6 (New Delhi: South Asian Publishers, 1985).

29 Ibid.

30 See S. P. Cohen, 'India Rising,' *The Wilson Quarterly*, 24, No. 3 (2000): 32–53; D. Scott, 'India's "Extended Neighborhood" Concept: Power Projection for a Rising Power,' *India Review*, 8, No. 2 (2009): 107–43; H. V. Pant, 'A Rising India's Search for a Foreign Policy,' *Orbis*, 53, No. 2 (2009): 250–64.

31 G. K. Tanham, *Indian Strategic Thought: An Interpretive Essay* (Santa Monica: RAND, 1992); K. Bajpai, 'Indian Strategic Culture,' in *South Asia in 2020: Future Strategic Balances and Alliances*, edited by M. R. Chambers, 250–80 (Carlisle: Strategic Studies Institute, 2002); R. Sagar. 'State of Mind: What Kind of Power Will India Become?' *International Affairs*, 85, No. 4 (2009): 801–16.

32 Bajpai, 'Indian Strategic Culture,' 251.

33 A. Kohli, *State-Directed Development: Political Power and Industrialization in the Global Periphery* (Cambridge: Cambridge University Press, 2004); V. Joshi, *India's Long Road: The Search for Prosperity*, 217–38 (Gurgaon: Penguin Allen Lane, 2016).

34 D. Markey, 'Developing India's Foreign Policy "Software",' *Asia Policy*, 8 (2009): 73–96; A. Sinha and J. P. Dorschner, 'India: Rising Power or a Mere Revolution of Rising Expectations?' *Polity*, 42, No. 1 (2010): 74–99; D. P. Fidler and S. Ganguly, 'India and Eastphalia,' *Indiana Journal of Global Legal Studies*, 17, No. 1 (2010): 147–64.

35 S. N. Maitra, 'A New Look at Foreign Policy,' *Economic and Political Weekly*, 2, No. 17 (1967): 793.

36 See S. Raghavan, *War and Peace in Modern India*, 267–310 (Ranikhet: Permanent Black, 2010).

37 Chakravarti, 'India,' 356.

38 P. Prabhakar, 'A Re-Examination of India's Foreign Policy,' *The Indian Journal of Political Science*, 24, No. 4 (1963): 373.

39 M. S. Rajan, 'India and World Politics in the Post-Nehru Era,' *International Journal*, 24, No. 1 (1968): 155.

40 K. R. Narayanan, 'Towards a New Equilibrium in Asia,' *Economic and Political Weekly*, 7, No. 5/7 (1972): 221.

41 Appadorai and Rajan, *India's Foreign Policy*, 50.

42 C. R. Mohan, *Crossing the Rubicon: The Shaping of India's New Foreign Policy*, 7 (New Delhi: Penguin, 2003).

43 K. Bajpai, 'Indian Grand Strategy: Six Schools of Thought,' in *India's Grand Strategy: History, Theory, Cases*, edited by K. Bajpai, S. Basit and V. Krishnappa, 113–50 (New Delhi: Routledge, 2014).

44 See, for example, N. K. Sarkar, 'Indian Foreign Policy and Economic Development,' *Economic and Political Weekly*, 2, No. 38 (1967): 1741–42.

45 See Narayanan, 'New Equilibrium,' 223.

46 Fidler and Ganguly, 'India and Eastphalia,' 149.

47 R. Thakur, 'India in the World: Neither Rich, Powerful, nor Principled,' *Foreign Affairs*, 76, No. 4 (1997): 15–22.

48 On the latter, see Rajan, 'India and World Politics,' 155.

49 N. Blarel, 'India's Soft Power: From Potential to Reality?' in *IDEAS Reports – Special Reports*, edited by N. Kitchen (SR010. LSE IDEAS, London School of Economics, 2012); I. Hall, 'India's New Public Diplomacy: Soft Power and the Limits of Government Action,' *Asian Survey*, 52, No. 6 (2012): 1089–110; J. Lee, 'Unrealised Potential: India's 'Soft Power' Ambition in Asia,' *Foreign Policy Analysis*, 4 (2010); D. Malone, 'Soft Power in Indian Foreign Policy,' *Economic and Political Weekly*, 46, No. 36 (2011): 35–39; R. D. Mullen and S. Ganguly, 'The Rise of India's Soft Power,' *Foreign Policy*, 8 May 2012; U. Purushothaman, 'Shifting Perceptions of Power: Soft Power and India's Foreign

Policy,' *Journal of Peace Studies*, 17 No. 2/3 (2010); S. Tharoor, 'India as a Soft Power,' *India International Centre Quarterly*, 35, No. 1 (2008): 32–45; C. Wagner, 'From Hard Power to Soft Power? Ideas, Interaction, Institutions, and Images in India's South Asia Policy,' Working Paper No. 26 (Heidelberg Papers in South Asian and Comparative Politics, 2005).

50 See J. S. Nye, 'Soft Power.' *Foreign Policy*, 80 (1990): 153–71; J. S. Nye, *Soft Power: The Means to Success in World Politics* (New York: Public Affairs, 2004).

51 P. B. Mehta, 'Still Under Nehru's Shadow? The Absence of Foreign Policy Frameworks in India,' *India Review*, 8, No. 3 (2009): 218.

52 Chakravarti, 'India,' 363.

53 J. K. Patnaik, 'International Political Economy and Regime Analysis: A Developing-Country Perspective,' in *Theorising the Region*, edited by K. Bajpai and S. Mallavarapu, 50.

54 D. Ollapally, 'Foreign Policy and Identity Politics: Realist versus Culturalist Lessons,' in *Theorising the Region*, edited by K. Bajpai and S. Mallavarapu, 131.

55 J. Bandyopadhyaya, *The Making of India's Foreign Policy: Determinants, Institutions, Processes and Personalities*, 4 (New Delhi: Allied Publishers, 1970).

56 Narayanan, 'New Equilibrium,' 219.

57 Appadorai and Rajan, *India's Foreign Policy*, 47.

58 J. Vivekanandan, '"Strategy, Legitimacy and the Imperium",' in *India's Grand Strategy*, edited by K. Bajpai et al., 79.

59 Mehta, 'Nehru's Shadow,' 210; S. D. Krasner, 'Structural Causes and Regime Consequences: Regimes as Intervening Variables,' *International Organization*, 36, No. 2 (1982): 185–205. See also K. Bajpai, 'India: Modified Structuralism,' in *Asian Security Practice: Material and Ideational Influences*, edited by M. Alagappa (Stanford: Stanford University Press, 1998).

60 Devdutt, 'Non-Alignment,' 384. See also A. P. Rana, 'The Intellectual Dimensions of India's Nonalignment,' *The Journal of Asian Studies*, 28, No. 2 (1969): 299–300.

61 See A. Harder, 'When Nehru Refused American Bait on a Permanent Seat for India at the UN,' *The Wire* (2016). Available at https://thewire.in/58802/when-nehru-refused-american-bait-on-a-permanent-seat-for-india-at-the-un/.

62 Devdutt, 'Non-Alignment,' 396.

63 Prabhakar, 'Re-Examination,' 372.

64 See R. Rajagopalan, 'Neorealist Theory and the India–Pakistan Conflict,' in *Theorising the Region*, edited by K. Bajpai and S. Mallavarapu, 142–72; T. V. Paul, *The India-Pakistan Conflict: An Enduring Rivalry* (Cambridge: Cambridge University Press, 2005); C. R. Mohan, 'India and the Balance of Power,' *Foreign Affairs*, 85, No. 4 (2006): 17–32; H. V. Pant, 'India in the Indian Ocean: Growing Mismatch between Ambitions and Capabilities,' *Pacific Affairs*, 82, No. 2 (2009): 279–97.

65 H. Morgenthau, *Scientific Man vs. Power Politics*, 16 (London: Latimer House, 1947).

66 Ibid.

67 John J. Mearsheimer. *The Tragedy of Great Power Politics* (New York: W. W. Norton, 2001).

68 P. N. Kirpal, 'Speculation on the International Relations of a Free and United India in the Post-War World,' *The Indian Journal of Political Science*, 7, No.1/2 (1945): 398–99.

69   T. B. Mukherjee, 'India's Foreign Policy,' *The Indian Journal of Political Science*, 10, No. 1/2 (1949): 47.

70   Chakravarti, 'India,' 355–56.

71   Rana, 'Intellectual Dimensions,' 306.

72   S. Kalyanaraman, 'Nehru's Advocacy of Internationalism and Indian Foreign Policy,' in *India's Grand Strategy*, edited by K. Bajpai et al., 153.

73   E. Asirvatham, 'How Sound Is India's Foreign Policy?' *The Indian Journal of Political Science*, 16, No. 4 (1955): 383.

74   Rana, 'Intellectual Dimensions,' 305.

75   D. Lal, 'Indian Foreign Policy, 1947–64, (Part 1),' *Economic and Political Weekly*, 2, No. 19 (1967): 881.

76   R. Khan, 'Crisis of National Interest in India,' *Economic and Political Weekly*, 3, No. 26/28 (1968): 1097.

77   D. Lal, 'Indian Foreign Policy, 1947–64, (Part 2),' *Economic and Political Weekly*, 2, No. 20 (1967): 936.

78   Asirvatham, 'How Sound', 377.

79   Lal, 'Indian Foreign Policy' (Part 2), 937.

80   R. Harshe, 'India's Non-Alignment: An Attempt at Conceptual Reconstruction,' *Economic and Political Weekly*, 25, No. 7 (1990): 400.

81   A. Nandy, 1973. 'The Making and Unmaking of Political Cultures in India,' *Daedalus*, 102, No. 1 (1990): 119.

82   Ibid.

83   Ibid.

84   Harshe, 'India's Non-Alignment,' 400.

85   Chakravarti, 'India,' 358.

86   Rana, 'Intellectual Dimensions,' 309.

87   Fidler and Ganguly, 'India and Eastphalia,' 151.

88   Mohan, *Crossing the Rubicon*, xxii

89   P. B. Mehta, 'Five Balancing Acts,' *Seminar*, 560 (2006). Available at http://www.india-seminar.com/2006/560/560%20pratap%20bhanu%20mehta.htm, accessed on 26 February 2017.

90   S. P. Cohen, *India: Emerging Power*, 35 (Washington, D.C.: The Brookings Institutions, 2001). See also A. J. Tellis, 'India as a Leading Power', Carnegie Endowment for International Peace, Washington, D.C.; B. Karnad, *Why India Is Not a Great Power (Yet)* (New Delhi: Oxford University Press, 2015); R. Guha, 'Will India Become A Superpower?' *Outlook*, 30 June 2008.

91   G. Perkovich, 'The Measure of India: What Makes Greatness?' *Seminar*, 529 (2003). Available at http://www.india-seminar.com/2003/529/529%20george%20perkovich.htm, accessed on 26 February 2017.

92   Defense expenditure figures calculated from the Stockholm International Peace Research Institute (SIPRI) Military Expenditure Database, https://www.sipri.org/databases/milex, accessed on 26 February 2017.

93   S. Khilnani, R. Kumar, P. B. Mehta, P. Menon, N. Nilekani, S. Raghavan, S. Saran and S.

Varadarajan, *Nonalignment 2.0: A Foreign and Strategic Policy for India in the Twenty First Century*, 9 (2012). Available at http://www.cprindia.org/research/reports/nonalignment-20-foreign-and-strategic-policy-india-twenty-first-century.

94 Ibid., 10.

95 Baldwin, 'Power Analysis', 163.

96 See W. P. S. Sidhu, P. B. Mehta and B. Jones, *Shaping the Emerging World: India and the Multilateral Order* (Washington, D.C.: Brookings Institution Press, 2013); D. Malone, *Does the Elephant Dance? Contemporary Indian Foreign Policy*, 249–73 (New York: Oxford University Press, 2011); A. Narlikar, 'Peculiar Chauvinism or Strategic Calculation: Explaining the Negotiation Strategy of a Rising India,' *International Affairs*, 82, No. 1 (2006): 77–94.

97 For a very preliminary step in this direction, see A. Narlikar, 'All That Glitters Is Not Gold: India's Rise to Power,' *Third World Quarterly*, 28, No. 5 (2007): 983–96.

98 B. Karnad, 'An Elephant with a Small "Footprint": The Realist Roots of India's Strategic Thought and Policies,' in *India's Grand Strategy*, edited by K. Bajpai et al., 200.

99 Khilnani et al., *Nonalignment 2.0*, 9.

100 K. M. Chenoy and A. M. Chenoy, 'India's Foreign Policy Shifts and the Calculus of Power,' *Economic and Political Weekly*, 42, No. 35 (2007): 3553.

101 On great powers and their political projects, see B. Hansen, *Unipolarity and World Politics: A Theory and Its Implications* (New York: Routledge, 2011).

102 For an example in the case of the US, see J. Ruggie, 'International Regimes, Transactions, and Change: Embedded Liberalism in the Postwar Economic Order,' *International Organization*, 36, No. 2 (1982): 379–415.

103 See M. Bhagavan, *The Peacemakers: India and the Quest for One World* (New Delhi: HarperCollins, 2012); R. Sagar, '"Jiski Lathi, Uski Bhains": The Hindu Nationalist View of International Politics,' in *India's Grand Strategy*, edited by K. Bajpai et al., 234–57; R. Sagar and A. Panda, 'Pledges and Pious Wishes: The Constituent Assembly Debates and the Myth of a "Nehruvian Consensus",' *India Review*, 14, No. 2 (2015): 203–20.

104 For an example of this kind of research in the case of Japan, see R. Samuels, *Securing Japan: Tokyo's Grand Strategy and the Future of East Asia* (Ithaca: Cornell University Press, 2007).

3

Constructivism and Indian Foreign Policy

Priya Chacko

This chapter seeks to examine how scholars have used constructivist approaches in International Relations (IR) to further the study of India's foreign policy. Constructivist approaches to the study of foreign policy focus on the social construction of foreign policy interests. They differ from rationalist, realist and liberal approaches because they do not see foreign policy interests as pre-given and unchanging and take foreign policy discourses and practices of representation seriously rather than dismissing them as 'mere rhetoric'. Constructivist approaches are also distinct from approaches in foreign policy analysis (FPA) that analyse 'belief systems', 'operational codes' and 'national role conceptions' because these are usually cognitive perspectives that attribute discourses and representations to the individual minds of policymakers.[1] Constructivists question the individualist ontology that informs these accounts, arguing that individuals are fundamentally social beings. They also reject the false assumption that material facts have objective meanings and singular interpretations and point to the empirical impossibility of getting into the individual decision-maker's mind. Instead, constructivist scholars analyse foreign policy discourses – groups of statements that produce particular kinds of knowledge about a topic – and norms – shared ideas about appropriate behaviour – as they are reproduced in public and private statements and foreign policy actions. Rather than being epiphenomenal, discourses and norms are seen by constructivists as key to the process of communication and persuasion with which state officials constitute a world. Moreover, constructivists argue that discourses and norms provide insights into the domestic and international political and cultural environment because they are viewed as inter-subjective structures of rules rather than the product of individual cognitive processes. By using constructivist concepts, like identity and norms, and methodologies, like critical discourse analysis, to analyse the domestic and international social relations that underpin the foreign policy interests and practices, scholars have deepened our understanding of established and new issues in Indian foreign policy. The chapter proceeds as follows. The first part details the emergence of constructivist approaches in IR and discusses the characteristics of the two major variants of conventional constructivism and critical constructivism. The second part of the chapter overviews the ways in which scholars have utilized constructivist approaches in the study of Indian foreign policy. The final part of the chapter illustrates how a constructivist framework can be used, by applying it to understand India's approach to Pakistan, Kashmir and cross-border terrorism under the Narendra Modi regime.

Constructivism and foreign policy

The development of IR theory has been strongly shaped by the global social and historical context. Structural realism's dominance during the Cold War, for instance, was related, in part, to its seeming ability to explain the dynamics of the relationship between the United States (US) and the Soviet Union. Likewise, it is no coincidence that constructivist approaches emerged at the end of the 1980s and rose to prominence in the 1990s as the Cold War ended. The collapse of the Soviet Union, which was infamously unforeseen by mainstream IR scholars, and its internal reform through *glasnost* and *perestroika,* was interpreted by constructivist scholars like Alexander Wendt as demonstrating the importance of ideas, identities, and their ability to transform foreign policy interests and, therefore, the conflictual nature of the international system.[2] Wendt, along with Friedrich Kratochwil and Nicholas Onuf, who introduced the term 'constructivism' to IR, is often considered one of the founding figures of the constructivist tradition.[3] Constructivism, however, is less a theory than an approach and, as such, there are different variants. This is, of course, not unique to constructivism. Realism too is better conceived as an approach, given that it comes in defensive, offensive, classical and neo-classical variants. Likewise, liberalism includes variants like neoliberal institutionalism, liberal interdependence and liberal preference theory. There have been a number of attempts to classify the different variants of constructivism in IR.[4] Here, I follow Ted Hopf in demarcating between two major variants, critical constructivism – which builds on the work of Onuf and Kratochwil – and conventional constructivism – which builds on Wendt and has become the dominant strand of constructivism in North American IR. Both variants draw insights from critical social theories; they both place importance on the role of language in social life to reveal the social construction of practices, identities and institutions, and they both utilize interpretivist methodologies such as discourse analysis and narrative analysis. However, as Hopf has argued, conventional constructivism 'is a collection of principles distilled from critical social theory' but without critical constructivism's 'more consistent theoretical or epistemological follow-through'.[5] The differences are clear in the divergent approaches the two variants take to the key constructivist concept of 'state identity' – the identity promoted by leaders and officials, as reflected in foreign policy discourses, which underpins foreign policy interests. As Hopf summarises:

> Conventional constructivists wish to discover identities and their associated reproductive social practices, and then offer an account of how those identities imply certain actions. But critical theorists have a different aim. They also wish to surface identities, not to articulate their effects, but to elaborate on how people come to believe in a single version of a naturalized truth. In other words, critical theory aims at exploding the myths associated with identity formation, whereas conventional constructivists wish to treat those identities as possible causes of action.

Hence, for conventional constructivists, certain types of identity lead to particular forms of behaviour, whereas for critical constructivists, identities provide social constraints and conditions of possibility for foreign policy action. Rather than seeking to uncover the 'real reasons' behind foreign policy decisions, which critical constructivists consider an impossibility given that we cannot get into individual minds, they seek to reveal how it becomes possible – through an analysis of language and discourses – for certain foreign policy actions to be undertaken over others.[6] Conventional constructivist analyses, moreover, has tended to focus on inter-state interaction, collective identity formation and global 'norms' – particularly norms that are seen as progressive such as humanitarianism or cooperation – and their 'diffusion' and 'localization' in the international system.[7] Critical constructivist analyses, by contrast, have critiqued the neglect of politics and power in the construction of identities and norms in conventional constructivist accounts. They have also questioned the assumption by scholars like Wendt that all states have certain 'core interests' such as 'survival' and that some interests, such as security and economic interests, can be treated as being 'pre-social'. Hence, critical constructivist work has tended to emphasize the domestic context and the patterns of domestic and international power relations – drawing on work by Foucault, Wittgenstein and Althusser among others to conceptualize power in critical terms – and how they shape state identity formation.[8] The liberal-idealist concerns of much conventional constructivist scholarship and the focus on power and the creation of dangerous 'Others' in critical constructivism means that the former could be characterized as a 'liberal' form of constructivism while the latter is a 'realist' form of constructivism.[9] Indeed, in her seminal work on critical constructivism, Jutta Weldes explicitly built on an overlooked insight in the classical realist scholarship of Hans Morgenthau who noted in his *Politics Among Nations* that 'the kind of interest determining political action in a particular period of history depends upon *the political and cultural context* within which foreign policy is formulated. The goals that might be pursued by nations in their foreign policy can run the whole gamut of objectives any nation has ever pursued or might possibly pursue'.[10]

Critical and conventional constructivist approaches continue to undergo conceptual development through internal dialogue and by using concepts from outside IR to address the weaknesses and limitations in the constructivist research agenda. Critical constructivists, for instance, have engaged with the conventional constructivist concepts of 'norms' and 'socialization', to address the lack of attention to agency and the tendency towards teleology in understanding norm diffusion in the international system. They have done so by returning to the conceptual origins of these notions in sociology, showing these to be less reductionist and more dynamic than their mobilization in IR would suggest. By advocating processual-relational approaches that draw on insights from sociology or postcolonial theory, this literature has highlighted the agency of 'socialisees', the relational nature of agency and the inherent dynamism and indeterminacy of norms.[11] Constructivist research has also sharpened understandings of identity construction by delving into sociological research on 'ontological security' and emotions to go beyond the conceptualization of identity as requiring the negative identification of an 'Other' and pointing instead to the processes of positive identification and the affective dimensions of both state identity formation and collective inter-state identity formation.[12] A recent 'practice turn' focusses on foreign policy practices, such as the formation of security communities like the North Atlantic Treaty Organization as 'socially meaningful patterns of action, which...reify background knowledge and discourse in and on the material world'.[13]

Constructivism and Indian foreign policy

There is a small but growing literature on Indian foreign policy which either explicitly uses constructivist frameworks or relies on constructivist methodologies. Scholars of Indian foreign policy were, in fact, at the forefront of the emergence of critical constructivism in IR. Himadeep Muddipi's contribution to a seminal volume of critical constructivist analysis, *Cultures of Insecurity*, underscored the 'added value' of constructivism for Indian foreign policy analysis and of Indian foreign policy case studies for the development of the constructivist research agenda.[14] Drawing on Althusser's notions of interpellation and articulation, Muppidi pointed to the inability of mainstream liberal and realist approaches to account for India's persistently insecure Cold War relationship with the United States and its friendly relationship with the Soviet Union and underscored the importance of taking account of India's colonial history and postcolonial 'security imaginary'. Likewise, Sankaran Krishna's (1999) book on India's intervention in Sri Lanka's civil war argued that 'an entity called "India" is coeval with a discourse called "Indian foreign policy"'.[15] Since these early contributions, scholars have used critical constructivist frameworks and insights to analyse India's foreign policy in South Asia, its stance on international intervention, its regional engagement and conflicts, its bilateral relationships and the foreign policy of the Bharatiya Janata Party (BJP).[16] An important feature of critical constructivist accounts of Indian foreign policy and a contribution to constructivist scholarship has been its utilization of literature in postcolonial studies. The work of scholars such as Homi Bhabha, Dipesh Chakrabarty and Partha Chatterjee has been used to theorize the impact of colonial legacies on contemporary global order and on the shaping of India's identity. Notions of 'mimicry' and 'ambivalence' have been particularly important in understanding the construction of India's postcolonial identity and the distinctive aspects of its foreign policy such as its persistent claims to exceptionalism, its entrenched territorial conflicts with Pakistan and China and its long-held emphasis on autonomy.[17]

The use of conventional constructivist frameworks has been less common in studies of Indian foreign policy. This perhaps reflects the central focus of this literature on Eurocentric accounts of global norms and socialization. India's rejection of alliance relationships and collective identity formation for much of its postcolonial history and its resistance to many aspects of the post-World War II liberal order served to challenge rather than validate conventional constructivist assumptions about state behaviour. The emergence of more sophisticated concepts of 'norm contestation' and 'norm localization' in conventional constructivist literature, however, seems to be facilitating more engagement. As India has moved away from non-alignment and towards the building of strategic partnerships and regional multilateralism, moreover, conventional constructivist literature on collective identity formation has become more relevant. Recent works have used conventional constructivist notions of state identity, norm contestation and norm localization to understand Indian debates on the Responsibility to Protect doctrine, India's relationship with the United States, India's engagement with climate change governance, its attempt to portray itself as a responsible nuclear power and India's approach to regional multilateralism in South Asia.[18]

By far the most popular issue area to which both conventional and constructivist approaches and methodologies have been applied, however, is nuclear weapons and, in this regard, scholars of Indian foreign policy have made distinctive contributions to understanding the politics of nuclear weapons, nuclear orders and nuclear technology. India's path to nuclear weapons had an unusual trajectory. The two-decade gap between nuclear tests, India's long-standing espousal of nuclear disarmament, and its continuing refusal to sign the Nuclear Non-Proliferation Treaty and the Comprehensive Test Ban Treaty, despite being one of the first countries to propose these regimes, have all proven ripe for constructivist analysis. An early contribution, Haider Nizamani's account of nuclear discourses in India and Pakistan, utilized constructivist methodologies of narrative analysis.[19] Since then, scholars of Indian foreign policy, using constructivism, have analysed the domestic politics of nuclear policy, the gendered and racialized nature of nuclear debates, India's engagement with the non-proliferation regime and the global nuclear order and the domestic and international context which prompted the nuclear tests of 1998, after which India declared itself a nuclear weapons state.[20] Recent work has also explored India and Pakistan's nuclear diplomacy and India's nuclear relations with the United States and Australia, with whom it has agreements for civilian nuclear technology cooperation and uranium sales.[21]

Another notable aspect of constructivist work on Indian foreign policy has been its attentiveness to political economy and capitalism. Like much mainstream IR theory, constructivist approaches tend to treat 'economics' and 'security' and ideas and material factors as distinct phenomena.[22] In conventional constructivism, for instance, 'cultural' factors are kept separate from material factors and economics is only relevant if commerce and trade can help to socialize states into cooperative relationships.[23] The focus on practices of representation in most critical constructivist approaches has come at the expense of theorizing the role of the socio-economic context in the formation of state identities. Several constructivist accounts of Indian foreign policy, however, have made attempts to foreground the economics–security nexus and the mutual constitution of material and ideational factors in novel ways. Muppidi, for instance, has sought to link India's nuclear policies to the broader construction of the global political economy and India's place within it by Indian political elites.[24] Specifically, he has argued that India's rejection of the nuclear non-proliferation regime is a part of its resistance to a hierarchical or colonial global order that places it in a subordinate political and economic position. Latha Varadarajan has argued for a view of state identity as constituted 'in and through a relationship with the global economy' and has illustrated this approach by drawing connections between India's nuclear tests and its decision to liberalize its economy in the 1990s which created new forms of insecurity.[25] Jalal Alamgir has argued that the commitment of successive Indian governments to economic liberalization, despite domestic resistance, was the outcome of India's 'globalist' identity and its perceptions of rivalry with China.[26] Using a framework that synthesizes constructivist foreign policy analysis and economic sociology, Chacko has argued that India's changing approach to international intervention, which has shifted from support for multilateral interventionism in the 1950s and 1960s, to the practice of unilateral intervention in the 1970s and 1980s, to resistance to notions of humanitarian intervention in the 1990s and heavily qualified support for the Responsibility to Protect doctrine in the 2000s, is linked to political and economic changes in its state-building project and the global political economy in which it is embedded. Below, I use this framework to analyse recent developments in India's foreign policy in relation to Pakistan and Islamist militancy in order to demonstrate the utility of a constructivist approach.

Case study: From strategic restraint to 'surgical strikes'

In November 2016, India announced that it had undertaken pre-emptive 'surgical strikes' against Pakistan-based militants across the Line of Control in Kashmir who the government claimed were preparing to launch attacks in Indian cities and in the Indian state of Jammu and Kashmir. There had been several militant attacks against Indian military targets since the election of the BJP-led National Democratic Alliance (NDA) in 2014. The worst attack, in the town of Uri, resulted in the deaths of 19 Indian soldiers, and was alleged by India to have been carried out by the Pakistan-based group Jaish-e-Mohammad (JEM). The use of 'surgical strikes' constituted a departure from the previous Congress Party-led United Progressive Alliance (UPA) government's policy of strategic restraint. While officials associated with the UPA government have admitted that it undertook cross-border raids these were not publicized and they went unacknowledged by the army. The limited and defensive nature of the 'surgical strikes', however, suggested that the government had modified rather than abandoned strategic restraint altogether. How do we theorize the BJP-led government's decision to publicize and escalate India's responses to cross-border attacks and how do we understand the government's unwillingness to undertake more extensive action?

A critical constructivist approach to foreign policy analysis should be well-placed to account for foreign policy change given its emphasis on the inherent instability and dynamism of state identities and, hence, the construction of the national interest.[27] Yet much critical constructivist work tends to emphasize the persistence of key features of state identities, without an adequate explanation of why this is the case.[28] This is the outcome of the deliberate emphasis in critical constructivist work on discourse and representation rather than socio-political and socio-economic conditions. Weldes, for instance, argues that constructions of the national interest develop in specific social, political and economic contexts that include non-linguistic practices that exist in a reciprocal relationship with discursive practices.[29] Yet, '[d]espite the undeniable importance of non-linguistic practices' her objective was 'to demonstrate that linguistic practices also have real and independent effects' because these are frequently given little regard in studies of foreign policy and international relations.[30] As Laffey notes, however, the reproduction of state identities through foreign policy leads to materializations and sedimentations in a changing 'landscape of institutions, apparatuses, and social relations' and this has consequences for both identities, and the foreign policy interests they give rise to as different actors and ideas are differentially empowered over time.[31] To develop a critical constructivist approach to understanding continuity and change in foreign policy, I draw from economic sociology and, in particular, Bob Jessop's 'cultural politial economy' approach.

Drawing on Marx and Foucault's later work on the state, Jessop argues that there are three key 'moments' in the development of power relations in societies: 'variation in the objects, subjects, purposes, and technologies of power; selection of some technologies and practices rather than others; and retention of some of these in turn as they are integrated into broader and more stable strategies of state and/or class (or national or racial) power'.[32] These three moments are constituted by both discursive and non-discursive factors, and the second and third steps reintroduce social classes, capital and the state, although these are not considered to be pre-constituted forces by Foucault but rather 'emergent effects of multiple projects, practices, and attempts to institutionalize political

power relations'.[33] Still, Foucault linked 'the retention of particular forms of
disciplinary and governmental power explicitly to bourgeois recognition of
their economic profitability and political utility'.[34] Using this framework,
continuity and change in foreign policy can be understood as being shaped
by (1) continuous *variation* in discourses and practices of foreign policy;
(2) the *selection* of certain foreign policy discourses and practices, either new
or existing, for interpreting events and legitimating foreign policy actions;
and (3) the *retention* of resonant foreign policy discourses and practices in
the identities of actors, institutional structures, hegemonic visions and state
projects. All of these mechanisms involve national and international discursive
and non-discursive factors. Foreign policy variation can occur when national
and international events and actors challenge the reproduction of dominant
state identities and foreign policy discourses and practices. The discursive
framing of new and old ideas and practices will help determine the selection
of foreign policy interests by influencing the extent to which they resonate
with key actors, in institutions and with broader metanarratives of state
identity. Non-discursive factors 'also operate here through conjunctural or
entrenched power relations, path-dependency, and structural selectivities'.[35]
In other words, the stronger the promotion of new foreign policy ideas
and practices by actors in existing power structures and the exclusion or
discrediting of alternative discourses and practices, the more likely they are
to be institutionalized and reinforced.

Identity and foreign policy under the Congress:
The emergence of a 'transformational' identity

An analysis of the foreign policy discourse and practices under the Congress-led
UPA government reveals the production of a state identity that can be described
as 'transformational'. This identity was constituted by a long-standing economy
of identity/difference that defined India by its civilizational exceptionalism
and against its pre-modern past, its non-democratic neighbours and external
colonialism. It was also significantly constituted by the more recent outcomes
of India's integration into the global economy from the 1990s and a change in
international representations of India as a 'rising power' from the mid-2000s
in particular.[36] India's global integration was the product of a change in the
dominant 'social imaginary', which is made up of policymakers' interpretations
of the world and the nature of power relations.[37] This shift was due to a fiscal
crisis in the late 1980s, economic growth in China and East Asia, and the
demise of the Soviet Union, all of which led to new insecurities and anxieties

about India's 'backwardness'. These developments empowered pro-economic reform policymakers and political leaders to promote and select new foreign policy ideas and discourses. The turn away from policies of import-substituting industrialization and towards economic liberalization was represented by policymakers as a technical change that was necessary for India to achieve its long-term goals of self-reliant economic development, political stability and international autonomy and, therefore, a rearticulation of its postcolonial state identity.[38] However, through this process of rearticulation, key 'signifiers' such as 'self-reliance' took on different meanings, leading to the production of an altered identity. In semiotics, discourses consist of 'signifiers' or words that gain meaning from their differential or associative relation with other signifiers and they work to constitute subject positions or social identities. Discourses and identities, therefore, change when these differential or associative relations are altered.

In the case of economic reforms in India, policymakers such as Manmohan Singh, who was Finance Minister when economic reforms were introduced, and Pranab Mukherjee, another pro-reform senior Congress leader, sought to associate self-reliance with 'economic growth' and 'liberalization' while the opposite of self-reliance – dependency – was associated with the need to resort to conditional loans from multilateral institutions as a result of fiscal deficits.[39] For instance, Singh argued in his 1996 budget speech that, '…in an interdependent world, swadeshi [self-reliance] must not be interpreted to mean economic isolation but rather self-reliance in building a prosperous India which interacts as an equal with other countries in the world'.[40] This rearticulated identity faced resistance from both the left and the right, with the Communist Party arguing that globalization was a new form of colonialism and the Hindu nationalist BJP arguing for internal liberalization and external protectionism in a bid to protect its traditional voter base of small farmers and traders.[41] Ultimately, however, policies of economic liberalization were adopted by the BJP when it won the elections in 1998 and these were institutionalized in various government ministries through the adoption of policies encouraging private and foreign investment and the use of market mechanisms in formerly state-dominated sectors. They also served to create an expanding middle class and corporate sector which formed a small but powerful domestic support base for economic reforms.

Discontent about the outcomes of economic reforms, such as 'jobless' growth and the scaling back of formerly universal social welfare programmes, continued to grow, however, and contributed to the defeat of the BJP-led NDA government in 2004. The new Congress-led government came to power on an electoral platform that promised 'inclusive growth' through continued reforms and the expansion of welfare programmes. Long-standing signifiers in India's foreign policy discourse like 'self-reliance' and 'non-alignment' under the Congress-led government were now linked with poverty alleviation and liberalization. As the National Security Advisor, Shivshankar Menon, put it:

> ... our primary task now and for the foreseeable future is to transform and improve the life of the unacceptably large number of our compatriots who live in poverty, with disease, hunger and illiteracy as their companions in life. This is our overriding priority, and must be the goal of our internal and external security policies. Our quest is the transformation of India, nothing less and nothing more. If we have consistently sought to avoid external entanglements or outside restraints on our freedom of choice and action it is because we have been acutely conscious of this overriding priority and wanted nothing else to come in the way of its pursuit. This was and remains the essence of the policy of non-alignment.... In other words, India would only be a responsible power if our choices bettered the lot of our people... There are several significant corollaries to this simple sounding proposition. It is certainly not a recipe for turning our backs on the world and trying for pure autonomy. We tried that for a while and it led to a growth rate of 3.5%. Instead it implies the active pursuit of our interests in the world, always bearing in mind our goal.[42]

The Congress's 'transformational' identity formed the basis of an economic growth-focussed foreign policy that placed emphasis on regional peace and stability. As Manmohan Singh, now Prime Minister, put it, '[o]bjective conditions point to South Asia emerging as a growth pole of the world economy. India and Pakistan, the two largest economies in the region, can give concrete shape to this vision and can find the pathway to a future of shared peace and prosperity'. This transformational identity made possible the UPA's strategy towards Pakistan and the Kashmir dispute which involved 'back channel' talks, a composite dialogue that focused on building economic and people-to-people links and a policy of strategic restraint. This meant that even after the 2008 terrorist attack in Mumbai by the Pakistan-based group Lashkar-e-Taiba led to a suspension of talks, the government and army downplayed subsequent military tensions and failed to publically acknowledge ongoing cross-border raids. The UPA's tenure was also a period in which

India emerged in Western discourses and foreign policies, particularly that of the United States, as a benign 'rising power' and a potential balancing force against a rising China.[43] These characterizations buttressed long-standing Indian discourses on the responsibility and exceptionalism of the Indian state as an international actor. They were rearticulated in the statements of Indian officials through an emphasis on India as a 'different' sort of big power: 'India will not be like the traditional big powers. Mrs Indira Gandhi used to say India will be a different power, a power that works for development, peace and international understanding, in its own interest and in that of its friends and partners abroad, Asia is not Europe and our indigenous strategic cultures are strong and lasting.'[44]

Identity and foreign policy under the BJP: From a 'transformational' to an 'aspirational' identity

Corruption scandals, slowing economic growth and rising inflation served to undermine the legitimacy of the UPA government in its second term and contributed to the election of the Congress-led government led by the BJP in 2014. In the lead-up to the election, the BJP indicated that there would be significant changes in India's foreign policy were it to be elected. The BJP's election manifesto pledged to 'create a web of allies' which suggested the end of India's long-held stance of non-alignment. It also promised 'zero tolerance' for terrorism and a reconsideration of India's 'no first use' nuclear policy. Yet, there has been no shift in India's nuclear policy and though India signed on to a Joint Strategic Vision for the Asia-Pacific and Indian Ocean Region with the Obama Administration, the Prime Minister, Narendra Modi, asserted in a 2016 interview that '[t]here is no reason to change India's non-alignment policy that is a legacy and has been in place'.[45]

There has, thus, been significant continuity in the BJP-led government's foreign policy. Like the UPA government it has emphasised economics, regional cooperation, 'soft power', engaging the diaspora and forming strategic partnerships while maintaining strategic autonomy. However, the addition of signifiers such as 'aspiring power' and 'leading power' in foreign policy statements from 2015 does reflect an important change.[46] As the former Foreign Secretary, S. Jaishankar, noted in a speech in 2015 outlining the 'foreign policy implications of a government led by Prime Minister Modi':

You would have already noted more energetic diplomacy that seeks a larger
and deeper footprint in the world, supported by soft-power initiatives like
the International Day of Yoga. The transition in India is an expression of
greater self-confidence. Its foreign policy dimension is to aspire to be a
leading power, rather than just a balancing power. Consequently, there is
also a willingness to shoulder greater global responsibilities.[47]

This 'aspirational' identity reflects and reinforces the new structures of class
and societal power relations that have emerged with the election of the Hindu
nationalist government. Specifically, a significant factor in the BJP's victory
in the 2014 election was its Prime Ministerial candidate, Narendra Modi,
whose key political constituency in the state of Gujarat where he was Chief
Minister, before becoming a national leader, was what he called the 'neo-middle
classes'.[48] These classes are newly urbanized, aspirational, and imbued with
Hindu religiosity.[49] Modi views them as the future driver of entrepreneurship-
driven economic growth and they were earmarked as a key group requiring
special attention at a national level in the BJP's 2014 election manifesto.[50]
The emphasis on India as an 'aspiring leading power' reflects the BJP's new
'aspirational' Hindu nationalism and its desire to appeal to this neo-middle
class constituency. Moreover, the nature of the BJP's foreign policy strategies,
such as the emphasis on using yoga as a 'soft power' initiative, strengthens the
association of Indian identity with Hinduism. Although the government has
sought to separate yoga from Hinduism, these efforts were undermined by
the religious significance of the chosen date of 21 June, which according to
Hindu beliefs is the day Lord Shiva became the first yogi, and its emphasis on
mass-drill yoga sessions. Mass-drill yoga sessions have long been promoted
by the Bharatiya Yog Sansthari (Indian Yoga Society), which grew out of the
Hindu nationalist organization the Rashtriya Swayamsevak Sangh (RSS) as a
'nationalist therapy' that 'denotes health in terms of the holistic integration of
country and consciousness, body and society'.[51]

The consolidation of the social imaginary that has given rise to this aspirational
identity, however, has faced various challenges. The Modi government's focus
on markets and economic liberalization and its inability to find solutions for
fundamental economic problems like stagnating private investment, exports,
and jobs growth has led to divisions in the Hindu nationalist movement and
broader discontent. The RSS finds its core support among the traditional
Hindu nationalist constituency of small traders, small business people and
small farmers and it has actively opposed policies that are seen as too much

in favour of the corporate sector and foreign capital.[52] This is the background in which the BJP's 'surgical strikes' against Pakistan-based militants, and its sustained diplomatic pressure against Pakistan in international fora, needs to be understood. The 'surgical strikes' were characterized by Hindu nationalist leaders like Ram Madhav as a 'jaw for tooth' response aimed at teaching Pakistan 'to behave'.[53] Criticism of the government's approach was declared 'anti-national' and Indian diplomats made a sustained effort to have Pakistan censured as a sponsor of terrorism.[54] These responses should be seen in the context of the BJP's desire to appeal to and unite the neo-middle classes, the RSS, and its traditional supporters. The strikes featured prominently in the BJP's electoral campaigns for important state elections.[55] The limited nature of the military response, however, ensured that the government's core foreign policy priorities were not displaced, though they also reduced the impact of the surgical strikes. Pakistan was able to deny that the strikes took place, which allowed de-escalation to occur, but this dented the BJP's credibility as questions were repeatedly raised by opposition politicians and the media about the veracity of the government's claims to military prowess and a distinctive foreign policy. Hence, it remains to be seen whether 'surgical strikes' will be retained as a new element of India's foreign policy.

Conclusion

While constructivist literature on Indian foreign policy is still relatively small, as this chapter has shown, scholars of Indian foreign policy were among the earliest to contribute to the development of constructivist theories; they have developed constructivism in distinctive ways through Indian case studies and they have made valuable contributions to the study of Indian foreign policy, by highlighting the broader social relations that produce India's foreign policy interests and behaviour. India's foreign policy is now firmly directed at the global integration of India's economy which has entailed greater global political engagement but also new forms of domestic political contention. Constructivist frameworks, methodologies and concepts will be essential in elucidating the changing construction of India's foreign policy interests and its ability to achieve its foreign policy goals as its global engagement grows and domestic political contention deepens. In turn, the study of Indian foreign policy will be vital in further developing constructivist approaches in IR.

Notes

1   It is often claimed, however, that constructivist literature owes an unacknowledged debt to FPA literature on national role conceptions. This is because Kal Holsti, who introduced the notion to the study of international politics, sought to incorporate a social element in the creation of national role conceptions, though this was under-developed in his work. His successors have sought to develop this further, which brings contemporary renderings of national role conceptions closer to the constructivist concept of identity. See K. J. Holsti, 'National Role Conceptions in the Study of Foreign Policy,' *International Studies Quarterly* 14, No. 3 (1970): 233–309; C. Shih, 'National Role Conception as Foreign Policy Motivation: The Psychocultural Bases of Chinese Diplomacy,' *Political Psychology* 9, No. 4 (1988): 599–631.

2   See A. Wendt, 'Anarchy Is What States Make of It: The Social Construction of Power Politics,' *International Organization* 46, No. 02 (1992): 391–425. For a critique of Wendt's interpretation of Soviet 'New Thinking' see V. Kubalkova, 'Soviet "New Thinking" and the End of the Cold War: Five Explanations,' in *Foreign Policy in a Constructed World*, edited by Vendulka Kubalkova (New York: Routledge, 2015).

3   F. Kratochwil, *Rules, Norms, and Decisions: On the Conditions of Practical and Legal Reasoning in International Relations and Domestic Affairs* (Cambridge: Cambridge University Press, 1989); N. Onuf, *World of Our Making: Rules and Rule in Social Theory and International Relations* (Columbia: University of South Carolina Press, 1989).

4   Ruggie, for instance, identifies postmodernist, neoclassical and naturalistic variants; Adler distinguishes between modernist, rule-based, narrative knowing and postmodernist approaches; Katzenstein, Keohane and Krasner identify conventional constructivism, critical constructivism and postmodernist approaches; Kubalkova distinguishes between soft constructivism, postmodern and rule-oriented constructivisms; Weldes distinguishes between modernist constructivism, critical constructivism and poststructural approaches. See J. G. Ruggie, 'What Makes the World Hang Together? Neo-utilitarianism and the Social Constructivist Challenge,' *International Organization* 52, No. 04 (1998): 855–885; E. Adler, 'Seizing the Middle Ground: Constructivism in World Politics,' *European Journal of International Relations* 3, No. 3 (1997): 319–363; P. J. Katzenstein, R. O. Keohane and S. D. Krasner, 'International Organization and the Study of World Politics,' *International Organization* 52, No. 04 (1998): 645–685; Kubalkova, 'Soviet "New Thinking" and the End of the Cold War: Five Explanations'; J. Weldes, 'Bureaucratic Politics: A Critical Constructivist Assessment,' *Mershon International Studies Review* 42, No. 2 (1998): 216–225.

5   T. Hopf, 'The Promise of Constructivism in International Relations Theory,' *International Security* 23, No. 1 (1998): 183.

6   R. L. Doty, 'Foreign Policy as Social Construction: A Post-Positivist Analysis of U.S. Counterinsurgency Policy in the Philippines,' *International Studies Quarterly* 37, No. 3 (1993): 298.

7   See for instance, M. N. Barnett and M. Finnemore, 'The Politics, Power, and Pathologies of International Organizations,' *International Organization* 53, No. 04 (1999): 699–732; A. Acharya, 'How Ideas Spread: Whose Norms Matter? Norm Localization and Institutional Change in Asian Regionalism,' *International Organization* 58, No. 02 (2004): 239–375; R. Jepperson, A. Wendt and P. Katzenstein, 'Norms, Identity and

Culture in National Security,' in *The Culture of National Security*, edited by Peter Katzenstein (New York: Columbia University Press, 1996).

8   See, for instance, J. Weldes, *Constructing National Interests: The United States and the Cuban Missile Crisis* (Minneapolis and London: University of Minnesota Press, 1999); D. Campbell, *Writing Security: United States Foreign Policy and the Politics of Identity* (Manchester: Manchester University Press, 1992); Doty, 'Foreign Policy as Social Construction: A Post-Positivist Analysis of U.S. Counterinsurgency Policy in the Philippines'; Jutta Weldes, Mark Laffey, Hugh Gusterson and Raymond Duval (eds), *Cultures of Insecurity: States, Communities and the Production of Danger* (Minneapolis: University of Minnesota Press, 1999).

9   P. T. Jackson and D. H. Nexon, 'Constructivist Realism or Realist-Constructivism?' *International Studies Review* 6, No. 2 (2004): 337–41.

10 Morgenthau quoted in Weldes, *Constructing National Interests: The United States and the Cuban Missile Crisis* (Minneapolis and London: University of Minnesota Press, 1999).

11 A. Wiener, *A Theory of Contestation* (Berlin: Springer, 2014); C. Epstein, 'Stop Telling Us How to Behave: Socialization or Infantilization?,' *International Studies Perspectives* 13, No. 2 (2012): 135–45; M. Hofferberth and C. Weber, 'Lost in Translation: A Critique of Constructivist Norm Research,' *Journal of International Relations and Development* 18, No. 1 (2015): 75–103; H. Niemann and H. Schillinger, 'Contestation "All the Way Down"? The Grammar of Contestation in Norm Research,' *Review of International Studies* 43, No. 1 (2017): 29–49.

12 B. J. Steele, *Ontological Security in International Relations* (London: Routledge, 2007); F. Berenskoetter, 'Friends, There Are No Friends? An Intimate Reframing of the International,' *Millennium* 35, No. 3 (2007): 647–76.

13 E. Adler and V. Pouliot, 'International Practices,' *International Theory*, 3, No. 01 (2011): 4.

14 H. Muppidi, 'Postcoloniality and the Production of International Insecurity: The Persistent Puzzle of U.S.–Indian Relations,' in *Cultures of Insecurity: States, Communities and the Production of Danger*, edited by Jutta Weldes, Mark Laffey, Hugh Gusterson and Raymond Duval (Minneapolis: University of Minnesota Press, 1999).

15 S. Krishna, *Postcolonial Insecurities: India, Sri Lanka, and the Question of Nationhood*, 4 (Minneapolis and London: University of Minnesota Press, 1999).

16 S. Singh, *India in South Asia: Domestic Identity Politics and Foreign Policy from Nehru to the BJP* (London and New York: Routledge, 2013); P. Chacko, *Indian Foreign Policy: The Politics of Postcolonial Identity from 1947 to 2004* (London and New York: Routledge, 2012); P. Chacko, 'A New "Special Relationship"? Power Transitions, Ontological Security, and India–US Relations,' *International Studies Perspectives* 15, No. 3 (2014): 329–46; 'Foreign Policy, Ideas and State-building: India and the Politics of International Intervention,' *Journal of International Relations and Development*, DOI:10.1057/jird.2016.15 (2016); P. Chacko and A. E. Davis, 'The Natural/Neglected Relationship: Liberalism, Identity and India–Australia Relations,' *The Pacific Review* 30, No. 1 (2017): 26–50; S. Singh, 'From a Sub-Continental Power to an Asia-Pacific Player: India's Changing Identity,' *India Review* 13, No. 3 (2014): 187–211; C. Ogden, *Hindu Nationalism and the Evolution of Contemporary Indian Security: Portents of Power* (New Delhi: Oxford University Press, 2014); W. W. Widmaier, 'The Democratic Peace Is What States Make of It: A Constructivist Analysis of the US–Indian 'Near-Miss' in the 1971 South Asian Crisis,' *European Journal of International Relations* 11, No.

3 (2005): 431–55; S. Chatterjee, 'Ethnic Conflicts in South Asia: A Constructivist Reading,' *South Asian Survey* 12, No. 1 (2005): 75–89.

17   Chacko, *Indian Foreign Policy: The Politics of Postcolonial Identity from 1947 to 2004*; H. Muppidi, *The Politics of the Global* (Minneapolis: University of Minnesota Press, 2004); S. Biswas, '"Nuclear Apartheid" as Political Position: Race as a Postcolonial Resource?' *Alternatives: Global, Local, Political* 26, No. 4 (2001): 485–522; R. Das, 'A Post-colonial Analysis of India–United States Nuclear Security: Orientalism, Discourse, and Identity in International Relations,' *Journal of Asian and African Studies* 52, No. 6 (2017): 741–759; R. Mathur, 'Sly Civility and the Paradox of Equality/Inequality in the Nuclear Order: A Post-colonial Critique,' *Critical Studies on Security* 4, No. 1 (2015): 57–72; A.E. Davis, 'A Shared History? Postcolonial Identity and India–Australia Relations, 1947–1954,' *Pacific Affairs* 88, No. 4 (2015): 849–869.

18   A. Michael, *India's Foreign Policy and Regional Multilateralism* (Springer, Basingstoke: Palgrave Macmillan, 2013); A. Bloomfield, *India and the Responsibility to Protect* (Farnham, Surrey, England: Ashgate Publishing, Ltd., 2016); H. Stevenson, 'India and International Norms of Climate Governance: A Constructivist Analysis of Normative Congruence Building,' *Review of International Studies* 37, No. 03 (2011): 997–1019; K. Sasikumar, 'Branding India: Constructing a Reputation for Responsibility in the Nuclear Order,' *Place Branding and Public Diplomacy* 13, No. 3 (2017): 242–254. DOI:10.1057/s41254-016-0038-2 (2017); Z. Selden and S. Strome, 'Competing Identities and Security Interests in the Indo-US Relationship,' *Foreign Policy Analysis*, DOI: 10.1093/fpa/orw029 (2016).

19   H. K. Nizamani, *The Roots of Rhetoric: Politics of Nuclear Weapons in India and Pakistan* (New Delhi: India Research Press, 2001).

20   P. Chacko, 'The Search for a Scientific Temper: Nuclear Technology and the Ambivalence of India's Postcolonial Modernity,' *Review of International Studies* 37, No. 1 (2011): 185–208; P. Malik, *India's Nuclear Debate: Exceptionalism and the Bomb* (New Delhi: Routledge, 2014); R. Das, 'State, Identity and Representations of Nuclear (In)Securities in India and Pakistan,' *Journal of Asian and African Studies* 45, No. 2 (2010): 146–169; K. Frey, *India's Nuclear Bomb and National Security* (London and New York: Routledge, 2006); Muppidi, *The Politics of the Global*; Mathur, 'Sly Civility and the Paradox of Equality/Inequality in the Nuclear Order: A Post-colonial Critique'; L. Varadarajan, 'Constructivism, Identity and Neoliberal (In)security,' *Review of International Studies* 30, No. 3 (2004): 319–341; Biswas, '"Nuclear Apartheid" as Political Position: Race as a Postcolonial Resource?'; S. Biswas, *Nuclear Desire: Power and the Postcolonial Nuclear Order* (Minneapolis and London: University of Minnesota Press, 2014).

21   M. E. Carranza, *India–Pakistan Nuclear Diplomacy: Constructivism and the Prospects for Nuclear Arms Control and Disarmament in South Asia* (Lanham: Rowman & Littlefield, 2016); Chacko and Davis, 'The Natural/Neglected Relationship: Liberalism, Identity and India–Australia Relations'; R. Das, 'The United States–India Nuclear Relations after 9/11: Alternative Discourses,' *Asian Journal of Political Science* 20, No. 1 (2012): 86–107; Das, 'A Post-colonial Analysis of India–United States Nuclear Security: Orientalism, Discourse, and Identity in International Relations.'

22   P. Chacko and Jayasuriya, 'A Capitalising Foreign Policy: Regulatory Geographies and Transnationalised State Projects,' *European Journal of International Relations* 24, No. 1 (2018): 82–105.

23 Jepperson, Wendt and Katzenstein, 'Norms, Identity and Culture in National Security';
    A. Wendt, *Social Theory of International Politics* (Cambridge: Cambridge University
    Press, 1999).
24 Muppidi, *The Politics of the Global.*
25 Varadarajan, 'Constructivism, Identity and Neoliberal (In)security,' 328.
26 J. Alamgir, *India's Open-Economy Policy: Globalism, Rivalry, Continuity* (New York and
    London: Routledge, 2009).
27 This section draws on Chacko, 'Foreign Policy, Ideas and State-building: India and
    the Politics of International Intervention.'
28 M. Laffey, 'Locating Identity: Performativity, Foreign Policy and State Action,' *Review
    of International Studies* 26, No. 3 (2000): 429–444.
29 Weldes, *Constructing National Interests: The United States and the Cuban Missile Crisis,*
    109–10.
30 Ibid., 112.
31 Laffey, 'Locating Identity: Performativity, Foreign Policy and State Action,' 441.
32 B. Jessop, 'Constituting Another Foucault Effect: Foucault on States and Statecraft,'
    in *Governmentality: Current Issues and Future Challenges*, edited by U. Bröckling, S.
    Krasmann and T. Lemke, 65 (New York and London: Routledge, 2011).
33 Ibid., 67.
34 Ibid., 68.
35 B. Jessop, 'Cultural Political Economy and Critical Policy Studies,' *Critical Policy Studies*
    3, Nos 3–4 (2010): 341.
36 Chacko, 'The Search for a Scientific Temper: Nuclear Technology and the Ambivalence
    of India's Postcolonial Modernity'; Alamgir, *India's Open-Economy Policy: Globalism,
    Rivalry, Continuity*; Muppidi, *The Politics of the Global*; Krishna, *Postcolonial Insecurities.*
37 Muppidi, *The Politics of the Global*, 25; Weldes, *Constructing National Interests: The
    United States and the Cuban Missile Crisis*, 10.
38 Muppidi, *The Politics of the Global.*
39 A. Padmanabhan, 'Self-reliance Has Different Meanings for India's Polity,' Rediff,
    20 August 2001. Available at http://www.rediff.com/money/2001/aug/20man.htm,
    accessed 8 February 2017.
40 M. Singh, 'Speech of Shri Manmohan Singh, Minister of Finance Introducing the
    Budget for the Year 1996-97', Ministry of Finance. Available at http://mof.gov.in/
    press_room/fm_speech/bs4.htm, accessed on 2 February 2017.
41 Padmanabhan, 'Self-Reliance Has Different Meanings for India's Polity'; P. Chacko,
    'Marketising Hindutva: The State, Society and Markets in Hindu Nationalism,' *Modern
    Asian Studies* (2018) (in press).
42 S. Menon, 'India and the Global Scene: Prem Bhatia Memorial Lecture,' National
    Maritime Foundation, 11 August 2011. Available at http://maritimeindia.org/article/
    india-and-global-scene, accesed on 30 January 2012.
43 Chacko, 'A New "Special Relationship"? Power Transitions, Ontological Security, and
    India–US Relations.'
44 S. Menon, "India Will Be a Different Power,' *Outlook*, 8 December 2011. Available at
    http://www.outlookindia.com/article.aspx?279270, accessed on 2 February 2017.
45 *Wall Street Journal*, 'Read an Edited Transcript of The Wall Street Journal's Interview
    With Indian Prime Minister Narendra Modi,' 26 May 2016. Available at http://

blogs.wsj.com/indiarealtime/2016/05/26/read-an-edited-transcript-of-the-wall-street-journals-interview-with-indian-prime-minister-narendra-modi/, accessed on 6 February 2017.

46 S. Jaishankar, 'Indian Foreign Secretary Subrahmanyam Jaishankar's Remarks,' Carnegie India, 6 April 2016. Available at http://carnegieindia.org/2016/04/06/indian-foreign-secretary-subrahmanyam-jaishankar-s-remarks/iwq7, accessed on 2 February 2017.

47 S. Jaishankar, 'IISS Fullerton Lecture by Dr. S. Jaishankar, Foreign Secretary in Singapore,' Ministry of External Affairs, 20 July 2015. Available at http://mea.gov.in/Speeches-Statements.htm?dtl/25493/IISS_Fullerton_Lecture_by_Foreign_Secretary_in_Singapore, accessed on 2 February 2017.

48 P. Chhibber and R. Verma, 'The BJP's 2014 "Modi Wave": An Ideological Consolidation of the Right,' *Economic and Political Weekly* XLIX, No. 39 (2014): 53–5.

49 C. Jaffrelot, 'What "Gujarat Model"? – Growth without Development – and with Socio-Political Polarisation,' *South Asia: Journal of South Asian Studies* 38, No. 4 (2015): 835.

50 Bharatiya Janata Party, 'Election Manifesto 2014,' 17. Available at http://bjpelectionmanifesto.com/pdf/manifesto2014.pdf, accessed on 2 July 2014.

51 J. S. Alter, 'A Therapy to Live By: Public Health, the Self and Nationalism in the Practice of a North Indian Yoga Society,' *Medical Anthropology* 17, No. 4 (1997): 314.

52 M. U. Shaikh, '100% FDI in Retail Is "Anti-national": RSS Affiliate Group Hits Out at Narendra Modi Government,' India.com, 20 June 2016. Available at http://www.india.com/news/india/100-fdi-in-retail-is-anti-national-rss-affiliate-group-hits-out-at-narendra-modi-government-1274002/, accessed on 30 June 2016.

53 R. Madhav, 'A Different Leader…,' *Indian Express*, 30 September 2016. Available athttp://indianexpress.com/article/opinion/columns/surgical-strikes-india-pkaistan-uri-attack-pathankot-attack-narendra-modi-nawaz-sharif-3056843/, accessed on 2 February 2017.

54 *Indian Express*, 'India Can't Go to War with Pakistan till 'Anti-national' Arvind Kejriwal Is CM: Subramanian Swamy,' *Indian Express*, 5 October 2016. Available at http://indianexpress.com/article/india/india-news-india/india-cant-go-to-war-with-pakistan-while-anti-national-arvind-kejriwal-is-cm-subramanian-swamy-3066703, accessed on 2 February 2017.

55 A. Shukla, 'Army Mute as BJP Election Posters Feature Soldier, Surgical Strikes,' *The Wire*, 9 October 2016. Available at https://thewire.in/71973/army-silent-surgical-strikes-bjp-election-posters, accessed on 2 February 2017.

4

Exploring Historical Memory and
Indian Foreign Policy

Manjari Chatterjee Miller

In 2015, it was claimed that the India–UK bilateral relationship is affected by 'a colonial mind set' that has led to a 'growing disconnect' between the two nations.[1] Correspondingly, the UK dropped from being India's third largest trading partner in 2000 to its twelfth largest in 2015.[2] There are many factors that one could point to for the cool bilateral relationship, including as has been suggested, India's rise, which implies that India's need for a strong bilateral relationship is less than the UK's.[3] But another, somewhat overlooked, factor is the historical relationship between the two as colonizer and colony, which continues to crop up in the relationship.

In 2013, for example, when British Prime Minister David Cameron visited India, the Indian media and public avidly discussed whether he would formally apologise for the Jallianwala Bagh massacre of 1919.[4] This incident in which hundreds of innocent Indian citizens were shot dead on the orders of British Brigadier-General Reginald Dyer is seen as a symbol of the brutalities committed during the two hundred years of British colonial rule in India. When Mr Cameron visited the site, and expressed regret for the 'shameful event',[5] he was strongly condemned for his half-hearted response.[6] In July 2015, Congress Member of Parliament, Shashi Tharoor, in a speech to the Oxford Union Society that quickly went viral and earned the praise of Prime Minister Narendra Modi, declared that Britain should financially and symbolically compensate India for its colonial rule:

> By the end of (the) nineteenth century, the fact is that India was already Britain's biggest cash cow – the world's biggest purchaser of British goods and exports and the source for highly paid employment for British civil servants. We literally paid for our own oppression. Colonialists like Robert Clive brought their rotten boroughs in England on the proceeds of their loot in India while taking the Hindi word loot into their dictionary as well

as their habits. And the British had the gall to call him Clive of India as if he belonged to the country, when all he really did was to ensure that much of the country belonged to him.[7]

In November 2015, a lobby group of Indian businessmen and Bollywood celebrities declared they would legally challenge the British monarchy's possession of the valuable Kohinoor diamond. This group of activists hired British lawyers to initiate High Court proceedings against Queen Elizabeth II. In an interview, David de Souza, co-founder of the Indian leisure group Titos and one of the funders of the legal action, explained:

> The Koh-i-Noor is one of the many artefacts taken from India under dubious circumstances. Colonization not only robbed our people of wealth, it destroyed the country's psyche itself. It brutalised society, traces of which linger on today in the form of mass poverty, lack of education and a host of other factors.[8]

These incidents suggest that despite the demise of colonialism over five decades ago, and despite India having led an influential anti-colonial movement from which it emerged independent, historical memories of colonialism persist. Although colonialism is only one facet of the multitude of historical experiences that India has undergone, it is an important legacy.[9] Yet the identification of specific historical experiences and memories, the mechanisms of collective memory and their ongoing effects, including but not limited to colonialism, have mostly been very lightly explored in the Indian international relations (IR) and foreign policy literature. This is despite the fact that, in both the general IR and area studies literature, there is precedence for such exploration, and despite the evidence showing that historical memories have often been institutionalized in India. This chapter offers a brief overview of the ways in which writers of Indian foreign policy have dealt with historical memory before turning to its treatment in the IR and area studies literature. Finally, it shows how the historical memory of colonialism has been institutionalized in India, examines why memory and its institutionalization is an important tool for the study of Indian foreign policy and offers avenues for further research.

Historical memory and Indian foreign policy

If we examine how historical memory and legacies have been treated with respect to Indian foreign policy, generally speaking, we find three bodies of work.

In the oldest and most established body of work, academics have implicitly examined India's post-1947 identity. In essence, this literature explores whether India as a nation asserted its identity to be more than a newly independent post-colonial state. The focus here has been on broad identity-shaping ideas such as non-alignment/idealism and realism. In terms of the former, scholars have argued that Indian foreign policy was characterized by a Nehruvian idealism, stemming from the historical legacy of India's first Prime Minister, Jawaharlal Nehru. Nehruvianism emphasized India's commitment to a number of principles including but not limited to 'liberal internationalism',[10] 'eradicating colonialism and racism',[11] 'organizing the uplift of the world's poor and dispossessed' (Ganguly, 2003, 42), a 'suspicion of superpowers',[12] and a commitment to remaining non-aligned and aloof from great power politics in the Cold War world.[13] In terms of the latter, an argument is made that in the 1990s India turned to a realist foreign policy, free from the 'manacles…of Cold War thinking…and real and imagined grievances'.[14] This thinking implied the recession of the historical legacy of Nehruvianism, both due to a realization of its failures, and/or the rise of the BJP, which in turn led India to grasp the 'significance of power as the most important dynamic in world politics'.[15]

The notion of historical memory and mechanisms is very implicit in this body of work. For those who expounded India's commitment to idealism, the 'mechanism' as it were of Nehruvianism, emanated primarily from the beliefs of a single leader, Jawaharlal Nehru, who was undoubtedly a powerful factor in Indian foreign policy. But there is little in-depth exploration of how and why his beliefs were propagated and institutionalized, such that even after his death, his legacy impacted India until the 1990s. The post-Cold War body of literature on the turn to realism obviously expounds a move away from the historical legacy of Nehru but again, it implies the recession of historical memories without an exploration of either the mechanisms and/or their de-emphasis or de-institutionalization. Moreover, there is little 'accompanying discussion of agency or an unpacking' of this ideational framework with reference to 'social ideas or individual beliefs'.[16]

Second, there has been work that explicitly rejects the idea of institutionalized historical memory and suggests that Indian strategic thought is notable chiefly by its absence. The work of George Tanham argues, for example, that although India has 'developed elements of a defence strategy, it has produced little formal strategic thinking and planning'.[17] While Tanham's argument is not that history or historical memory is irrelevant, he suggests that in the Indian case the lack of an overarching Indian political entity meant that there was no institutionalized belief in a 'greater India' – 'there was little thought of India as even a collection of states that might gain from…cooperative action or agreed on interstate norms'.[18] In essence, Tanham implies that any institutionalization of historical memory was localized. His work, however, does not trace or provide evidence of either this localized institutionalization or whether local institutionalized memory produced local elites or localized strategic thought. Nor does it explain why even the largest and most powerful Indian political entities, such as the Mughal Empire, would not have impacted Indian strategic thought.

Third, there been newer work that more explicitly explores historical memory and agency by examining the legacy of political elites, parties and decision makers. Sagar's work explicitly refutes Tanham and examines pre-1947 ideas about war, peace and international relations by influential leading Indian thinkers. Looking at the beliefs of Keshub Chandra Sen, Swami Vivekananda, Dadabhai Naoroji, Bankimchandra Chattopadhyay, Mahatma Gandhi and Rabindranath Tagore, among others, Sagar traces how elites learnt, agreed and disagreed about the nature of international relations.[19] His conclusion is that although Indian elites 'collectively failed to reckon with the responsibilities of statehood' this was the result of rather than the absence of particular kinds of beliefs about international relations.[20] Along similar lines, Sullivan argues that, since the nineteenth century, Indian elites have differentiated India from other nations and civilizations and seen it as a unique state.[21] On one hand, these elites see India as internally exceptional because it is itself morally and spiritually distinctive and superior. On the other, they see it as externally exceptional because it is a shining and emulable example of a plural and peaceful society.[22] These beliefs, Sullivan argues were institutionalized through pre-independence discourses, and the post-independence creation of particular kinds of diplomatic institutions leading to the emergence of an intellectual consensus.[23]

Most recently, Ian Hall has probed how the historical traditions of Hindutva, or Hindu nationalist ideology, have informed Indian Prime Minister Narendra Modi's approach to foreign policy. He argues that while Nehru drew upon an amalgamation of British socialist ideas, Buddhism and Gandhian thought to create a 'normative agenda' for India that endured through subsequent leadership changes, Modi is 'steeped in the Hindu nationalist intellectual tradition', particularly as propagated by Swami Vivekananda.[24] However, the limited nature of this historical intellectual repertoire means that Modi has been unsuccessful in setting a new normative agenda for Indian foreign policy.[25]

While this newest body of work is very promising with regard to understanding historical memory and Indian foreign policy, there are three modes of inquiry that are either not included in its purview or explored in passing. First, there is little work on what such historical ideas concretely mean for foreign policy decision making. How do these beliefs matter and impact foreign policy? Second, and more importantly, there is again little attention paid to the mechanisms of institutionalization. If the ideas of elites such as Indian Foreign Service officers or nineteenth-century thinkers are important how were these ideas transmitted and institutionalized, and why were some ideas privileged over others? Last, the connection between historical memory and Indian foreign policy is mostly confined to beliefs and ideas held by elites, whether they be Nehruvianism, realism, or Hindutva. There is little work done on historical experiences and events and their impact. If we turn to the general IR and area studies literature, however, we find the work on historical memory includes not just the historical ideas and legacies of elites but also an emphasis on historical events and experiences, and their institutionalization which in turn informs national identity.

Remembering and responding to the past

The work of Legro among others has shown that ideational structures or collectively held ideas, that is, 'concepts or beliefs held by groups (that is, states)' are 'social and holistic', 'have an inter-subjective existence that stands above individual minds and is typically embodied in symbols, discourse and institutions'.[26] Because these ideational structures are institutionalized, they can be 'sticky'. Institutionalization implies that these ideas are embedded in tangible organizations as well as in 'social norms, patterns of discourse, and collective identities'.[27] Empirically, there has been much work done on these 'sticky' ideational structures. Many have explored, for example, the impact of specific historical experiences, particularly traumatic history, and their memorialization.

One of the richest and most detailed empirical bodies of work that one can point to as an example of focusing on both a single country and its historical experiences is the literature that probes the traumatic history of the Holocaust, and how and why it is remembered. This literature focuses on the different processes of institutionalization of experiences and memories, the variation in and commemoration of individual and collective memory, and its impact on the Israeli nation. There are certain significant points that emerge from this literature that we can use to understand how historical experiences in a country are remembered and institutionalized. To begin with, the mass murder, imprisonment and torture of the European Jews by the Nazi regime in Germany were individual experiences but they were also a shared experience of individuals. In other words, it was a 'multifaceted' memory. There were individual voices, which formed group voices, and eventually national voices that through shared stories, remembrances, commemorative monuments and museums led to the establishment of a 'meta memory' of the Holocaust.[28] Thus, mediated by representations and media, individual trauma informed and shaped a collective remembrance of trauma.[29]

This collective memory was 'a central factor in constructing the memory of the Holocaust' for those who had undergone it but it was equally importantly constructed and perpetuated for those who had never experienced it.[30] The process of transmission of memory, particularly inter-generationally, to those who had not first-hand experienced the horror of the Holocaust was key to the eventual construction of state/national memory and identity in Israel.

It has been pointed out that there is a distinction between social memory and historical memory. The former refers to the memories of an event of people or a group to which they belong who have experienced it personally while the latter is 'memory that has been mediated, by films, and books, and schools and holidays'.[31] These representations constructed a national experience – 'in the case of the Holocaust, only a small minority who experienced Nazism is alive. For all the rest of us it is an experience mediated by representations.' This does not mean that such representations are not authentic but rather they are the 'basis of that authenticity'.[32] For example, representations such as the military cemeteries, military memorials, Yad Vashem and memorial sites were instrumental in constructing a national identity.[33] Moreover, post-World War II events such as Israel's trial of the Nazi, Adolf Eichman, where personal survival stories were repeatedly shared, granted not just state recognition to the victims, but transformed the general identity of the Israeli public from 'victims' to 'accusers'.[34] Even more significantly, the state of Israel itself was enshrined as the answer to the trauma Jews had undergone – 'the Holocaust memory in Israel was articulated in its Declaration of Independence which determined the state to be the ultimate response to the Holocaust.'[35] The collective memory of trauma was, thus, enfolded into a national narrative.

Even though there were different national narratives that emerged at different (and sometimes overlapping) points of time from this trauma – for example, sympathy for the suffering of the victims, lionization of the ghetto fighters and the transformation of the Israeli public from victims and refugees to accusers and heroes[36] – a significant factor that pulled together these differences was the eventual emergence of the Holocaust as a symbol of national, and even transnational, solidarity.[37] As Levy and Sznaider point out, in the aftermath of World War II, the destruction of the European Jewry was incorporated into the atrocities of war time – during the Nuremberg trials of 1945, the extermination of nearly six million Jews was merely one of a long list of horrific Nazi crimes.[38] The idea of the Holocaust and its representation as a singular event came later when it 'became a symbol for (Israel's) existential fears and (its) necessity to conduct and maintain a strong military state'.[39] As Rothberg states, 'the English word "Holocaust" only belatedly became the singular, capitalized name of an event considered unique, and this belated naming probably took place sometime in the 1960s.[40] Thus, even though it was a multifaceted traumatic historical experience that was not perceived as a stand-alone event in the immediate aftermath of its occurrence, its emergence as 'the Holocaust' demonstrates the importance of 'cosmopolitan memory', that is, the formation of both nation-specific and nation-transcending commonalities[41] that provide a universal frame of reference.

Thus, this literature on individual, collective and national memories of the Holocaust gives us insight not just into how historical experiences are remembered in a country but how and why it can be folded into a national narrative that persists. 'Memory is not a thing but a continuous process that links the past and the present in dialogically contingent ways'[42] and its very fluidity is its strength.[43]

The persistence of individual and collective memory has also been harnessed by states in an attempt to 'control' the national narrative. One of the most powerful tools for forging a national identity is the manipulation and management of the past. The construction and maintenance of the collective memory of a nation is crucial for nation building.[44] This is because shared historical myths and trauma can define in and out groups – who is a part of the group, what it means to be part of the group and, equally importantly, who is *not* a part of the group – thus building ethnic, religious and national identities.[45] Collective memories can be objective or subjective, and both the real and perceived past matter for national identity.[46] As Smith points out, '[N]o memory, no identity. No identity, no nation'.[47] The past is not just about the past – it is purposefully reconstructed to serve the needs of the present.[48]

The work of Zheng Wang and He Yinan shows, for example, how memories of Japanese colonialism have been not only institutionalized but also 'purposefully reconstructed' by the Chinese government. Under the regime of Mao Zedong, historical narratives emphasized the role of the Chinese Communist Party (CCP) in securing a victory against the Guomindang (KMT) and foreign imperialism[49] rather than individual memories. Narratives about the 'many good Japanese and the few bad Japanese'[50] blamed Japanese aggression on a small military clique and the nefarious role of the US and the KMT, and served to promote the seminal role of the CCP in the Chinese civil war rather than its suffering at the hands of Japan. This memory was revised in later decades when Japan was now reviled as an 'immoral other'[51] and China began to conduct a 'national humiliation' education campaign about China's suffering under a hundred years of colonialism.[52]

The research programme that examines the persistence of historical memory also includes work that looks at the mitigation of historical memory, most notably in the transitional justice literature, which examines the processes and practices by which nations can move forward from traumatic history. The concept of transitional justice has been both narrowly and broadly defined. One of the earliest definitions categorized it as 'a concept of justice associated with periods of political change, characterized by legal responses to confront the wrongdoings of repressive predecessor regimes'.[53] The broadest view of transitional justice, on the other hand, encompasses any measure taken by a state to come to terms with a historical legacy of atrocities and human rights violations[54] – 'the search for a just society in the wake of...oppressive and even violent systems'.[55] At its core it is

> a range of practices that address the pervasive negative psychological, social, and political effects of past injustices (usually involving human rights violations) committed by the state or in the name of the state and that aim to amend these effects in order to establish the rule of law, democracy, peace, reconciliation, and respect for individual and collective rights, either domestically and/or internationally.[56]

In the view of some the very act of remembrance can be interpreted as a step towards recovery or mitigation of the historical experience through either re-institutionalization or de-institutionalization. Martha Minow's seminal work, for example, discusses the struggle of societies to acknowledge, punish and recover from historical traumas like genocide and mass violence. She points out the difficulties of too much and too little remembrance – 'too much enshrinement of victimhood; too little acknowledgement of the past'[57] – and explores instead the path between 'vengeance and forgiveness'.[58] Specifically, she explores legal and cultural institutions that could offer this path to healing – trials, truth commissions and reparations. She concludes that the past is still very much present for many countries and a key to recovery is 'not memory but remembering...a process for reinterpreting what cannot be made sensible, for assembling what cannot be put together, and for separating what cannot be severed from both present and future'.[59]

There are certain lessons that we can deduce from this literature. First, extrapolation from individual historical experiences to collective and national historical experiences is a common path for countries that have undergone a significant historical event.[60] After all, 'nations like individuals...develop visions, dreams and prejudices about themselves and the world that shape their intentions...the mind sets of leaders and peoples'.[61] Second, despite the variations in narratives of a history, countries often institutionalize and eventually treat the entire history as a unitary unique event. China's treatment of Japanese colonialism or Israel's treatment of the Holocaust are cases in point. Third, the 'purposeful reconstruction' and institutionalization of historical memory, particularly traumatic history, is common, and is not easily dismissed as mere propaganda by states. Moreover, it may be done through a variety of practices, some of which are related to transitional justice including memorialization through history textbooks.

Remembering and institutionalizing memories of colonialism

Turning now to India, we can show that important historical experiences, such as colonialism, have, in fact, been institutionalized. Nationalists emphasized they were not only economically and politically exploited by 200 years of British colonialism but also suffered from the sting of social and cultural humiliation and subjugation. India for its part has not used the legal and institutional practices of transitional justice to remember the colonial past. Despite its many grievances, and recorded objective as well as subjective memories of suffering, there have been no trials or truth commissions and no official calls for restitution, reparations, or apologies. However, memories of colonialism have been institutionalized through public commemorations and, particularly, history textbooks to create a national narrative of self and other.

One of the most important vehicles for the institutionalized transmission of historical memory is history teaching through textbooks. 'The powerful link between history and memory is especially salient in the educational system which is responsible for implanting knowledge and values in the younger generation.'[62] The appropriation of the past through history teaching conveys a consciousness of resilient national identity[63] and gives students an idea of who they are and what it means to be a part of a particular nation.[64] Textbooks, which are the predominant means of history teaching, are not only 'the modern version of village storytellers'[65] but function as a 'sort of historical supreme court whose task it is to decipher from all the (different) pieces of the past the "true" collective memories which are appropriate for inclusion in the national historical narrative'.[66] India too has used textbooks for history teaching including about its colonial past.

India has a federal system of government, with power shared between the centre and the states. The Indian Constitution (Entry 11, List II, 7th Schedule) lays down that 'education including universities, subject to the provisions of Entries 63, 64, 65 and 66 of List I and Entry 25 of List III' is a state subject. Nonetheless, since independence in 1947, the centre has 'shown an unprecedented activity and interest in the field of education'.[67] Thus, education has devolved to be a shared responsibility between the centre and states.[68]

India's educational system is driven by a government body, the National Council for Educational Research and Training (NCERT), which promotes a national curriculum that is adopted into a syllabus, and generates a set of corresponding textbooks for every grade.[69] These textbooks are then recommended to 42 different educational/examination boards including the Central Board of Secondary Education (CBSE), the Indian Certified School Examination (ICSE) and various State Boards of examinations. Public and private schools may use any of these boards but the most widely used are CBSE and ICSE.[70]

I examined the volumes of Indian history that are written and published by NCERT as part of the National Curriculum Framework (NCF). The NCERT was set up in 1961 to guide the central and state governments in building a 'national system of education'.[71] It is headed by the Minister of Human Resource Development. NCERT text books are used by private and public schools in India, and in some cases NCERT textbooks are required reading. For example, schools that follow the CBSE[72] system have to use NCERT books.[73] The NCERT textbooks in use today were last revised in 2006. Examining the state production, institutionalization and endorsement of narratives of history that are imparted to millions of young adults over long periods of time offers a method of establishing on a national basis whether there is narration and reconstruction of an historical experience, that is, institutionalization of historical memory.[74]

The NCERT history textbooks reveal a strong sense of 'self' and foreign 'other'. The recounting of colonial history is, in addition to the detailing of an exploitative system set in place by the British, also repeatedly accompanied by the narration of painful violent events and trauma. For example, the chapter on the impact of colonialism in the Indian countryside constructs ruthless British policies including the decimation of local populations:

[T]he British embarked on a brutal policy of exploitation, hunting the Paharias down and killing them...the experience of pacification campaigns and memories of brutal repression shaped (the Paharias') perception of British infiltration into the area. Every white man appeared to represent a power that was destroying their way of life and means of survival.[75]

The chapter on the Revolt of 1857 constructs the change in British sensibilities towards the sepoys in the 1840s: 'The officers developed a sense of superiority and started treating the sepoys as their racial inferiors, riding roughshod over their sensibilities. Abuse and physical violence became common, and thus the distance between sepoys and officers grew.'[76] The response to the Revolt is also detailed with an examination of British paintings and media that depicted the alleged mass rapes of British women by the rebels which were in turn used to justify the use of brute force to repress the rebels.

There were innumerable pictures and cartoons in the British press that sanctioned brutal repression and violent reprisal...the urge for vengeance and retribution was expressed in the brutal way in which the rebels were executed. They were blown from guns, or hanged from the gallows. Images of these executions were widely circulated through popular journals.[77] The repression of the rebels meant the silencing of their voice.[78]

The narrative of colonial trauma is quite intense and linked strongly to British injustices cementing a sense of the British 'other'. If we examine the NCERT history volume on the pre-colonial period in Indian history which was also often one of conquest by foreign dynasties, it is clear that the development of Indo-Islamic and other forms of cultural and traditional accommodation[79] preclude any, even implicit, treatment of this period as the 'other'.[80] The sharp distinction that is made between the absolute construction and consolidation during the pre-British period, and the absolute deconstruction and trauma during the colonial period is very clear from the texts. To give an example, the treatment of a supposedly neutral topic – architecture – in the two periods is very different. The capital of Vijaynagara, for example, is seen as 'impressive'[81] and 'beautiful'.[82] The colonial capitals of Madras, Calcutta and Bombay, however, are seen as grandeur for the sake of impressing the authority of colonial power.[83]

Moving forward with historical memory as a tool

The NCERT history textbooks show us that an important historical experience, the British Raj, has been institutionalized by the state in India. This begs the question of how this matters, if at all, for foreign policy. To begin with, we already know that despite different colonial experiences, ex-colonies like India have a common sense of victimhood because they treated and responded to colonialism in a similar fashion – as collective trauma. The narrative of suffering and the language of victimhood that emerged in India after the demise of colonialism is consistent with the theories of collective trauma as outlined in the psychology literature and this impacts its foreign policy decisions in bounded cases.[84] The NCERT textbooks show an acute awareness of this sense of exploitation, and a strong distinction between pre-colonial and post-colonial self, which makes a post-colonial emphasis on victimhood plausible.

Additionally, however, it suggests that there is ample opportunity to analyse what other historical events mattered and why, and trace their institutionalization. For example, it has been argued that the concept of India as a non-aligned nation is still de facto the most discernible discourse that governs India's foreign policy. This does not mean that non-alignment has not been 'de-emphasized', particularly after 1998[85] but rather that no distinct discourse has emerged to replace it or move away from it.[86] Rather than taking this as a given through India's foreign policy behaviour, it would be fruitful to examine what the institutionalization of the legacy of non-alignment entailed – the education of Indian Foreign Service (IFS) officers perhaps? or doctrines studied by the military? – that could explain its pervasiveness. Looking at how the Mughal Empire's military doctrines were institutionalized or perhaps even de-institutionalized by the British would give us an idea of whether there was ever a corresponding strategic culture in India that stemmed from it. In the case of colonialism, we could reasonably point to institutionalization of memories as a reason why in 2005, when Prime Minister Manmohan Singh stated in a speech delivered in the UK that 'India's experience with Britain had its beneficial consequences too',[87] he was roundly criticized. While Singh was explicitly citing India's railways, bureaucracy, rule of law and freedom of press as examples, and even though his speech also repeatedly acknowledged that India's 'grievance against the British empire had a sound basis',[88] he was criticized back home for 'eulogizing colonial rule and humiliating freedom fighters'.[89]

There are also three important lessons to be noted from any study of historical memory with respect to Indian foreign policy. First, emphasizing the role of historical memory and its institutionalization should not be understood as a claim that states are trapped by the past. With reference to colonialism, Indian textbooks correctly emphasizing India's victimization and exploitation in the past neither precludes the simultaneous embracing of new identities nor the acknowledgement that an absolute 'othering' of the colonizer can lead to the loss of India's own historical complexity. For example, the NCERT textbooks accurately detail how the rape of British women by Indian sepoys during the Revolt of 1857 was not just exaggerated but used by the British government to justify brutal and violent retribution against the rebels.[90] However, in using only one narrative the voices of the women, both Indian and British, who faced traumatic violence from both sides in the inevitable chaos of rebellion, are lost.[91]

Second, institutionalized frameworks – whether through history textbooks, popular narratives, or domestic political bases matter – can make it difficult for any individual leader to affect drastic shifts. Manmohan Singh's nuanced speech at Oxford is an example of the constraints faced by a leader. His speech clearly referenced the exploitative nature of British colonialism yet he was strongly condemned for referring to any perceived benefits. Third, by examining historical memory and its institutionalization can we examine how and why there are shifts in national identity. In India's case, the label of 'rising power' is now increasingly applied. The identity of rising power suggests victor rather than victim as Miller[92] has previously argued. And India has indeed taken some steps that have been suggestive of newfound confidence. For example, in December 2013 the Khobragade case became a very public example of the distrust in the Indo-US relationship. Devyani Khobragade, an Indian diplomat stationed in New York, was arrested and strip-searched by American authorities on the charge of illegally hiring and underpaying her children's nanny. Rage against the United States at the violation of an Indian official's diplomatic immunity and, particularly, the coarse treatment of an educated middle class

Indian woman united political parties across the spectrum. It led the Indian government to take a series of retaliatory steps that severely dented the India–US relationship. The most serious action was pulling away the security barriers from around the US embassy in New Delhi. The crisis and India's response, which baffled and frustrated the US,[93] was lauded not just in India but by commentators who believed that very few countries had the 'geopolitical heft or the moral legitimacy to look the American government in the eye and demand such absolute reciprocity'.[94] Much to the delight of the Indian public, the Indian government succeeded in persuading the US government to allow Khobragade to return home and not face charges in an American court. One could argue that India took an assertive step that was severely damaging to its bilateral relationship with the world's only superpower because of an increasing confidence that comes from a new externally imposed identity of rising power.

As the historical experiences recede further into the past it would be interesting to observe how newer identities emerge and whether they exist in parallel with these memories or whether they succeed in replacing them. This offers a rich avenue for further exploration.

Notes

1   *The Independent*, 'Colonial Mindset Harming British Trade with India', 26 October 2015.

2   BBC, 'The Links between UK and India', 12 November 2015.

3   David Sott, 'The Rise of India: UK Perspectives,' *International Affairs* 93, no. 1 (2017): 165–88.

4   *The Guardian*, 'David Cameron Defends Lack of Apology for British Massacre at Amritsar', 20 February 2013.

5   Reuters, 'British PM Regrets "Deeply Shameful" Colonial Indian Massacre', 20 February 2013.

6   *First Post*, 'A Sorry Apology: David Cameron at Jallianwala Bagh', 20 February 2013.

7   *The Wall Street Journal*, 'Should Britain Pay Reparations to India?' 24 July 2015.

8   *The Hindu*, 'Queen May Face Legal Challenge over Kohinoor', 8 November 2015.

9   Manjari Chatterjee Miller, *Wronged By Empire: Post-Imperial Ideology and Foreign Policy in India and China* (Stanford CA: Stanford University Press, 2013).

10 Stephen P. Cohen, *India: Emerging Power* (Washington D.C.: Brookings Institution Press, 2001), 38.

11 James Chiriyankandath, 'Realigning India: Indian Foreign Policy after the Cold War,' *Round Table: The Commonwealth Journal of International Affairs* 93, no. 374 (April 2004): 200.

12 Cohen, *India*, 40.

13 Kanti Bajpai, 'Indian Conceptions of Order and Justice: Nehruvian, Gandhian, Hindutva, and Neo-Liberal,' in *Order and Justice in International Relations*, edited by Rosemary Foot, John Gaddis and Andrew Hurrell, 236–61 (Oxford, UK: Oxford University Press), 241.

14 Sumit Ganguly, 'India's Foreign Policy Grows Up,' *World Policy Journal* 20, no. 4 (Winter 2003/2004): 41–47, 42.

15 C. Raja Mohan, *Crossing the Rubicon: The Shaping of India's Foreign Policy* (India: Viking by Penguin Books India), xxii.

16 Manjari Chatterjee Miller and Kate Sullivan de Estrada, 'Pragmatism in Indian Foreign Policy: How Ideas Constrain Modi,' *International Affairs* 93, no. 1 (2017): 27–49, 33–34.

17 George K. Tanham, *Indian Strategic Thought: An Interpretive Essay* (Santa Monica, CA: RAND, 1992), 50.

18 Ibid., 51.

19 Rahul Sagar, 'Before Midnight: Views on International Relations, 1857–1947,' in *The Oxford Handbook of Indian Foreign Policy*, edited by David M. Malone, C. Raja Mohan and Srinath Raghavan, 65–79 (Oxford UK: Oxford University Press, 2015).

20 Ibid., 78.

21 Kate Sullivan, 'Exceptionalism in Indian Diplomacy: The Origins of India's Moral Leadership Aspirations,' *South Asia: Journal of South Asian Studies* 37, no. 4 (2014): 640–55; Kate Sullivan (ed.), Competing Visions of India in World Politics: India's Rise beyond the West (Palgrave MacMillan, 2015).

22 Ibid.

23 Sullivan, 'Exceptionalism in Indian Diplomacy,' 642.

24 Ian Hall, 'Narendra Modi and India's Normative Power,' *International Affairs* 93, no. 1 (2017): 113–31.

25 Ibid.

26 Jeffrey W. Legro, 'The Transformation of Policy Ideas,' *American Journal of Political Science* 44, no. 3 (July 2000): 419–32, 420.

27 Sheri Berman, 'Review: Ideas, Norms, and Culture in Political Analysis,' *Comparative Politics* 33, no. 2 (January 2001): 231–50, 238.

28 Dalia Ofer, 'We Israelis Remember, But How?: The Memory of the Holocaust and the Israeli Experiences,' *Israel Studies* 18, no. 2 (Summer 2013): 70–85, 82.

29 Neta Kligler-Vilenchik, Yariv Tsfati and Oren Meyers. 'Setting the Collective Memory Agenda: Examining Mainstream Media Influence on Individuals' Perceptions of the Past,' *Memory Studies* 7, no. 4 (2014): 484–99.

30 Ofer, 'We Israelis Remember, But How?' 83.

31 Daniel Levy and Natan Sznaider, 'The Holocaust and the Formation of Cosmopolitan Memory,' *European Journal of Social Theory* 5, no. 1 (2002): 87–106, 91.

32 Ibid.

33   Mooli Brog, 'Victims and Victors: Holocaust and Military Commemoration in Israel Collective Memory,' *Israel Studies* 8, no. 3 (Fall 2003): 65–99, 67.

34   Ibid., 76.

35   Ibid., 71.

36   Ibid., 65–99.

37   Levy and Sznaider, 'The Holocaust and the Formation of Cosmopolitan Memory,' 93.

38   Ibid., 94

39   Ibid., 96.

40   Michael Rothberg, 'Trauma, Memory, Holocaust,' in *Memory: A History*, edited by Dmitri Nikulin, 280–90 (Oxford and New York: Oxford University Press, 2015), 284.

41   Levy and Sznaider, 'The Holocaust and the Formation of Cosmopolitan Memory,' 92.

42   Akiko Hashimoto, 'Review: The Politics of Regret,' *Social Forces* 87, no. 1 (2008): 603–04, 604.

43   Yael Zerubavel, *Recovered Roots: Collective Memory and the Making of Israeli National Tradition* (Chicago IL: University of Chicago Press, 1995).

44   Elie Podeh, 'History and Memory in the Israeli Education System,' *History and Memory* 12, no. 1 (2000): 65–100, 65; Yinan He, 'Remembering and Forgetting the War: Elite Mythmaking, Mass Reaction, and Sino-Japanese Relations,' *History and Memory* 19, no. 2 (2007): 43–74.

45   Anthony D. Smith, *The Ethnic Origins of Nations* (Oxford, UK: Basil Blackwell, 1986).

46   James Pennebaker, 'Introduction,' in *Collective Memory of Political Events: Social Psychological Perspectives*, edited by J. W. Pennebaker, Dario Paez and Bernard Rimé, vii–xi (Mahwah, N.J.: Lawrence Erlbaum Associates, 1997).

47   Anthony D. Smith, 'Memory and Modernity,' *Nations and Nationalism* 2, no. 3 (1996): 371–88, 383.

48   Maurice Halbwachs, *On Collective Memory*, translated by Lewis A. Coser (Chicago IL: University of Chicago Press, 1992), 224.

49   He, 'Remembering and Forgetting the War', 47; Zheng Wang, 'National Humiliation, History Education, and the Politics of Historical Memory: Patriotic Education Campaign in China,' *International Studies Quarterly* 52, no. 4 (2008): 783–806, 789.

50   He, 'Remembering and Forgetting the War,' 47.

51   Ibid., 54.

52   Wang, 'National Humiliation, History Education, and the Politics of Historical Memory.'

53   Ruti G. Teitel, 'Transitional Justice Genealogy,' *Harvard Human Rights Journal* 16 (2003): 69–94, 69.

54   Naomi Roht-Arriaza, 'The New Landscape of Transition Justice,' in *Transitional Justice in the Twenty-First Century: Beyond Truth Versus Justice*, edited Naomi Roht-Arriaza and Javier Mariezcurrena, 1–16 (Cambridge, UK: Cambridge University Press, 2006), 2.

55   Alexander L. Boraine, 'Transitional Justice: A Holistic Interpretation,' *Journal of International Affairs* 60, no. 1 (2006): 17–28, 18.

56   Michal Ben-Josef Hirsch, 'And the Truth Shall Make You Free: The International Norm of Truth-seeking,' PhD dissertation, Massachusetts Institute of Technology, 2009.

57   Martha Minow, *Between Vengeance and Forgiveness: Facing History After Genocide and Mass Violence* (Boston MA: Beacon Press, 1998), 2.

58   Ibid., 4.

59   Ibid., 120.

60   Judy Barsalou, *Trauma and Transitional Justice in Divided Societies* (Washington D.C: The United States Institute of Peace, 2005); Robert I. Rotberg and Dennis Thompson (eds), *Truth v. Justice: The Morality of Truth Commissions: The Morality of Truth Commissions* (Princeton NJ: Princeton University Press, 2010); John Sigal and M. Weinfeld, *Trauma and Rebirth: Intergenerational Effects of the Holocaust* (New York: Praeger, 1989); Yael Danieli (ed.), *International Handbook of Multigenerational Legacies of Trauma* (New York and London: Plenum Press, 1998); James Wertsch, *Voices of Collective Remembering* (Cambridge, UK: Cambridge University Press, 2002); Jeffrey C. Alexander, 'Toward a Theory of Cultural Trauma,' in *Cultural Trauma and Collective Identity*, edited by Jeffrey C. Alexander, Ron Eyerman, Bernhard Giesen, Neil Smelser, Piotr Sztompka and Björn Wittrock, 620–39 (Berkeley, California: University of California Press, 2004).

61   Akira Iriye quoted in David Scott, *China Stands Up: The PRC and the International System* (Abingdon, UK: Routledge, 2007), 4.

62   Podeh, 'History and Memory in the Israeli Education System', 65.

63   John Dorschner and Thomas Sherlock, 'The Role of History in Shaping Collective Identities in India and Pakistan,' in *Teaching the Violent Past: History Education and Reconciliation*, edited by Elizabeth A. Cole, 275–315 (New York: Rowman & Littlefield, 2007), 276.

64   Michael Gottlob, 'Changing Concepts of Identity in the Indian Textbook Controversy,' *Internationale Schulbuchforschung* 29, no. 4 (2007): 341–53, 341.

65   Howard D. Mehlinger, 'International Textbook Revision: Examples from the United States,' *Internationale Schulbuchforschung* 7 (1985): 287–98, 287.

66   Podeh, 'History and Memory in the Israeli Education System', 66.

67   J. P. Naik, *The Role of the Government of India in Education* (New Delhi: Government of India, Ministry of Education, 1962), 2.

68   Sylvie Guichard, 'The Indian Nation and Selective Amnesia: Representing Conflicts and Violence in Indian History Textbooks,' *Nations and Nationalism* 19, no. 1 (2013): 68–86, 70.

69   Amita Gupta, 'Schooling in India,' in *Going to School in South Asia*, edited by Amita Gupta, 66–111 (Westport CT: Greenwood Press, 2007), 92.

70   Ibid.

71   National Council of Education and Research Training, 'Leading the Change: 50 Years of NCERT'. Available at http://www.ncert.nic.in/oth_anoun/leading_the_change.pdf.

72   One of several Boards of Education in India. CBSE falls under the Union Government of India while other boards, such as the West Bengal Board, may fall under the purview of the relevant state, that is, West Bengal.

73 *India Today*, 'CBSE Schools to Use Only NCERT Books: Minister of State School Education', 19 May 2014.

74 I use *Themes in Indian History* Parts I, II and III, NCERT 2006. The books issued in 2006 appear to still be in use today.

75 *Themes in Indian History*, Part III, NCERT, 269.

76 Ibid., 299.

77 Ibid., 310–11.

78 Ibid., 300.

79 Sugata Bose and Ayesha Jalal, *Modern South Asia: History, Culture, Political Economy*, third edition (New York, NY: Routledge, 2011).

80 Ibid., Part II, NCERT.

81 Ibid., 180.

82 Ibid., 181.

83 Ibid., Part III, NCERT, 338.

84 Miller, *Wronged by Empire*.

85 Mohan, *Crossing the Rubicon*, 261–64.

86 Frank O'Donnell and Harsh V. Pant, 'Managing Indian Defence Policy: The Missing Grand Strategy Connection,' *Orbis* 59, no. 2 (2015): 199–214; Manjari Chatterjee Miller, 'India's Feeble Foreign Policy,' *Foreign Affairs* (May/June 2013): 14–19; Pratap Bhanu Mehta, 'Still under Nehru's Shadow? The Absence of Foreign Policy Frameworks in India,' *India Review* 8, no. 3 (2009): 209–33.

87 Text of Manmohan Singh's Speech, Oxford UK, 12 July 2005. Available at http://www.rediff.com/news/2005/jul/12spec.htm.

88 Ibid.

89 *The Economic Times*, 'BJP Raises Din over Manmohan's Colonial Musings', 14 July 2005.

90 *Themes in Indian History*, Part III, NCERT, 308–12.

91 Rudranghsu Mukherjee, 'Satan Let Loose upon Earth: The Kanpur Massacres in India in the Revolt of 1857,' *Past and Present* 128, no. 1 (August 1990): 92–116.

92 Miller, *Wronged by Empire*.

93 Ashley Tellis, 'India–US Relations: The Rupture Is Certainly Real and Quite Tragic', Rediff, 17 February 2014.

94 Kishore Mahbubani, 'Two Shades of Immunity', *The Indian Express*, 12 January 2014.

5

A Doubled Geography
Geobody, Land and Sea in Indian Security Thought

Itty Abraham

Geography plays an intimate and largely unacknowledged role in shaping Indian thinking on security, defence and foreign policies. While nearly all scholars and analysts who write about India and its place in the world address disputes and problems emanating from geophysical-spaces-made-political-objects – think of Kashmir, Siachen or the Indus River treaty – and confront resilient spatial images and metaphors – for example, homeland, *punyabhumi* or infiltrators – remarkably few acknowledge the power of spatial concepts and logics in shaping Indian security discourses.[1] Simply put, India has no explicit geopolitical tradition, yet geography is everywhere in its political thought.[2]

For a characteristic example of the ubiquity of spatial thinking in Indian foreign policy, consider Prime Minister Jawaharlal Nehru, bemoaning the breakdown of relations with China in an informal conversation with President Nasser of Egypt in 1960:

> Before the Chinese came to Tibet, we had no trouble...The frontier which was dead for thousands of years has now become alive with armies facing each other...Another peculiar feature of the problem [with China] is that from times immemorial, mountains have formed an intimate part of our culture. The Himalayas, for example, occupy [first] place in the minds and hearts of our people. It is inconceivable that a chunk of Himalaya may cease to be a part of India.[3]

This short statement spills over with language joining geography and nation across multiple registers. The physical is made coterminous with the cultural, embodying the nation in the form of a mountain chain. A political geography is animated when the Chinese arrive in Tibet, bringing a 'dead' frontier to life and making the Himalayas a living metonym of the Indian nation. For Nehru, the strength of the bond between mountains and the emotions of the

Indian people is so strong that losing a 'chunk' of the Himalayas becomes an 'inconceivable' loss to the Indian nation. Giving up these treasured lands comes to mean the same as giving up a part of the nation: it is beyond imagination.[4] President Nasser could no doubt have reflected similarly on the place of the Nile in shaping the dominant Egyptian self-image.

From language comes political consequence. The power of geography in making sense of and giving shape to the strategic choices facing India are nowhere more visible than in Nehru's statement above, the inconceivability of giving up the Himalayas for the effect it would have on Indian 'minds and hearts'. Although it is widely accepted today that long-standing territorial disputes could easily become a trigger for a much more serious conflict between India and its neighbours, possibly including even the use of nuclear weapons,[5] the practical response of resolving disputes over these flashpoints by exchanging one piece of land for another is rarely taken seriously in New Delhi as a political possibility. A piece of the national territory, given its intimate identification with the nation and its culture, can have no possible equivalence with other goods, even a net improvement in security, making a trade-off impossible to imagine. This affective combination of nation and territory has been named a 'geobody' in historian Thongchai Winichakul's apt term.[6]

Taken as a whole, this chapter can be read in two ways. Most obviously, it is a reflection on the doubled place of geography in Indian security, its familiar presence in discourse joined by its absence as an explicit category of analysis, and the political consequences of that doubling.[7] The chapter proceeds by first framing and then unpacking a dominant trope in the representation of Indian security space, namely the idea of the national geobody as the prime object of national security. After historicizing the idea of the national geobody as a distinctively terrestrial object and identifying its origins in anti-colonial thought and practices, the chapter goes on to discuss a different spatial ontology, the oceans and seas, to highlight future challenges facing the country if the terrestrial geobody continues to define the unconscious core of Indian strategic thinking.

Less obviously, this chapter offers a tacit introduction to post-structural and postcolonial analyses of foreign policy.[8] It addresses two modes of spatial representation in Indian security discourse, the metaphoric-linguistic and the material-ontological. The discussion of the national geobody highlights the power of language as a metaphor, and shows how dominant frames of reference – 'truth regimes' – are produced through the intersection of distinct spatializing practices. The material-ontological expression of geography is also produced through discourse, but the analytic concern in this chapter is with two contrasting ontologies, terrestrial and marine.[9] The material difference and challenges embodied by the sea is discussed through the work of three Indian geopolitical thinkers who have reflected on maritime spaces and what a non-terrestrial ontology means for geopolitics. In the end, this chapter is concerned to show that, *contra* the first rule of conventional geopolitics, geography is not destiny, indeed, it is not even fixed or permanent as a geophysical signifier such as a mountain is typically assumed to be.[10] Rather, what gets called geography turns out to be fluid, malleable, and shifting: no matter its everyday and familiar representations in language, geography is neither natural nor has it been around for times immemorial.[11] It is a discursive manifestation of power and knowledge with its own socially constructed history that changes with time and interests.[12]

Geography as a truth regime

Geography has always been over-determined in Indian strategic thought. Leave aside for the moment the immediate problem at the country's independence of the breakdown of the imperial geopolitical scheme composed of extended frontiers and buffer zones that had kept potential invaders far from India's heartland.[13] There is a far more profound existential problem to consider. As will be discussed at greater length below, international recognition of Indian claims to national self-determination had been won, in no small part, by a successful claim that India met the Wilsonian criteria for national self-determination, namely of being an identifiable nation with a singular national homeland.[14] However, due to the religious fault lines dividing the independence movements and the form of their eventual political resolution, British India's struggle for political freedom would end with the territorial division of the imperial territory into two sovereign states, India and Pakistan.[15] The price of India's independence was the loss of one of its key foundations, a defined national territory. Political success would forever inseparably be joined with territorial breakdown. Through this contradictory process, geography acquired its doubled status: always present as a condition of India's creation, and in the same instant, made absent by its nature: unmentionable for the cost it had endured and the trauma it had produced.

This complex of cause and explanation, contradiction and self-evident truth, constitutes what Stuart Hall, following Foucault, calls a 'regime of truth'.[16] A regime of truth is a discourse: it is an organized system of meaning that constitutes a particular way of making sense of the world by giving authoritative meaning to particular terms and their relations with each other.[17] Discourses are world-making technologies. While they are immensely powerful, they are also necessarily selective. Discourses produce imaginative worlds by creating authoritative structures of meaning, but also by leaving things out. Absences become vital tools for critical analyses seeking to unravel the foundations of dominant discourse. What is left out can be discerned by paying close attention to discourse's internal contradictions. By focusing on moments and conditions when contradictions erupt into view, a critical absence of the Indian security discourse, namely geography's doubled form, becomes visible. Adopting this approach allows this chapter to undo and re-present – make unnatural – the national geobody as a regime of truth.

Outline of the national geobody

The idea of the national geobody emerged as a discursive supplement to the political struggle for Indian independence from colonial rule.[18] The national geobody was a collective product of imperial, visual, religious, cultural and infrastructural practices, each assuming or seeking to establish a territorial basis for Indian distinctiveness and sovereignty. The idea of the national geobody is discursively inscribed through the simultaneous nationalization of geography and spatialization of the nation. When it comes to the latter, pride of place inevitably goes to the Himalayas, the lofty snow-capped mountain ranges in the north of the country, which roughly coincide with India's northern frontiers, as the Nehru quote above reminds us. Running a close second to the great northern mountain ranges are references to the immense oceans that fringe the country's southern peninsula. The pioneering geopolitical writer and diplomat, K. M. Panikkar, would wax eloquent about India's intimate and historic relationship with the sea:

> From the ports on the East coast of India argosies have sailed this sea from the dawn of history and the colonization of the Pacific islands by the Hindus shows the extent to which this sea has been explored and navigated at least 2,000 years ago... [Indian] supremacy in [the Bay of Bengal] was naval and political, based on an extensive colonization of the islands and this supremacy ceased only with the breakdown of Chola power in the thirteenth century...

the period of Hindu supremacy in the Ocean was one of complete freedom of trade and navigation.[19]

Through these renderings of the country's national geography, nation and territory are joined seamlessly. India comes to be imagined as a natural fortress, guarded on all sides by elements of the natural landscape, reinforcing a profound sense of national distinctiveness. Panikkar states:

> The geographic structure of the Indian Ocean is particularly important. For the most part, its area is walled off on three sides by land, with the southern side of Asia forming a roof over it...the vital feature which differentiates the Indian Ocean is...the subcontinent of India which juts out far into the sea for a thousand miles to its tapering end at Cape Comorin.[20]

In this discourse, high and long mountain ranges and deep and wide oceans enforce natural barriers to the uninvited incursions of outsiders, creating a haven of ancient civilization able to flower for millennia, producing in its wake great knowledge and a unique national culture. The turning points in Indian history, by the same token, come when these great natural redoubts have been violated or bypassed by crafty outsiders, whether European colonial powers or Muslim invaders from Central Asia. The sublime majesty of these natural boundaries thus carries with it a heightened sense of national dread when physical barriers are transgressed in real or imagined ways, invoking an abhorrent contamination of the pristine motherland with all its associations of violence and violation.[21] National security becomes a necessary supplement to the physical protections provided by a benevolent Nature.[22]

Legacy of imperial geopolitics

Terrestrial imaginations of India come from two primary sources: the imperial-political and the cultural-social. The dominant form of territoriality associated with the modern Indian state owes its origins to imperial state practices most directly expressed in the geopolitical vision put forward by Lord Curzon, viceroy of India at the end of the nineteenth century.[23] Curzon's account of the geopolitical forces shaping Indian political space was deeply self-serving insofar as it conveniently erased the long history of British maritime incursions into what would become their greatest colony, a movement that began from small and vulnerable holdings on the southern and western Indian coasts. In his famous Romanes lecture delivered at Oxford after stepping down as viceroy, Curzon would dismiss these humble beginnings in favour of a description of the growth of British power in India that described it as an immense natural force upon which no human restrictions could be placed.[24] One of the most striking features of imperial geopolitics as propounded by Curzon is how the country's oceanic boundaries disappear, to be replaced by powerful forces emanating from the terrestrial heartland of the country. The forces of expansion that drove the British Indian Empire began from the centre and looked north and west; the south of the country with its oceanic boundaries was entirely ignored. This tendency to look away from the seas to the mountains would become a characteristic feature of postcolonial Indian geopolitical thinking.

Perhaps not surprisingly, given this tendency, among the first foreign policy acts of the postcolonial Indian state would be to bind the northern Himalayan kingdoms of Nepal, Sikkim and Bhutan to India with unequal treaties that restricted their sovereignty and made India the guarantor of their external security.[25] India's new neighbour, Pakistan, would become India's most serious security problem, due not only to the bloody legacy of Partition, but also because Pakistan's newly marked territorial boundaries meant that the mountainous frontiers of the Hindu Kush and the buffer state of Afghanistan no longer stood as geophysical protectors of the Indian heartland.

Domestic sources of territoriality

Imperial geopolitical visions were joined by narratives of territoriality produced by anti-colonial nationalists, working through a variety of different registers.[26] As mentioned above, nationalists sought international recognition for India's right to be free of colonial rule, even as intellectuals and social movements produced visions of a sovereign and independent country across multiple domains, including the visual, spiritual and infrastructural. What joined these very different forces into a single discourse was the territorial base of the national geobody each independently helped establish.

For those seeking international recognition of India's right to be free of British rule, what was critical was the claim that India had been in existence for centuries, hence, demanding national independence was nothing more than a *restoration* of a sovereignty that was all too well known. For anti-colonial nationalists, foregrounding the geophysical features of the country as the natural home of the Indian people had the political consequence of conveniently shifting the nation's origins far back in historical time.[27] The slippage between the immutability and timelessness of a physical geography and a people who had inhabited this space for as long as the mountains and seas had been around allowed nationalists to meet the terms of political independence laid down by Woodrow Wilson in the lead up to the Versailles conference of 1919.[28] The commonsense of India's historicity would be engendered through reference to the geological time of mountains and oceans rather than the calendar time of the modern era, pushing back the origins of the nation to a moment when it becomes difficult to separate geological, human and mythic histories from each other, producing a field for the supernatural and the hypernatural to cohabit. In the process, the ancient texts of the Hindus would become re-inscribed as ur-texts of an Indian nation that was yet to be, providing textual evidence of the homeland of the Hindu people, an identifiable race that was yet to become a nation.[29]

Visual, religious and infrastructural spatial practices

It must be remembered that from 1857 onwards, India was both 'British' and 'Native', a congeries of kingdoms and principalities subordinated by imperial treaties, directly ruled territories including the three Presidencies, suzerain areas and loosely controlled frontier regions, as well as small enclaves under the jurisdiction of France, Portugal and other European states.[30] Indian political space was, to put it mildly, heterogeneous. The homogenization and nationalization of Indian geography began from multiple ideational and material sources, including new representations and imaginations of the country as well as the infrastructural investments of the colonial state.

Sumathi Ramaswamy's work demonstrates the significance of the visual image in establishing this new spatial construction.[31] She focuses on the emergence of *Bharat Mata* (Mother India), a mass-produced image of a sari-clad female goddess superimposed on pictorial representations of the country, with her head crowned by the Himalayas and her feet bathed by the Indian Ocean. This new and mass-produced vision of Mother India in the form of 'calendar art', Ramaswamy argues, was immensely popular, circulated widely, and became a powerful supplement to the purely cartographic map by adding a symbolic and deeply resonant image of what India had come to mean and would be. The most important element of her argument is the claim that once the modern cartographic map of India became the dominant visual representation of the country in people's minds, all other forms of visual codes had to conform to its parameters. Ramaswamy argues that 'all discourses of territory, especially non-scientific, sentimental, and sacral ones, have necessarily to contend with the scientific map form'.[32] This sacralization of Indian national space was further reinforced by the emergence of new spaces of religious circulation, a popular 'sacred geography', produced by a qualitative rise in the numbers of pilgrims travelling across the country.[33] The privileging of specific journeys, particularly to the Ganges at Banaras and to shrines and monasteries around the country, was both a cause and symptom of Hindu revival movements characteristic of the period. Pilgrimages in turn were made much easier by extensive colonial investments in infrastructure, especially the railways, which apart from binding the country together through a network of steel and coal, had the additional effect of producing uniform times across the country, another step in homogenizing a variegated national space.[34]

The writings of religious nationalists played an important part in the process of materializing a national geography.[35] The turn of the century was a time when new maps of the Indian subcontinent were very much in vogue. Perhaps the most efficacious of these maps from a political standpoint were those cartographic representations produced by the votaries of a new country called Pakistan, a proposed homeland for India's Muslim populations. These maps were contested directly by Hindu ideologues such as Golwalkar who built on earlier polemics by Damodar Sarvarkar, founder of the Rashtriya Swayamsevak Sangh (RSS). The latter had argued for a vision of India as a fatherland in the European geopolitical idiom, while Golwalkar sought to re-imagine India as the holy land of the Hindu race or *punyabhumi*. This exclusive vision would go beyond map-making in a narrow sense. In this latter re-inscription, India's boundaries would stretch to include the Himalayas to the north, Afghanistan to the west, Burma and the Irrawaddy basin in the east and the peninsular cape of Kanyakumari to the south. Supplementing this expansive geography was a distinct vision of who could be considered an authentic Indian. For Hindu nationalists, true Indians could only be those individuals had been born within India's sacred geography *and* whose holiest places of worship lay within India. In other words, Hindus, Sikhs and Jains could be considered legitimate residents of India but not Christians or Muslims, whose holy places lay outside the territorial borders of the country.

Imaginations of a revised Indian political space were not restricted to religious visions alone. Manu Goswami has shown how the writings of early modernists and nationalists built on the administrative reforms and infrastructural investments of the colonial government.[36] Among the most important of these visions was the critique of imperial and colonial financial and trade policies by a future member of the British Parliament, Dadabhai Naoroji. Naoroji's economic forensics drew attention to the 'drain' of wealth away from India to the metropole. Using the colonial government's own data he would argue that as much as 200 million pounds sterling – an extraordinary figure for the times – was being extracted from India annually. Beyond the angry political reaction this critique obviously engendered, in the process of removing India from imperial accounts, Naoroji's vision produced a latent image of India as a bounded economic space, another means of stabilizing the idea of India as an independent territory.

It is important to recall that these visual, spiritual, and infrastructural imaginations of a terrestrial geobody were not restricted to cultural and anti-colonial domains. The temporal and political transition to a sovereign state would join a discourse of national geography to practices of state territoriality. Given how deliberately independent India sought to define itself against its colonial past, it is ironic that no small part of the spatial underpinnings of postcolonial strategic imaginaries owed their origins to an imperial legacy of geopolitics and, more disturbingly, shared very similar ends.

Maritime geopolitics: New boundaries of the geobody

The one exception to the general rule that Indian geopolitical thinkers ignored the sea, following in the footsteps of their imperial predecessors, is found in early writings of K. M. Panikkar.[37] Panikkar, the first of modern India's geopolitical writers, was a Malabar-born and Oxford-trained historian who had an extraordinary public career spanning the late colonial and early independence periods. Starting as a professor at the famed Aligarh Muslim University, he would go on to become the founding editor of a major Indian newspaper, *Hindustan Times*, the advisor and prime minister (*Dewan*) to a number of prominent princely states, independent India's ambassador to China, Egypt and France, and eventually vice chancellor of Benaras Hindu University after his diplomatic career ended. All through his busy life 'Sardar' Panikkar would write voluminously, in English and in Malayalam, on a wide range of historical, literary, religious and contemporary political subjects, most notably geopolitics.[38]

An early study of his, *India and the Indian Ocean* (1946), is noteworthy not only for its prescience in outlining the future contours of the Asia-Pacific maritime region, but also for its critical assessment of the flaws in Indian security thinking due to the prevailing obsession with its land frontiers.[39] While the influence of the American geopolitical writer, Admiral T. H. Mahan, is all too visible in the book's subtitle, *An Essay on the Influence of Sea Power on Indian History*, the book is more than just an application of Mahan's ideas to another ocean. The monograph can be read as a postcolonial historical reconstruction of Indian history seen from the standpoint of the seas surrounding the southern peninsula.

In this slim volume, Panikkar sought not only to revive memories of the long maritime traditions of India, commercial as well as military, but also to sketch a geopolitical map of the region, outlining those places that particularly affected the defence of India, from the island of Socotra in the Gulf of Aden to Singapore and the Malacca Straits. He was careful to highlight India's special place at its centre of this ocean, dominating both the eastern and western fringes of the ocean, and hence controlling the maritime passages between the Arabian peninsula, Africa, southern and eastern Asia. Over and over, Panikkar seeks to remind his readers that 'sea [has had] a preponderant influence on [India's] destiny' and 'whoever controls the Indian Ocean has India at his mercy'.[40] The larger problem is that, as he bluntly states, 'Indian histories so far have been written not from the point of view of India as a whole, but from the point of view of Delhi and its changing dynasties'.[41] In a direct riposte to Curzon, Panikkar argued that the rapid expansion of the Japanese empire during the Second World War proved that 'the strategic area of Indian warfare was not so much the Burmese [land] frontier as Malaya, Singapore, and the neglected Andaman Islands'.[42] Writing as the end of formal British rule in India was imminent, Panikkar called for India to take on a greater responsibility in controlling the seas around the peninsula, to complement the Royal Navy in the first instance, but with an eye to long term dominance over what in his mind was without question an Indian 'lake'. As he wrote, '[b]ut by slow stages, this situation [Britain's dominance] will change. The interests of the new countries will become increasingly important…clearly it is India, with her geographical position and greater resources that will have a major part to play'.[43] For this to come about, he argued, a small and modest navy that was little more than a coast guard was more than useless. It had to be a force capable of force projection: its objective was to 'protect the seas, not the land, and if it cannot…better not to have a navy at all'.[44]

Maritime geopolitics: Liquid ontologies

Although Panikkar's early efforts to refocus the orientation of India's defence policies towards the sea were articulate and thoughtful, few visible or material changes came of them. The next major effort to take the maritime zone seriously emerged in a study prepared by the geopolitical strategist Bhabani Sen Gupta and his colleagues at Delhi's Centre for Policy Research, in the wake of claims by Indonesia and Malaysia to territorialize the Straits of Malacca in 1971.[45] Their study sought to place the Malacca Straits in larger strategic, legal and political context and is significant for a number of reasons. While it did not seek to speak directly to Indian strategy in favour of outlining the larger issues at stake for international law and the region, the study stands as a landmark in outlining the revised geopolitical map of the Indian Ocean region following the end of British post-war naval hegemony. An important insight of the study was to see the enlargement of the Indian Ocean into what would later come to be called the Indo-Pacific as a product of change engendered by new technologies of communication, logistics, transport and industrial growth. Oceanic space was being transformed by a new materiality, it argued. This study is extremely important as the first Indian study to reference the sea as a liquid space, turning away from the dominant conception of a physical geography shaped by a terrestrial ontology.

After the Suez crisis in 1956, the Indian Ocean was no longer limited to the space imagined in *India and the Indian Ocean*, bounded on the west by the eastern African coast, Iran and the Arabian peninsula to the north and west, and the Kra peninsula to the east. Sen Gupta et al.'s focus on the Malacca Straits returned attention to the maritime connections between the Indian and Pacific Oceans, bringing the South and East China Seas and the Bay of Bengal into mutual correspondence again, as they had been before the period of European dominance.[46] As Panikkar had pointed out, in the pre-modern period, this oceanic region had been one continuous commercial space, with oceanic dominance shaped by competition between the southern Indian Chola kingdom and the Sri Vijaya empire of contemporary Southeast Asia. Sen Gupta's study, written at a moment when regional orders were in flux, defined the boundaries of this expanded maritime space as extending from Japan in the east to the new Chinese-built railroad joining Tanzania and Zambia in the west.

The 1968 announcement of the withdrawal of the Royal Navy 'east of Suez' had created what some consider a power vacuum in the maritime control of the Indian Ocean region.[47] The international community was debating whether to use 3 or 12 miles from the shore as the extent of state territorial control, with opinion divided between the established maritime powers who preferred the smaller figure against newly independent countries and the Soviet Union who opted for the larger figure. India was still reacting with outrage at the movement of the US Seventh Fleet into the Bay of Bengal during the war with Pakistan that led to the creation of Bangladesh in 1971. A proposal by Ceylon (Sri Lanka) to declare the Indian Ocean region a zone of peace was well received by the non-aligned countries. Littoral countries of the seas east of India were keen to establish greater control over shipping in this region, especially the movement of foreign naval ships, including nuclear-powered and nuclear-armed submarines, and increasingly massive oil tankers. Indonesia and Malaysia were envious of the economic and political rents obtained by Singapore from its strategic location and hoped to convert the Malacca straits from an international waterway into territorial jurisdiction. Both now claimed their territorial waters extended to 12 miles.

The ontological condition of the sea as a 'liquid territory' was raised by Indonesia and the Philippines as a matter of national integrity.[48] Both island nations now sought to establish the archipelago as a distinct kind of national territory in international law. In the process of discussing how to measure the territorial extent of archipelagic countries, it became clear that other issues needed clarification as well, especially the status of 'internal' waters, the marine areas between islands. Indonesia argued that, 'if in some parts of the world, the sea and the water may have become [a] separating factor, for Indonesia it has become a unifying factor. Maintaining the principle of archipelago means maintaining the principle of the unity of the Indonesian islands'.[49] Accepting this claim would not affect the movement of foreign vessels, however, as Indonesia permitted innocent passage between the islands (through what they saw as their internal waters) as long as the principle of the archipelago as a single territorial unit was accepted in international law. In other words, water as well as land had to be seen as inseparable elements of the national territory. This claim, if accepted, meant that some part of the Straits of Malacca would become part of Indonesia's internal waters, subject to Indonesian territorial sovereignty. The desire to keep the straits as an international waterway was of deep concern to many parties, most notably the United States and an economically resurgent Japan, as so much of the latter's international trade, including especially vital petroleum supplies, was channeled through the Malacca Straits.

The core legal issue that Sen Gupta and his colleagues sought to grapple with was the right of 'innocent passage' of foreign vessels through a country's territorial waters. By contrast with the passage of foreign aliens through sovereign lands, a situation where no one questions the right of the state in question to ascertain their bona fides and to permit or block their movement, controlling movement across the sea is far less easy. Based on the practical difficulties of monitoring and controlling foreign traffic in maritime space and keeping in mind the foundational legal principle of freedom of movement on the high seas, the idea of 'innocent passage' gives ships and other maritime vessels the right to move through a state's territorial waters as long as they have no ulterior motive for doing so. Sen Gupta and colleagues point out that the complexity of 'innocent passage' arises from a number of sources, including whether a state's claim to territorial waters is recognized internationally, whether the waters in question are coastal seas that fall under the 12 mile limit, are straits that join oceans, or are sea passages that lead only into closed territorial waters.

The law of the sea's privileging of unconstrained movement of 'innocent' vessels is deeply misleading. In fact, 'innocent passage' is international law's way of saying that the sea is always incompletely territorialized and that there is little that terrestrial political authority can do about it. The easiest way to see the problem produced by liquid territoriality is if we transpose the issue to land. Imagine a world in which we land at an international airport whose immigration control system is based on random selection. Most travellers will pass through without molestation and will never be checked at all, some will be checked and found to be 'innocently' passing through, with valid papers and reasons, while a very small number of those checked will be found to be in violation of some national rule and held to account. Such a radically unlikely situation describes the everyday condition of ship traffic through territorial waters. States simply cannot physically check more than a handful of the vessels passing through their territorial waters for practical reasons. What is not often appreciated is that the state's ability to impose what we now think of as a normal regime of immigration control is predicated on being able to create physical bottlenecks (chokepoints in geopolitical language) that passengers must pass through. Airports, border posts, boundary walls and checkpoints are forms of artificial terrain that are deployed in order to block, control, channel, or monitor the movement of people and goods across territory.[50]

Building terrain on water is a very different and difficult problem. States may want to control their territorial waters but at the best of times find it difficult to do so, not only as the history of smuggling tells us on a daily basis, but as we are also reminded by the enormous difficulty of getting rid of Somali pirates off the east coast of Africa.[51] These pirates, who appeared to be merely a ragtag group of marine subalterns, armed with only light weapons and small arms, were able to hold the world's shipping fleets to ransom for years precisely due to the extra advantages given to them by their mobility, local knowledge, creative use of satellite phones and digital navigation devices, and the physical difficulties of constraining movement over the high seas. Eventually it would take the navies of a dozen countries to control the pirates, and the problem has still not disappeared entirely.[52]

'Innocent passage' makes legal virtue out of practical necessity. Since states cannot control all traffic through their claimed territories, and at the same time also cannot give up their claims of territorial sovereignty, innocent passage becomes a way of finessing the problem. Rather than reminding us of the state's (in)ability to control movement through its claimed territorial space, the legal focus shifts to the moving vessel and places the burden of 'innocent passage' on the ship passing through domestic waters. If the vessel violates this rule, it can be held to account, but the real secret being covered up here is that the terrestrial state has little means of establishing to what extent passage is in fact innocent, short of stopping all ships, a physical and practical impossibility. The fluid and open ontology of the sea makes it impossible for states to control all movement through their territorial waters: hence, the problem of liquid territoriality.

It would take another three decades before a fuller appreciation of the spatial and material changes touched on by Sen Gupta and his colleagues became apparent to a wider audience. C. Raja Mohan's recent study of India–China relations, *Samudra Manthan* (lit. trans: The Churning Sea) was the first to carry those initial insights into a robust discussion of what he has termed the 'Indo-Pacific', a region now transforming into a zone of potential conflict that extends from East Africa to East Asia.

Maritime geopolitics: China and the Indo-Pacific

Raja Mohan's purpose in this important study is to examine potential causes of future conflict between India and China in the Indo-Pacific maritime zone.[53] The Indo-Pacific runs from the eastern African littoral to northern Japan, but also extends well into the Pacific, especially the second 'island chain' that runs in a 'north south line from the Kurils through Japan, the Bonins, the Marianas, the Carolinas, and [Papua]'.[54] This chain is the more distant of two sets of archipelagos that Chinese strategists see as natural containers of their oceanic aspirations, and include a number of islands that have been dominated by the US and its allies since the Second World War. Traditional hotspots remain but are supplemented by other areas of concern in this new conflict space. Closer to the mainland, the Indo-Pacific region includes familiar sectors of long-running concern to China, most notably the 'renegade province' of Taiwan, but also the multi-disputed island groups of the South China Sea, the Spratlys and Paracels. With the passage of time, the Malacca Straits has become even more important as the key choke point or geopolitical fulcrum of this oceanic complex, channeling as it does no less than one third of the world's trade, including vital oil supplies from the Persian Gulf to points east. In addition, new areas within the western oceanic region have become of strategic and political importance since Sen Gupta's study. These include the weakly governed Somali and East African coast, adjoining French, US and Chinese military bases in Djibouti, an unsettled Yemeni peninsula, and the strategically located Indian Ocean archipelagos of the Seychelles and Mauritius.

Raja Mohan notes that for both China and India, the present historical moment marks a move away from their 'traditional obsession with controlling land frontiers',[55] namely the western expanses of China and the northwest of India. His study begins from the premise that as these two Asian powers become even more important, especially in economic terms, they are 'likely to step on each other's toes and those of the Americans, the world's dominant maritime power'.[56] Raja Mohan is particularly interested in an emerging 'maritime rivalry', as he terms it, which is most likely to have its 'sharpest expression in the Bay of Bengal, the South China Sea, and the Straits of Malacca'.[57] Although he does not say so explicitly, the heightened prospect of conflict comes because overlapping components of these seas are also considered to be marine geobodies by India, China, Taiwan, Indonesia, Malaysia, Singapore, Philippines and Vietnam.

According to Raja Mohan, although the region of potential China–India conflict has expanded across the Indo-Pacific due to heightened expectations and obligations, greater logistical challenges and new threats leading to the growth of naval power in both countries, the most likely danger spots remain all too familiar and close to the territorial homeland.

To understand why, two points need to be borne in mind. First, even during the decades when each country was far more concerned about land frontiers populated by restive ethnic margins than the seas and oceans, the Bay of Bengal (for India) and the South China Sea (for China) never lost their status as homeland (albeit maritime) territories for each country. These coastal seas were considered marine extensions of their land territories, naturally belonging to them and falling under their control. These seas are politically and emotionally vital because they are seen as integral parts of the national geobody, yet being liquid spaces, as I have discussed above, achieving sovereign control was far more difficult than on land. Second, although the identification of three danger zones appears to be a reference to three discrete sectors, it should be remembered that from a geophysical standpoint the Bay of Bengal and South China Sea form a single continuous maritime zone, thanks to the connecting role played by the Malacca Straits. Countries see sovereignty at stake when geobodies are in question and are likely to act forcibly when national homelands are encroached upon. For other states, however, these seas are part of an open and continuous marine space governed by the law of the sea, and are not the property of any state. Innocent passage allows them to travel up to the territorial edge of another country without violating international law.

The original source of anxiety for both states is the gap between the lack of international recognition of the Bay of Bengal and the South China Sea as territorial extensions of each state and domestic understandings within India and China that the Bay and the Sea respectively are integral parts of the national geobody. During the Cold War, the Indian navy was unable to prevent foreign naval forces from repeatedly encroaching into the Indian Ocean. US and Soviet nuclear submarines regularly passed through the region in search of each other, while the US converted Diego Garcia in the Chagos archipelago into an important naval base that in all likelihood also stockpiled nuclear weapons. By far the most dramatic event demonstrating the lack of Indian control over the neighboring seas, an event still imprinted on the Indian mind – public and official – was the passage of the US aircraft carrier *Enterprise* and the Seventh Fleet through the Bay of Bengal during the 1971 Bangladesh war. Ostensibly sent to East Pakistan in aid of trapped citizens during the war, the term 'USS Enterprise' has become a rank metonym for American gunboat diplomacy in South Asia. More recently, the devastations of the 2004 tsunami that affected the Nicobar Islands and the southern Indian peninsula has once again exposed the vulnerability of this region, albeit from an entirely new and unexpected source, namely climate change.

From the Indian standpoint, ongoing Chinese investments in ports, pipelines, roads, terminals and other logistical infrastructure in Myanmar, Pakistan, Maldives and Sri Lanka have produced official insecurities about being encircled by a 'string of pearls', a dubious metaphor coined by an international consultancy group that has come to represent Indian fear of being contained by China in the Indian Ocean region. The most significant Indian response has been to increase naval budgets and visibility, and to reaffirm the strategic importance of the Andaman and Nicobar islands, an archipelago that lies to the east of the Bay of Bengal and dominates the entrance to the Malacca Straits.[58] Especially under BJP governments in Delhi, the reach and scope of naval and aviation resources stationed at different sites in the island chain has expanded considerably while the Andaman and Nicobar territory has been re-classified as the first joint services 'tri-command'.[59] With these and other capital investments, the Bay of Bengal is on its way to becoming territorialized as a coastal sea dominated by Indian naval power, as the South China Sea is to China.

Turning to China, the unresolved issue of Taiwan's identity cannot be delinked from its maritime character, as noted earlier. In partial response to the existential problem of a divided Chinese homeland, the entirety of the South China Sea has been claimed by China as its territory since the end of the Second World War, outlined by the infamous 'nine dash line'.[60] This general claim as well as specific claims on groups of islands such as the Spratlys and Paracels are actively contested by the Philippines, Vietnam and other littoral countries. For several decades the dispute remained *in potentio*, ebbing and flowing with external circumstances. In the last two decades and especially in the last five years, China has left little doubt that it intends to back up its claim to the South China Sea with the military muscle needed to end all disputes in its favour. It has been building up its naval forces with capital investments and foreign equipment purchases, it has launched its first aircraft carrier, expanded its Hainan Island naval station into a major submarine base and, most important, has unilaterally taken over reefs, banks and uninhabited islands in the South China Sea and converted them into manned military outposts. Intense building activity over the last few years that included reclaiming areas of sea around these contested islands have led to the creation of new 'facts on the ground', including full length airstrips, extensive supply depots, and living quarters to be used by military personnel.[61] Even the recent adverse judgment of the International Court of Justice in the case brought by the Philippines against China did little to stop the ongoing momentum of its conversion and construction work. The South China Sea has finally, and perhaps more than at any other time in its history, become a Chinese lake.

Summing up, the insights of these three Indian geopolitical thinkers set
against recent developments in the Indo-Pacific maritime zone point to an
emerging and dangerous contradiction. On the one hand, the boundaries of
national geobodies have been constantly expanding into surrounding seas
while, on the other hand, the difficulties of imposing sovereign control over
such spaces have never been more acute with the enormous growth of marine
traffic, civilian as well as military, in these regions in the present and future.
This outcome is both unstable and unsustainable.

Conclusion

This chapter is an exploration of the simultaneous absence and presence
of geography in Indian security discourse, a contradictory condition I have
termed 'doubling'. Geography's doubling is manifested through over-
determination in explaining India's security dilemmas and its relative absence
as an explicit mode of analysis. The links between these two manifestations
is explored through an extended discussion of the national geobody, its
origins and futures. That the national geobody's origins lie firmly within a
terrestrial frame dominated by metaphor, while its future is most likely to be
played out in ontologically distinct maritime space, makes this a complicated
exploration. Two findings follow from this analysis of the expanding national
geobody: first, the deep roots of why it appears politically impossible for
India to exchange territory for security, and, second, the likelihood of naval
conflict in the Indo-Pacific maritime zone as long as Indian and Chinese
security thought is informed by an uncritical and ahistorical conception of
their respective national geobodies.

Notes

1   For an important exception, see Sanjay Chaturvedi, 'Indian Geopolitics: "Nation-State"
    and the Colonial Legacy', in *International Relations in India: The Region and the Nation*,
    edited by Kanti P. Bajpai and Siddharth Mallavarapu, 238–83 (Delhi: Orient Longman,
    2004).
2   The handful of self-consciously geopolitical writers include K. M. Panikkar, Bhabhani
    Sen Gupta, Admiral Raja Menon, C. Raja Mohan, Bharat Karnad and Jaswant Singh.
3   Prime Minister's Talks with President Nasser, 29–31 March, 1960. File 111. Subimal
    Dutt Papers, Nehru Memorial Museum and Library, New Delhi.
4   Yet, as we know, India has given away land to other countries in order to improve
    bilateral relations. Itty Abraham, *How India Became Territorial: Foreign Policy, Diaspora,*

Geopolitics (Stanford, CA: Stanford University Press, 2014). Available at http://www. sup.org/books/title/?id=23245.

5   Xuecheng Liu, *The Sino-Indian Border Dispute and Sino-Indian Relations* (Lanham, MD: University Press of America, 1994).

6   Thongchai Winichakul, *Siam Mapped: A History of the Geo-Body of a Nation* (Honolulu: University of Hawaii Press, 1997).

7   Careful readers will note the Derridean reference; this chapter can also be read as an exercise in tracking the 'spoor' of geography in Indian security thinking. Jacques Derrida, *Writing and Difference*, translated by Alan Bass (New York: Routledge).

8   For a longer discussion, see Sankaran Krishna, *Globalization and Postcolonialism: Hegemony and Resistance in the Twenty-First Century* (Lanham, MD: Rowman and Littlefield, 2008).

9   Outer space (the upper atmosphere and beyond) too would qualify in this latter category, although it is notable that for all its achievements in space flights, satellite technology, and rocket launches, India has not developed a language to naturalize outer space as an extension of its territorial holdings, in the way the US has used the trope of the frontier to describe and legitimize its missions in outer space.

10 Gearóid Ó. Tuathail, *Critical Geopolitics: The Politics of Writing Global Space* (Minneapolis: University of Minnesota Press, 1996).

11 Stuart Elden, 'Land, Terrain, Territory', *Progress in Human Geography* 34, No. 6 (2010):799– 817. Available at https://doi.org/10.1177/0309132510362603.

12 Michel Foucault, *Power/Knowledge: Selected Interviews and Other Writings*, 1972–1977 (Pantheon Books, 1980).

13 Peter John Brobst, *The Future of the Great Game: Sir Olaf Caroe, India's Independence, and the Defense of Asia* (Akron, Ohio: University of Akron Press, 2005).

14 Erez Manela, *The Wilsonian Moment: Self-Determination and the International Origins of Anticolonial Nationalism* (New York: Oxford University Press, 2007).

15 Ayesha Jalal, *The Sole Spokesman: Jinnah, the Muslim League and the Demand for Pakistan* (Cambridge: Cambridge University Press, 1994).

16 Stuart Hall, *The Fateful Triangle: Race, Ethnicity, Nation*, edited by Kobena Mercer, W.E.B. Du Bois Lectures (Cambridge, Mass.: Harvard University Press, 2017). Available at http://www.hup.harvard.edu/catalog.php?isbn=9780674976528.

17 Michel Foucault, *Society Must Be Defended: Lectures at the Collège de France, 1975-76*, Translated by Graham Burchell (New York: Picador, 2003).

18 For a longer discussion, see Abraham, *How India Became Territorial*.

19 Kavalam Madhava Panikkar, *India and the Indian Ocean: An Essay on the Influence of Sea Power on Indian History*, 28, 35 (London: G. Allen & Unwin, 1962).

20 Panikkar, *India and the Indian Ocean*, 19.

21 Ritu Menon and Kamla Bhasin, *Borders and Boundaries: Women in India's Partition* (New Brunswick: Rutgers University Press, 1998).

22 Jaswant Singh, *Defending India* (Delhi: Macmillan India, 1999).

23 Brobst, *The Future of the Great Game*.

24 George N. Curzon, *Frontiers: The Romanes Lecture, 1907* (Oxford: Clarendon Press, 1907).

25   Achin Vanaik, *The Painful Transition: Bourgeois Democracy in India* (London: Verso, 1990).
26   Abraham, *How India Became Territorial.*
27   Gyan Prakash, *Another Reason: Science and the Imagination of Modern India* (Princeton: Princeton University Press, 1999).
28   Manela, *The Wilsonian Moment.*
29   Thomas R. Trautmann, *Aryans and British India* (Berkeley: University of California Press, 1997).
30   Barbara Ramusack, *The Indian Princes and Their States* (Cambridge: Cambridge University Press, 2008).
31   Sumathi Ramaswamy, *The Goddess and the Nation: Mapping Mother India* (Durham, NC: Duke University Press, 2010).
32   Ramaswamy, *The Goddess and the Nation*, 30.
33   Diana Eck, *India: A Sacred Geography* (New York: Three Rivers Press, 2012).
34   Manu Goswami, *Producing India* (Chicago: University of Chicago Press, 2004).
35   Christophe Jaffrelot, *The Hindu Nationalist Movement and Indian Politics, 1925 to the 1990s: Strategies of Identity-Building, Implantation and Mobilisation* (*with Special Reference to Central India*) (London: C. Hurst & Co. Publishers, 1996).
36   Goswami, *Producing India.*
37   K. M. Panikkar, *Asia and Western Dominance: A Survey of the Vasco Da Gama Epoch of Asian History, 1498–1945* (London: George Allen and Unwin, 1953).
38   Not surprisingly, Panikkar's writings were absorbed and reproduced anew by Indian naval strategists for decades without much success in changing the country's dominant landward orientation or affecting inter-service budgetary allocations, until relatively recently. Ironically, Panikkar himself contributed to restoring the landward frame of Indian geopolitics in his later writings, turning his back on these early and powerful arguments for the importance of seeing India as a marine power, and returning to the time-honored position that in the end land power would always trump sea power. Kavalam Madhava Panikkar, *Geographical Factors in Indian History* (Delhi: Bharatiya Vidya Bhavan, 1969).
39   Ibid.
40   Ibid., 14, 84.
41   Ibid., 83.
42   Ibid., 85.
43   Ibid., 82.
44   Ibid., 97.
45   Bhabani Sen Gupta, T. T. Poulose and Hemlata Bhatia, *The Malacca Straits and the Indian Ocean: A Study of the Strategic and Legal Aspects of a Controversial Sea-Lane* (Delhi: Macmillan, 1974).
46   Janet L. Abu-Lughod, *Before European Hegemony: The World System A.D. 1250–1350* (New York: Oxford University Press, 1989).
47   Anita Inder Singh, *The Limits of British Influence: South Asia and the Anglo-American Relationship, 1947–56* (London: Pinter Publishers, 1993).
48   John Butcher and R. E. Elson, *Sovereignty and the Sea: How Indonesia Became an Archipelagic State* (Singapore: NUS Press, 2017). Available at https://nuspress.nus.edu.sg/products/sovereignty-and-the-sea-how-indonesia-became-an-archipelagic-state.

49 Sen Gupta, Poulose and Bhatia, *The Malacca Straits and the Indian Ocean*, 42.
50 Max Hirsch, *Airport Urbanism: Infrastructure and Mobility in Asia*. (Minneapolis: University of Minnesota Press, 2016).
51 Jack Lang, 'Report of the Special Advisor to the Secretary General on Legal Issues Related to Piracy off the Coast of Somlia', S/2011/30 (New York: United Nations, 2011).
52 Colin Freeman, 'Somali Pirates Hijack First Commercial Ship in Five Years', *The Telegraph*, 14 March 2017. Available at http://www.telegraph.co.uk/ news/2017/03/14/ somali-pirates-hijack-first-commercial-ship-five-years/.
53 C. Raja Mohan, *Samudra Manthan: Sino-Indian Rivalry in the Indo-Pacific* (Washington D.C.: Carnegie Endowment for International Peace, 2012).
54 Ibid., 56.
55 Ibid., 2.
56 Ibid., 4.
57 Ibid., 6.
58 Sunil Raman, 'The Strategic Importance of the Andaman and Nicobar Islands', *The Diplomat*, 3 January 2016.
59 A. K. Singh, 'The Andaman and Nicobar Islands – From a Strategic Outpost to Springboard: Security and Development Issues', Veer Sawarkar Memorial Lecture, Pune, Savitribai Phule University, 2015.
60 Gerard Sasges, 'Absent Maps, Marine Science, and the Reimagination of the South China Sea, 1922–1939', *Journal of Asian Studies* 75, No. 1 (2016): 157–80.
61 Ian Storey and Cheng-Yi Lin, *The South China Sea Dispute: Navingating Diplomatic and Strategic Tensions* (Singapore: ISEAS-Yusof Ishak Institute, 2016).

6

Foreign Policy Analysis and Indian Foreign Policy

Harsh V. Pant and *Avinash Paliwal*

In a town-hall type address to citizens in August 2016, Prime Minister Narendra Modi stated that India's foreign policy was all about 'India First'.[1] Though this can be inferred in myriad ways, the statement underlined two well-known assumptions about Indian foreign policy. First, as noted in the first such study by J. Bandyopadhyaya, Prime Ministers play a critical role in steering the direction of Indian foreign policy.[2] This has been evident in the articulation of doctrines around the persona and political temperament of different Prime Ministers. If foreign policy 'emerged whole from the head and heart' of Jawaharlal Nehru, Indira and Rajiv Gandhi overshadowed, if not stepped upon, the bureaucracy in charting India's relationship with the world.[3] More recently, terms such as Rao Doctrine, Gujral Doctrine, Manmohan Doctrine, and Modi Doctrine typify the diplomatic style and policy substance of different Indian Prime Ministers.[4] Second, external affairs are a policy domain wherein both the Indian public and policymakers seek – and believe there exists – consensus. Even during periods of extreme political polarisation, few would disagree that India should indeed focus on 'India First' when it comes to international politics. For it underlines the basic tenet of political realism in an anarchic world.[5] It can be argued that Nehru's Non-Alignment, Narasimha Rao's pragmatism and Modi's assertiveness are all manifestations of this deep realist foundation of India's foreign policy outlook.

Most existing scholarly analyses of India's foreign policy revolves around these two broad facets. Be it debates around the role of institution or about the drivers of India's foreign policy, the issue is assessed by focusing on what policy output looks like rather than how it is formulated. Both India's position in the world and its shifting policy pronouncements in the context of a constantly evolving world order are aspects that have been well researched, and shall continue to elicit vibrant debate and discussion. Similar to works on other rising powers, studies on India's foreign policy address a diverse set of questions. What are the ideological underpinnings of Indian foreign policy? Does India offer a vision to the world? What is the state of India's relationships with major global powers? Why does India continue to have problems in emerging as a 'benign' regional power in South Asia? What factors have made it possible to conceive of India as a rising global player? How does India's foreign policy compare to other emerging powers like Brazil, China and Russia? These questions provide a broad canvas for research. Whereas some of them have been addressed in detail, others remain relatively neglected.

One of the key questions relate to the process of foreign policymaking. How is India's foreign policy made? The issue is not simply of describing the role and purpose of various state institutions and non-state elements that contributes towards this end. As the following sections show, that aspect is well documented. The issue that remains, however, is how these institutions and entities interact with each other, how this interaction influences policy output (in conjunction with external factors) and what lessons can be learnt about the shaping of India's foreign policy by observing and analysing this process. These questions are central to Foreign Policy Analysis (FPA), a sub-field in the discipline of International Relations. Giving primacy to processes over outcomes, FPA tries to cement the link between conventional IR theories and empirical data on policymaking.[6] It identifies linkages between the global, regional and domestic factors that inform foreign policymaking strategies and processes of a state.

This chapter argues that application of FPA to Indian foreign policy is a 'new direction' that holds tremendous merit despite methodological difficulties related to lack of good primary sources of information. First, it shows how different ideas compete for influence over policy output on different thematic issues and in varying contexts, that is, crisis policymaking and during non-crisis situations. Second, acknowledging the Prime Minister's role in shaping policy course, analysis of the policymaking process shows that Prime Ministers are not always 'free agents' working towards their vision of India in the world. They are constrained by political and institutional pressures that can play both a limiting and a liberating role in shaping policy output on critical issues. Third, analysis of India's foreign policymaking helps in unpacking operational level debates and nuances therein rather than focus on the narrative of Indian strategic practices or the structural determinants of India's foreign policy. Fourth, by highlighting the complexity of the processes and nuances of policy motivation, FPA allows for challenging a long held myth of foreign policy consensus in India, but underscores the continuities in India's strategy formation since 1947.

This chapter is divided into three sections. The first section locates FPA within the larger IR literature and articulates its merits and limitations related to methodological difficulties of its application in the Indian case. Ranging from bureaucratic theory to organizational politics and the rational actor model, this section shows that the study of Indian foreign policy could also gain from conceptual frameworks offered by the discipline of public policy processes. The second section delves into the literature that focuses on India's foreign policymaking processes and discusses how this strand can be developed further. It discusses the challenges posed by limited sources, difficulties of conducting fieldwork and framing questions suitable for the purpose of process tracing, and how these issues can be overcome. Corresponding with the broader aim of this volume, this final section argues that emphasis on foreign policymaking process will not just enrich the study of Indian foreign policy, but will also allow using the case of India to shape theories of FPA itself.

Foreign policy analysis and change

Foreign policy behaviour of states has been studied in considerable detail within the discipline of political science and IR. Ranging from theories like realism/ neo-realism, liberalism/neoliberalism and constructivist approaches to IR, considerable amount of work has been done to decode, explain and sometimes predict behaviour of states.[7] Realism and neo-realism, for instance, simply put, argue that the world is an anarchic place with 'states' being paramount sovereign actors shaping international relations.[8] Relations between states are necessarily antagonistic given the human nature of 'greed' and 'expansionism'.[9] More than cooperation, a drive to 'survive' guides the behaviour of states that are interested in expanding their interests, authority, and power.[10] Highly persuasive but also vigorously contested realism and neo-realism provide the vocabulary of power, and at times rationale, to contemporary policymakers. This is not to say that this theory has come to guide international politics or that it simply states objective facts about interstate relations. However, the inherent pessimism of the realist school of thought often mirrors the frustration faced in solving conflicts using diplomatic means. Moreover, the focus of this school on human imperfections often makes its logic irresistible.

Opposing the pessimism of the realist school are the liberals and the neoliberals. While agreeing with realist tenets such as 'anarchy' in world order and 'states' being the key referent objects whose security is paramount, neoliberals offer an optimistic picture of world politics.[11] Rather than being caught in an antagonistic relationship, states can (and do) cooperate to achieve mutually beneficial outcomes. One state, according to this logic, can help in the development of other states, till the time this process advances its own interests as well. Modern global institutions such as the United Nations (UN), the World Bank (WB) and the International Monetary Fund (IMF) are bodies that help in facilitating mutually beneficial interactions between states. Known as the 'neo-neo' debate, there are many examples to demonstrate successes and failures of both the realist and liberal schools of thought. As we will see in the following section, realism and liberalism have deeply informed the study of Indian foreign policy.

Constructivists challenge the realist's pessimism and a the liberal's optimism. They argue that most aspects of IR are 'historically and socially constructed, rather than being inevitable consequences of human nature'.[12] Interpretations, historical beliefs, norms and other subjectivities determine IR more than human antagonism or cooperation. IR, then, lies somewhere at the interaction of individual beliefs, historical antecedents, rational thought, material capacity, and the subjectivities of human nature. It is neither black nor white. But it can surely be black and/or white, if people 'choose' to treat it as such. Constructivists depart from the realists and the liberals by connecting individual agency to larger structural factors. As famously argued by Alexander Wendt, IR is shaped by constant interaction between the 'agent' and 'structure'.[13] The agent and the structure have a constitutive relationship rather than being disjointed, that is, while the structure provides the wider framework to an agent's actions and thought, constant interaction between various agents shapes the global structures as well.[14] None of these structural theories of IR, however, explain how their core assumptions and arguments get translated into operational level policy debates and actions.

Foreign Policy Analysis (FPA) fills this gap. An actor-specific theory, FPA offers a powerful 'connection to the empirical ground' upon which other IR theories are based.[15] Based on the premise that all occurrences between nations are 'grounded in human decision makers acting singly or in groups', FPA allows IR to 'reclaim its ability to manifest human agency, with its attendant change, creativity, accountability, and meaning'.[16] It argues that human agency and not states is the most important intersection point between the material and ideational determinants of state behaviour. Developed during the Cold War, most case studies within FPA are West centric, and mostly applied using modernist approaches such as rational choice theory, bureaucratic politics and organizational behaviour. The rational actor model, based on the rational choice theory, posits that states are rational entities seeking profit maximization. They set their goals, consider options and assess consequences before opting for the most beneficial policy course.[17] The concern with the rational actor model is the definition of rationality. It does not include aspects such as emotions, group think, selective attention, or even bureaucratic pressures within a state.[18]

Bureaucratic politics and organizational process models offer themselves as alternatives instead. Within the former, individuals and groups belonging to different bureaucratic structures within a government vie for influence over foreign policy output. Allowing for personal interests such as professional rewards and promotion coupled with profit maximization of a specific ministry or government department overshadows larger national interests.[19] Complicating the idea of rationality as proposed in rational choice, the bureaucratic politics model throws light on the parochialism of foreign policy making in modern states. Organizational behaviour frameworks, however, argues that foreign policy takes shape in the light of certain 'standard operating procedures' of one or more organizations that are critical within the policy domain, that is, based on an organization's structure and procedural rules. All these models, and more, have been applied extensively in the case of developed countries. For instance, a study of the US policymaking process during the Vietnam War gives an excellent account of internal politics within the US Department of Defence by dynamically applying the rational actor paradigm, bureaucratic politics and organizational politics.[20]

Another account uses organizational behaviour model to show how internal dynamics of an organization becomes enmeshed with personal aspirations of individuals or group of policymakers in building a lobby for a particular decision within the security and foreign policy sphere of the US.[21] Analysis of the US participation in the Korean War sheds further light on the behavioural aspect of foreign policy formulation and how the subjectivities of the decision makers play an essential role in shaping policies.[22] Drawing from the rational actor model this study argues that a policymaker's 'definition of the situation' is the critical aspect of policy formulation.[23] In such a scenario the decision maker is assumed to represent the state as a unitary actor. One of the most seminal studies, however, is on the Cuban Missile Crisis between the US and the Soviet Union in 1962. The analysts apply most existing models of FPA to understand US foreign and security policy during crisis situations from different perspectives.[24]

In an interesting departure from widely used FPA models are recent works on foreign policy change. Occurring in the wake of traditional IR theories' inability to predict structural shifts – like the end of the Cold War – scholars developed newer models that could better explain change. Jeffrey Legro's two-step model to assess changing foreign policy orthodoxies is one such framework.[25] According to Legro, 'old orthodoxy' must collapse and be replaced by a 'new orthodoxy' for policy change to occur. Identifying various causal variables for policy change, this model explains how these variables interact with each other to determine continuity and change in a state's foreign policy. Similar to Legro's work, though outside the field of FPA, is the Advocacy Coalition Framework (ACF). The ACF emphasize policy change, learning and coalition behaviour. At the macro-level it assumes that specialists within a particular 'policy subsystem' play an important role in most of the policymaking.[26] Behaviour of these specialists, nonetheless, is affected by the broader socioeconomic and political system. It further assumes that the individual is heavily impacted by social psychology and that multiple actors in a subsystem should be aggregated into 'advocacy coalitions'. These assumptions are determined by the relationship between the dependent variables, that is, 'belief systems' and 'policy change', and the independent variables, that is, 'policy-oriented learning' and 'external shocks', as well as 'negotiated agreements'.[27]

The belief system according to the ACF is a three-tier system that includes core beliefs, policy core beliefs and secondary beliefs.[28] Core beliefs here refer to ontological and normative assumptions about human behaviour and the weight given to basic values such as equality, welfare of people, relative role of the government and the market, and so on.[29] An outcome of social conditioning that a person undergoes from childhood, core beliefs are considered as difficult to change. Again, developed by studying US foreign policy, some applications of the ACF include examination of 'legislative hearings data concerning US foreign policy and the creation of Israel' to ascertain reasons for a particular political tilt of US policies before the creation of Israel.[30] Other cases include determining changes in Swiss foreign policy in different cases by conducting a comparative analysis of Swiss policy vis-à-vis South Africa (1968–94) and Iraq (1990–91).[31] The Swiss government had imposed sanctions against Saddam Hussein's regime during the First Gulf War; however, it did not buckle under severe international pressure to impose similar sanctions against the apartheid government of South Africa for years. More recently the ACF has been applied to explain different US approaches towards the erstwhile Soviet Union using the Yalta and Riga Axioms through belief systems of different advocacy coalitions.[32] There are many more theoretical analyses on foreign policy formulation and change for developed countries and serious research is being conducted to build on existing literature.

FPA's core strength of connecting structural IR theories to empirical realities can push the study of Indian foreign policy to newer horizons. First, it would allow challenging the dominant Prime Minister centric analysis of Indian foreign policy. Despite the fact that every Indian Prime Minister has her or his signature style, the foreign policymaking process in India is complex. Both in terms of diversity of bureaucratic opinion and rivalry, as well as organizational cultures and influence of non-governmental entities, the way in which foreign policy decisions are made reflects much more about India's strategic thoughts and practices rather than focusing simply on the Prime Minister. Indian states that have borders with neighbouring countries, for instance, have become powerful over the years in shaping New Delhi's geopolitical calculus. Second, rigorous study of the policymaking process would allow highlighting whether there truly is a consensus among Indian politicians and policymakers on issues of foreign affairs. The intensity of protests in India over the India–US nuclear deal in 2005, for instance, belied this consensus.[33] Or, as underlined by a recent study, even during Nehru's time as Prime Minister, there were multiple strands of opinion within India's strategic community – most of which were brushed aside by Nehru's dominant personality.[34]

There are, however, some methodological challenges related to FPA's application to the Indian case. First, and the biggest, challenge relates to the lack of available sources. Though there are archives available in India till 1971, good quality primary data for the period after that is difficult to access. One of the biggest sources of primary information are the ministerial reports and Parliamentary debates – none of which discuss the policymaking process – or leaked documents from Western countries such as the US and the UK. For instance, the archives of the UK Foreign and Commonwealth Office hold a treasure trove of material on British engagement with and assessment of South Asian politics, especially during the Soviet War in Afghanistan between 1979 and 1987. The National Security Archives at the George Washington University also offer primary data on events surrounding the so-called War on Terror, and the rise of Islamist militancy across the world in the 1990s. Though valuable, most of these sources are issue and area specific. Moreover, they highlight Indian thinking – and to some extent decision-making – from an external perspective rather than an internal one. Indian media archives, political biographies and autobiographies, as well as interviews with retired and serving officials, then become important sources of information. Conducting interviews in India about sensitive topics has its own layers of challenges, and even at times runs the risk of compromising objectivity.

Studies in Indian foreign policymaking

As discussed in the Introduction, most existing literature on Indian foreign policy is either empirical in nature or uses traditional IR lenses such as realism and liberalism to make sense of these issues, apart from occasional historical analyses. There are few studies that use foreign policy analysis in the case of India. In a less celebrated but important work, Jeffrey Benner approaches India's foreign policymaking process using a 'jurisdictional methodology' called 'neo-reductionism'.[35] Benner gives a detailed map of India's external affairs establishment and its relationship with different political leaders.[36] According to this methodology, 'bureaucratic influences are assumed to be dominant within certain classes of international relations behaviour'.[37] His study, however, is not restricted to the MEA itself, but analyses the whole foreign policy 'community'.[38] Drawing from J. D. Singer and James N. Rosenau's works, Benner suggests that foreign policy studies have been divided into five levels of analysis, that is, idiosyncratic/psychological, decision-making/small group, bureaucratic, national/domestic and systemic.[39] He argues that there are two ways to study policy formulation – the dynamic approach that looks at the 'chain of decision making' (or the flow of the policy), and the static approach that looks at institutional structures through which ideas get refracted into legally binding policies. Benner opts for the former for its novelty, and for being more useful to understand crisis decision-making.

While Benner's study is unique given the fact that there is hardly any such work on India, there are limitations to the approach he uses. In fact, the strongest aspect of his approach, that is, focus on bureaucratic organizations responsible for formulating legally binding decisions, becomes a weakness as well. There are different non-jurisdictional organizations and constituencies in India that play an equally important role in formulating foreign policies in their own way and this is what is missing in Benner's work. A comparison of Benner's and Bandyopadhayaya's works shows that while the former places tremendous emphasis on bureaucracy, the latter keeps it centered on the Prime Minister and his coterie of advisors. In contrast, Vipin Narang and Paul Staniland trace 'the core elements in the foreign and security policy worldviews of India's policymaking elite'.[40] They argue that despite 'heterogeneity across individuals and over time, a "strategic core" has nevertheless emerged' in India, which directs its world affairs.[41] Though this study refrains from explicating India's foreign and security policymaking from a theoretical straightjacket, it emphasizes the existence of a strategic core by analysing the interplay between ideas and personalities.[42] Narang and Staniland's study is unique in its articulation of interplay between ideas, institutions and patronage. Of particular interest is how decentralization of India's democracy in the post-Cold War era impacts this interplay.[43] The 1989–98 period marked the initiation of coalition politics in India and an entry of regional parties at the national level.

Regional parties came to form critical interest groups altering the national government's regional policy calculus, but they contributed little to India's grand strategic thought.[44] However, clear strategic tenets emerged with the rise of Hindu nationalism marked by the BJP-led government during 1998–2004 and the following rule of the Congress-led UPA post 2004. While there are differences between the visions of these political coalitions, there is considerable overlap on certain strategic goals. Theoretically, Narang and Staniland's work provides an opening to delve into linkages between domestic ideology and institutions in the shaping of Indian foreign policy. Adding to this, Sumit Ganguly underscores the role of personalities in India's foreign policymaking from a constructivist perspective.[45] Looking at structure and agency in the making of India's foreign policy Ganguly places the 'agents', that is, different Prime Ministers, in the changing 'structural' context after independence. Though his work provides an interesting narrative, it remains theoretically underdeveloped.

Shrikant Paranjpe provides an overview of India's strategic culture since independence based on the similar agent-structure model, though implicitly.[46] Unlike Ganguly, Paranjpe problematizes the idea of nation and subsequently explicates national security policy formulation both externally and internally. Keeping personalities in perspective, Paranjpe incorporates institutional and structural pressures in the national security policymaking of India. By juxtaposing arguments made by different ministries and individual personalities over issues ranging from Left-wing extremism to security threats from external sources, the role of state in policymaking is delineated systematically. This study is also important in understanding the historical and institutional foundation of India's strategic culture. However, in complete contrast to Ganguly's and Paranjpe's works is that of Pramoda K. Panda, who employs the specific case study methodology to understand foreign policymaking.

Studying the decision-making process during the Sino-Indian war of 1962 and the India–Pakistan war of 1971, Panda applies a 'holistic approach to foreign policy analysis' and uses a 'case study method' and a 'comparative method'.[47] Given that the cases being studied are wars and the lead-up to them, the period of analysis remains restricted to short periods of time. Deconstructing the cases into different phases, Panda looks at the 'flow' of decision-making and 'adopts maximalist conception about the period of their (the conflicts) occurrence.'[48] In case of the Bangladesh War, for example, Panda claims that Indian foreign policy 'evolved through four distinct phases', that is, support (to the Mukti Bahini movement), military involvement, local war and war. Interaction between policymakers, that is, the Prime Minister and his/her coterie of advisors and trouble-shooters, is given particular weight. The role played by domestic political constituencies and interest groups is implicitly accounted for in Panda's study. An interesting study given its relevance in terms of academic enquiry, the sole focus on crises restricts its scope, especially if foreign policymaking is to be understood as a process of evolution over time. Nonetheless, despite focusing on actors and their personal motivations in deciding a policy, the study keeps larger systemic factors in sight.

Dixit and Rana provide an insider's perspective on the working of the MEA and the dynamics of decision-making.[49] While the latter explains the internal structure of the MEA and its functioning, the former gives a brief but insightful account of the foreign policy decision-making processes. Adding to the list of insider's view was K. Subrahmanyam, who wrote about defence planning in India.[50] Subrahmanyam's work gives an interesting look into the decision-making culture of the security establishment and how it impacts foreign policy decisions. For instance, the leadership of Field Marshal Sam Manekshaw in the India–Pakistan war of 1971 and India's defence planning played a major role in convincing Indira Gandhi to declare war that led to the creation of Bangladesh. In addition to this are works by Paranjpe and Misra who look at the role of the Parliament in the making of India's nuclear policy and the overall foreign policy planning in India respectively. On similar lines but more critical of the establishment are works by Shashi Tharoor and Surjit Mansingh who look at intra-state politics during Indira Gandhi's tenure as Prime Minister and its impact on the policy processes.[51]

M. G. Gupta does a similar study during Rajiv Gandhi's leadership and shows how different domestic and external variables defined Rajiv Gandhi's policies with respect to Sri Lanka, among others.[52] Moreover, works by Steve Hoffman, Nancy Jetley, Neville Maxwell, D. R. Mankekar, John Garver, Yascov Y. I. Vertzberger and Alka Acharya provide a wide-ranging analysis of Indian policymaking during the 1962 war with China, and India's China policy in general.[53] Among these authors, Hoffman's work stands out for its balanced but incisive critique of India's China policy. One of its most important, and contested, conclusions is that India lacked a well-developed decision-making structure in 1962 due to little political development.[54] Sisson and Rose on the other hand provide an excellent comparative analysis of policy formulation in New Delhi and Islamabad during the 1971 India–Pakistan war.[55]

Chris Ogden provides a normative analysis of India's foreign and security policymaking, particularly during the BJP-led government from 1998 to 2004.[56] Based on a detailed historical account based on extensive interviews in India, Ogden conceptualizes and articulates India's 'security identity' and shows how this identity plays a definitive role in shaping foreign and security policy decisions.[57] One of the only studies that uses normative theory to study Indian foreign and security policymaking, Ogden highlights in detail how (a) 'concepts of security identity help to explain the BJP-led NDA's security policy'; (b) 'whether India's security identity constrain the BJP-led NDA's desired policy norms; and (c) whether the BJP-led NDA influence the norms structuring India's security identity'.[58] This is done by examining India's foreign policy until 1998, and then deconstructing New Delhi's approach towards its neighbours and the world in general, and towards the nuclear question in particular. In another piece Ogden analyses the cases of India's approach towards Pakistan and its decision to test nuclear bombs in 1998 under the BJP-led Vajpayee government; he argues that 'Pakistan's support of various insurgencies and terrorism against India has … entrenched the contemporary Pakistan-terrorism nexus within India's (foreign and domestic) security perspectives'.[59] Based on primary interviews with various Indian policymakers, Ogden confirms that the BJP plays a critical role in informing and influencing the present-day trajectory of India's security outlook.[60] An important and original work on the role of norms in impacting operational policymaking, Ogden's work will resonate in this thesis. The focus on beliefs, as explained later, and their interaction with external events and domestic capacities has links with the larger study of norms and foreign policymaking.

In addition to Ogden's work, Daniel Markey provides a critique of India's foreign policymaking institutions and suggests mechanisms to develop India's foreign policy 'software'.[61] Markey claims that the foreign policy establishment of India is a major obstacle to India's rise as a global power for four main reasons. First, the Indian Foreign Service (IFS) is a rather small service wing, given India's size, and has stringent selection criteria while it remains closed to external expertise. Second, the public universities are poorly funded, highly bureaucratic and the quality of education is low. Third, the think-tank culture in India is relatively new and lacks access to information. And last, private firms and Indian media institutions are not built to conduct sustained foreign policy research.[62] While this study does not talk about policymaking per se, it gives an idea about the efficacy of Indian institutions and bureaucratic culture. In addition to Markey's work is that of David Mitchell who examines the leadership styles of Nehru, Indira Gandhi, Rajiv Gandhi and A. B. Vajpayee.[63] Mitchell's focus on the leadership style of different Prime Ministers and its impact on foreign policy puts him in league with Bandyopadhyaya and others who focused on the personality of the Prime Minister. The strength of his profiling approach, however, sets his study apart from the rest. Using Margaret Hermann's distance technique and the automated profiling software Profiler+, Mitchell reaches the conclusion that 'Indian prime minister's leadership styles vary between being "strategic" and "opportunistic" in nature'.[64] For example, whereas Nehru and Vajpayee 'demonstrated opportunistic leadership styles' while dealing with Pakistan, Indira and Rajiv Gandhi, despite having opportunistic traits, 'challenged constraints and were open to ideas and information'.[65] Mitchell's work is a unique study of Prime Ministerial leadership traits and, in conjunction with other works, enriches the study of Indian foreign policy and the role played by both Vajpayee and Singh who, like their predecessors, were critical in shaping India's foreign policy.

   The literature above covers empirical and theoretical ground in terms of outlining political (role of personalities and coalition politics), bureaucratic, structural, systemic, as well as ideational and normative factors in determining foreign policymaking. These studies, however, miss the role played by critical non-governmental factors and groups including civil society activists, private business, think tanks, media, and increasingly the diaspora in shaping India's foreign policy. C. Raja Mohan, for instance, delves into the 'relationship between international relations scholarship, Indian public opinion and foreign policymaking in India'.[66] He argues that unlike in other developed countries, India still lags behind in having a 'permanent establishment' that constitutes of policymakers, academicians, media persons and an active political class that churns out constructive and effective foreign policy recommendations.[67] While there is scope for it to emerge in the near future, what exists at the moment is an 'informal network' of a small group of policy activists within and outside the government. Three key reasons for the non-existence of this 'establishment' are: First, an elusive domestic foreign policy consensus. Second, the Indian strategic community's conformism to a few leaders that gives personalities dominance over processes. Third, changing institutional balance in which non-governmental institutions including academics and media persons are more confident and aware about global politics and have started making their opinions heard openly.[68] Devesh Kapoor's work on India's foreign policy and public opinion provides the hitherto unarticulated link between foreign policy and public opinion in India.[69] Based on a survey conducted across the country Kapoor concludes that political elite dominates foreign policymaking in India and mass public is poorly informed about the same.[70] However, the impact of public opinion is taken into account when taking a big policy decision such as the India–US nuclear deal.

Bridging the gap between public opinion or civil society and foreign policy is the proactive and opinionated media houses as well as business conglomerates. While on one hand media is often 'managed' to steer public opinion in a certain pro-government direction, it has increasingly provided a platform for counter-narratives and critique of the government's foreign policy. Moreover, business houses and often converging interests between the government, media and the business houses, help the three actors determine a mutually beneficial policy path – and steer public narrative in accordance with those needs. According to Sanjaya Baru, private business and trade as well as national (English) and regional (regional language) media plays a critical role in India's foreign policymaking in the twenty-first century.[71] This is particularly true in a liberalized economy, which has witnessed a serious bulge of professional middle class. Additionally 'international trade and capital flows as well as the importance of Indian migrants abroad, have increased the importance of people-to-people and business-to-business relations in India's state-to-state relations with other countries.'[72] This is visible in the rise of India's engagement in multilateral economic groupings including the BRICS (Brazil-Russia-India-China-South Africa) and the Association of Southeast Asian Nations (ASEAN) internationally and the South Asian Association for Regional Cooperation (SAARC) and the Bay of Bengal Initiative for Multi Sectoral Social, Technical, and Economic Cooperation (BIMSTEC). Rajiv Kumar, however, challenges this narrative and argues that despite liberalization India's protectionist tendencies severely limit the corporate's influence on foreign policy.[73]

The way forward

Honing in on concepts rooted in foreign policy analysis and change in the Indian case, a new strand of literature has recently emerged. Focused on the evolution of India's bilateral relationships over longer time periods, these studies have attempted to overcome methodological challenges to articulate and understand foreign policymaking processes in India. One such study is Nicolas Blarel's work on the making of India's Israel policy from 1922 till 2012.[74] At an intersection of history and FPA, Blarel's work uses Legro's two-step model to show how the 'old' orthodoxy in India favouring Palestine was overshadowed by the 'new' orthodoxy that viewed Israel as a key strategic partner over the course of a century. Without compromising on detail and based on a mix of archival research and primary interviews, Blarel is able to show how ideas flow and develop within India's foreign policy circuits. In a separate study Blarel further analyses the role of coalition politics and federalism on the shaping of India's foreign policy.[75] Significant works given India's growing weight both in the world and certainly in the region, these studies form an important part of the study of Indian foreign policy and can be developed further.

Similarly, Avinash Paliwal uses the ACF to understand the shaping of India's Afghanistan policy from 1979 till 2015.[76] Developing a new analytical framework, Paliwal argues that India's Afghanistan policy debates occur on a spectrum of ideas with two broad policy coalitions, that is, the 'partisans' and the 'conciliators'.[77] Whereas the former argues for active containment of Pakistan in Afghanistan, the latter are more accommodative. Though not a binary, the partisans versus conciliators debate is impacted by India's desire of striking a strategic balance between Afghanistan and Pakistan, availability of local Afghan partners towards this endeavour, and evolving international postures towards Afghanistan. Conceptualization of policy debates and drivers helps in understanding policymaking processes on one hand and explaining policy change on the other. Whether this framework helps in explaining only one case study, that is, Afghanistan, or can be applied to other neighbours as well is yet to be seen. Both Blarel's and Paliwal's works are unique in the fact that they deal with long time frames (rather than just crisis situations), that is, dealing with contemporary diplomatic history on one hand, and using theoretical frameworks within the field of FPA and public policy processes on the other to decode India's foreign policymaking processes.

An overview of the literature on India's foreign policy in this chapter demonstrates the dearth of literature on policymaking processes but also underlines the value such an analysis imparts. Use of FPA in the Indian case, then, is truly a 'new direction' worth exploring further despite the want of quality sources. A combination of historical analysis based on archival research and fieldwork involving rigorous interviews with retired and serving policymakers, in combination with publicly available official documents and leaked and declassified dossiers of various Western governments (for example, Wikileaks and CIA archives) makes such studies viable.[78] Though conducting fieldwork in India is not always easy, scholars must be encouraged to undertake field trips and policymakers be made aware of the value of deeper engagement with academics. For the aforementioned literature, based on multiple interviews with policymakers, comprehensively establish that not only do multiple ideas compete for influence on policy output within India, but that Prime Ministers, however powerful in the foreign policy domain, are not necessarily 'free agents'. Constrained by political and institutional pressures both within and outside India, they are often the products of their environment, even if their personalities and temperaments differ. These works unpack operational level debates rather than focusing on the grand narrative of Indian strategic practices or the structural determinants of India's foreign policy. And by doing so, they also challenge a long held myth of foreign policy consensus in India, while also underscoring important continuities in India's strategy formation since 1947.

Notes

1   *Hindustan Times*, 'Foreign Policy, Good Governance,' 16 August 2016. Available at http://www.hindustantimes.com/india-news/from-foreign-policy-to-good-governance-top-10-quotes-from-pm-modi-s-town-hall-event/story-dkfPG5NKdieaFnWRvG2NRO.html, accessed on 11 December 2017.
2   J. Bandopadhyaya, *The Making of India's Foreign Policy: Determinants, Institutions, Processes, and Personalities* (Bombay: Allied Publishers, 1971), 220–276.
3   David Malone, *Does the Elephant Dance? Contemporary Indian Foreign Policy*, 48–49 (Oxford: Oxford University Press, 2011); Shashi Tharoor, *Nehru: The Invention of India*, 183 (New York: Arcade Publishing, 2012). On Indira Gandhi, see Surjit Mansingh, *India's Search for Power: Indira Gandhi's Foreign Policy, 1966–1982* (New Delhi: Sage Publishers, 1984). On Rajiv Gandhi, see Harish Kapoor, 'Indian Foreign Policy under Rajiv Gandhi', *The Round Table: Commonwealth Journal of International Affairs*, 304 (1987), 469–80.
4   On the Gujral Doctrine, see I. K. Gujral, *Matters of Discretion: An Autobiography* (New Delhi: Replika Press, 2011). On the Manmohan Doctrine, see Siddharth Singh, 'The Manmohan Doctrine', *Live Mint*, 19 November 2013. Available at http://www.livemint.com/Opinion/1P5ZiAwokDqqPjAZRA0EyI/The-Manmohan-doctrine.html, accessed on 12 December 2017. On the Modi Doctrine, see Sreeram Chaulia, *Modi Doctrine: The Foreign Policy of India's Prime Minister* (New Delhi: Bloomsbury, 2016).
5   On anarchical society, see Hedley Bull, *The Anarchical Society: A Study of Order in World*

Politics (London: Palgrave Macmillan, 2002). On realism, see Kenneth Waltz, *Theory of International Politics* (Illinois: Waveland Press, 2010).

6   Valerie Hudson, 'Foreign Policy Analysis: Actor Specific Theory and the Ground of International Relations', *Foreign Policy Analysis Journal*, 1, No. 1 (2005): 1–30.

7   For an analysis of international relations theories, see Robert Jackson and Georg Sorensen, *Introduction to International Relations: Theories and Approaches* (Oxford: Oxford University Press, 2010).

8   Kenneth Waltz, 'Structural Realism after the Cold War', *International Security*, 25, No. 1 (2000): 8–9.

9   Hans J Morgenthau, *Politics Among Nations: The Struggle for Power and Peace*, 7th edition, 23–26 (US: McGraw Hill, 2005).

10   Ibid.

11   Michael Doyle, 'Kant, Liberal Legacies and Foreign Affairs,' *Philosophy and Public Affairs*, 12, No. 3 (Summer 2003): 207–10.

12   Patrick T. Jackson and Daniel H. Nexon, 'Whence Causal Mechanisms? A Comment on Legro' Dialogue, *International Organization*, 1, No. 1 (2002): 82.

13   Alexander E Wendt, 'The Agent-Structure Problem in International Relations Theory,' *International Organization*, 41, No. 3 (Summer edition): 338 (USA: MIT Press, 1987).

14   Ibid.

15   Hudson, 'Foreign Policy Analysis: Actor Specific Theory and the Ground of International Relations', 1.

16   Ibid.

17   Graham T. Allison and Philip Zelikow, *Essence of a Decision: Explaining the Cuban Missile Crisis* (US: Pearson, 1999).

18   M. Clarke, 'The Foreign Policy System: A Framework from Analysis', in *Understanding Foreign Policy: The Foreign Policy Systems Approach*, edited by M. Clarke and B. White, 27–59 (Cheltenham: Edward Elgar, 1989).

19   Jackson and Georg, *Introduction to International Relations*, 252–68.

20   Jaya Krishna Baral, *The Pentagon and the Making of US Foreign Policy: A Case Study of Vietnam, 1960–1968*, 8–15 (New Delhi: Radiant Publishers, 1978).

21   Morton H. Halperin, Priscilla Clapp and Arnold Kanter, *Bureaucratic Politics and Foreign Policy*, 25–62 (Washington DC: Brookings Institution Press, 2006).

22   Richard C. Snyder and Glenn D. Paige, 'The United States Decision to Resist Aggression in Korea: The Application of an Analytical Scheme,' *Administrative Science Quarterly*, 3, No. 3 (1958): 343–51.

23   Ibid.

24   Allison and Zelikow, *Essence of a Decision*, 45–78.

25   Jeffrey Legro, *Rethinking the World: Great Power Strategies and International Order* (Ithaca, NY: Cornell University Press, 2005).

26   Paul A Sabatier (ed.), *Theories of the Policy Process* (US: Westview Press, 2007); and Paul Sabatier and Hank Jenkins-Smith (eds), *Policy Change and Learning: An Advocacy Coalition Approach* (Boulder, CO: Westview, 1994).

27   Sabatier and Wieble, *Theories of the Policy Process*, 195–98.

28   Ibid, 204–05.

29   The term 'normative' here implies establishing, relating to, or deriving from a standard norm, specifically on behaviour. For a detailed reading on norms in international relations see Annika Bjorkdahl, 'Norms in International Relations – Some Conceptual

and Methodological Reflections', *Cambridge Review of International Affairs*, 15, No. 1 (1998): 9–15.

30 Jonathan J Pierce, 'Coalition Stability and Belief Change: Advocacy Coalitions in the U.S. Foreign Policy and the Creation of Israel, 1922–44,' *Policy Studies Journal*, 39, No. 3 (2011): 411–34.

31 Christian Hirschi and Thomas Widmer, 'Policy Change and Policy Stasis: Comparing Swiss Foreign Policy towards South Africa (1968–94) and Iraq (1990–91),' *Policy Studies Journal*, 38, No. 3 (2010): 537–63.

32 Su-Mi Lee, 'Understanding the Yalta Axioms and Riga Axioms through the Belief Systems of the Advocacy Coalition Framework,' *Foreign Policy Analysis Journal*, 11, No. 3 (1 July 2015): 295–315.

33 *BBC News*, 'Bush Arrives to India Protests', 1 March 2006. Available at http://news.bbc.co.uk/1/hi/world/south_asia/4761956.stm, accessed on 15 December 2017.

34 Rahul Sagar and Ankit Panda, 'Pledges and Pious Wishes: The Constituent Assembly Debates and the Myth of a "Nehruvian" 'Consensus', *India Review*, 14, No. 2 (2015): 203–20.

35 Jeffrey Benner, *Structure of Decision: The Indian Foreign Policy Bureaucracy*, 5 (New Delhi: South Asia Publishers, 1984).

36 Ibid.

37 Ibid.

38 Ibid., 3–5.

39 James N. Singer (ed.), *Linkage Politics: Essays on the Convergence of National and International Systems*, 113–26 (New York: Free Press, 1969).

40 Vipin Narang and Paul Staniland, 'Institutions and Worldviews in Indian Foreign Security Policy,' *India Review*, 11, No. 2 (2012): 76–94.

41 Ibid.

42 Ibid., 80–86.

43 Rob Jenkins, 'India's States and the Making of Foreign Economic Policy: The Limits of the Constituent Diplomacy Paradigm,' *Journal of Federalism*, 33, No. 4 (2003): 63–81.

44 Ibid., 76.

45 Sumit Ganguly, 'Structure and Agency in the Making of Indian Foreign Policy,' ISAS Working Paper 116, November 2010.

46 A. Paranjpe, *India's Strategic Culture: The Making of National Security Policy*, 3–10 (New Delhi: Routledge).

47 Pramoda Kumar Panda, *Making of India's Foreign Policy: Prime Ministers and Wars*, 20 (New Delhi: Raj Publications, 2004).

48 Ibid.

49 J. N. Dixit, *The Making of India's Foreign Policy: Raja Ram Mohun Roy to Yashwant Sinha*, 5–12 (India: Allied Publishers, 2003).

50 K Subrahmanyam, *Perspectives in Defence Planning*, 5–23 (New Delhi: Abhinav Publications, 1972).

51 Shashi Tharoor, *Reasons of the State: Political Development and India's Foreign Policy under Indira Gandhi* (New Delhi: Vikas Publishing House, 1982); Surjit Mansingh, *India's Search for Power: Indira Gandhi's Foreign Policy, 1966–82* (New Delhi: SAGE Publishers, 1984).

52   M. G. Gupta, *Rajiv Gandhi's Foreign Policy: A Study in Continuity and Change*, 30–55 (Agra: M G Publishers, 1987).

53   Nancy Jetley, *India–China Relations (1947–1977): A Study of Parliaments Role in the Making of Foreign Policy* (New Delhi: Radiant Publishers, 1979); Neville Maxwell, *India's China War* (Bombay: Random House Publications, 1970); D. R. Mankekar, *The Guilty Men of 1962* (Bombay: Penguin Books, 1968); Yascov Y. I. Vertzberger, *Misperception in Foreign Policy Making: The Sino-Indian Conflict, 1959–1962* (Colorado: Westview Press, 1984); Alka Acharya, 'Prelude to Sino-Indian War: Aspects of the Decision-Making Process during 1959-62', *China Report*, October–December (New Delhi: SAGE Publications, 1996).

54   Steve A. Hoffman, *India and the China Crisis*, 43–116 (USA: University of California Press, 1990).

55   Richard Sisson and Leo E. Rose, *War and Secession: Pakistan, India and the Creation of Bangladesh*, 134–53 (California: University of California Press, 1990).

56   Chris Ogden, *Hindu Nationalism and the Evolution of Contemporary Indian Security: Portents of Power*, 21–47 (Oxford: OUP, 2014).

57   Ibid.

58   Ibid., 20.

59   Chris Ogden, 'Tracing the Pakistan-Terrorism Nexus in Indian Security Perspectives: From 1947 to 26/11,' *India Quarterly: A Journal of International Affairs*, 69, No. 1 (2013): 35–50.

60   Chris Ogden, 'A Lasting Legacy: The BJP-led National Democratic Alliance and India's Politics,' *Journal of Contemporary Asia*, 42, No. 1 (2012): 22–38.

61   Daniel Markey, 'Developing India's Foreign Policy Software,' *Asia Policy*, No. 8 (July 2009): 73–96 (Washington: National Bureau of Asian Research).

62   Ibid., 76–83.

63   David Mitchell, 'Determining Indian Foreign Policy: An Examination of Prime Ministerial Leadership Styles,' *India Review*, 6, No. 4 (2007): 251–87 (London: Routledge).

64   Ibid., 252.

65   Ibid., 281–82.

66   C. Raja Mohan, 'The Making of Indian Foreign Policy: The Role of Scholarship and Public Opinion,' ISAS Working Paper No. 73, 13 July, Singapore: Institute for South Asian Studies, National University of Singapore, 2009).

67   Ibid., 7.

68   Ibid., 14.

69   Devesh Kapur, 'Public Opinion and Indian Foreign Policy,' *India Review*, 8 (July 2009): 286–315 (London: Routledge).

70   Ibid., 290.

71   Sanjaya Baru, 'The Influence of Business and Media on Indian Foreign Policy,' *India Review*, 8, No. 3 (2009): 266–85 (London: Routledge).

72   Ibid.

73   Rajiv Kumar, 'Role of Business in India's Foreign Policy', *India Review*, 15, No. 1 (2016): 98–111.

74   Nicolas Blarel, *The Evolution of India's Israel Policy: Continuity, Change, and Compromise since 1922* (New Delhi: Oxford University Press, 2015).

75　Nicolas Blarel, 'Inside Out? Assessing the Domestic Determinants of India's External Behaviour', in *Theorizing Indian Foreign Policy*, edited by Mischa Handsel, Melissa Levaillant and Raphaelle Khan (London: Routledge, 2017).

76　Avinash Paliwal, *My Enemy's Enemy – India in Afghanistan from the Soviet Invasion to the US Withdrawal* (New York: Oxford University Press, 2017).

77　Ibid.

78　George Perkovich's seminal work on India's nuclear bomb, among others, shows that this is within academic reach. George Perkovich, *India's Nuclear Bomb: The Impact on Global Proliferation* (Los Angeles: University of California Press, 1999).

Part II
Emerging Themes

7

Non-Alignment and Beyond

Harsh V. Pant and *Julie M. Super*

The release of a report titled *Nonalignment 2.0* in 2012 brought a seemingly antiquated debate back to the forefront of Indian policy circles. Yet as any close examination of Indian foreign policy over the past six decades will underscore, Indian policymakers' fixation with non-alignment never truly petered out. It has remained a central component of Indian identity in global politics that is manifest in continuities: India has been in pursuit of strategic autonomy since Independence, which in practice has led to semi-alliances fashioned under the cover of non-alignment and shaped by regional dynamics. In this setting, the rise of China now raises an interesting conundrum for Indian policymakers as New Delhi seeks to balance the benefits and risks of an increasingly assertive neighbour and a network of alliances with like-minded countries.

This chapter provides an overview of what non-alignment has meant in practice for India, from the early roots of the policy, through the Cold War era, and into the modern day international system. The focus of the chapter is narrowed primarily to the role of external factors in shaping Indian policy, especially the ongoing challenges posed by Pakistan and China and the role of power politics in the global system. Though domestic factors have had a significant influence on the trajectory of Indian foreign policy, the continuities of non-alignment have prevailed through changes in leadership and domestic vicissitudes. By exploring the foundation of non-alignment and how India has operationalized the policy through time, this chapter maintains that to some extent continuity has persisted into the twenty-first century: despite the revival of non-alignment rhetoric with the 2012 policy prescription, India moved closer to the West and its allies in practice. Yet, amid China's growing influence, the success of India's modern-day pursuit of strategic autonomy may well rest on a strong foundation of strategic partnerships that move beyond the limited commitments of non-alignment. The coming to office of the NDA government led by Narendra Modi in May 2014 has signaled a move away from even the rhetoric of non-alignment with significant implications for the future of Indian foreign policy.

Origins

Many factors contributed to the development of non-alignment in India, but the origins of non-alignment can be traced to three main factors, drawn from nationalist leanings, proximity to the Soviet Union, and economic troubles on the eve of independence.

First, tracing back to the early twentieth century, the Indian National Congress leaders deemed there were no natural military threats of significance to India. From this point of view, the biggest security risk was being drawn into the conflicts of other nations, meaning that the armed forces would be better applied to ensuring internal security than supporting a forward British policy.[1] This estimation carried into the independence movement, forming a pillar of the call for non-alignment. Pakistan had become a buffer between India and Afghanistan, and the Congress did not consider China to be a serious security concern, despite doubts among some officials.[2] China was in the midst of recovering from a civil war and, according to Nehru, offered little reason to believe in the early 1950s that there was a dispute over their shared border or any other imminent grounds for hostilities.[3]

With minimal external threats, the newly created state of Pakistan formed India's dominant security concern. Tensions surrounding partition in 1947 had led to violence in divided areas and an armed conflict in Kashmir that ended with an inconclusive UN-sponsored ceasefire in 1949. Still, Pakistan was not a substantial enough military threat to necessitate armed support from an external power. The Congress estimated that non-alignment would allow India to devote resources to deterring threats from Pakistan while minimizing other external threats by not aggravating political or economic differences. In addition to the general absence of provocation due to friendly policies, the political cost to a nation threatening war with an independent and non-aligned India would be high – and with negligible economic return.[4] India's peaceful emergence and non-threatening existence would thus serve as measures of security.

Second, India's proximity to the Soviet Union, in terms of interests as well as geography, required close consideration in developing a foreign policy and ultimately supported the adoption of non-alignment. As the world's largest democracy and with close links to Britain, India seemed a natural fit in the

Western bloc. Yet Nehru admired the Soviet Union's rapid industrialization and apparent socio-economic progress. Rajen Harshe identifies this apparent contradiction in India's domestic set-up, explaining that even in its nascent stage, Indian development represented a mélange in which structures of democracy and a partially planned economy worked in tandem. Given this, Harshe maintains, India was not well-positioned to decisively reject the ideology of either Cold War camp.[5] India's geographic proximity to the Soviet Union and China added an impetus to reducing any chances of hostilities based on ideology.

The socio-economic situation in India formed a third factor underlying non-alignment. India's economy in 1947 was stagnant and heavily dependent on an under-developed agricultural sector.[6] Likewise, an already insufficient industrial sector was worsened by partition, and the creation of Pakistan led to an influx of millions of refugees. Faced with widespread hunger and poverty, Nehru believed that peace was requisite for development and non-alignment was requisite for peace.[7] By establishing a non-threatening existence, non-alignment would theoretically allow India to minimize defence expenditures, reduce chances of costly conflict, and draw from multiple sources of aid without strict preconditions. Throughout the 1950s and 1960s, India was indeed successful in drawing financial and technical assistance from a variety of industrialized countries and had received some $70 million in support from the World Bank by 1960.[8]

The decision to adopt non-alignment was thus not merely an idealistic dream of neutrality, but was rather based on a realistic assessment of India's geopolitical situation. Nehru intended to give India room to manoeuvre according to its own interests, rather than be entrenched in the limitations of a Cold War alliance. The benefit of hindsight reveals the consequences of this approach. Although providing flexibility, non-alignment gave way to an inward-looking foreign policy that only gave real credence to Pakistan as a threat. This in turn created a reactive foreign policy.

Non-alignment in an aligned world

In the early years of independence, non-alignment formed the foundation of Indian foreign policy with apparent success. As intended, India was able to secure support from both camps of the Cold War, albeit mostly in the form of diplomacy and economic aid.

The Soviet Union began a bid for friendly relations as early as 1951, with food aid to India. A 1953 trade deal with India expanded this effort, with India–Soviet trade reaching $1.6 million in the first year of the agreement and $94.6 million by 1958.[9] As Nikita Khrushchev rose to prominence, Soviet openness towards India continued to grow alongside a more engaged foreign policy. 1955 brought an amiable exchange of official visits, during which time Soviet leaders voiced support for non-alignment and, notably, expressed recognition of Kashmir as a part of India.[10] In an apparent sign of reciprocal friendship, India remained quiet the following year when the Soviet Union invaded Hungary, and abstained from a vote demanding the withdrawal of Soviet troops.

Non-alignment garnered a cooler reception from Washington. The American Secretary of State, Dean Acheson, did not view Nehru favourably, and his successor, John Foster Dulles, was vocal in his disdain for non-alignment, which he considered neutralism. Dulles openly chided India's policy in 1955, calling neutrality 'an obsolete conception', and again in 1956 when he described neutrality as being 'except under very exceptional circumstances . . . an immoral and short-sighted conception'.[11] Nevertheless, India remained important to the US in its efforts to curb the spread of communism, and India's continuation of membership in the British Commonwealth and democratic values likely helped assuage Western concerns. Likewise, India retained hopes of a strategic relationship with the US that would benefit its own developmental ambitions without the restraints of a formal alliance. Despite nuances of frustration, relations between the US and India were thus affable overall through the 1950s, during which time the US became the largest aid donor to India.[12]

Yet India's lack of formal commitment to either power was not without consequence. Perhaps the greatest repercussion was the decision of the US to arm Pakistan after it joined the Central Treaty Organization (CENTO) and the Southeast Asia Treaty Organization (SEATO) in 1955. In the short term, this increased the perceived threat from Pakistan in India. In the long term, this shift in perception fed an increasingly regionally focused policy consumed by Pakistan.

Outside the major powers, non-alignment gave India pre-eminence among the developing countries, as noted by the success of the 1955 Bandung Conference, which laid the groundwork for the Non-Aligned Movement and exhibited a spirit of cooperation between China and India. The friendly air of Bandung contributed to India's approach of mutual friendship and trust towards China that had progressed since the early 1950s. China's annexation of Tibet was met with reticence in India, which tacitly recognized the move as legitimate in a 1954 agreement with Beijing that promoted exchanges with the 'Tibet region of China'. In the same agreement, China and India agreed to five principles of peaceful coexistence, or *panchsheel*, which included mutual respect for territorial integrity, non-aggression, and non-interference in internal affairs. Nehru also pushed for China's international recognition and tended to downplay the significance of Chinese border movements, despite China's rejection of the McMahon line in the latter part of the decade.

Nehru's conciliatory policy towards China was not simply one of idealism. Although an exchange of letters with Chinese Premier Zhou En-lai beginning in 1958 brought the border dispute to the forefront of contention, Nehru had taken at least some prior actions to address a potential Chinese threat, including border infrastructure improvements, troop reinforcements and a more direct government role in administrating border areas.[13] Nehru was not opposed to the use of force, but India was not in a position to take on a major war, especially with a comparatively stronger country like China.[14] Acknowledging China as a threat would have demanded a huge increase in defence spending and necessitated greater support from the Western bloc.[15] Further obfuscating the situation was the decision of the US to arm Pakistan. With a growing threat from Pakistan, India had measured interest in devoting military resources to its western border while trying to avoid hostilities on two fronts. Nehru's attempts to assuage tensions with China were thus in accordance with a key goal of non-alignment: to reduce chances of hostilities for the sake of economic growth.

Still, Nehru did erroneously discount the possibility of a major attack from China, and India's two-pronged approach of strategic preparedness and trust, with diplomacy at the helm, ultimately proved insufficient. That the country's foreign policy was largely defined by, and vulnerable to, regional dynamics within the context of great power politics came into sharp focus when China invaded India in 1962.

India's pivot

The surprise of the 1962 conflict called the efficacy of non-alignment into question. One of the clearest challenges was Nehru's reaching out to the US during the conflict. At his behest, Washington provided India with arms and ammunition and the State Department considered an embargo against China if hostilities did not cease.[16] US support to India extended beyond the immediate conflict with pledges of some $310 million in grants and loans from 1962 to 1965 and another $500 million in 1964 that was to be spread over a five year period in support of India's defence.[17] Though the US stopped short of providing modern combat weapons and failed to follow through on its 1964 pledge, American support during the conflict, subsequent economic and food aid, and pledges of continuing assistance undermined Nehru's policy by demonstrating overt dependency on the US.

A second challenge arose as it became apparent that policies of friendship were not sufficient in ensuring security. Rapprochement towards China did not prevent a hostile invasion, and friendship towards the Soviet Union served little benefit in the light of a military threat from China. Nehru lamented China's betrayal of 'good faith' and attributed the attack to a Chinese foreign policy based on a stark view that the world was divided into communists and imperialists, between whom war was inevitable.[18] For him, the conflict was not a consequence of non-alignment, but did prove that India must be prepared to fend off hostility from other nations by building up defence capabilities, which in the short term would require assistance from other countries. For many members of Parliament, however, the future value of non-alignment was dubious, and members from opposition parties and the Congress alike voiced support for India to join the US-led military bloc.[19]

These challenges ultimately did not terminate India's commitment to non-alignment, but did begin to redefine it. Recognizing the limits of friendship, Nehru increased defence spending as part of India's development objectives. In addition to American pledges, India garnered support from the UK, Canada, France, and Australia, and increased defence imports from the Soviet Union.[20] New Delhi applied these procurements to its 1964 rearmament plan with an eye on building defence against the Chinese threat, which intensified with China's first nuclear test in 1964, while also working to resolve the Kashmir dispute with Pakistan as part of a broader effort to assure President Ayub Khan that rearmament was not a measure of hostility towards Pakistan.[21] In a broader sense, the shock of the war indicated that India could no longer fully avoid taking sides. Domestic limitations meant that substantial external support was necessary for security.

Taking sides

India–US cooperation was short-lived, and Pakistan and China became key factors in India's move towards the Soviet Union. An early driver was the 1965 war, in which Pakistan used American-supplied arms against India, leading to thousands of casualties on each side. The conflict added to the growing disenchantment with US defence cooperation. After 1962, US military aid to India had become contingent upon settling the Kashmir dispute with Pakistan, and American defence inspectors were placed on the ground to ensure American-supplied equipment did not end up along the Pakistani front.[22] Frustrations deepened when border skirmishes in early 1965 met no punitive action by the US and plummeted with the subsequent onslaughts of August and September.[23] A 1965 American arms embargo against India and Pakistan added to this deterioration, as did post-conflict efforts by the US to make vital food aid to India contingent upon government-led agricultural reforms and efforts to temper criticism of American policy in Vietnam.[24] The continuation of economic aid from the US, paired with an unwelcomed Soviet warming towards Pakistan amid crumbling Soviet–China ties, kept India manoeuvring between the two states through the 1960s, but the gap between New Delhi and Washington had expanded.

1971 solidified India's shift from non-alignment with a nadir in relations between India and the US. Sudden American rapprochement towards China and the prospect of a third war with Pakistan responding to a military crackdown in East Pakistan prompted India to enter a 20-year treaty of peace, friendship, and cooperation with the Soviet Union. In an immediate sense, the treaty allowed India to take action in East Pakistan by providing security against Chinese intervention and a shield from international censure in the United Nations Security Council.[25] But more broadly, the treaty signaled a firm shift away from the West. American support for Pakistan in the subsequent 1971 war, though limited, deepened the India–US wedge, and following the Indian victory in East Pakistan, American influence on the subcontinent waned.

Though not an explicit military alliance, the India–Soviet treaty was a sharp departure from non-alignment. It maintained that neither country would enter into a military alliance or hostile actions against the other. If either side were subjected to an attack or threat, the two countries agreed to 'enter into mutual consultations in order to remove such a threat and to take appropriate effective measures to ensure peace and security of their countries', hinting that the treaty allowed room for a military alliance in any circumstance that constituted a threat to peace.[26] Equivocal language allowed India to maintain a semblance of non-alignment, but the treaty in effect created deterrence against any form of a US–China–Pakistan détente and fostered near-dependency on the Soviet Union for India's defence capabilities.

India used its move towards the Soviet Union to secure its place as a regional powerbroker. The treaty had paved the way for India to successfully engage

Pakistan militarily and divide the state with the creation of Bangladesh. Soviet deterrence, paired with its veto of three votes against India in the Security Council, allowed this to be a very much bilateral move.[27] Having secured assurance of the same protection moving forward, India's success in the conflict demonstrated New Delhi's ability to manipulate power politics to increase its regional clout. This push to build security in its immediate neighbourhood without the interference of external powers became a central component of India's diplomatic efforts after the success of the 1971 war.[28]

Closer ties with the Soviet Union also ensured a steady supplier for defence equipment. There is marked continuity in this aspect of the relationship that carries through leadership changes and periods of heightened and cooled relations. Under Indira Gandhi in the 1970s, concerns about over-dependency and the quality of products from the Soviet Union were offset by depleted foreign exchange reserves, which left little alternative for procurement.[29] Increasing efforts to diversify supply under the Janata government in the late 1970s brought more Soviet offers, and the reversal of US sanctions against Pakistan following the 1979 Soviet invasion of Afghanistan tempered Indian objections to the invasion itself. With renewed American support after 1979, Pakistan was able to revitalize its nuclear programme and modernize its military which ignited an unprecedented level of Indian arms purchases from France and the Soviet Union, including an agreement with the Soviet Union in 1980 for the transfer of $1.63 billion in defence equipment to India.[30] Rajiv Gandhi's election after his mother's assassination renewed interest in reducing dependency on Soviet arms and signaled a warming towards the US. Yet his defence policy was still marked by continuity; economic limitations continued to favour Soviet offers, and the challenge of shifting to Western suppliers proved difficult because of technology gaps and delayed Soviet deliveries.[31]Adding to the continuity of relations throughout the Cold War were other measures of Soviet collaboration, including its support for India's economic plans, favourable oil prices, the launching of two satellites for India, generous loan rates, and a willingness to accept goods in exchange for military equipment.[32]

Even at the zenith of relations with the Soviet Union, India retained space for leverage by reaching out to the West. By the 1980s, this was accompanied by an improvement in political relations. This was partially due to Ronald Reagan's efforts to mend the divide between the US and India as part of a broader strategy to undercut Soviet influence.[33] But there was also a growing overlap of interests. Although he was limited in his ability to shift away from Soviet dependency, the US welcomed Rajiv Gandhi's more liberal economic policies, and there were elements of agreement regarding Pakistan, especially following the Soviet withdrawal from Afghanistan and growing concerns over a possible nuclear weapon. This relationship remained tenuous through the end of the Cold War because of lingering suspicions of loyalties and intentions, and continuity in relations with the Soviet Union ultimately prevailed owing to India's ongoing regional concerns and economic limitations. But the warming in relations was indicative of a gradual shift away from Soviet Union dependency, which was fast-tracked with the Soviet collapse in 1991.

Turn of the century: Looking East, leaning West

The loss of its key patron and economic distress in the 1990s pushed India towards the economic liberalization initiated under Rajiv Gandhi and contributed to a warming of ties with Washington. With economic liberalization came opportunities for greater foreign investment and an effort to diversify defence relationships. By the end of the 1990s, India had secured defence agreements with Italy, South Africa, the UK, and the US, and between 2000 and 2008, New Delhi would secure another 19 defence agreements – a staggering change from the seven total agreements secured in the first 53 years of independence.[34] Pakistan's slip from its privileged position in American foreign policy upon the collapse of the Soviet Union also injected energy in bilateral ties with the US, but this boost was limited by a gap in stances on nuclear proliferation.[35] The Clinton Administration's push for non-proliferation and Indian reluctance to oblige led to mounting vexations on both sides that peaked with India's rejection of the US-led comprehensive test ban treaty in 1996 and a nuclear weapon test in 1998. In a strange twist, it was Pakistan that pushed India and the US back together through its incursions into Kargil in 1999. This marked the first time Washington supported India against Pakistan and was followed by a momentous visit by President Clinton in 2000 – the first visit by an American president in more than two decades.

Bilateral cooperation accelerated in the 2000s amid converging interests. The September 2001 attacks against the US and the attack on Indian Parliament by Pakistani gunmen later that year spurred India–US cooperation on counter-terrorism measures, leading to regional security dialogues and US pressure on Pakistan to curb cross-border attacks. Despite an upsurge in aid to Pakistan as part of the US-led war on terror, that relationship remained rocky and did not substantially hinder a closer relationship with India. In part, this demonstrates a shift in US interests: conflict with Pakistan would devastate India's economy and thus undercut increasing US interest in India as a balance to China.[36] More broadly, it is a reflection of increasing US support for India as a regional powerbroker and progress in cooperation over India's nuclear programme. 2005 was a major pivot in this relationship. In the course of the year, India and the US finalized the Next Steps in Strategic Partnership Initiative, which expanded bilateral cooperation and commerce in space, civilian nuclear activities, and high-technology trade, and signed a landmark defence agreement calling for bilateral military exercises, an expansion of two-way defence trade and an increase in intelligence sharing. Perhaps the most substantial pivot came with the unveiling of a new framework for nuclear cooperation in 2005, which led to the 2008 US–India Civil Nuclear Agreement and reversed India's status as a nuclear pariah.[37]

The enthusiasm of the 2000s somewhat dampened at the turn of the decade, but bilateral relations retained importance on both sides, particularly with the US strategic pivot to Asia under the Obama Administration. Despite some vacillations in moving forward, the policy was directed at prioritizing a balance of power in Asia by strengthening existing alliances and expanding partnerships throughout the region. The strategy pointed to India as a pillar, with hopes that it would be 'a regional economic anchor and provider of security in the broader Indian Ocean region'.[38] This support for India's rise and regional leadership helped revive the bilateral momentum of the previous decade.

At the same time, Indian policymakers continued to place emphasis on strategic autonomy, a relic of non-alignment, as a means of mitigating the potential costs of a strategic partnership with the US. This balancing act was evident in relations with China: despite interest in cooperation with the US, India wished to avoid antagonizing its more powerful neighbour by serving as the linchpin of the US pivot to Asia, which the Chinese broadly perceived as a measure of containment.[39] Concerns also lingered over US reliability, not only due to its continued relationship with Pakistan but also because of its vulnerability to China during the 2008–09 financial crisis.[40] Likewise, India balanced its still-strong defence relationship with Russia against its interests in cooperation with the US. New Delhi sided with Russia, China, and Iran in their initial avoidance of interference in Syria's civil war and aligned with Russia over its actions in Ukraine in 2014 through equivocations and a lack of support for US measures against Russia.[41]

Echoes of the past: *Nonalignment 2.0*

Non-alignment made a clear reappearance in 2012 with the release of *Nonalignment 2.0*, a document produced by prominent strategic thinkers in India that pulls the post-Cold War threads of strategic autonomy into a full revival of Nehru's non-alignment for modern times. The report echoed Nehru by calling for a focus on internal development by maximizing room to manoeuvre in the global scene. The reasoning was familiar, as the document based the decision to revive non-alignment on a regional threat assessment within the context of global politics, a desire for strategic autonomy, and a need to address problems of poverty. To this end, the report called for wide-ranging economic engagement, the strengthening of domestic institutions, an active role in shaping global norms, and a continual effort to avoid provoking hostility. The document warned that although the US may seem to be a likely ally, a formal alliance risks eroding strategic autonomy, as the US can be 'too demanding in its friendship and resentful of other attachments India might pursue'.[42] The essence of the report suggested that India would benefit most from keeping equal distance from the US and China, pursuing friendship with each but using its potential as a partner as leverage against both.

As in years past, this policy prescription is largely centred on China and Pakistan. The writers rightly identify China as one of the most significant foreign policy and security challenges facing India. They give credence to the many potential points of conflict: the disputed border, Chinese interest in the Indian Ocean, asymmetry in economic and trade relations, unpredictability in US–China ties, and Chinese wariness over India–US cooperation. And they fittingly recommend building India's naval capacity, in part by strengthening cooperation with countervailing powers such as Indonesia, Vietnam, and Australia. The report also points to a nuclear umbrella in relations between China, India, and Pakistan, which, along with China's focus on internal stability and economic growth, limits the likely scale of warfare. Thus, three of the key takeaways are for India to reallocate resources from the Pakistan border to the Chinese border, be strategically prepared to leverage asymmetric advantages in case of conflict, and to generally avoid provoking hostility and punitive policies from China by not moving irrevocably close to the US or Japan. The report's take on Pakistan also evokes past notions of non-alignment by hardly making mention of the role of outside powers. Though it mentions engagement with China on this front, acknowledging China's robust friendship with Pakistan, the report ultimately focuses on reducing chances of terrorism through diplomacy, the promotion of dialogue and military exchanges, and a strengthening of Indian police, intelligence, and counter-terrorism capabilities. Each is presented on a bilateral level, implying there is little room for external powers.

The report acknowledges changing circumstances in the global scene and places much significance on the rise of China, but the rhetoric and recommendations are old; this manner of pushing for strategic autonomy is evident throughout the history of independent India. India may not be quick to drop the idea of non-alignment, as it forms a part of its national identity. Yet this has never truly precluded relations resembling alignments, as apparent in the 1962 war, during the remainder of the Cold War, and even into the post-Cold War era. Even *Nonalignment 2.0* encourages defence cooperation with regional players for the sake of balancing China's maritime ambitions.

Yet China's impressive rise suggests that the old practice of non-alignment may not be sufficient as India works to secure its place as a regional and global player. Other states are looking to India to step up its role in the region as a balance to an increasingly assertive China; but if India steps up to the plate, it will be required to make hard decisions at times – quite contrary to the report's recommendation to avoid 'sharp choices'. Indeed, as Ashley Tellis has argued, India's strategic circumstances with China and Pakistan make an avoidance of sharp choices potentially dangerous.[43] Beyond this, maritime disputes flaring up in East and Southeast Asia mean that tighter security cooperation with Asian states may compel India to articulate support for its quasi-allies, particularly as they become more central to India's own security policy. This should not be viewed as a loss of strategic autonomy, but rather as an exercise of it; though India wants to continue engaging China, it cannot be afraid of provoking hostilities at every corner.

India is facing a shift in power dynamics with the rise of China that adds impetus to building relations with the US and its Asian allies. From the perspective of Indian policy, concerns over China are multidimensional. First, the border dispute between the two remains unresolved. There was progress on this front with the signing of a defence cooperation agreement in October 2013, which called for communication about border movements and restraint in situations of conflict. Yet the Doklam crisis of 2017 which resulted when the Indian Army and the People's Liberation Army confronted each other along a mountainous disputed region of the tri-junction between India, China and Bhutan underlined the fact that fundamental tensions between the two neighbours remain unresolved. A second concern for India stems from China's increasing presence in its neighbourhood, where smaller neighbours looking to balance India's regional hegemony, such as Sri Lanka, Bangladesh, Nepal, and Pakistan, have welcomed Chinese soft power and investments. This has led to a sense of encirclement by China in India's immediate vicinity. While expanding its regional influence, China has also demonstrated assertiveness in territorial disputes, as seen in its confrontation with Japan over the Senkaku islands in 2014. Meanwhile, China and Russia have stepped up cooperation, especially in the light of a growing wedge between the US and Russia over Syria and Ukraine.

Also of concern to India is Beijing's relationship with Pakistan. China has replaced the US as Pakistan's leading trading partner, with the volume of Pakistan's overall trade with China reaching $10.03 billion in the fiscal year 2015–16.[44] China has also made purposeful strides in Pakistan through investment projects such as a port at Gwadar, which opened in 2007 along the Arabian Sea with some $200 million of Chinese funding. The operation of the port was transferred to China Overseas Port Holdings in 2013, adding to concern that the port is part of a larger network of strategic bases and diplomatic ties reaching from the Middle East to the South China Sea. China is Pakistan's top supplier of weapons, selling 51 per cent of the weapons Islamabad imported in 2010–14.[45] Chinese investments in Pakistan's nuclear infrastructure add to Indian apprehension. China is a key enabler of Pakistan's nuclear programme and has repeatedly demonstrated willingness to violate its obligations as a Nuclear Suppliers Group (NSG) member by providing Pakistan nuclear reactors, claiming that its support to Pakistan predates Chinese NSG membership and is thus acceptable under a grandfather clause. Adding to general concerns over advancements in Pakistan's nuclear capability is the troubling reality that its facilities are expanding in an unstable environment where they are subject to militant attacks.

India has long aspired to rise as a major player in the global system and is, in some ways, positioned to do so as an economic giant, a responsible nuclear weapon state, and a dominant presence in the Indian Ocean. But India is unlikely to independently balance China's rise. China's GDP far outstrips that of India and has consistently recorded higher percentages of growth, and this gap carries over into defence spending and capabilities.[46] Given this, a strategy that focuses on engaging China economically, while resting on a quasi-alliance with the US, is not sufficient. In contrast to the idea put forward by *Nonalignment 2.0*, alignments and strategic autonomy no longer need to be mutually exclusive in today's increasingly multi-polar world. India would benefit from a more comprehensive strategy to balance China and foster its own rise by stepping up wide-ranging cooperation with other regional players.

India's 'Look East' policy, established in 1991, was an early step in this direction and gained momentum in the 2000s as Asian states began turning to India as a potential counterbalance to China.[47] Along these lines, India increased its presence and role in regional organizations such as ASEAN, in which it became a full dialogue partner in 1995 and a strategic partner in 2012. Indian bilateral trade with ASEAN increased from $2.9 billion in 1993 to $71.8 billion in 2012, during which time the partnership also expanded to include dialogue and cooperation in security and political dimensions.[48]

India also made rapid strides in regional bilateral cooperation. New Delhi stepped up its role as a provider of military equipment in the region in the 2000s, as especially evident in increasing sales to Indonesia and Vietnam, and has conducted joint military exercises with a majority of regional players while deepening naval ties with countries that share concern over piracy and Chinese influence in the Indian Ocean and South China Sea. Recent years have transformed India's relationship with Japan into a robust strategic partnership with substantial efforts in maritime cooperation and have brought India and South Korea together in tighter cooperation, again, with great value placed in building naval capabilities.[49] Elsewhere, India also deepened bilateral economic and defence cooperation in the 2000s. In states such as Japan, Malaysia, Vietnam and the Philippines, maritime disputes with China helped energize interest in India as a regional partner. In Australia, relations with India were boosted by deepening trade ties and amplified maritime cooperation, and by former Prime Minister Julia Gillard's state visit in 2012, when she named India as an integral part of Australia's future in Asia.[50]

Changing course

Since 2014, the government under Narendra Modi has initiated a sharper departure from India's past manner of balancing relations; though India's foreign policy objectives under Modi are not dramatically different from those of past administrations, New Delhi has become more assertive in its actions and less attached to the ideals and rhetoric of non-alignment.[51]

Modi demonstrated assertiveness in his approach to China early in his tenure as Prime Minister. During an official visit to Japan in 2014, he offered a barely veiled criticism of China when he claimed that 'everywhere around us, we see an 18th-century expansionist mind-set: encroaching on another country, intruding in others' waters, invading other countries and capturing territory'.[52] Less than a month later, he welcomed Xi Jinping to India and described the two countries as being at the brink of great potential. Around the same time, he extended a message of confidence to Southeast Asia by rebranding India's Look East policy as 'Act East', suggesting a new energy in India's approach to regional partnerships.

India–China relations have always followed a pattern of cooperation and confrontation, where both the nations have sought to cooperate on the issues of coinciding interests while maintaining their differences, essentially with regard to border disputes. Two issues continue to act as major irritants in India–China relations. The first is the continuance of Chinese veto over inclusion of Maulana Masoor Azhar in the UN designated list of terrorists. The second is China's determined opposition to include India as a member of the Nuclear Suppliers Group. The Doklam standoff between the two nations in 2017, arguably the worst in decades, represents a new low in the relations and stands as a true test of Modi's China policy.

Since the coming to office of the Modi government, however, there has been a more assertive posturing while articulating India's stand. In dealing with China, the Modi government worked on two fronts – the first was an assertive bilateral diplomacy and the second was attempting to forge strategic partnerships in Asia and with crucial island states in the Indian Ocean region, which would give India the necessary bargaining leverage to deal with China. Immediately after becoming Prime Minister, Modi attempted to reach out to China by trying to seek investments and attempting to build cooperation on the economic front. But when it came to the border dispute and continuing skirmishes along the border, Modi categorically articulated India's position that 'peace was a pre-requisite for a better all-round relationship'. This was seen as a departure from the earlier Indian position that better relations between the two nations would eventually lead to peace.[53] Similarly, Modi has been articulating India's stand on freedom of navigation and overflight in the seas while calling for respect of the United Nations Convention on the Law of the Sea (UNCLOS) by all nations. This was a direct signal to China for its belligerence in the South China Sea, and was appreciated by the affected nations.[54]

Aware of the relentless rise of China and its implications for India, Modi has sought to develop defence and strategic partnerships with nations that are crucial for India's interests. Modi has deepened the defence and strategic ties with Japan. He also invited Japan to be a part of the 'Malabar' exercises conducted with the US yearly, despite China's express displeasure in the past at multilateral naval exercises in the region.[55] Similarly, India has deepened its defence ties with Vietnam over the years. The most critical component of this relationship, however, is India considering selling surface-to-air missile to Vietnam. If the deal comes through, it would be the first time such a sale is carried out in the region by India, and it will take defence ties with Vietnam to the next level.[56] Modi also attempted to bolster India's ties with key island states like Maldives, Seychelles, Mauritius, and Sri Lanka in the Indian Ocean region by personally visiting these states to deepen ties. This is seen as an attempt to reorient India's approach towards this crucial region and to maintain the balance of power in the light of growing Chinese assertiveness.

In Sri Lanka, where India has faced complicated relations for decades due to its unsuccessful peacekeeping role in the Sri Lankan civil war, Modi's visit was the first by an Indian Prime Minister in twenty-eight years, and one that came at an opportune time. Over the past few decades, Sri Lanka developed an unambiguous tilt towards China, as evident in its reliance on Chinese support in infrastructure development under former President Mahinda Rajapaksa. The scope of China's involvement is well demonstrated by its key role in the $1.4 billion Colombo Port City development project. Sri Lanka has also proactively supported China's Maritime Silk Road Initiative, spearheaded by Xi Jinping to build economic links throughout Southeast Asia and the Indian Ocean, and stirred concern in India by allowing the docking of Chinese submarines in Colombo in 2014.

The election of Maithripala Sirisena as Sri Lanka's President in January 2015 opened an opportunity to rejuvenate ties between New Delhi and Colombo, especially as Sirisena called for a review of Chinese investments in Sri Lanka on suspicion of corruption and made India his first visit abroad as President. With a timely visit in March 2015, Modi made progress on this front, reaching four agreements and pledging some $1.5 billion in a currency swap with Sri Lanka and more than $300 million in support of developing the Sri Lankan railway sector. Perhaps aware of shifting dynamics in the region and scepticism regarding its motives, China took steps to promote trilateral cooperation with India in facilitating Sri Lankan development.[57]

Since then, there have been frequent high-level official visits as both the countries attempt to deepen their relations on multiple fronts, which includes collaboration in different areas such as energy, infrastructure, and special economic zones. India and Sri Lanka are also working on sorting out issues related to FTA and initiating the much discussed Economic and Technological Cooperation Agreement (ETCA), which proposes to increase trade and investment with India's five crucial southern states of Karnataka, Tamil Nadu, Kerala, Andhra Pradesh, and Telangana.[58] By launching a South Asian satellite entirely funded by India, Modi attempted a novel approach in boosting ties with neighbours including Sri Lanka, as the satellite would be used by all the South Asian neighbours (excluding Pakistan) to improve their broadcasting and telecommunication services.

Beyond economic and commercial aspects, Modi attempted to explore cultural and civilizational ties as a means of rejuvenating the connection between India and Sri Lanka, which has had strategic implications. Modi's second visit, to participate in International Vesak Day, was significant in this respect, as he leveraged Buddhism as a common heritage to bolster ties. The visit was a potent indication of improved ties between the two countries that have shown favourable signs for India, especially as Colombo appeared sensitive to India's concern over a growing Chinese presence in the Indian Ocean region. This is prominently evident in Sri Lanka's refusal to allow Chinese submarines to dock at Colombo port.[59] Sri Lanka also limited China's role in Hambantota to only commercial purposes, barring any military activity after express concern from India and other countries like Japan.[60]

Modi's assertiveness in foreign policy also continues to be apparent in strategic cooperation with the US. In addition to a successful summit in September 2014, Obama's participation in India's 2015 Republic Day celebrations demonstrated a new willingness by New Delhi to showcase the India–US partnership on the world stage, particularly as such an invitation is commonly reserved for India's closest partners. Obama's visit additionally brought progress in bilateral defence cooperation by finalizing the renewal of the US–India Defence Relationship framework for another 10 years, which will include strengthened cooperation in military-to-military and maritime matters and in developing new opportunities in trade and technology.

Modi attempted to make a strong case for a new phase in India–US relations when he, in his address to the US Congress in June 2016, declared that the relationship has 'overcome the hesitations of history'. This reflects the apparent desire of the Modi government to upgrade the relations between the two countries into a robust strategic partnership. One of the most critical components of India–US relations under Modi is the signing of the Logistics Exchange Memorandum of Agreement (LEMOA), which allows both countries to use each other's military facilities for repair and replenishment of supplies. Seen as a foundational agreement to build on future such cooperation, LEMOA is indeed a departure from India's conventional approach of reluctance in getting into military agreements with major powers. This has been followed by the signing of the COMCASA or Communications Compatibility and Security Agreement in September 2018, allowing the two nations to share high-end encrypted communication and satellite data and giving a legal framework for defence technology transfer.

The Trump administration has been especially vocal about China's growing might. This convergence of strategic interest was once again reflected in Prime Minister Modi's visit to the US to meet President Trump in June 2017. The joint statement noted that both leaders 'agreed that a close partnership between the United States and India is central to peace and stability in the region'.[61] The rise of China and the ensuing security and strategic concerns thus offer strong rationale for both states to devise ways to deal with this issue in a manner that would avert unnecessary escalation.

Another area of convergence for both the countries is ensuring lasting peace in Afghanistan. While the US wants to end its protracted war in Afghanistan and ensure a smooth retrieval, a peaceful and stable Afghanistan in the region is in India's national interest. The South Asia policy of the Trump Administration, announced in August 2017, calls for a more proactive role for India in Afghanistan and takes a tougher line on Pakistan. There are no signs to suggest that India will contribute troops on ground in Afghanistan, but it is clear that Afghanistan offers space for a deepening of ties between the US and India, as both share a common goal of a peaceful and stable Afghanistan.

As throughout its history, India has vested interest in a variety of partners, many of whom do not always see eye-to-eye. China has huge economic potential for India, and with a difficult neighbour to the west, lingering tensions over Tibet, and a shared border that extends well over 2,500 kilometres, it is not in India's interest to provoke hostilities with China. But passivity is not a sufficient approach, and in the absence of a strictly bi-polar world, stronger cooperation with the US and its allies does not preclude deepening engagement with China. Engagement with China may help India emerge as a regional interlocutor and add stability to a potentially volatile region; indeed these two factors would also be in the interest of the US and its regional allies. The Modi government is redefining strategic autonomy as an objective that is attainable through strengthened partnerships rather than the avoidance of partnerships. By doing so, it seems to be underlining that in today's complicated global scene, strategic autonomy and non-alignment are not necessarily a package deal.

Conclusion

Finding an effective grand strategy inevitably requires a balancing act. Non-alignment has been India's answer to this challenge and an influential tenet of its foreign and security policy since emerging from colonization. This approach successfully allowed India to avoid many of the limitations and entanglements of a formal alliance in the past, but it has also left the country in a position of shaping policy in a reactive manner, often based on Pakistan and China.

India is now at a juncture. China's rise and assertiveness as a regional and global power and the simultaneous rise of middle powers in the region means that this balancing act is at once increasing in complexity and importance. China's growth presents great opportunities for positive engagement, but territorial disputes and a forward policy in the region raise concerns for New Delhi, particularly in the Indian Ocean region and with Pakistan. The region itself is riddled with rivalries; a desire to balance China may push states together while other issues divide them. This is true on the global level as well, as noted by a degree of unpredictability in US–China relations.

The revival of non-alignment in 2012 recommends handling the changing global system by pursuing friendship with, but keeping safe distance from, major powers while building naval cooperation with regional states. In reality, India stands to benefit from being more assertive. Already, cooperation with regional players is aiding India's economy and defence capabilities, and as a pillar of the US pivot to Asia, India is finding support for an increased role as a regional powerbroker. These growing partnerships do not need to bar engagement with China; rather, assertiveness in regional and global relations may actually carve more room for India to pursue the strategic autonomy it values.

India's rising global profile is reshaping New Delhi's approach to its major partnerships in the changing global order. Though it may not be quick to drop its attachment to non-alignment in theory, New Delhi is showing signs of pursuing strategic autonomy separately from non-alignment under Narendra Modi. This separation is overdue in India's foreign policy and the country stands to benefit from leveraging partnerships rather than shunning them. Under the Modi government, India is charting new territory in its foreign policy, predicated on the belief that rather than proclaiming non-alignment as an end in itself, India needs deeper engagement with its friends and partners if it is to develop leverage in its dealings with its adversaries and competitors. India is today well positioned to define its bilateral relationships on its own terms and would do well to continue engaging more closely with those countries that can facilitate its rise to regional and global prominence.

Notes

1	Lorne J. Kavic, *India's Quest for Security: Defence Policies, 1947–1965*, 21 (Berkeley: University of California Press, 1962).

2	Vallabhbhai Patel warned Nehru of a 'united and strong' China with expansionist ambitions under 'a cloak of ideology which makes it ten times more dangerous'. See Ramachandra Guha, *India after Gandhi: The History of the World's Largest Democracy*, 168–69 (London: Macmillan, 2007).

3	Jawaharlal Nehru, 'Changing India', *Foreign Affairs*, 41, No. 3 (April 1963): 457.

4	Chris Smith, *India's Ad Hoc Arsenal: Direction or Drift in Defence Policy?* 42 (Oxford: Oxford University Press, 1994).

5	Rajen Harshe, 'India's Non-Alignment: An Attempt at Conceptual Reconstruction', *Economic and Political Weekly* 25, No. 7/8 (1990): 399–400.

6	David M. Malone, *Does the Elephant Dance? Contemporary Indian Foreign Policy*, 76 (Oxford: Oxford University Press, 2011).

7	Raju G. C. Thomas, 'Nonalignment and Indian Security: Nehru's Rationale and Legacy', *Journal of Strategic Studies* 2, No. 2 (1979): 158.

8	'World Bank Group Historical Chronology', World Bank Archives. Accessed on 12 December 2017. Available at http://web.worldbank.org/WBSITE/EXTERNAL/EXTABOUTUS/EXTARCHIVES/0,,contentMDK:20035657~menuPK:56307~pagePK:36726~piPK:437378~theSitePK:29506,00.html.

9	Smith, *India's Ad Hoc Arsenal*, 83.

10	Guha, *India after Gandhi*, 163.

11	As quoted in John Lewis Gaddis, *Strategies of Containment: A Critical Appraisal of American National Security Policy during the Cold War*, 151 (Oxford: Oxford University Press, 2005); Thomas, 'Nonalignment and Indian Security', 160.

12	Ashley J. Tellis, 'The Transforming U.S.–Indian Relationship and Its Significance for American Interests', 1–2. Accessed on 16 October 2006. Nonproliferation Policy Education.

13	Kavic, *India's Quest for Security*, 47–51.

14	Bharat Karnad, *Nuclear Weapons and Indian Security: The Realist Foundations of Strategy*, 166 (New Delhi: Macmillan, 2002).

15	Smith, *India's Ad Hoc Arsenal*, 54.

16	Jeff M. Smith, 'A Forgotten War in the Himalayas', *Yale Global*, 14 September 2012. Available at https://yaleglobal.yale.edu/content/forgotten-war-himalayas.

17	K. Subrahmanyam, 'Indian Security: The Absence of Conceptual Evolution', *India International Centre Quarterly*, 23, No. 1 (1996): 84.

18	Nehru, 'Changing India', 458–60.

19	Thomas, 'Nonalignment and Indian Security', 162.

20	Smith, *India's Ad Hoc Arsenal*, 81; Soviet data based on SIPRI trade registers. Accessed on 12 December 2017. Available at http://armstrade.sipri.org/armstrade/page/trade_register.php.

21	These efforts ultimately ended with Nehru's death in 1964. See Guha, *India after Gandhi*, 347–61.

22	Subrahmanyam, 'Indian Security', 84; Thomas, 'Nonalignment and Indian Security', 162.

23 Subrahmanyam, 'Indian Security', 85.

24 Tellis, 'Transforming U.S.-Indian Relationship', 2; U.S. Department of State ,Office of the Historian. 'USAID and PL–480, 1961–1969'. Accessed on 12 December 2017. Available at https://history.state.gov/milestones/1961-1968/pl-480.

25 Sumit Ganguly, 'Wars without End: the Indo-Pakistani Conflict', *Annals of the American Academy of Political and Social Science*, 541, Small Wars (1995): 175.

26 Ashok Kapur, 'India–Soviet Treaty and the Emerging Asian Balance', *Asian Survey*, 12, No.6 (1972): 464.

27 Ganguly, 'Wars without End', 175.

28 Kapur, 'India–Soviet Treaty', 471–72.

29 Smith, *India's Ad Hoc Arsenal*, 95–96.

30 Ibid., 109–11; Subrahmanyam, 'Indian Security', 94.

31 Smith, *India's Ad Hoc Arsenal*, 113.

32 Harshe, 'India's Non-Alignment', 402; Santosh K. Mehrotra, *India and the Soviet Union: Trade and Technology Transfer*, 66–68 (Cambridge: Cambridge University Press, 1990).

33 Tellis, 'Transforming U.S.–Indian Relationship', 2.

34 Brian K. Hedrick, 'India's Strategic Defense Transformation: Expanding Global Relationships', *Strategic Studies Institute* (2009): 11–12, 42.

35 Tellis, 'Transforming U.S.–Indian Relationship', 2.

36 For more, see Daniel S. Markey, 'Reorienting U.S. Pakistan Strategy: From Af-Pak to Asia', *Council on Foreign Relations, Special Report no. 68* (2014).

37 A detailed discussion of the US–India civil nuclear energy cooperation agreement can be found in Harsh V. Pant, *The US–India Nuclear Pact: Policy, Process, and Great Power Politics* (Oxford: Oxford University Press, 2011).

38 U.S. Department of Defense, *Sustaining U.S. Global Leadership: Priorities for 21st Century Defense* (Washington, D.C., 2012). Accessed on 12 December 2017. Available at http://www.defense.gov/news/defense_strategic_guidance.pdf.

39 This view was expressed by several Indian policymakers that the authors interviewed.

40 A detailed examination of how India has responded to the US 'pivot' to the Asia-Pacific can be found in Harsh V. Pant and Yogesh Joshi, 'Indian Foreign Policy Responds to the US Pivot', *Asia Policy*, No. 19 (January 2015): 89–114.

41 Tanvi Madan, 'India's Reaction to the Situation in Ukraine: Looking Beyond a Phrase', Brookings Institution, 14 March 2014. Accessed on 12 December 2017. Available at http://www.brookings.edu/blogs/up-front/posts/2014/03/14-ukraine-india-madan.

42 Sunil Khilnani et al., *Nonalignment 2.0: A Foreign and Strategic Policy for India in the 21st Century* (Center for Policy Research, 2012). Accessed on 12 December 2017. Available at http://www.cprindia.org/sites/default/files/NonAlignment%202.0_1.pdf.

43 Ashley Tellis, 'Can India Revive Nonalignment?' *Yale Global*, 28 August 2012. Accessed on 12 December 2017. Available at https://yaleglobal.yale.edu/content/can-india-revive-nonalignment. Accessed on 12 December 2017. Available at http://www.bbc.com/news/world-asia-india-29639950.

44 Shahid Iqbal, 'Trade Deficit with China Swells to $6.2bn', *Dawn*, 16 August 2016. Accessed on 12 December 2017. Available at https://www.dawn.com/news/1277774.

45 Reuters, 'PM Approves Deal to Buy Eight Chinese Submarines', 2 April 2015.

46 Based on World Bank GDP and military spending data, http://data.worldbank.org/.

47   For a more detailed discussion, see Harsh V. Pant, *China Rises, India Ponders: India's 'Look East' Policy Gathers Momentum*, 13 (Australia India Institute, 2013). Accessed on 12 December 2017. Available at http://www.aii.unimelb.edu.au/sites/default/files/China%20Rises,%20India%20Ponders.pdf.

48   'Overview of ASEAN–India Dialogue Relations', ASEAN. Accessed on 12 December 2017. Available at http://www.asean.org/asean/external-relations/india/item/overview-of-asean-india-dialogue-relations.

49   Pant, 'China Rises, India Ponders', 7–9.

50   Philip Hudson, 'Julia Gillard Will Elevate India to the Highest Priority for Australia', *The Australian*, 17 October 2012.

51   Sumit Ganguly, 'Has Modi Truly Changed India's Foreign Policy?', *The Washington Quarterly*, 40, No. 2 (2017): 131–43.

52   Mitsuru Obe and Niharika Mandhana, 'India and Japan Pursue Closer Ties to Counter China', *Wall Street Journal*, 1 September 2014.

53   Kanti Bajpai, 'Narendra Modi's Pakistan and China Policy: Assertive Bi-lateral Diplomacy, Active Coalition Diplomacy,' International Affairs 93, No. 1 (2017). Accessed on 12 December 2017. Available at https://www.chathamhouse.org/sites/files/chathamhouse/publications/ia/INTA93_1_05_Bajpai.pdf.

54   *Indian Express*, 'Vietnam Top Leaders Hail India's Position on Disputed South China Sea,' 3 September 2016; *India Today*, 'Philippines Hails India's Support India's South China Sea Support as Modi Heads to China,' 1 September 2016.

55   *Times of India*, 'India Shuns China, Allows Japan in Malabar Naval Drill', 13 July 2015.

56   Reuters, 'India Says in Talks with Vietnam for First Missile Sale', 15 February 2017.

57   P. S. Suryanarayana, 'Neighbourliness in India–Sri Lanka Ties – Analysis', *Eurasia Review*, 21 March 2015.

58   *Financial Express*, 'India, Sri Lanka Likely to Finalise ETCA by the Year End,' 17 May 2017.

59   Reuters, 'Sri Lanka Rejects Chinese Request for Submarine Visit', 11 May 2017.

60   Reuters, 'Sri Lanka's Cabinet Clears Port Deal with China Firm after Concerns Addressed,' 25 July 2017.

61   Government of India, Ministry of External Affairs, 'Joint Statement – United States and India: Prosperity Through Partnership' (2017). Accessed on 12 December 2017. Available at http://www.mea.gov.in/bilateral-documents.htm?dtl/28560/Joint+Statement++United+States+and+India+Prosperity+Through+Partnership.

8

India and Multilateralism
Concepts, New Trajectories and Theorizing

Arndt Michael

In Asia it seems inevitable that two or three huge federations will develop. [...] India is going to be the centre of a very big federation.

Jawaharlal Nehru, 1946[1]

[The] BJP believes a resurgent India must get its rightful place in the comity of nations and international institutions. The vision is to fundamentally reboot and reorient the foreign policy goals, content and process, in a manner that locates India's global strategic engagement in a new paradigm and on a wider canvass, that is not just limited to political diplomacy, but also includes our economic, scientific, cultural, political and security interests, both regional and global, on the principles of equality and mutuality, so that it leads to an economically stronger India, and its voice is heard in the international fora.

Bharatiya Janata Party, *Election Manifesto*, 2014[2]

Introduction

From being a leading member of the Non-Aligned Movement (NAM) to being one of the largest contributors to peacekeeping troops in the United Nations (UN), from being a member of the largest regional organization in the world in terms of population (South Asian Association for Regional Cooperation, SAARC) as well as territorial scope (Indian Ocean Rim Association, IORA), the Indian approach towards and involvement in multilateralism has an impressive history and trajectory. Today, major changes in India's role in multilateralism are underway, making India's present-day role in multilateralism an intriguing work in progress.

India's historical 'tryst' with multilateralism started when India sent a delegation – albeit as part of the British delegation – to the United Nations

Conference on International Organisation (UNCIO), responsible for drafting the UN charter in 1945.[3] Since then, India has shown a virtually unwavering commitment to the principles and concomitant obligations stipulated in the UN charter.[4]

At independence, India's international position was weak, her financial and military resources low. After independence, multilateralism under the framework of the UN was consequently used by India as a means of protecting her hard-won sovereignty as well as strengthening the economy, while at the same time coming to realize that fora like the UN were in no small measure used as an arena for continuing great-powers politics.[5] Still, whenever possible India used global multilateralism to exert influence and impress upon the world her idiosyncratic normative and universalist approach.

With the emergence of the Cold War, Indian leaders were convinced that multilateral engagement could further enhance India's international position and enable her to garner crucial support by states who had just been freed from colonialism, making India the almost natural leader of like-minded states in international organizations. After all, India had become the first state after the Second World War to gain independence.[6] Concomitantly, for India her Nehru-inspired policy of non-alignment meant she did not want to ally herself with any state and wanted to retain her autonomy in decision-making. Regionally, the existing structural asymmetry and India's natural primacy in the South Asia region, the ramifications of the partition of British India, the presence of multiple cross-border identities and a colonial legacy of porous and nebulous borders made efforts at South Asian regional multilateralism difficult at best, if not impossible. All in all, India's approach towards multilateralism was exclusively global in the 1940s and 1950s.

From the late 1960s, internationally and in multilateral settings, India was increasingly criticised on grounds of her seemingly erratic and contradictory strategic behaviour: India's invasion of East Pakistan in 1971 contradicted non-interventionist norms which India had constantly championed; the 1971 Treaty of Friendship and Cooperation with the Soviet Union contradicted non-alignment; the 1974 Peaceful Nuclear Explosion (PNE) contradicted Indian calls for universal disarmament; and, crucially, Indian lack of public criticism of the Soviet Union's 1979 invasion of Afghanistan contradicted her incessant calls for worldwide peace. Unsurprisingly, in the 1980s India's multilateral influence waned and she became largely marginalized in international fora.

After the Cold War and in the wake of economic liberalization, a policy shift and a shift in regional focus gradually developed, most prominently with the Gujral Doctrine and the Look East policy in the early 1990s. Coupled with an increased need for foreign direct investment (FDI), upgrading of outdated technology and tapping into new markets, a changed and much more pragmatic attitude towards both global and regional multilateralism was adopted. Indian policy ultimately became more realistic, leaving behind abstract notions of universalism and idealism. For India, economic growth became key for her global aspirations and attempts to gradually ascend international hierarchies. The acquisition of nuclear weapons in 1998, an increased economic clout and a period of domestic stability (and the emergence of regional parties) led to India's international engagement increasing in scope and depth.

Today, India has become actively involved in discussions of global issues and has been transformed into an international stakeholder, shareholder and agenda-setter, successfully leaving her mark in agreements related to climate change, world trade, nuclear proliferation and international terrorism. Alongside India's engagement in large multilateral settings, India has also become active in smaller groups of nations, such as the BRICS (Brazil, Russia, India, China and South Africa) or the IBSA (India, Brazil, South Africa) Dialogue Forum, all of which aim at creating a counterweight to Western dominance.

Overall, Indian involvement in global and regional multilateralism has witnessed multiple ties in multiple institutions over multiple issues. Multilateralism at the global and regional levels has been an important part of India's foreign policy agenda as well as her international identity and profile, with a drastic increase in activities at both levels in the recent past, albeit with varying degrees of success. Together with this increase in the praxis of multilateralism, Indian scholarship on multilateralism has also proliferated and introduced new concepts and ideas for analysing multilateralism, challenging 'Western' conceptions of multilateralism. This chapter seeks to contribute to the discourse on India's role in the theory and praxis of multilateralism. In what follows, the chapter will first look at India's current role in global institutions, followed in the third section by an analysis of India's role in select regional institutions. The penultimate section will take theorizing multilateralism into focus and look at Western 'versus' Indian scholarship. The chapter concludes by outlining a future research agenda for multilateralism.

Indian engagement in global multilateralism: Concepts and institutions

Global multilateralism takes place in different settings and institutions, dealing with global questions such as peace, international trade and finances, climate change, anti-terrorism, human security, and so on. For India, participation in global multilateralism has served different purposes, depending on the respective objectives and set-up of the institutions; hence, for her the most important global institutions today are the following six: the NAM (third world solidarity), the UN (international peace and development; environment), the World Trade Organization (WTO) (international trade), the BRICS (rising powers and financial influence), IBSA (rising powers) and the Shanghai Cooperation Organization (SCO) (regional security).

The Conference of Heads of State or Government of Non-Aligned Countries (Non-Aligned Movement)[7] met for the first time in Belgrade in 1961, after having been initiated at the Bandung Conference in 1955. Jawaharlal Nehru assessed that 'the power of nations assembled here is not military power or economic power, nevertheless it is power. Call it moral force.'[8] The objectives of the NAM were to counter great-power politics, to safeguard national autonomy, circumvent military pacts and/or alliances and to 'obstinately defend and project genuine independence, the real power to choose and not [to] be compelled to accept the policies of other states'.[9] NAM was glued together mainly by an anti-imperialism sentiment and the aim of ending colonialism,[10] and created an independent international voice for mainly non-Western states. All in all, non-alignment did not purport to be isolationist or neutral; rather, the idea of autonomy in international affairs was key. Indian leadership role among erstwhile colonies also made it possible for India to turn the NAM into a platform for an increased international role, and India, for example, criticized a great number of states regarding their policies in Korea, Congo, Suez and Vietnam (although not the Soviet Union's invasion of Hungary in 1956).

After the Cold War, many, even Indian policymakers, questioned the relevance of NAM. Prime Minister I. K. Gujral famously asked: 'It is a mantra that we have to keep repeating, but who are you going to be nonaligned against?'[11] Still, the NAM has persisted until today. It now represents critical development issues, for example global warming, economic disparities and terrorism, taking the perspective of the developing world. At the same time, the fundamental aim of maintaining strategic independence in India's international affairs lives on, with former Indian Prime Minister Manmohan Singh stating in 2006: 'Our stand is in full conformity with our founding fathers [...] Non-alignment is a state of mind and ability to exercise an independent judgement on issues.'[12]

Despite NAM's significance for India's international identity, Narendra Modi chose not to attend the 17th NAM Summit in September 2016 and sent the Indian Vice President instead, only the second time in the history of NAM that an Indian Prime Minister did not participate. This decision was heavily criticised by many,[13] a criticism that was to be expected and could not have caught the Modi government by surprise. It was a clear demonstration that the Indian government had changed key features of its foreign policy outlook and decided to focus on other international organizations instead, especially the United Nations.

India was a founding member of the United Nations and a vocal advocate of anti-colonialism and a co-sponsor of the 1960 UN Declaration on the Granting of Independence to Colonial Countries and Peoples. Besides, India strongly supported global and especially nuclear disarmament, for example with the Indian 'Action Plan for Ushering in a Nuclear-Weapon Free and Non-Violent World Order' in 1988. Regarding trade, in 1964 India was instrumental in establishing the UN Conference on Trade and Development, which later led to the emergence of the Group of 77 (the G77), the largest organization of developing states at the UN, as well as the UN Industrial Development Organization in 1966. India promoted the 'Comprehensive Convention on International Terrorism' in 1992. Crucially, India has devoted a great deal of development resources to the UN and has been one of the largest contributors to the United Nations Development Programme (UNDP) and a major contributor to United Nations Population Fund (UNFPA) and United Nations Children's Fund (UNICEF), as well as the United Nations Conference on Trade and Development (UNCTAD) Trust Fund for least developed countries.

Importantly, India has been engaged in several peacekeeping operations and related activities, for example the Neutral Nations Repatriation Commission in Korea, the International Control Commission in Vietnam and United Nations Peace Keeping Operations (UNPKO) in the Belgian Congo and Suez. Between 1950 and 2017, India contributed to 45 out of 71 UNPKO missions, with approximately 195,000 troops.[14] In April 2017, India was the second-highest overall contributor to UNPKO, sending 7,648 troops and police out of the UN's then total deployment of 96,865 troops and police.[15]

Also, India has been active in dealing with climate change: India is a party to the United Nations Framework Convention on Climate Change (UNFCC) and the Kyoto Protocol as part of which India voluntarily pledged to reduce its carbon emission by 20 to 25 per cent over the 2005 levels by 2020. During the 2009 Copenhagen negotiations, India, Brazil, China and South Africa founded the BASIC group[16] and brokered a secret deal with the USA,[17] a move that alienated many developing countries. The BASIC group was hence instrumental in reaching the Copenhagen Agreement in which it was agreed, inter alia, to have voluntary instead of mandatory reductions in greenhouse emissions. India's crucial role in climate negotiations needs to be highlighted in this context: India's traditional insistence on differentiated responsibilities in controlling carbon emissions has practically embedded this idea (or norm) in the discourse on climate change,[18] confirming that India has become a global norm entrepreneur. And in the same vein, on the occasion of the Paris Climate Accord in December 2015, *Time Magazine* wrote: 'No country matters more than India at the Paris Climate Talks.'[19]

India has held a non-permanent seat in the United Nations Security Council (UNSC) for seven terms in 1950–52, 1965–67, 1970–72 1976–78, 1983–85, 1990–92 and 2011–13,[20] showcasing her intentions to gain a permanent seat in the UNSC. Today, India sees herself as a responsible great power, a role that has at times conflicted with the UN's 'responsibility to protect',[21] especially as the latter contradicts the norm of non-intervention, an important normative concept for India. Also, India's assessment of the work of the International Criminal Court (ICC) can best be described as critical.[22] Nonetheless, India's influence in the BASIC group has the potential of increasing India's role as a veto-player in international negotiations. Shashi Tharoor noted that the UN should be used as 'a platform for establishing India's place in the world'.[23] In line with this reasoning, in 2015, Narendra Modi successfully campaigned at the UN for the introduction of an International Day of Yoga, a major milestone in India's soft power outreach via global multilateralism.

India's role in the WTO as the most important institution responsible for global trade has evolved over the years, showing that India was gradually able to use her hard-line, persevering positions for exerting increased leverage. In October 1947, India belonged to the founding Contracting Parties to the General Agreement on Tariffs and Trade (GATT), concluding in 1947 and culminating in the WTO in 1995. In the past, India largely stuck to her older ideological position of standing with the developing countries and arguing for justice.[24] With reference to India's negotiating style in GATT trade rounds and those of the WTO, Amrita Narlikar writes that 'India's hard-line positions […] have contributed greatly to its position as a leader of the developing world [...] [via] the idea that "India is the voice of the voiceless in the WTO'".[25]

For India, protecting her national self-sufficiency has been key in international negotiations, and concomitantly protecting Indian domestic constituencies. In the initial GATT years, India refused to commit to reciprocal tariff reduction and asked for special exemptions. During the Tokyo Rounds that took place in the 1980s, India opposed regulations dealing with trade-related aspects of intellectual property rights (TRIPS) and trade-related investment measures (TRIMs). By opposing GATT tariffs, asking for concessions and insisting on the inclusion of services in GATT negotiations, India became the leader of the G10 (Argentina, Brazil, Cuba, Egypt, India, Nicaragua, Nigeria, Peru, Tanzania and Yugoslavia) in the 1980s and 1990s. While nine members of this group eventually agreed to concessions, India stood her ground.

In 1996, during the Uruguay Round (the eighth GATT round launched in 1985), the Like-Minded Group (LMG) comprising Cuba, Egypt, India, Indonesia, Malaysia, Pakistan, Tanzania and Uganda was formed, only to be practically dissolved at the Doha Ministerial Conference in 2001. It was only India that refused to accept bilateral agreements, but, after Indian concerns had been addressed, she eventually signed the November 2001 Doha Declaration on TRIPS and Public Health. India, together with Brazil, then became the leader of the G20 grouping of developing nations when the Cancun Ministerial Conference took place in 2003 where agricultural policies were the contentious centre of negotiations.

The Doha talks collapsed in 2008 and negotiations have stalled since then. After prolonged negotiations, a Bali package was agreed upon in December 2013 and 150 states reached a Trade Facilitation Agreement (TFA) in December 2013. India agreed under the condition that final decisions on the status of state-supported food programmes are to be postponed until 2017; in 2014, New Delhi changed its position and rejected the TFA, but later signed a pact with the USA in November 2014 according to which the 'peace clause' in the TFA was extended, which means that a final deal on the subject must be reached first.

All in all, India has developed her own peculiar strategy in the WTO: it has begun to work with specific country coalitions built around a specific issue area (so called hybrid coalitions) and has adopted was has been termed a distributive strategy and used 'framing devices' based on notions of fairness.[26]

A new breed of global multilateral frameworks or institutions are BRICS and IBSA. BRICS was formed in September 2006 by Brazil, Russia, India and

China. The group conducted its first annual summit in June 2009; South Africa then joined in December 2010. The objective of BRICS is the creation of a more equitable international financial system. At the same time, BRICS member-states want to use their international influence collectively and, among other objectives, synchronize specific policies. Member-states have agreed to regularly meet on the sidelines of meetings of the United Nations General Assembly (UNGA), the International Monetary Fund (IMF), the World Bank, the G20 and other multilateral fora. Furthermore, there is now a New Development Bank 'for mobilizing resources for infrastructure and sustainable development projects in BRICS and other emerging economies and developing countries, [and] to supplement [...] multilateral and regional financial institutions'.[27]

Formalized in June 2003 through the adoption of the Brasilia Declaration, the first IBSA Summit took place in September 2006. IBSA objectives have been the strengthening of trilateral collaboration in areas such as trade, environment and defence. IBSA countries want to work together on the 'proposed reforms of the UN, peace and security, terrorism, globalization, and sustainable and social development [...]' and "aspires to make a significant contribution to the framework of South-South cooperation [...] by promoting potential synergies among the members'".[28]

And finally, India is a member of the Shanghai Cooperation Organisation (SCO). Founded upon principles of combating terrorism, separatism and extremism, membership of the SCO is made up of China, Kazakhstan, Kyrgyzstan, Russia, Tajikistan and Uzbekistan (with Afghanistan, Iran and Mongolia as observers). The objective of the SCO is to promote regional stability, military cooperation, counterterrorism as well as economic and cultural cooperation. India and Pakistan who both had observer status since 2005 joined in June 2017. Considering that Pakistan acceded to the organization at the same time as India, the success or failure of the SCO will be an interesting topic of future analysis against the backdrop of worsening Indo-Pak ties, although the SCO charter explicitly prohibits raising of bilateral issues.

On the whole, India's current role in multilateral institutions is that of an emerging global power acutely aware of its rising global influence. These six institutions show that India has used multilateralism, sometimes judiciously, sometimes arbitrarily, to advance specific Indian ideas and norms. Especially India's role in peacekeeping and global trade are cases in point, as is the Indian success in shaping the global environmental agenda. India's negotiating position in the WTO has made India a veto player to be reckoned with. India today is an indispensable power in global institutions, but she has, as some authors have suggested, begun to show a predilection for participating in 'global governance by oligarchy'.[29] While this new trend might seem at odds with India's professed support of the developing world, there is a certain logic behind India's new sympathy for institutions such as BRICS, IBSA, BASIC, and so on. They increase Indian leverage, allow her to pool resources and give her more influence in the still West-dominated multilateral institutions. Also, Modi's absence in the 2016 NAM summit is an indicator that India ranks global multilateral organizations and prioritizes those which wield genuine global influence, unlike the NAM which has wielded only a rhetorical one.

Indian engagement in regional multilateralism: Concepts and institutions

India's regional multilateral policy had initially been geared towards Asia rather than its immediate neighbourhood, that is, South Asia. Before independence, Nehru already spoke about a South Asian Federation consisting of India, Iraq, Iran, Afghanistan and Burma. In 1947, the Asian Relations Conference dealt with the possible framework of an Asian organization, even an 'Eastern Federation' was discussed, with Indian and China as leaders. Several multilateral conferences took place in the 1950s, all of which discussed (but did not implement) how regional cooperation could look like, for example the Baguio Conference of May 1950 on economic and cultural cooperation, the Colombo Plan of July 1951 on economic and technological cooperation (and even collective security), involving India, Pakistan, Burma, Indonesia and Ceylon (Sri Lanka).[30]

Four regional organizations or regimes are key to understanding India's position vis-à-vis regional multilateralism, namely the South Asian Association for Regional Cooperation (SAARC), the Indian Ocean Rim Association (IORA), the Bay of Bengal Initiative for Multi-Sectoral Technical and Economic Cooperation (BIMST-EC) and the Mekong Ganga Cooperation (MGC) Initiative. While regional multilateralism had been gradually implemented in practically every region of the world until the 1980s, South Asia was the one world region where such cooperation remained at large. The SAARC was eventually founded in 1985, after seven years of protracted negotiations, with Bangladesh as its initiator.[31] Since the inception of SAARC, there have only been eighteen summit meetings, hundreds of ministerial meetings with little concrete to show for, and, as of 2018, seven major conventions and thirteen official agreements. Membership is composed of Afghanistan, Bangladesh, Bhutan, India, Maldives, Nepal, Pakistan and Sri Lanka. The secretariat is in Kathmandu, with a staff of about fifty, in theory responsible for an organization that is home to 1.5 billion people. The SAARC charter stipulates that no bilateral and contentious issues are to be discussed and that the Panchsheel are the guiding principles underlying the work of the organization. The institutional set-up is based on a pyramidal structure with regular summits at the apex, supported by Council of Ministers meetings and standing committees comprising foreign secretaries.[32]

In terms of security cooperation, SAARC has proven to be of little significance.[33] The India–Pakistan antagonism, lack of political will and mutual distrust have been major stumbling blocks towards achieving a closer security cooperation – and a security community along the lines of Karl W. Deutsch[34] is more than utopian. In truth, the administrative chains in form of the SAARC charter – not least on the diplomatic pressure of India – have severely limited the organization's ability to advance any form of inter-state cooperation going beyond low politics. There is general accord that SAARC has been somewhat useful as a forum for informal talks between, for example, India and Pakistan, but the major economic objective of a South Asian Free Trade Area (SAFTA), though officially in existence since 2004, has been confronted with severe administrative and technical problems and has not yet been implemented. Former Indian Prime Minister Manmohan Singh matter-of-factly commented in 2005 that after twenty years, SAARC had clearly not fulfilled the dreams of its founding fathers.[35] And even the National Democratic Alliance (NDA) government under Narendra Modi has not changed the relevance of SAARC as an organization. Modi invited the SAARC heads of state or government to his swearing-in ceremony on 26 May 2014[36] and held bilateral talks with each of them on his first day in office, including Pakistani Prime Minister Nawaz Sharif. At the time, this move was hailed as the beginning of a new era in regional multilateralism. However, after participating in the 2014 Summit, India decided to boycott the next SAARC Summit which was scheduled to take place in Islamabad in November 2016, with other SAARC member-states also declaring their boycott. Until the middle of 2018, no date for the next SAARC summit had been agreed upon and SAARC activities remain at large.

A second regional organization with Indian membership is IORA, until 2013 known as the Indian Ocean Rim-Association for Regional Cooperation (IOR-ARC). IORA was an Australian initiative in 1995 and was meant to encompass economic as well security coordination for all countries of the Indian Ocean Rim. IORA now has twenty-one members. Since its founding after seven years of extensive deliberations, the unusual institutional design of the organization has stymied all efforts at cooperation. The Indian-crafted charter prescribes a so-called tripartite model of cooperation: representatives from governments, the academia and the business world are all responsible for furthering cooperation in different areas. An utterly understaffed secretariat exists in Mauritius. Altogether seventeen Council of Minister meetings have taken place until 2018. In 2012, Shashi Tharoor, the then Indian Minister of State for External Affairs, commented after attending a Council of Ministers meeting that even after seventeen years of existence, cooperation had still not left the declaratory phase.[37] IORA has economic and social objectives, but has achieved little in terms of practical implementation and visible successes.

A third regional organization is BIMST-EC. It was founded in 1997, with Thailand as its originator. It took seven years before the first official summit meeting between the members of the organization was held, and another eight years before the necessity of a coordinating secretariat was finally acknowledged. The secretariat is in Dhaka since 2014, with a minuscule staff number. Members are Bangladesh, India, Myanmar, Sri Lanka, Thailand, Bhutan and Nepal. Officially, there are fourteen priority sectors of cooperation. In theory, BIMST-EC could serve as an important bridge between South Asia and Southeast Asia and could support India's Act East policy.[38] However, the envisaged BIMST-EC free trade agreement (BIMST-EC FTA) remains at large. Except for four summits until 2018, BIMST-EC has remained more of an idea than a functioning organization.

And finally, the Mekong Ganga Cooperation (MGC) forum encompasses six riparian countries of the Mekong and Ganga (Cambodia, India, Laos, Myanmar, Thailand and Vietnam). The original promoter was Thailand. At the time of its founding in 2000 in Vientiane, it was agreed to cooperate in the fields of tourism, education, human resource development, culture, communication and transport. Though not conceived of as a genuine 'organization' but rather as a multilateral forum for regional cooperation, the MGC represents regional cooperation at its most basic. It was agreed to have 'Annual Ministerial Meetings', back to back with 'ASEAN Ministerial Meetings' and regular 'Senior Officials' Meeting'. There have only been six ministerial meetings so far, but no effective tangible achievements. The then Minister for Foreign Affairs of Myanmar, Nyan Win, observed in 2007 that despite seven years of efforts, progress had been very slow.[39]

While each of these four organizations must be seen in the light of their respective geographical regions, distinctive historical and socio-economic developments and dissimilar objectives, they still showcase three commonalities, all of which illustrate that India's policy towards regional multilateralism has been contradictory at best. First, there is a tendency towards competing regionalism, meaning that membership as well as sectors of cooperation overlap.[40] BIMST-EC and its objectives, for example, are basically SAARC minus Pakistan plus Thailand. The MGC has overlapping membership and objectives with BIMST-EC and SAARC, and several SAARC countries are also members of the IORA. Second, all four initiatives originated from India's neighbours. India subsequently started a diplomatic offensive and influenced the respective negotiations and founding documents, removing high politics such as security cooperation from the agenda. And third, one of the key features of cooperation is non-institutionalization. While three of the organizations have a small secretariat of sorts, the lack of manpower and financial resources render it impossible to advance cooperation, even within the narrow confines of the respective charters.

In the past, a lively debate in academic and media circles has raged on how regional cooperation can be improved, deepened, expanded, strengthened, rejuvenated, and so on, but to no avail. Especially the future of SAARC and IORA is highly uncertain, as the former is practically hostage to the Indo-Pak antagonism and the latter suffering from ill-defined objectives and dramatic lack of resources. In regional multilateralism, bilateralism is still India's preferred way of dealing with neighbours, and while new concepts that address the overall paralysis currently existing are urgently needed, these seem elusive at best.

Theorizing multilateralism and regionalism: Western 'versus' Indian scholarship

Multilateral practice by India within the parameters provided by the UN, NAM and to a lesser degree regional organizations has informed Indian theorizing on multilateralism. Complex processes of decision-making, the search for consensus-building and finding means of exercising leverage at international multilateral fora have been amply analysed in the writings of Indian authors, whereas the concept of multilateralism as such was mostly viewed as part of an institutional and regulatory system. However, there is as of now no genuine Indian theory of International Relations (IR),[41] nor a cohesive body of Indian literature on multilateralism. The majority of works on India's involvement in global and regional multilateralism has been descriptive and mostly followed political realist assumptions. Still, Indian authors, scholars and practitioners, residing in India or abroad, have begun to elaborate on concepts of multilateralism from different theoretical vantage points and IR schools, enriching traditional arguments of IR scholarship and providing new angles of analysis.

The theoretical study of multilateralism – as part of the general system of IR theories – started in the 1990s in Western academia. Prominent theoretical analyses of the concept of multilateralism were conducted, inter alia, by Keohane,[42] Caporaso,[43] Ruggie,[44] Cox[45] and Rosenau.[46] While Cox's and Rosenau's works are based on the reflectivist school of IR, Keohane followed the rationalist tradition, with Ruggie combining both schools.

Looking at arguments advanced by the rationalist IR school of thought first, multilateralism is defined as the 'practice of coordinating national policies in a group of three or more states'.[47] Institutional arrangements possess 'persistent set of rules that constrain activity, shape expectations and prescribe roles'. According to Ruggie 'multilateralism depicts a generic institutional form in international relations that coordinates relations among three or more states on the basis of generalized principles of conduct'.[48] Two consequences of the generalized principles of conduct are: 'indivisibility' among the members of a collectivity with respect to the range of behaviour in question; and 'diffuse reciprocity' expected by each member to yield a rough equivalence of benefits in the aggregate and over time.

The framework provided by Keohane and Ruggie suggests two main features – an institutional structure with a specific, perpetual regulatory framework and a universal, state-centric appeal. In Indian theorizing, especially the aspects of perpetuality and universality are questioned. In his study on global governance, Deepak Nayyar[49] only partially agrees with the framework proposed by Keohane/Ruggie and argues that it is necessary to adapt multilateral institutions and rules: institutions or rules need to be created to account for global issues such as international financial structures, transnational corporations, cross-border movement of people, and so on. For Nayyar, different rules have been implemented for different issue areas and institutions. For example, regarding the WTO, trade flows are treated differently from technology flows. Also, rules are not universally applicable. Regarding the IMF or the World Bank, there are no rules for surplus or deficit countries from the industrialized world that do not borrow from multilateral financial institutions, but such rules exist for borrowers in the developing world or for transitional economies. Finally, the agenda for new rules is partisan. For Nayyar, there is an urgent need to make rules uniformly applicable to all states and create symmetry across issue areas. Hence, for Nayyar uniformity exists to a much wider degree, and the features of perpetuality as well as the scope of diffuse reciprocity are both questionable. Authors such as Shashi Tharoor[50] and J. N. Dixit,[51] writing from their professional backgrounds as diplomats, have also elaborated on the concept of multilateralism, but mostly in terms of regulatory issues that come into play within the deliberations in universal multilateral institutions such as the UN.

Looking at the long-standing debate of regionalism 'versus' multilateralism, different strands of arguments have been forwarded. Representatives of 'Western' approaches – for example practitioners such as Barroso,[52] Groom[53] or Zadek[54] – do not see a major cleavage between multilateralism and regionalism, as, for example, exemplified by the European Union (EU). On the other hand, authors such as Winters[55] or Ornelas[56] beg to differ and assess that regionalism causes a number of problems. Several Indian scholars take more nuanced viewpoints: B. S. Prakash[57] writes that the universal character of 'traditional' multilateralism is under pressure because of changes in multilateralism (especially regarding the UN) which has led to 'sub-regionalism' or 'pan-regionalism'. Indian scholars like Jagdish Bhagwati,[58] Nipun Agarwal[59] and Sayantan Gupta[60] argue that regionalism might actually be a stumbling block for the evolution of multilateralism. Scholars such as Manoj Pant and Amit Sadhukaran[61] differ in their assessment and argue that regionalism is not a hurdle to multilateralism. A somewhat neutral position can be found by Andriamananjara[62] and Aghion et al.[63] They write that regionalism (for example in the form of the so-called Regional Trade Agreements [RTAs]). strengthens multilateralism. The major argument for them is that economic rents which arise as a consequence of multilateral trade negatively affect the interests of regional special-interest lobby groups. In turn, these groups exert pressure on their respective governments and attempt to influence them towards making more and more concessions. Hence, governments are confronted with a 'multi-objective' decision-making scenario. They are required to factor in cultural, environmental, economic or social factors rather than the economic factor. Therefore, the complexity of multi-objective decision-making has the potential of leading to governmental decisions which are essentially incompatible with the objectives of multilateralism. All in all, Indian scholarship acknowledges the rift between regional and universal multilateral interest, and hence questions the notion of Ruggie's 'indivisibility'.

Shifting the perspective towards reflectivist theorizing regarding multilateralism, there are at least two distinctive features – a specific historic trajectory and transformations and the existence of social forces that are linked dialectically. Reference authors are Cox and Rosenau: Cox's[64] 'historical dialectics' looks at multilateralism using both a historical perspective and a dialectical process. Cox[65] examines the creation of a 'new multilateralism' based upon social forces which transcend the boundaries of nation-states and encompasses global society. Rosenau[66] analyses multilateralism by considering both 'globalizing' and 'localizing' forces; for Rosenau, the nation-state and the authority it normally has are both under pressure from an 'imagined community', in the form of sub-national, supra-national or trans-national communities. For Rosenau, different levels of ethnic, religious and familial affiliations are all linked to multilateralism.

Indian reflectivist thinking is represented by Ramesh Thakur and Amitav Acharya. Newman, Thakur and Tirman[67] argue that multilateralism is a function of changes in environmental dynamics. Demands and power configurations are not static, but evolve over time; multilateral institutions (or norms) must adapt and cannot remain static. Acharya[68] argues that multilateralism is a function of norms rather than institutions, an argument in part based upon Kratochwil's works.[69] Changes which occur in the institutional dimensions of multilateralism can best be understood when considering normative shifts in multilateral practice. However, such shifts are spatially contingent. Acharya[70] argues that norms in multilateralism are likely to adapt, depending on the regional context. Acharya[71] builds his argument on the framework of norm localization to explain how foreign norms diffuse in regional and local contexts. He describes 'norm localization' as the active construction of locally applicable multilateral norms by local actors through discourse, framing, grafting and cultural selection of foreign ideas.[72] He elaborates that the resulting behaviour of the recipient can be understood more in terms of the former than the latter, although it can be fully understood in terms of both. Norm localization will lead to congruence between foreign and local beliefs as well as practices.

Summarizing the major ideas of Indian scholarship, the following arguments have been forwarded. First, multilateralism is not static; rather, it is embedded in dynamic institutions and rules, and a process of institutional and issue-area adaptation is hence expedient. Second, multilateralism is normative; occurring normative shifts can be analysed through processes of norm localization, essentially fusing local/regional norms with global ones. As the body of Indian theorizing constantly grows, there is an increased likelihood that Indian theorizing will eventually contribute to IR theorizing in general and to multilateralism theorizing in particular.

India and multilateralism: A future research agenda

Multilateralism takes place in various institutional settings, and (theoretically) analysing the different objectives, issue areas and regional or global scope ultimately necessitates an approach that allows incorporation of differences in state approach, normative orientations and political objectives. At the same time, such an approach should offer a cohesive perspective and a new analytical framework for assessing India's idiosyncratic position(s). The so-called 'cultural turn' in social sciences and the rise of constructivist scholarship in IR has opened new vistas for much more nuanced analyses of policies in Western and non-Western regions. Endogenous preference building highlighted by reflexivist scholarship allows comprehension of foreign policy decisions in a path-dependent manner, not least because of previous historical experiences which are deeply rooted in the collective memory of nations and their policymakers. An ideational perspective can provide more context-sensitivity and possibly avoid a Western-centric bias often inherent in mainstream IR analyses of non-Western regions. The following three approaches could prove a fertile ground for further practical and theoretical analyses of India's role in multilateralism.

First, addressing a possible Western-centric bias, Peter Katzenstein's 'analytic eclecticism'[73] is a response to what Katzenstein identified as a compartmentalization of knowledge that 'overlooks and questions causal mechanisms that do not fit comfortably' into existing paradigms, resulting in 'a degree of specialization that makes academic scholarship irrelevant to the concerns of a broader policy community'.[74] Rather than arguing within the boundaries provided by one theoretical perspective or research tradition alone, 'analytic eclecticism takes components of different research traditions and combines them to produce new analytical frameworks'.[75] Analytic eclecticism deals with the complexity of social phenomena and is an 'attack on incompleteness'.[76] However, it is more than just a 'theoretical synthesis of existing research traditions';[77] instead, the approach 'selectively adopts and reinterprets concepts, causal mechanisms, explanations and prescriptions from particular research traditions',[78] leading to 'novel frameworks' and enabling scholars 'to capture a more nuanced understanding of a complex world'.[79]

As a research framework 'analytic eclecticism' is particularly useful when concepts derived from Western experiences encounter historically and culturally different experiences such as those made in regions of the Global South.[80] Hence, Katzenstein's approach could serve a double purpose: it could incorporate India's historically based normative and ideational orientations (as exemplified by the NAM or the Panchsheel principles), while at the same time opening a venue for choosing specific elements of specific IR theories useful for analysing the behaviour of an emerging power in different multilateral settings.

Second, the significance of institutions for conflict resolution and policymaking in the international arena markedly increased with the end of the Cold War, exemplified by the emergence of a rapidly proliferating structure of global governance. Yet, to cite Barnett/Duvall, institutions are no 'antidotes to power'.[81] This was shown by the fact that states have increasingly used institutions in a strategic manner, for example to find better means of increasing their own power in certain fora, or to limit the influence of other states, for example the Great Powers. In this process, institutions have become devices for 'hedging',[82] 'soft balancing'[83] and arenas for negotiating issues such as membership, mandates, cooperative norms or decision-making procedures.[84] In other words: views associated with political realism have now entered institutions. The resultant uncertainties surrounding institutional politics might hence be analysed by what Kai He has termed 'institutional realism',[85] an approach which seems especially pertinent for a rising power like India which is in the process of partly reorienting her foreign policy outlook.

Third, theoretical approaches towards India's position in multilateralism could make use of (liberal) institutionalist approaches. The observable fragmentation of institutions impacts global governance as a whole.[86] A group of scholars highlight complementary effects of fragmentation, interpreting the latter as a model of social differentiation and a possible sign of institutional division of labour.[87] Other scholars see a conflictive nature in the realm of institution-building, with a possible institutional paralysis.[88] Related to this, the concepts of 'governance costs' and 'opportunity costs' could be used for evaluating the impact of some of the above-mentioned global and regional institutional arrangements on global governance per se,[89] highlighting India's distinctive role.

All things considered: Indian power and influence in global and regional multilateralism are on the rise. India has successfully introduced specific normative and ideational concepts into multilateralism, but preferred global over regional institutions. The analysis of India's future behaviour will thus necessitate focusing on select issue areas in India's dealings with global or regional institutions respectively. India's different approaches in her multilateral priorities eventually render difficult the application of a single (novel) theoretical approach and make a good case for approaches that transcend compartmentalization. Global multilateralism has clearly served India well in her ongoing quest to achieve great-power status, a major foreign policy objective still at large. Looking at the past seventy years, India has shown that she can judiciously and responsibly use her influence in multilateral institutions – a positive harbinger of things to come.

Notes

1   See Jawaharlal Nehru, 'Inter-Asian Relations,' *India Quarterly* 2, No. 4 (1946): 323–327.

2   Bharatiya Janata Party, *Election Manifesto* (2014). Available at http://bjpelectionmanifesto. com/pdf/manifesto2014.pdf, accessed on 10 June 2014.

3   V. S. Mani, 'An Indian Perspective on the Evolution of International Law on the Treshhold of the Third Millennium,' in *Asian Yearbook of International Law*, Volume 9, edited by B. S. Chimni, Masahiro Miyoshi and Surya Subedi, 31–77 (Martinus Nijhoff Publishers: 2000).

4   J. N. Dixit, 'India's Approach to Multilateralism,' in *United Nations: Multilateralism and International Security*, edited by C. Uday Bhaskar, K. Santhanam, Uttam K. Sinha and Tasneem Meenai (IDSA/Shipra, 2005)

5   B. S. Prakash, 'Strengthening and Restructuring Multilateral Institutions: A Perspective,' in *United Nations: Multilateralism and International Security*, edited by C. Uday Bhaskar, K. Santhanam, Uttam K. Sinha and Tasneem Meenai, 442–456 (IDSA/Shipra, 2005).

6   Rajendra K. Jain, 'From Idealism to Pragmatism: India and Asian Regional Integration,' *Japanese Journal of Political Science* 12 No. 2 (2011): 213–31, 226.

7   See Chapter 6, 'Non-Alignment and Beyond' by Harsh V. Pant and Julie M. Super, in this volume.

8   Manmohan Singh, 'Prime Minister's Address,' 15th Non-Aligned Movement Summit. *Sharm El-Sheikh* (15 July 2009, Egypt). Available at http://www.satp.org/satporgtp/ countries/india/document/papers/primeministersaddress_alignedmovement_ summitEgypt.htm, accessed on 4 October 2013.

9   David Malone, *Does the Elephant Dance? Contemporary Indian Foreign Policy*, 252 (New Delhi: Oxford University Press, 2011).

10 Arjun Appadorai, 'Non-Alignment: Some Important Issues,' *International Studies* 20, No. 1 and 2 (1981): 3–11.

11 Cited in Sumit Ganguly and Manjeet S. Pardesi, 'Explaining Sixty Years of India's Foreign Policy,' *India Review* 8, No. 1 (2009): 4–19, here 11.

12 *Economic Times*, 'Indo-US Ties Not at the Cost of Other Nations,' September 2006.

Available at http://economictimes.indiatimes.com/news/politics-and-nation/indo-us-ties-not-at-the-cost-of-other-nations/articleshow/1983638.cms, accessed on 10 December 2012. Chandra Prakash Bhambhri, 'Non-Alignment in the Changing Context of Twenty-First Century,' *India Quarterly* 62, No. 3 (2006): 95–109.

13 *The Hindu*, 'The Margarita Mirror,' 13 September 2016. Available at http://www.thehindu.com/opinion/op-ed/The-Margarita-mirror/article14634932.ece, accessed on 10 January 2017.

14 See UN, 'UN Peacekeeping Fact Sheet' (2017). Available at http://www.un.org/en/peacekeeping/resources/statistics/factsheet.shtml, accessed on 20 May 2017.

15 UN, 'India: Troop and Police Contributors' (United Nations Peacekeeping: 2017). Available at http://www.un.org/en/peacekeeping/resources/statistics/contributors.shtml, accessed on 5 May 2017.

16 Kathryn Ann Hochstetler, 'The G-77, BASIC, and Global Climate Governance: A New Era in Multilateral Environmental Negotiations,' *Revista Brasileira De Politica Internacional* 55 (2012): 53–69.

17 Per Meilstrup, 'The Runaway Summit: The Background Story of the Danish Presidency of COP15, the UN Climate Change Conference,' *Danish Foreign Policy Yearbook 2010*, 113–135 (Copenhagen: Danish Institute for International Studies, 2010).

18 Sandeep Sengupta, 'Defending "Differentiation" India's Foreign Policy on Climate Change from Rio to Copenhagen,' in *India's Foreign Policy: A Reader*, edited by Kanti Bajpai and Harsh V. Pant, 389–414 (Oxford: Oxford University Press, 2013).

19 *Time*, 'Why No Country Matters More Than India at the Paris Climate Talks,' 11 December 2015. Available at http://time.com/4144843/india-paris-climate-change, accessed on 28 January 2016.

20 Malone, *Does the Elephant Dance? Contemporary Indian Foreign Policy*, p. 260.

21 See Chapter 9, 'India and the Responsibility to Protect' by Ian Hall, in this volume.

22 Yeshi Choedon, 'India and the Current Concerns of UN Peacekeeping: Issues and Prospects,' *India Quarterly* 63, No. 2 (2007): 150–184.

23 Harsh Pant, *Indian Foreign Policy – An Overview*, 226 (New Delhi: Orient BlackSwan, 2016).

24 Amrita Narlikar, 'India and the World Trade Organization,' in *India's Foreign Policy: A Reader*, edited by Kanti Bajpai and Harsh V. Pant, 415–437 (Oxford: Oxford University Press, 2013).

25 Amrita Narlikar, 'Peculiar Chauvinism or Strategic Calculation? Explaining the Negotiating Strategy of a Rising India,' *International Affairs* 82, No. 1 (2006): 59–76, 75.

26 Narlikar, 'India and the World Trade Organization', 433.

27 See BRICS Summit Delhi Declaration (2012). Available at https://www.brics2017.org/English/AboutBRICS/DOPS/201701/t20170114_1117.html, accessed on 10 October 2015.

28 Chris Alden and Marco Antonio Vieira, 'The New Diplomacy of the South: South Africa, Brazil, India and Trilateralism,' *Third World Quarterly* 26 No. 7 (2005): 1077–1095, 1089.

29 Poorvi Chitalkar and David M. Malone, 'India and Global Governance,' in *The Oxford*

Handbook of Indian Foreign Policy, edited by David M. Malone, C. Raja Mohan and Srinath Raghavan, 581–595, 591 (New Delhi: Oxford University Press, 2015)

30 Arndt Michael, *India's Foreign Policy and Regional Multilateralism*, 48–56 (Basingstoke: Palgrave Macmillan, 2013).

31 Sukh D. Muni and Anuradha Muni, *Regional Co-operation in South Asia* (New Delhi: National Publishing House, 1984).

32 See Lawrence Sáez, *The South Asian Association for Regional Cooperation (SAARC): An Emerging Collaboration Architecture*, 8–29 (Abingdon, Oxon: Routledge, 2012).

33 Arndt Michael, 'Sovereignty vs. Security: SAARC and Its Role in the Regional Security Architecture in South Asia,' *Harvard Asia Quarterly* 15, No. 2 (2013): 37–45.

34 See Karl W. Deutsch, et. al., *Political Economy in the North Atlantic Area: International Organisation in the Light of Historical Experience* (Princeton, 1957).

35 Michael, *India's Foreign Policy and Regional Multilateralism*, 1.

36 Ankit Panda, 'Modi Reaches Out to SAARC Leaders Ahead of Swearing-In as Prime Minister,' *The Diplomat*, 22 May 2014. Available at http://thediplomat.com/2014/05/modi-reaches-out-to-saarc-leaders-ahead-of-swearing-in-as-prime-minister, accessed on 24 May 2014.

37 Michael, *India's Foreign Policy and Regional Multilateralism*, 1–2.

38 *Hindustan Times*, 'All You Need to Know About BIMSTEC, the Huddle of Bay of Bengal Nations,' 14 October 2016. Available at http://www.hindustantimes.com/india-news/all-you-need-to-know-about-bimstec-the-huddle-of-bay-of-bengal-nations/story-vaZIQ2o6Mwh5Yj3Ki1rzsI.html, accessed on 10 December 2016.

39 Michael, *India's Foreign Policy and Regional Multilateralism*.

40 Arndt Michael, 'Competing Regionalism in South Asia and Neighbouring Regions under Narendra Modi: New Leadership, Old Problems,' *Stosunki Międzynarodowe – International Relations* 51, No. 4 (2015): 179–197.

41 See Navnita Chadha Behera, 'Re-Imagining IR in India,' *International Relations of the Asia Pacific* 7, No. 3 (2007): 341–368; Siddharth Mallavarapu, 'Development of International Relations Theory in India: Traditions, Contemporary Perspectives and Trajectories,' *International Studies* 46, Nos 1 and 2 (2009):165–183.

42 Robert O Keohane, 'Multilateralism: An Agenda for Research,' *International Journal* 45, No. 4 (1990): 731–764.

43 James A. Caporaso, 'International Relations Theory and Multilateralism: The Search for Foundations,' *International Organization* 46, No. 3 (1992): 599–632.

44 John Gerard Ruggie, 'Multilateralism: The Anatomy of an Institution,' in *Multilateralism Matters: The Theory and Praxis of an Institutional Form*, edited by John Gerard Ruggie, 3–36 (Columbia University Press, 1993).

45 Robert W. Cox, 'Multilateralism and World Order,' in *Approaches to World Order*, edited by Robert W. Cox and Timothy Sinclair, 494–523 (Cambridge: 1996).

46 James N. Rosenau, 'The Person, the Household, the Community and the Globe: Notes for a Theory of Multilateralism in a Turbulent World,' in *The New Realism: Perspectives*

on *Multilateralism and World Order*, edited by Robert W. Cox (St. Martin's Press/United Nations University Press, 1997).

47 Robert O Keohane, 'International Institutions: Two Approaches,' *International Studies Quarterly* 32 No. 4 (1988): 379–396. Robert O. Keohane, 'The Contingent Legitimacy of Multilateralism,' GARNET Working Paper No. 9 (2000).

48 John Gerard Ruggie, 'Multilateralism: The Anatomy of an Institution,' in *Multilateralism Matters: The Theory and Praxis of an Institutional Form*, edited by John Gerard Ruggie, 3–36 (Columbia University Press, 1993).

49 See Deepak Nayyar (ed.), *Governing Globalization* (Oxford: Oxford University Press, 2002).

50 Shashi Tharoor, 'Why America Still Needs the United Nations,' *Foreign Affairs* (2003). Available at http://www.foreignaffairs.com/articles/59184/shashi-tharoor/why-america-still-needs-the-united-nations, accessed 4 on April 2010.

51 J. N. Dixit, 'India's Approach to Multilateralism,' in *United Nations: Multilateralism and International Security*, edited by C. Uday Bhaskar, K. Santhanam, Uttam K. Sinha and Tasneem Meenai (IDSA: Shipra, 2005).

52 Jose Manuel Barroso, 'Asian Giants Can Imbibe Europe's Values,' *Times of India*, 24 January 2010. Available at http://timesofindia.indiatimes.com/home/sunday-times/all-that-matters/Asian-giants-can-imbibe-Europes-values/articleshow/5493466.cms, accessed on 30 September 2016.

53 A. J. R. Groom, 'Multilateralism as a Way of Life in Europe,' in *Multilateralism under Challenge? Power, International Order and Structural Change*, edited by Edward Newman, Ramesh Thakur and John Tirman (United Nations University Press, 2009).

54 Simon Zadek, 'Collaborative Governance: The New Multilateralism for the 21st Century,' (2007). Available at http://www.zadek.net/collaborative-governance, accessed on 4 April 2016.

55 L. Alan Winters, 'Regionalism versus Multilateralism,' Policy Research Working Paper No. 1687 (Washington, DC: World Bank, 1996).

56 Emanuel Ornelas, 'Feasible Multilateralism and the Effects of Regionalism,' 25 April 2005. Available at https://ssrn.com/abstract=385704, accessed on 28 March 2017.

57 B. S. Prakash, 'Strengthening and Restructuring Multilateral Institutions: A Perspective,' in *United Nations: Multilateralism and International Security*, edited by C. Uday Bhaskar, K. Santhanam, Uttam K. Sinha and Tasneem Meenai, 442–456 (IDSA: Shipra, 2005).

58 Jagdish Bhagwati, 'Regionalism Versus Multilateralism,' *The World Economy* 15, No. 15 (1992): 535–556. Jagdish Bhagwati, 'Preferential Trading Areas and Multilateralism: Strategies, Friends or Foes?' in *The Economics of Preferential Trade Agreements*, edited by Jagdish Bhagwati (AEI Press, 1996).

59 Nipun Agarwal, 'Why Multilateralism Can't Exist: Is the WTO Mandate Wrong?' (2007). Available at http://papers.ssrn.com/sol3/papers.cfm?abstract_id=957765, accessed on 28 July 2016.

60 Sayantan Gupta, 'Changing Faces of International Trade: Multilateralism to Regionalism,' *Journal of International Commercial Law and Technology* 3, No. 4 (2009): 260–273.

61 Manoj Pant and Amit Sadhukaran, 'Does Regionalism Hinder Multilateralism: A Case Study of India,' Discussion Paper 09-03 (New Delhi: Centre for International Trade and Development, SIS, JNU, 2008).

62 Soamiely Andriamananjara, *On the Relationship Between Preferential Trade Agreements and the Multilateral Trading System* (Washington D.C.: US International Trade Commission, 2003).

63 Philippe Aghion, Pol Antràs and Elhanan Helpman, 'Negotiating Free Trade,' NBER Working Paper 10721 (Cambridge: National Bureau of Economic Research, 2004).

64 Robert W. Cox, 'Multilateralism and World Order,' in *Approaches to World Order*, edited by Robert W. Cox and Timothy Sinclair, 494–523 (Cambridge, 1996).

65 Robert W. Cox (ed.), *The New Realism: Perspectives on Multilateralism and World Order* (St. Martin's Press/United Nations University Press, 1997).

66 James N. Rosenau, 'The Person, the Household, the Community and the Globe: Notes for a Theory of Multilateralism in a Turbulent World,' in *The New Realism: Perspectives on Multilateralism and World Order*, edited by Robert W. Cox (St. Martin's Press/United Nations University Press, 1997).

67 Edward Newman, Ramesh Thakur and John Tirman (eds), *Multilateralism Under Challenge? Power, International Order and Structural Change*, Chapters: Introduction, 1–18; Conclusion, 531–540 (United Nations University Press, 2009). Available at https://collections.unu.edu/eserv/UNU:2470/pdf9280811290.pdf, accessed on 18 October 2016.

68 Amitav Acharya, 'Multilateralism, Sovereignty and Normative Change in World Politics,' in *Multilateralism Under Challenge?*, edited by Ramesh Thakur et al., 95–118 (United Nations University Press, 2009).

69 Friedrich Kratochwil, 'Norms Versus Numbers: Multilateralism and the Rationalist and Reflexivist Approaches to Institutions,' in *Multilateralism Matters: The Theory and Praxis of an Institutional Form*, edited by John Gerard Ruggie, 443–474 (Columbia University Press, 1993).

70 Amitav Acharya, 'Multilateralism, Sovereignty and Normative Change in World Politics,' in *Multilateralism Under Challenge?* 95–118.

71 Amitav Acharya, 'How Ideas Spread: Whose Norms Matter? Norm Localization and Institutional Change in Asian Regionalism,' *International Organisation* 58, No. 2 (2004): 239–275.

72 See for an application on regional multilateralism especially Michael, *India's Foreign Policy and Regional Multilateralism*, 7–16.

73 Peter Katzenstein, 'Regionalism Reconsidered,' *Journal of East Asian Studies* 7 (2007): 395–412; Peter Katzenstein and Rudra Sil, 'Eclectic Theorizing in the Study and Practice of International Relations,' in *The Oxford Handbook of International Relations*, edited by Christian Reus-Smit and Duncan Snidal, 109–130 (Oxford: Oxford University Press, 2008).

74 Katzenstein, 'Regionalism Reconsidered', 397.

75 Ibid.

76 Ibid.

77 Ibid., 398.

78 Ibid.

79 Ibid.

80 Matthias Basedau and Patrick Köllner, 'Area Studies, Comparative Area Studies, and the Study of Politics: Context, Substance, and Methodological Challenges,' *Zeitschrift für Vergleichende Politikwissenschaft* 1, No. 1 (2007): 105–124. Mikko Huotari and Jürgen Rüland, 'Context, Concepts and Comparison in Southeast Asian Studies – Introduction to the Special Issue,' *Pacific Affairs* 87, No. 3 (2014): 415–440.

81 Michael Barnett and Raymond Duvall, 'Power in International Politics,' *International Organization* 59, No. 1 (2005): 39–77, 40.

82 Evelyn Goh, 'Understanding Hedging in Asia-Pacific Security,' *PacNet* 43 (31 August 2006). Available at http://www.stratad.net/downloads/PacNet%2043.pdf, accessed on 6 February 2011. Cheng-Chwee Kuik, 'The Essence of Hedging: Malaysia and Singapore's Response to a Rising China,' *Contemporary Southeast Asia* 30, No. 2 (2008): 159–185.

83 Robert A. Pape, 'Soft Balancing against the United States,' *International Security* 30, No. 1 (2005): 7–45.

84 Jürgen Rüland' 'The Rise of "Diminished Multilateralism": East Asian and European Forum Shopping in Global Governance,' *Asia Europe Journal* 9, Nos 2–4 (2012): 255–270.

85 Kai He, 'Does ASEAN Matter? International Relations Theories, Institutional Realism, and ASEAN,' *Asian Security* 2, No. 3 (2006): 189–214. Kai He and Huiyun Feng, 'If Not Soft Balancing, Then What? Reconsidering Soft Balancing and U.S. Policy toward China,' *Security Studies* 17, No. 2 (2008): 363–395.

86 Astrid Carrapatoso and Mareike Well, 'REDD+ Finance: Policy Making in the Context of Fragmented Institutions,' *Climate Policy* (August 2016). DOI:10.1080/14693062.20 16.1202096, accessed on 10 January 2017.

87 Michael Zürn and Benjamin Faude, 'On Fragmentation, Differentiation, and Coordination,' *Global Environmental Politics* 13, No. 3 (2013): 119–130. Thomas Gehring and Benjamin Faude, 'A Theory of Emerging Order Within Institutional Complexes: How Composition among Regulatory International Institutions Leads to Institutional Adaptation and Division of Labor,' *Review of International Organizations* 9 (2014): 471–498.

88 Frank Biermann, Philipp Pattberg, Harro Van Asselt and Fariborz Zelli, 'The Fragmentation of Global Governance Architectures: A Framework of Analysis,' *Global Environmental Politics* 9, No. 4 (2009): 14–40.

89 David A. Lake, 'Global Governance: A Relational Contracting Approach,' in *Globalization and Governance*, edited by Jeffrey A. Hart and Aseem Prakash, 31–53 (London and New York: Routledge, 1999).

9

India and the Responsibility to Protect

Ian Hall

India's response to the emergence and evolution of the doctrine of the Responsibility to Protect (R2P) – as well as its invocation in several recent crises – has generated a significant number of academic and policy-oriented studies.[1] It has attracted the attention of scholars interested in the effects the so-called 'rising powers' might be having on the international system. It has piqued the interest of think tank analysts and serious journalists concerned with assessing New Delhi's approach to foreign policy, especially when it comes to the management of key bilateral relationships and the multilateral processes of global governance. And it has also become a focus for researchers analysing how foreign policy is made in India – on its core players, their beliefs and preferences, the institutional contexts in which they operate, and the pressures they experience from parliamentarians, interest groups, electoral politics, the military, or the media, amongst others.

India's complex relationship with R2P is, in other words, not simply interesting in itself, but also important in terms of what this emerging body of research tells us about India's contemporary international relations in general, and its changing foreign policymaking processes in particular. Moreover the work this topic has so far prompted provides a useful snapshot of the present state of scholarship on Indian foreign policy – a field often criticized as theoretically underdeveloped by global standards.[2]

All the scholarship discussed in this chapter observes that the majority of India's foreign policymaking elite remains sceptical about key aspects of R2P and that a minority is straightforwardly hostile to some elements. They disagree, however, when it comes to explaining New Delhi's reluctance to embrace R2P, especially its so-called 'third pillar', which calls for international intervention in cases where states are manifestly failing to protect their populations. Some point to ideational factors, to the beliefs held by the policymaking elite, assuming that these drive Indian foreign policy preferences. Others point to domestic political imperatives, especially electoral politics and the challenges of managing ruling coalitions, as shaping India's approach to R2P. And still others argue that concerns over India's own handling of its internal security challenges underpin official scepticism about the doctrine. But whatever the reasons behind India's foreign policymaking elite remaining wary and critical of R2P, all agree that on this doctrine, at least, India's position has not shifted much, if at all, despite major changes in other areas over the past twenty years.[3]

This chapter explores each of the different explanations for this lack of change in turn, focusing not just on what they tell us about India's stance on R2P, but also on what they suggest about the ways in which foreign policy is made in India. That analysis is prefaced – for context – with a brief discussion of the origins and content of the R2P doctrine. The second section outlines the evolution of India's positions on human rights and humanitarian intervention, in theory and practice, in international relations, as well as its contemporary stance. The third section explores the explanations advanced by various scholars and policy analysts for India's official attitudes to R2P prior to and during the 2005 World Summit at which it was affirmed by the United Nations General Assembly (UNGA) and especially afterwards, when R2P was invoked during the Libyan and Syrian crises, in particular. It observes that those crises revealed not just divisions within the Indian elite about R2P itself, but also weaknesses in the institutions and processes of foreign policymaking that will have to be addressed if India is to be a 'leading power'.[4] The chapter concludes by charting some ways forward for the study of India and R2P that take the progress made elsewhere in the study of Indian foreign policy seriously.

The responsibility to protect

The doctrine of R2P emerged amidst the arguments that followed a series of military interventions in civil conflicts during the course of the 1990s and early 2000s.[5] It was a response both to a series of mass atrocities – in Somalia, the former Yugoslavia, Rwanda, the Democratic Republic of Congo, Sudan and elsewhere – and to substantive disagreement about what ought to be done in response by the international community. In the 1990s, some states had sought to stretch the bounds of peacekeeping, a practice established in the early 1960s, and normally mandated by the UN Security Council (UNSC), to encompass something akin to 'peace enforcement', in which international forces tried to make peace by disarming local combatants, rather than simply ensuring peace agreements were kept.[6] Others – notably in Europe – pushed harder, arguing for what, in the midst of the Kosovo crisis of 1998–09, the then British Prime Minister Tony Blair called a 'doctrine of humanitarian community' that justified military intervention in civil conflicts even without UNSC authorization.[7] This kind of thinking had led to UNSC-mandated interventions in Somalia (beginning in 1992), Bosnia (also beginning in 1992), East Timor (in 1999) and Sierra Leone (in 2000), as well as the unsanctioned NATO intervention in Kosovo.[8]

R2P was advanced as a means of overcoming divisions between Western states (and others, notably in Africa) and many non-Western states over the legitimacy and legality of external intervention in civil conflicts. It was originally formulated by the International Commission on Intervention and State Sovereignty (ICISS), a body created by the Canadian government in response to a plea from the then UN Secretary-General Kofi Annan in the wake of NATO's military action in Kosovo. The ICISS convened five meetings – in Ottawa, Maputo, New Delhi, Wakefield (also in Canada) and Geneva – over the course of a year between late 2000 and late 2001, chaired by the former Australian Foreign Minister, Gareth Evans, and the Algerian diplomat Mohamed Sahnoun, with 10 further Commissioners, including Ramesh Thakur, originally from India.[9]

The ICISS report argued that 'sovereign states have a responsibility to protect their own citizens from avoidable catastrophe – from mass murder and rape, from starvation – but that when they are unwilling or unable to do so, that responsibility must be borne by the broader community of states'.[10] The responsibility to protect, it argued, consisted of the responsibility to prevent conflicts by addressing their causes; to react to 'compelling human need' in a timely fashion when conflict occurred; and to rebuild, 'particularly after military intervention', to ensure that conflict did not break out again.[11] It derived its 'principles for military intervention' from both the great post-war humanitarian and human rights conventions – which implied that the international community had an obligation to respond to large-scale loss of life or ethnic-cleansing – and from Western just war theory, which held that intervening states should act with the right intention (that is, sincerely), use force as a last resort, apply proportional means and act only when there is a reasonable prospect of success. Crucially, the report also insisted – using the language of just war theory – that the 'right authority' that ought to decide whether military intervention was necessary was the UNSC, or, if the UNSC manifestly failed in its obligation to act, the UNGA under the so-called 'Uniting for Peace' process used during the Korean war, or regional organizations, which must nevertheless seek UNSC authorization after an initial response.[12] In this way, the ICISS report simultaneously opened up the possibility of further 'humanitarian interventions' while seeking to bring them fully under the UN's auspices.

This conception of R2P did not meet with immediate or universal approval, partly because its language was regarded by some, especially in the non-Western world, as too close to that of Western enthusiasts for humanitarian intervention, and partly because of unforeseen and somewhat inhospitable circumstances – the ICISS report was published, it must be noted, in the immediate aftermath of the terrorist attacks of 11 September 2001.[13] The US-led action in Iraq in 2003, however, provided a further catalyst for change, with the UN Secretary General convening a High-Level Panel on Threats, Challenges and Change (HLP), which included among its members Gareth Evans, earlier co-chair of the ICISS. The Panel's report (*A More Secure World*, 2004) brought R2P back onto the UN's agenda.[14] It made the argument that R2P was an 'emerging norm' and reaffirmed the principle that the UNSC, acting under Chapter VII of the UN Charter, is the proper authority to mandate military interventions 'as a last resort' if states were unwilling or unable to protect their populations from harm.[15]

With the backing of Kofi Annan, the HLP's thinking on R2P helped frame the discussion about sovereignty, human rights and intervention at the 2005 World Summit meeting, convened to debate UN reform, the millennium development goals, terrorism and a number of other issues. Ultimately, the World Summit Outcome Document endorsed R2P, but not after considerable negotiation and modification to what had been proposed by the ICISS and HLP. As Bellamy notes, the Permanent Five (P5) on the UNSC – China, France, Russia, the UK and the US – were divided among themselves. China and Russia took conservative views, arguing that the UNSC was already sufficiently empowered by the Charter and against the idea that R2P might be used as a means to circumvent a P5 veto. By contrast, France and the UK argued that interventions not authorized by the UNSC because of a P5 veto ought to be permitted in some circumstances. The US, for its part, was concerned about the prescriptiveness of the ICISS and HLPs' conceptualizations of R2P, which they feared might 'constrain', as Bellamy puts it, 'its right to decide when and where to use force'.[16]

In the end, the World Summit endorsed a watered-down version of R2P with what should be seen as significant concessions to the conservatives on the

UNSC and outside it. Paragraphs 138 and 139 of the Outcome Document summarized the compromise. The first affirmed that '[e]ach individual state has the responsibility to protect its populations from genocide, war crimes, ethnic cleansing, and crime against humanity', which involves a responsibility to prevent not just those crimes, but also their incitement. It noted that the UN should 'encourage and help states to exercise its responsibility' and required it to generate capacity to provide an 'early warning capability' to alert states and others to the possibility that such crimes might occur.[17] The second paragraph affirmed that the 'international community' also had a responsibility 'to use appropriate diplomatic, humanitarian and other peaceful means, in accordance with Chapters VI and VIII of the Charter, to help protect populations'. But it also noted that a willingness 'to take collective action, in a timely and decisive manner, through the Security Council...on a case-by-case basis and in cooperation with relevant regional organizations...should peaceful means be inadequate' and states were 'manifestly' failing to protect their populations. And it noted that the international community was committed to help 'states build capacity to protect their populations' and to assist states 'under stress before crises and conflicts break out'.[18]

As I will discuss in more detail below, India was very reluctant to endorse even this water-down concept of R2P, and its diplomats played a prominent role in seeking to have reference to it removed from the final Outcome Document. Moreover, in the aftermath of the World Summit, India's concerns were repeatedly challenged as activists and diplomats pushed the R2P agenda forward.

This work culminated in UN Secretary-General Ban Ki-moon's *Implementing the Responsibility to Protect* report, published in mid-January 2009. That document aimed to clarify the concept of R2P and to set out a means of realizing it in practice. It divided R2P into three pillars – the first covering state responsibilities, the second on the international community's responsibilities concerning capacity building, and the third on the proper response of the international community in the event that states were unable or unwilling to fulfil their responsibility to protect. It reemphasized the notion – designed to reassure conservative critics – that 'the responsibility to protect is an ally of sovereignty, not an adversary' and that it refers only to the 'four crimes and violations: genocide, war crimes, ethnic cleansing, and crimes against humanity'.[19] It also reemphasized that pillar-three responses could include peaceful interventions (covered by Chapter VI of the Charter) and regional institutional ones (covered by Chapter VIII), alongside or instead of Chapter VII's UNSC-mandated military interventions.[20]

Despite these efforts at clarification, however, the implementation of R2P prior to the Libyan crisis of 2011 remained patchy and arguably inconsistent. It played no role in UN responses to the humanitarian crisis generated at the close of the Sri Lankan civil war in 2009, for example.[21] The Libyan and, to a lesser extent, Côte d'Ivoire crises, however, focused attention on R2P in a way that none had done prior to 2011 and led, in the judgement of Bellamy, to a significant shift towards framing comparable humanitarian challenges in terms of R2P as the 'norm' rather than as an exception.[22] Resolutions 1970 and 1973 on Libya and 1975 on Côte d'Ivoire used R2P language to lay out the UNSC's responses to the conduct of Muammar Gaddafi's government and Laurent Gbagbo's use of force against civilians supportive of his political opponents. UNSCR 1973 was particularly significant because it not merely imposed a no-fly zone but also authorized the use of 'all necessary measures' to protect civilians under Chapter VII.

That provision – and indeed the whole resolution – was and continues to be contentious. When European militaries, supported by US forces, began to bomb regime targets in Libya in response, Russia, in particular, began to argue that UNSCR 1973 was being misinterpreted and that the UNSC had not in fact authorized the use of force.[23] India, as we shall see, also joined in the chorus of criticism. Conservative concern with the supposed misuse of R2P – together with Russian interests – helped to stymie an R2P-framed response to the Syrian civil war, which broke out in earnest in mid-2011.[24] As a consequence, R2P remains one of the more controversial and contested apparent 'norms' in international relations – much debated, but seemingly without a clear sense of how to reconcile liberal enthusiasm for the principle and conservative scepticism.

India, human rights and intervention: Independence to the World Summit

In the late 1940s and through the 1950s, postcolonial India was a strong advocate of the notion of human rights and a supporter of efforts to mitigate or eliminate egregious abuses of those rights.[25] Indian diplomats played significant roles on the UN's Human Rights Commission (HRC) that produced the Universal Declaration of Human Rights (1948) and pioneered attempts to realize those rights. Hansa Mehta, the Gujarati diplomat who served on the HRC, even at one point advocated that the UNSC be empowered to investigate human rights abuses and 'enforce redress'.[26] She also chaired the HRC's Working Group on Implementation, which was tasked with laying out the means by which rights could be realized and protected, and which ultimately recommended the creation of a standing UN committee to investigate abuses and an International Court, backed by the UNGA, in which cases could be heard against individuals, groups and states.[27]

At the same time, India pushed hard for the UN to intervene diplomatically in South Africa's internal affairs to dismantle the institutionalized racism of the *apartheid* system. This campaign began with Mohandas Gandhi urging the leader of India's United Nations delegation, Jawaharlal Nehru's sister Vijaya Laksmi Pandit, to pay attention to the plight of the people of Indian origin in South Africa – a long-standing concern of Gandhi's.[28] Pandit led a long debate in the UNGA on the issue during its first session and secured Resolution 44(I) calling on South Africa to abide by its 'international obligations' on the treatment of Indians.[29] The energetic and mercurial activist-turned-ambassador and long-time Nehru confidante, V. K. Krishna Menon, continued this effort through the mid-1950s, speaking in the UNGA every year that he was India's Permanent Representative on the need for international scrutiny and action on South Africa's racist laws.[30] His actions did not merely anger the South African – they generated significant and long-running arguments among both scholars and diplomats about the limits of sovereignty and the international community's rights (or otherwise) to debate, criticize or even intervene in the internal affairs of states that had laws inconsistent with international rules, norms or expectations.[31]

At the same time, however, India became markedly more defensive about external scrutiny, criticism or interference in its own internal affairs, partly because of the bruising experience of the UN's handling of the Kashmir crisis and its aftermath.[32] It embraced a statist and conservative understanding of international relations, most obviously in the so-called 'Five Principles of Peaceful Coexistence' embedded in the 1954 Treaty recognizing China's annexation of Tibet – principles that affirmed mutual respect for territorial integrity and sovereignty, non-aggression and non-interference, sovereign equality, and the desire for peaceful co-existence. Nehru and his diplomats, in particular Krishna Menon, grew increasingly critical of Western interventions, especially the disastrous Anglo-French initiative to seize the Suez Canal in Egypt in 1956, though more reticent when it came to Soviet behaviour, such as its military action in Hungary the same year.[33] Moreover, fear of foreign interference, especially by the United States, began to permeate the Indian political and bureaucratic establishment as the Cold War wore on.[34] Under

Indira Gandhi, Nehru's daughter, who governed for most of the period between 1966 and 1984, preserving and extending independence of action – sometimes conceived as 'strategic autonomy' – was elevated to become the highest foreign policy priority.[35]

At the same time, India's own behaviour generated its own challenges. Internally, it was beset by a series of separatist and anti-government insurgencies: in Nagaland, in the North-East after 1954, in Mizoram from the mid-1960s, in Punjab during the 1970s and 1980s, in Kashmir in the 1990s, to cite just a few cases. India's stretched, often poorly equipped police forces sometimes struggled to cope; the military – also stretched and often badly equipped – was periodically deployed in support of the civil power and at times acted heavy-handedly. Local and international activists have long complained that the security forces have abused the human rights of insurgents and civilians alike, engaging in extra-judicial killing, torture, rape, depravation of liberty, and so on. In the 1990s, alleged human rights abuses in Kashmir indeed became a particular focus of American diplomacy towards India.[36]

Just as India's behaviour at home raised questions about its professed commitments to human rights, so its foreign policy raised questions about its commitments to non-intervention and non-interference. Under Indira Gandhi and then her son, Rajiv Gandhi, India followed – not always wholly consistently – a kind of South Asian Monroe Doctrine that aimed to shut the superpowers out of the region and assert India's dominant position.[37] In 1971, India intervened in what was then East Pakistan to end a civil conflict that was sending hundreds of thousands of refugees across the border, effectively splitting Pakistan in half and helping to create the independent state of Bangladesh. While driven in large part by self-interest and a degree of opportunism, some have interpreted India's action as an early humanitarian intervention.[38] Moreover, as Sumit Ganguly has rightly noted, India was also supportive of similar interventions, notably that of Vietnam in Khmer-Rouge ruled Cambodia in 1978–79.[39] And India also repeatedly involved itself in the internal affairs of its neighbours – deploying peacekeepers in Sri Lanka in 1987 and then becoming mired in that country's civil war, as well as sending troops to the Maldives in 1988 to foil a coup d'état.[40]

Despite these forays into regional interventionism, however, India was deeply concerned by Western humanitarian interventions of the 1990s, suspicious of the motives that drove them and (more quietly) disturbed by the military power on display. Along with China and much of the Non-Aligned Movement, India did support the deployment of a multinational force to Somalia in 1992 as authorized under Chapter VII, but, as Kudrat Virk has argued, did so only because it assessed that there was no government to give consent.[41] It also provided troops for the UN mission to Sierra Leone in 1999.[42] But by that time, influential parts of official India had come to the view that acts like the NATO bombing of Serbia over Kosovo marked a 'return to anarchy', where might is right', as India's then-Permanent Representative to the UN put it.[43] At the same time, academic critics – notably the veteran scholar M. S. Rajan at Jawaharlal Nehru University (JNU) – denounced these kinds of Western actions as hypocritical and disingenuous, an egregious form of neocolonial paternalism.[44] Similarly, two more scholars from JNU concluded that Western intervention in Bosnia-Herzegovina had been driven not by humanitarian concern, but by the 'national interests of the intervening powers'.[45]

India's foreign policy establishment was equally sceptical about R2P. India struck an uncompromising stance at the 2005 World Summit, its Permanent Representative, Nirupam Sen, denouncing R2P's legal basis and its intent, which he believed was to facilitate greater Western interference in the affairs of others, and even the name itself.[46] 'Military humanism', Sen declared, 'was unacceptable.'[47] At the last minute, Sen even attempted to have the section on R2P struck from the Outcome Document.

Sen's successor, Hardeep Singh Puri, was a little more sympathetic, recognizing during the debate at the UN over the *Implementing the Responsibility to Protect* report that the World Summit had given R2P a 'cautious go ahead' but urging that it should never be used to 'provide a pretext for humanitarian intervention or unilateral action'.[48] India's position, he argued, was clear: avoiding the 'four mass atrocities' was best done by 'strengthening the capacity and ability of States through various means so that they can effectively fulfil their human rights obligations rather than devising a Secretariat driven mechanism without a focus on the promotion and protection of human rights and without the involvement of States'.[49] Puri was content, in other words, with pillars one and two, but not at all with the third.

India remained in this sceptical position when it took up a non-permanent seat on the UNSC on 1 January 2011 – the first time it had occupied a seat since 1984–85 and thus it was a significant moment for 'rising' India.[50] It faced difficult decisions concerning R2P almost at once. In February 2011, Libyans rose up against Muammar Gaddafi, and civil war soon followed. India's immediate concern was the fate of 18,000 or so Indian citizens working in Libya and the Ministry of External Affairs (MEA) began the difficult process of making arrangements for an evacuation. At the end of the month, the growing conflict was referred to the UNSC. On 26 February, UNSCR 1970 was passed. The Resolution reminded the Libyan government of its responsibility to protect its people, referred the regime's conduct to the International Criminal Court's (ICC) prosecutor, and imposed both an arms embargo and specific sanctions on Gaddafi's family and associates.[51] Somewhat reluctantly, expressing concerns that the ICC referral might push Gaddafi into a corner and lead to reprisals against its citizens and others, India voted for the resolution.[52]

India balked, however, when it came to the follow-up resolution in UNSCR 1973, which authorized European-led military action against the Libyan government. In the Security Council, Puri argued that India could not support the resolution on the grounds that the facts of the matter were unclear and that military action would likely have unintended consequences, probably escalating the violence.[53] A few days later, External Affairs Minister S. M. Krishna expressed his 'regret' over the bombing authorized by UNSCR 1973 and Indian Prime Minister Manmohan Singh issued a statement to call for peoples in the region to make their own decisions 'free from outside interference'.[54] Singh reiterated this message in his address to the UNGA in September 2011, arguing that 'actions taken under the authority of the United Nations must respect the unity, territorial integrity, sovereignty and independence of individual states'.[55]

Thereafter, India's official position on R2P with reference to both Libya and then Syria, as that civil war escalated through 2011 and beyond, was generally unsympathetic. In October 2011, it abstained in the vote on a resolution – vetoed by China and Russia – that framed the Syrian crisis in terms of R2P. Puri argued that India agreed with the underlying principles of R2P, but maintained that states also have a responsibility to 'protect their citizens from armed groups and militias'.[56]Although India indicated its support for a second draft resolution, championed by the Arab League, in early February 2012, Puri argued that it did so only because it was backed by that regional organization and because it did not authorize the use of force.[57] The resolution was in any case vetoed by China and Russia, as was a third draft in July 2012.

R2P and the making of Indian foreign policy

India's responses to the Libyan and Syrian crises stimulated much academic interest both inside the country and outside and generated a number of different theories purporting to explain its behaviour. The initial arguments were straightforward. Those sympathetic to India's opposition to Western military intervention in Libya suggested that its behaviour was either principled and ethical, or sagacious and pragmatic, or – for some – both. In the left-wing journal *Frontline*, John Cherian weighed in to condemn what he argued was a 'crude, colonial style intervention'.[58] Both Prem Shankar Jha and Brahma Chellaney defended India's stance on the grounds that military action could not but stir up more extremism in Libya, creating, as Chellaney put it, a 'terrorist citadel' on Europe's 'doorstep'.[59] The retired Indian Foreign Service officer, erstwhile Director of the Institute for Defence Studies and Analyses and Deputy National Security Advisor, Arvind Gupta, simply argued that India took its position on 'pragmatic grounds and not in opposition to the R2P doctrine per se'.[60]

As the debate developed, however, these arguments were questioned. Manoj Joshi of the Observer Research Foundation suggested that India's stance was not so much principled as, in his words, 'craven and cynical'. India's representatives at the UN and their political masters in New Delhi, he argued, knew perfectly well that the no-fly zone and other provisions of UNSC 1973 meant military intervention by Western powers; moreover, Joshi declared, the resolution was perfectly legal in terms of international law, 'imperfect' though it might be.[61]

C. Raja Mohan ran a similar line, arguing that there was 'no question of high principle' being involved in India's behaviour during the Libyan crisis in 2011; rather, it had been simply and straightforwardly 'self-interested'.[62] Indian rhetoric about the sacrosanct nature of the principle of non-intervention was mere wind, belied by India's own behaviour and its past positions in similar crises. For Mohan, India's opposition to the use of force by Western states was less an expression of lingering anti-colonial or anti-Western sentiment and more a factor of a generally prudent, risk-averse outlook in the foreign policy establishment.

Others were less generous. Sumit Ganguly implied that India's abstention in the vote on UNSC Resolution 1973 merely demonstrated that it was 'incapable of taking a clear-cut moral stance against a dictator intent on crushing a challenge to his regime'.[63] Harsh V. Pant agreed, noting that India's behaviour on this issue will likely stoke 'suspicion that the emerging power remains unwilling to contribute to the management of the global order' and condemning India's 'lack of leadership'.[64] Last but not least, Dhruva Jaishankar suggested that India's stance perhaps betrayed a lingering 'insecurity'. He also noted rumours that Muammar Gaddafi had made offers to India of 'favourable oil contracts'

– offers rebuffed by New Delhi, but which nevertheless reflected 'poorly on India's aspirations as a great power'.[65]

In sum, the first wave of commentary on India's behaviour during the Libya crisis, in which journalists, former practitioners and think tankers were prominent, alongside academics, explained it in terms of elite beliefs, perceptions of Indian interests, or ingrained patterns of behaviour – whether they involved adherence to high moral principle (Cherian), pragmatic calculation about the possible consequences (Gupta, but also, as we have seen, Puri, India's PR at the UN), cynicism (Joshi), prudence (Mohan) and weakness of either conviction or will (Ganguly, Pant, Jaishankar). These theories were generally underpinned by the assumption that the foreign policy 'establishment' (to use Mohan's term) makes Indian foreign policy and does so largely in isolation from other parts of Indian society; moreover, they imply – perhaps not intentionally – a high degree of homogeneity in the views held within it.

The second wave of analysis came mostly from academics. The explanations they offered for India's stance on the Libyan crisis, and then on the Syrian civil war, were much more varied than that of the first wave. While Kudrat Virk suggested that India's stance on R2P remained 'ambiguous', she agreed that over the past 20 years it had shifted away from what she called 'its "natural" preference for sovereignty as autonomy, non-intervention, and non-use of force' towards a more flexible position. India now accepted that humanitarian intervention might in principle be justified, including under the auspices of R2P, with the Libyan crisis in 2011 demonstrating that 'the issue had become one about the conditions under which intervention could occur'.[66] She explained this change in terms of a wider shift from a broadly ideological foreign policy towards a more pragmatic one, in line with the arguments of Mohan and others.[67]

This argument was soon followed by a series of articles advancing alternative explanations for India's position on R2P during and after 2011. According to Urvashi Aneja, India's behaviour demonstrated not a softening of its stance on intervention in general and intervention under R2P in particular, but rather an attempt to engage in 'norm containment' to further India's wider interests in a multipolar order in which the values of one set of states is not imposed on others, and a greater say in its management.[68] Having been defeated in its last-minute attempt to derail international agreement on R2P at the 2005 World Summit, Aneja argues, India has set itself the task of reinterpreting it in terms that align with its 'pluralist view of international order'.[69] It has done this by placing particular emphasis on pillar one – framing it, to use Samir Kumar Das's formulation, as 'the enhancement of sovereign capacity' – and on the responsibilities generated for the international community by pillar two, and de-emphasizing pillar three, concerning intervention.[70] 'India has also argued', Aneja notes, 'in contrast to the World Summit Outcome Document, that the three pillars do in fact have a set sequence.'[71] Moreover, India has 'attempted to link the successful implementation of R2P to the reform of the Security Council', maintaining that reform is 'critical' to that success.[72] Together, Aneja argues, this attempt at reframing R2P constitutes an effort at 'norm containment' informed by a deep commitment to a 'pluralist order' of sovereign states that contrasts with the vision of a solidarist order of peoples that arguably underpins some Western views of R2P.[73]

This reading of India's behaviour has – not surprisingly – generated some controversy, especially among Western advocates for R2P. Writing in the *Oxford Handbook of the Responsibility to Protect*, Sarah Teitt pushes back against the notion that India, together with China and other emerging powers, is seeking to 'contain' and reinterpret the norm to suit their preferences or interests. She argues that what we have seen is something different: 'a dynamic process of negotiation and compromise between international R2P norm advocates and Asia Pacific actors, which has witnessed concession and accommodation on both sides'.[74] This process has produced what Teitt calls, borrowing Amitav Acharya's term, 'norm localization', as well as 'norm containment'.[75] The R2P norm was accepted in 2005, she thinks, and has been accepted since then because it shifted the debate about human rights protection away from a debate about individuals or groups versus states, with which states like India were uncomfortable. Since the 'ultimate goal of R2P is to uphold sovereignty and build state capacity to prevent the four atrocity crimes' and because it entails a 'clear affirmation that R2P is based in existing international law and does not alter the UN Charter', Teitt argues that states like India might come to accept it and agree to work within its confines, to negotiate ways of making R2P work, however much they may not like some of the arguments put by more enthusiastic reformers.[76]

Teitt notes, indeed, that India's official positions on R2P have changed over time, contra the implication by Ganguly, Hall and others, that New Delhi's stance has remained fundamentally unchanged, moving from being one of the most 'vocal opponents' to a 'more conciliatory stance' and then on – during 2011 and after – to 'greater scepticism'.[77] In this, Teitt is not alone. Madhan

Mohan Jaganathan and Gerrit Kurtz, basing their analysis on an assessment of both public statements and a series of interviews with key actors in New Delhi, have suggested that India's position on R2P was less fixed and more ambiguous than some have implied. They argued that it shifted over time, as Virk had maintained, but – in contrast to Virk – they suggest the changes in attitude that can be seen from the early 2000s through the World Summit and on into the mid-2010s were not underpinned by a movement from an ideological foreign policy to a more pragmatic one. Instead, Jaganathan and Kurtz argue that India's changing positions on R2P are shaped by contingent interplays of ideational and institutional variables operating within the Indian state.

Constant in the background to Indian debates over R2P, Jaganathan and Kurtz thought, is the view – deeply ingrained in the minds of postcolonial elites ruling states with an earlier experience of Western imperial rule – that 'sovereign space', understood in formal terms and in terms of practical autonomy, must be defended.[78] This view has generated widespread doubt about ideas like R2P which was compounded by 'scepticism about the motives that underpinned' the 'humanitarian interventions' undertaken by Western powers in the 1990s and 'circumspection of the attendant consequences'.[79] But it did not predetermine, Jaganathan and Kurtz argued, India's official position on R2P at the 2005 World Summit or its responses to its invocation during the Libyan, Syrian and other subsequent crises. Instead, these were the product of specific factors.

The evidence collected by Jaganathan and Kurtz leads them to the conclusion that India's stance at the World Summit and its attempt to stymie agreement on R2P was 'strongly influenced by the personal style of its permanent representative, Nirupam Sen'. Because New Delhi was more interested in other issues discussed at the World Summit, especially UNSC reform, and because the MEA is under-staffed by global standards and over-stretched, Sen was apparently left without a brief on R2P.[80] Sen was thus able to craft a position that he believed aligned with India's earlier critical stance on Western interventions and that fitted his personal 'left-leaning' and 'anti-American' views.[81] Since his views also aligned with a number of Indian politicians, especially those belonging to the so-called Left Front, which formed part of Manmohan Singh's first government from 2004 to 2008, it seems he felt comfortable in advancing views that did not necessarily align with others in government or in the MEA, including those of the then Foreign Secretary, Shyam Saran.[82]

The replacement of Sen by Hardeep Singh Puri, Jaganathan and Kurtz think, was partly responsible for a change in the official Indian attitude to

R2P from 2009 until the Libyan crisis blew up in early 2011, despite the fact that Sen remained at the UN in the new capacity of special advisor on R2P to the UNGA President. A change of government, they argue, also played a part. In July 2008, the Left Front withdrew its support to the Congress-led United Progressive Alliance over the US–India Nuclear Deal; in the 2009 general election, however, the government (known thereafter as UPA-II) was returned with sufficient Members of Parliament to not need that support. Jaganathan and Kurtz argued that this generated a 'conducive environment' for a 'much more positive attitude towards R2P' that can be traced in Puri's statements at the UN and in India's support for UNSC Resolution 1970, though they also note that concerns about relations with Arab states and about Indian nationals working in the region were also elements in its decision-making.[83]

Jaganathan and Kurtz explain the decision to abstain from voting on Resolution 1973 and India's subsequent criticism of the Libyan intervention and call for UNSC action in Syria in similar terms, as products of combinations of ideational and institutional variables. They note the opposition to the use of military force in Libya voiced by some influential Muslim leaders, whose constituents generally vote for Congress, and argue that this may have swayed the government's views. But above all they emphasize the deep-seated concern, flowing from postcolonial anxieties, about the possible 'instrumentalization of R2P to justify regime change'.[84] At the same time, Jaganathan and Kurtz note the pressure from within elements of the Indian polity to take a more positive stance on R2P, especially with regard to Sri Lanka. They observe that India has voted for resolutions critical of Sri Lankans' treatment of its Tamil minority and ascribe that behaviour to – in part – the influence of the Dravida Munnetra Kazhagam (DMK) Party in the Indian state of Tamil Nadu.[85]

This explanation of India's changing positions on R2P has not gone unchallenged. Indeed, at least three alternatives have been advanced, all of which shift the focus of explanation away from institutional variables – particularly from the notion that parliamentary pressures and intra-coalition dynamics had significant influence – and back towards the perception held by the foreign policymaking of India's proper role and national interests.

In their article in *Asian Politics and Policy*, Mischa Hansel and Miriam Mölleruse put forward their 'role theory', which posits that state elites contrive foreign policy in accordance with the social roles they believe their state should act out, to assess India's positions on international humanitarian norms, including R2P, as expressed in a series of 42 speeches made by the

Prime Ministers, External Affairs Ministers, Foreign Secretaries and National Security Advisors in post between 2001 and 2012.[86] They suggest that India's policymakers conceive of at least eight different roles for India, each implying different stances on norms like R2P, including those of 'internal developer [that is, a state focused principally on its own social and economic development], regional integrator, advocate of developing nations, active independent, moral force, great power, liberal example, and democracy promoter'.[87] On R2P, this apparent confusion of roles leads to what they call 'intra-role policy contradiction' between advocates and arguments for a liberal role and one of democracy promoter and those who favour different roles. In line with a number of other scholars, Hansel and Möller argue that

> India's policies vis-à-vis international humanitarian norms can…be at least partially understood as being motivated by the desire to ameliorate the tensions between divergent and sometimes incompatible role expectations. In particular, this applies to the conflict between the roles of a liberal example and a democracy promoter, and that of an active independent.[88]

Hansel and Möller imply, in other words, that India's changing position on R2P might best be explained as the product of internal disagreement within the Indian foreign policy establishment about the role it ought to fulfil in international politics.

With a painstaking analysis of the 'identity-discourses' he thinks help shape Indian foreign policy, as well as the language used by Hardeep Singh Puri and other Indian officials, Alan Bloomfield makes a similar case in his discussion of India's handling of the Libyan crisis. He identifies three different possible identities for India: a liberal democratic one that would lead it to favour humanitarian interventions in line with Western states, an anti-imperial identity that would lead it to favour a hard interpretation of the norms of sovereignty and non-intervention, and a great power identity which he suggests would lead it to take a pragmatic, case-by-case approach to interventions, endorsing them if they fit Indian interests. He argues that the latter was most influential during 2011, as 'hard-realist logic shaped India's abstention strongly, and anti-imperialist logic – but only developing world solidarity, not anti-Westernism – was also very important, while soft liberal-democratic logic played a minor role' in the decision-making processes during the Libyan crisis in 2011.[89]

A similar argument is advanced by Sumit Ganguly. Like other analysts, Ganguly notes the long-standing tension between India's postcolonial anxiety

about sovereignty and non-intervention on one hand, and its repeated efforts
to try to influence the internal affairs of other states, like apartheid-era South
Africa and European-ruled colonies in the 1950s and 1960s, East Pakistan
in 1971, or, more recently, Sri Lanka in the late 1980s. Like Bloomfield, he
recognizes that India's foreign policy elite still, as he puts it, 'labours under the
weight of its Nehruvian anti-colonial legacy', which generates scepticism about
Western motives for interventions, but Ganguly argues that this does not fully
explain Indian concern about the third pillar of R2P.[90]

Other factors, Ganguly thinks, clearly play their part. One that he highlights
is the oft-noted Indian official concern about the possible effect that support
for repeated Western interventions in the Arab world might have on Muslim
opinion at home. But Ganguly also observes a factor that generally goes
unmentioned in discussions of Indian attitudes to humanitarian and human
rights norms, namely acute sensitivity to possible and actual criticisms of the
behaviour of its security forces in counter-insurgencies in Jammu and Kashmir
and elsewhere in India. New Delhi remains acutely conscious of the dangers
inherent in the possible multilateralization of internal security problems, having
seen the Kashmir dispute made the subject of UNSC Resolutions in the late
1940s.[91] Ganguly suggests that official attitudes might change once politicians
and bureaucrats are convinced that their increased investment in the police and
armed forces has reached a level at which India had 'capabilities to maintain
social peace and public order without a resort to widespread state-supported
coercion'. 'It is India's current inability to forestall and contain significant
domestic political violence', he concludes, 'that leads its policymakers to fear that
any departure from a firm commitment to the principle of national sovereignty
could rebound significantly to its disadvantage.'[92]

Conclusion

India's mixed and often sceptical response to the emergence and evolution of
the doctrine of the R2P has been seen by some as a measure of its commitment
to the West and to a 'liberal international order'.[93] Whether or not it should
be interpreted in that way, the story of India's reaction to R2P opens a window
on the attitudes that prevail among the foreign policy elite in New Delhi, its
broader understandings of how international relations do and ought to function,
and how these beliefs are changing, as the composition, training and experience
of that elite itself changes. It tells us something about the ability of the foreign
policy establishment to craft diplomatic strategies to manage circumstances in

which powerful states are seeking to advance new normative agendas and to lay out India's putative alternatives.[94]

Moreover, India's management of the challenge of R2P reveals much about foreign policymaking in New Delhi – especially about its persistent and emerging drivers – and also about the ways in which the analysis of Indian foreign policy is changing.[95] All the academic studies of India and R2P focus some or most of their attention on the beliefs and preferences of the foreign policymaking elite, implying that ideas play a significant role alongside perceived interests in generating policy outcomes. This accords with the more widespread view that Indian foreign policy continues to be shaped by postcolonial concerns about sovereignty and autonomy, in particular, and contestation over political values.[96] Implicitly or explicitly, they also note the substantial latitude given to high-ranking officials – notably Nirupam Sen, in 2005 and after – to drive policy in areas that are not the core focus of the Prime Minister, External Affairs Minister or Foreign Secretary, partly because the Indian Foreign Service remains understaffed and overstretched. The problem of state capacity is also evident in this context, especially concerning the ability of India's security forces to manage internal insurgencies in line with constitutional and international human rights commitments, which in turn generate elite anxieties and defensiveness about international humanitarian agendas.[97] Finally, the issue of R2P also highlights the partial and shifting influence of domestic politics over Indian foreign policy – and, implicitly, the slight and uneven erosion of the New Delhi-based elite's dominance over its making. Three issues are especially salient: coalition management, vote-blocs, and the interests of the states, evident in the apparent influence exercised over the Manmohan Singh government's stance on R2P by concerns over the Left Front, the support of Muslims for Congress and its allies and the particular worries in Tamil Nadu about the plight of Tamils in Sri Lanka.

Notes

1   Alan Bloomfield's *India and the Responsibility to Protect* (Aldershot: Ashgate, 2016) provides an excellent survey of the literature to date of publication.
2   See especially Rajesh M. Basrur, 'Scholarship on India's International Relations: Some Disciplinary Shortcomings', *International Studies* 46, Nos 1–2 (2009). For an excellent introduction to International Relations (IR) theory in India, see Siddharth Mallavarapu, 'Development of International Relations Theory in India Traditions, Contemporary Perspectives and Trajectories', *International Studies* 46, Nos 1–2 (2009).

3   The classic text on these changes remains C. Raja Mohan, *Crossing the Rubicon: The Shaping of India's New Foreign Policy* (New York: Palgrave, 2003), but see also David M. Malone, *Does the Elephant Dance? Contemporary Indian Foreign Policy* (Oxford: Oxford University Press, 2011) and Teresita C. Schaffer and Howard B. Schaffer, *India at the Global High Table: The Quest for Regional Primacy and Strategic Autonomy* (Washington, DC: Brookings, 2016).

4   This term has been used by Modi's Foreign Secretary, S. Jaishankar, to describe the role that India would wish to play in international relations. On the concept, see especially Ashley J. Tellis, 'India as a Leading Power', *Carnegie Endowment for International Peace*, 4 April 2016. Accessed on 30 June 2017. Available at http://carnegieendowment. org/2016/04/04/india-as-leading-power-pub-63185.

5   The classic text on R2P, which explores its origins, is Alex Bellamy, *Responsibility to Protect* (Cambridge: Polity, 2008). See also Ramesh Thakur, *The United Nations, Peace and Security: From Collective Security to the Responsibility to Protect* (Cambridge: Cambridge University Press, 2006), Gareth Evans, *The Responsibility to Protect: Ending Mass Atrocity Crimes Once and For All* (Washington, DC: Brookings, 2009) and Alex Bellamy and Tim Dunne (eds), *The Oxford Handbook of the Responsibility to Protect* (Oxford: Oxford University Press, 2016).

6   Jane Boulden, *Peace Enforcement: The United Nations Experience in Congo, Somalia, and Bosnia* (Westport, CT: Praeger, 2001).

7   'The Blair Doctrine', transcript of speech by Rt. Hon. Tony Blair, Chicago, 22 April 1999. Accessed on 30 June 2017. Available at http://www.pbs.org/newshour/bb/international-jan-june99-blair_doctrine4-23/. For context, see Oliver Daddow, '"Tony's War"? Blair, Kosovo and the Interventionist Impulse in British Foreign Policy', *International Affairs* 85, No. 3 (2009).

8   See especially Nicholas J. Wheeler, *Saving Strangers: Humanitarian Intervention in International Society* (Oxford: Oxford University Press, 2000).

9   International Commission on Intervention and State Sovereignty, *Responsibility to Protect*, 81 (Ottawa: International Development Research Centre, 2001).

10 Ibid., viii.

11 Ibid., xi.

12 Ibid., xii–xiii. For an analysis of why and how the ICISS came to these conclusions, see Bellamy, *Responsibility to Protect*.

13 Charles Cater and David M. Malone, 'The Genesis of R2P: Kofi Annan's Intervention Dilemma', in *The Oxford Handbook of the Responsibility to Protect*, edited by Alex Bellamy and Tim Dunne, 121 (Oxford: Oxford University Press, 2016).

14 'High-Level Panel on Threats, Challenges and Change', *A More Secure World: Our Shared Responsibility* (United Nations, 2004). Accessed on 30 June 2017. Available at http://www.un.org/en/peacebuilding/pdf/historical/hlp_more_secure_world.pdf.

15 Ibid., 66.

16 Bellamy, *Responsibility to Protect*, 67.

17 United Nations General Assembly, *2005 World Summit Outcome*, A/60/L.1, 31, 15 September 2005. Accessed on 30 June 2017. Available at http://responsibilitytoprotect. org/world%20summit%20outcome%20doc%202005(1).pdf.

18 UNGA, *2005 World Summit Outcome*, 31.

19   UNGA, *Implementing the Responsibility to Protect: Report of the Secretary-General*, A/63/677, 7–8, 12 January 2009. Accessed on 30 June 2017. Available at http:// responsibilitytoprotect.org/implementing%20the%20rtop.pdf.

20   Ibid., 9.

21   Alex Bellamy, 'The Responsibility to Protect Turns Ten', *Ethics and International Affairs* 29, No. 2 (2015): 165.

22   Ibid., 166. See also the table analysing the incidence of crises and R2P-framed UNSC responses on page 167.

23   Xymena Kurowska, 'Multipolarity as Resistance to Liberal Norms: Russia's Position on Responsibility to Protect', *Conflict, Security and Development* 14, No. 4 (2014): 489–508.

24   Derek Averre and Lance Davies, 'Russia, Humanitarian Intervention and the Responsibility to Protect: The Case of Syria', *International Affairs* 91, No. 4 (2015).

25   On the crucial role played by India's diplomats during this period, see especially Manu Bhagavan, 'A New Hope: India, the United Nations and the Making of the Universal Declaration of Human Rights', *Modern Asian Studies* 44, No. 2 (2010) and *India and the Quest for One World: The Peacemakers* (New York: Palgrave, 2013).

26   Bhagavan, 'A New Hope', 329.

27   Ibid., 330.

28   Ibid., 317–318.

29   UNGA Resolution, 'Treatment of Indians in the Union of South Africa', 8 December 1946, A/RES/44(I). Accessed on 30 June 2017. Available at http://www.un.org/en/ga/ search/view_doc.asp?symbol=A/RES/44(I).

30   Ian Hall, '"Mephistopheles in a Saville Row Suit": V. K. Krishna Menon and the West', in *Radicals and Reactionaries in Twentieth Century International Thought*, edited by Ian Hall (New York: Palgrave, 2015).

31   See especially Quincy Wright, 'Is Discussion Intervention?' *The American Journal of International Law* 50, No. 1 (1956).

32   For a contemporary view by a well-informed observer, see Michael Brecher, 'Kashmir: A Case Study in United Nations Mediation', *Pacific Affairs* 26, No. 3 (1953).

33   Sumit Ganguly, 'India and the Responsibility to Protect', *International Relations* 30, No. 3 (2016): 364.

34   See Paul Michael McGarr, '"Quiet Americans in India": The CIA and the Politics of Intelligence in Cold War South Asia', *Diplomatic History* 38, No. 5 (2014).

35   Indira Gandhi, 'India and the World', *Foreign Affairs* 51 (1972): 68.

36   Ganguly, 'India and the Responsibility to Protect', 365.

37   Mohammed Ayoob, 'India in South Asia: The Quest for Regional Predominance', *World Policy Journal* 7, No. 1 (1989).

38   Nicholas Wheeler argues that the East Pakistan intervention is best seen as a humanitarian intervention in his *Saving Strangers: Humanitarian Intervention in International Society* (Oxford: Oxford University Press, 2000). See also Gary J. Bass, 'The Indian Way of Humanitarian Intervention', *The Yale Journal of International Law* 40 (2015).

39   Sumit Ganguly, 'India and the Responsibility to Protect', 364. Ganguly notes that India had mixed motives: it also recognized that Vietnam's intervention would limit Chinese influence in Cambodia.

40 Kudrat Virk, 'India and the Responsibility to Protect: A Tale of Ambiguity', *Global Responsibility to Protect* 5, No. 1 (2013): 59. See also Devin T. Hagerty, 'India's Regional Security Doctrine', *Asian Survey* 31, No. 4 (1991).

41 Virk, 'India and the Responsibility to Protect', 67–68.

42 Ibid., 69.

43 Quoted in Satish Nambiar, 'India: An Uneasy Precedent', in *Kosovo and the Challenge of Humanitarian Intervention: Selective Indignation, Collective Action, and International Citizenship*, edited by Albrecht Schnabel and Ramesh Thakur, 263 (Tokyo: United Nations University Press, 2000).

44 M. S. Rajan, 'The New Interventionism?' *International Studies* 37, No. 1 (2000). See also the equally critical Rahul Rao, 'The UN and NATO in the New World Order: Legal Issues', *International Studies* 37, No. 3 (2000) and Shalini Chawla, 'NATO's Response to the Kosovo Crisis', *Strategic Analysis* 24, No. 6 (2000).

45 B. K. Shrivastava and Manmohan Agarwal, 'Politics of Intervention and the Bosnia-Herzegovina Conflict', *International Studies*, 40, No. 1 (2003): 83.

46 Ian Hall, 'Tilting at Windmills? The Indian Debate on Responsibility to Protect after UNSC 1973', *Global Responsibility to Protect* 5, No. 1 (2013): 93.

47 Quoted in Alan Bloomfield, 'India and the Libyan Crisis: Flirting with the Responsibility to Protect, Retreating to the Sovereignty Norm', *Contemporary Security Policy* 36, No. 1 (2015): 33.

48 Quoted in Hall, 'Tilting at Windmills?' 95.

49 Ibid., 96.

50 Rohan Mukherjee and David M. Malone, 'From High Ground to High Table: The Evolution of Indian Multilateralism', *Global Governance: A Review of Multilateralism and International Organizations* 17, No. 3 (2011).

51 UNSCR 1970, 20 February 2011, S/RES/1970.

52 Hardeep Singh Puri, *Perilous Interventions: The Security Council and the Politics of Chaos* (New Delhi: HarperCollins, 2016). Ganguly suggests that India came under significant pressure from the US to vote in favour ('India and the Responsibility to Protect', 368).

53 Puri's account of these events can be found in *Perilous Interventions*, 81–103.

54 Quoted in Hall, 'Tilting at Windmills?' 98.

55 Quoted in Ramesh Thakur, 'R2P after Libya and Syria: Engaging Emerging Powers', *The Washington Quarterly* 36, No. 2 (2013): 70.

56 Quoted in Tim Dunne and Sarah Teitt, 'Contested Intervention: China, India, and the Responsibility to Protect', *Global Governance* 21 (2015): 384. See also Puri, *Perilous Interventions*, 104–136.

57 Dunne and Teitt, 'Contested Intervention', 385.

58 John Cherian, 'Libya in the Crosshairs', *Frontline* 28, No. 8 (April 2011). Accessed on 30 June 2017. Available at http://www.frontline.in/navigation/?type=static&page=arc hiveSearch&aid=20110422280800400&ais=08&avol=28.

59 Prem Shankar Jha, 'Does the West have a Death Wish?', *Tehelka* 8, No. 13 (2 April 2011). Available at http://www.tehelka.com/2011/04/does-the-west-have-a-death-wish/.

60 Arvind Gupta, 'Mind the R2P', *Indian Express*, 22 April 2011. Available at http:// indianexpress.com/article/opinion/columns/mind-the-r2p/.

61 Manoj Joshi, 'Dodgy Stand on Libya Crisis', *India Today*, 24 March 2011. Available at http://indiatoday.intoday.in/story/dodgy-stand-on-libya-crisis/1/133200.html.

62 C. Raja Mohan, 'India, Libya and the Principle of Non-Intervention', ISAS Insights, 122, 13 April 2011. Available at https://www.isas.nus.edu.sg/ISAS%20Reports/ ISAS%20Insights%20122%20-%20Email%20-%20India,%20Libya%20and%20 the%20Princple%20of%20Non-Intervention.pdf.

63 Sumit Ganguly, 'A Pointless Abstention', *The Diplomat*, 23 April 2011. Available at http://thediplomat.com/2011/03/a-pointless-abstention/.

64 Harsh V. Pant, 'Libya Exposes New Faultlines in Indian Foreign Policy', *ISN Insights*, 21 April 2011.

65 Dhruva Jaishankar, 'India's Acute Abstinence Syndrome', Polaris, 19 March 2011. Available at http://polaris.nationalinterest.in/2011/03/19/acute-abstinence-syndrome/.

66 Virk, 'India and the Responsibility to Protect', 82.

67 See especially Mohan, *Crossing the Rubicon*.

68 Urvashi Aneja, 'India, R2P and Humanitarian Assistance', *Global Responsibility to Protect* 6 (2014).

69 Ibid., 234.

70 Ibid., 235.

71 Ibid., 236.

72 Ibid., 237.

73 Ibid., 243–245.

74 Sarah Teitt, 'Asia Pacific and South Asia', in *The Oxford Handbook of the Responsibility to Protect*, edited by Alex Bellamy and Tim Dunne, 373 (Oxford: Oxford University Press, 2016).

75 Ibid., 374. See also Amitav Acharya, 'How Ideas Spread: Whose Norms Matter? Norm Localization and Institutional Change in Asian Regionalism', *International Organization* 58, No. 2 (2004).

76 Teitt, 'Asia Pacific and South Asia', 376 and 378–379.

77 Ibid., 383. See also Dunne and Teitt, 'Contested Intervention', 377, 379, 381–382, 384.

78 Madhan Mohan Jaganathan and Gerrit Kurtz, 'Singing the Tune of Sovereignty? India and the Responsibility to Protect', *Conflict, Security and Development* 14, No. 4 (2014): 464. See also Manjari Chatterjee Miller's exploration of this issue in *Wronged by Empire: Post-Imperial Ideology and Foreign Policy in India and China* (Stanford, CA: Stanford University Press, 2013).

79 Jaganathan and Kurtz, 'Singing the Tune of Sovereignty?' 468.

80 On the MEA's weaknesses, see Daniel Markey, 'Developing India's Foreign Policy Software', *Asia Policy* 8, No. 1(2009): 73–96.

81 Jaganathan and Kurtz, 'Singing the Tune of Sovereignty?' 469–470.

82 Ibid., 470.

83 Ibid., 472.

84 Ibid., 475.

85 Ibid., 476–477.

86 Mischa Hansel and Miriam Möller, 'Indian Foreign Policy and International Humanitarian Norms: A Role-Theoretical Analysis', *Asian Politics and Policy* 7, No. 1 (2015): 82.

87 Ibid., 83.

88 Ibid., 95.
89 Alan Bloomfield, 'India and the Libyan Crisis: Flirting with the Responsibility to Protect, Retreating to the Sovereignty Norm', *Contemporary Security Policy* 36, No. 1 (2015): 44.
90 Sumit Ganguly, 'India and the Responsibility to Protect', *International Relations* 30, No. 3 (2016): 367.
91 Ibid., 365.
92 Ibid., 371.
93 See, for example, Tara McCormack, 'The Responsibility to Protect and the End of the Western Century', *Journal of Intervention and Statebuilding* 4, No. 1 (2010): 69–82 and Jason Ralph and Adrian Gallagher, 'Legitimacy Faultlines in International Society: The Responsibility to Protect and Prosecute after Libya', *Review of International Studies* 41, No. 3 (2015): 553–573.
94 On these debates, see also Ian Hall, 'Narendra Modi and India's Normative Power', *International Affairs* 93, No. 1 (2017): 113–131.
95 On the latter, see Siddharth Mallavarapu, 'Theorizing India's Foreign Relations', in *The Oxford Handbook of Indian Foreign Policy*, edited by David M. Malone, C. Raja Mohan and Srinath Raghavan, 35–48 (Oxford: Oxford University Press, 2015).
96 Kanti Bajpai, 'Five Approaches to the Study of Indian Foreign Policy', in *Oxford Handbook of Indian Foreign Policy*, edited by David M. Malone, C. Raja Mohan and Srinath Raghavan, 23–25 and 28–30 (Oxford: Oxford University Press, 2015).
97 See especially Sumit Ganguly and William R. Thompson, *Ascending India and Its State Capacity: Extraction, Violence, and Legitimacy* (New Haven: Yale University Press, 2017).

10

India and the Indo-Pacific Discourse

David Scott

In November 2017 Foreign Secretary Subrahmanyam Jaishankar noted 'the growing appreciation and acceptance of the concept of Indo-Pacific'.[1] Followers of Indian foreign policy would not have encountered the term *Indo-Pacific* before 2006, but a decade later it has become a 'new template of analysis' for Indian security and foreign policy analysis.[2] Media use has also become common.[3] Indeed Indian figures talk of 'the Indo-Pacific imperative' for India.[4] The Indian ambassador to Singapore emphasized 'our vision of the Indo-Pacific region as our natural habitat [...] and our strategic commitment to the region'.[5] His choice of words around the term 'Indo-Pacific' were revealing – *our vision*, of a *region* that was India's *natural habitat*.

In a broad generalized sense, the term 'Indo-Pacific' involves both Indian and Pacific Oceans (for India especially the eastern Indian Ocean and western Pacific), with the South China Sea as a joining buckle.[6] The 'Indo' bit of the term 'Indo-Pacific' points not only to the Indian Ocean but also to India. Whereas India is marginal to the term *Asia-Pacific* (that is, the Pacific basin and the Pacific Rim), it is self-evidently politically and geographically right in the Indo-Pacific.

Geopolitically the adoption of the term 'Indo-Pacific' reflects a shift of focus by India from land (the Indian subcontinent) to maritime concerns.[7] It reflects further development in India's own foreign policy formulations. First was the formulation since the 1990s that India's strategic horizons were no longer restricted to its *immediate neighbourhood* of South Asia, but instead also involved what was styled as India's *extended neighbourhood*. This was also described as an *omni-directional diplomacy*, which consisted of a Look West to the Middle East, a Look North to Central Asia, a Look South to the Indian Ocean and a Look East to Pacific Asia. India's Indo-Pacific pivot in effect represents a fusion of its *Look South* and *Look East* horizons established and gradually widened since the 2000s.[8] India's self-defined strategic interests are Indo-Pacific wide, stretching from established interests in the Indian Ocean, to growing interests in the South China Sea, and indeed into the South/West Pacific.[9] The election of a new BJP-led administration headed by Narendra Modi brought a new eastwards emphasis encapsulated with the mantra *Act East*.[10]

This chapter looks at three overlapping fields, namely India as an Indo-Pacific 'actor', the Indo-Pacific strategic discourse 'around' (that is, on) government, and the Indo-Pacific language and policies used 'inside' (that is, by) government.

An Indo-Pacific actor

India is an 'Indo-Pacific power' in four ways.[11] First, as already noted, India is geographically located in the Indo-Pacific. Its west coast (and its Western Naval Command) faces the Arabian Sea, its south coast (and its Southern Naval Command) juts deep into the Indian Ocean and its east coast (and its Eastern Naval Command) faces the Bay of Bengal. In addition, India's Andaman and Nicobar Islands sit on top of the Strait of Malacca, and are described by the government as a 'springboard to Southeast Asia and the Pacific Ocean'.[12]

Second, the Indian navy has regularly deployed into the South China Sea since 2000 and into the Western Pacific since 2007. Third, India has shaped various bilateral security partnerships with countries around the South China Sea and Pacific Rim, namely Singapore, Indonesia, Vietnam, Australia,[13] Japan,[14] France[15] and the United States.[16] Trilateral dialogues also involve India with both Japan and the US (IJUS), which reflect for India 'the growing convergence of their respective countries' interests in the Indo-Pacific region';[17] and more recently with Australia and Japan (IAJ), which is similarly Indo-Pacific in its spread of members.[18] India's involvement in November 2017 with the revived quadrilateral mechanism with Australia, Japan and the US was described by the Ministry of External Affairs as involving 'consultations on issues of common interest in the Indo-Pacific region', aiming to shape 'a free, open, prosperous and inclusive Indo-Pacific region' and 'highlighted India's Act East Policy as the cornerstone of its engagement in the Indo-Pacific region'.[19] All this makes for a rising India of increasing importance within the Indo-Pacific balance of power.[20]

Fourth, India is already involved in various de facto Indo-Pacific bodies that include members from the Indian and Pacific Oceans. Such bodies include the East Asia Summit (EAS), the ASEAN Regional Forum (ARF) and the ASEAN Defence Ministers' Meeting-Plus (ADMM-Plus). India is also a member of the Asia-Pacific Fishery Commission (APFC), which had previously operated from 1948 to 1976 as the Indo-Pacific Fisheries Council (IPFC).

India is also an observer in the West Pacific Naval Symposium (WPNS) and is a leading member of the Indian Ocean Naval Symposium (IONS). Finally, India is involved in the RIC (Russia–India–China) Consultation on Asia-Pacific Affairs (CAPA), which first met in December 2016, but with no indications of actual substance. In addition, India is involved in two particular Indo-Pacific sub-regional mechanisms. First is the Mekong–Ganga Cooperation (MGC) grouping set up in 2000, which brings India and Myanmar together with the South China Sea littoral states of Thailand, Cambodia and Vietnam. Significantly the MGC does not have China as a member. Second is the Forum for India Pacific Island Countries (FIPIC) set up in 2014, an Indian initiative which brings India together with the Cook Islands, Fiji, Kiribati, Marshall Islands, Micronesia, Nauru, Niue, Palau, Papua New Guinea, Samoa, Solomon Islands, Tonga, Tuvalu and Vanuatu.

India is also a maritime security partner in various Indo-Pacific settings.[21] India's organization of the MILAN naval exercises in the waters around the Andaman and Nicobar Islands started off as a modest meet between India, Indonesia, Singapore and Thailand in 1995. By 2018, the MILAN framework was involving navies from both wings of the Indo-Pacific – in the shape of South Africa, Mozambique, Tanzania, Kenya, Oman, Seychelles, Maldives, Mauritius, Sri Lanka, Bangladesh, Myanmar, Thailand Malaysia, Singapore, Cambodia, Vietnam, Philippines, Brunei, Indonesia, Timor Leste, Papua New Guinea, Australia and New Zealand. Pakistan and China remained absent. In turn, India has also joined other Indo-Pacific multilateral ventures in the South China Sea and the Pacific Ocean. With regard to the latter, India joined the ADMM-Plus naval Exercise on Maritime Security and Counter Terrorism (EMSCT), held in the South China Sea in May 2016. With regard to the latter, Indian warships participated in 2014, 2016 and 2018 in the RIMPAC exercises held off Hawaii which India considered 'a demonstration of India's commitment to peace and prosperity of the Indo-Pacific region and Indian Navy's increasing footprint and operational reach'.[22]

Various bilateral exercises have an Indo-Pacific nature to them. India's SIMBEX exercises with Singapore have alternated since 2005 between the Bay of Bengal and the South China Sea. The INDRA exercises with Russia took place in the Indian Ocean in 2003, 2005, 2009 and 2015, and in the Western Pacific in 2007, 2014, 2016 and 2017. The India–Japan JIMEX naval exercises took place in the Western Pacific in 2011 and the Eastern Indian Ocean in 2013. Since 2007 the bilateral MALABAR exercises between India and the US alternated between the Indian Ocean and the Western Pacific. Trilateral MALABAR exercises with Japan and the US have taken place in the Bay of Bengal in 2015 and 2017, and the Western Pacific in 2007, 2009, 2014, 2016 and 2018.[23]

Around government: strategic debate

Indian usage of the term 'Indo-Pacific' arose in naval circles. This was prefigured in India's formal 2004 *Naval Doctrine* which noted 'the shift in global maritime focus from the Atlantic–Pacific combine to the Pacific–Indian Ocean region'.[24] The first 'Indo-Pacific' reference in India came in 2006 from Premvir Das, the former Chief of Eastern Naval Command.[25] This was quickly followed by Gurpreet Khurana, former Commander in the Indian Navy and subsequent Executive Director of the National Maritime Foundation. He used the term 'Indo-Pacific' in 2007 in connection with maritime cooperation with Japan, and in 2008 in connection with competition with China.[26] By 2009, Arun Prakash, the Chief of Naval Staff 2004–06 and subsequent Chairman of the National Maritime Foundation, was arguing that it was 'time for our diplomats to take a stand and suggest through regional and international forums that the Indian Ocean is now significant enough to be hyphenated with the Pacific, in order to create a new term, "Indo-Pacific"'.[27] Two years later the call was maintained by Prakash, 'I would suggest that it is time to coin a new term, the "Indo-Pacific".'[28]

By 2011 the rising prominence of the 'Indo-Pacific' as a term was signaled and further strengthened in the widely noticed piece *Mapping the Indo-Pacific*:

> Over the past year, the term 'Indo-Pacific' has gained currency in strategic discourse in India. From a geopolitical perspective it represents the inclusion of the Western Pacific within the range of India's security interests, thus stretching beyond the traditional focus on the Indian Ocean theatre. It is a logical corollary to India's Look East policy.[29]

This was written by Shyam Saran, the former Foreign Secretary 2004–06, official advisor to the Prime Minister 2006–10, and subsequent Chairman of the National Security Advisory Board.

Indian think tanks have been a noticeable vehicle since 2011 in furthering Indo-Pacific terms of reference in Indian strategic discourse (Table 10.1), in particular the Observer Research Foundation (ORF) and the National

Maritime Foundation (NMF). Such think tanks form a semi-official bridge from outside government into government, and their Indo-Pacific conferences often include ministers, officials and diplomats. Think tank logic in organizing these conferences was simple, the 'Indo-Pacific is the new geopolitical reality'.[30]

Table 10.1: Indian think tanks – Indo-Pacific seminars, workshops and conferences

2011	United Service Institute	*Japan-India-US Trilateral Strategic Dialogue on Security Issues in the Indo-Pacific Region*
2013	National Maritime Foundation	*Geopolitics of the Indo-Pacific Region*[31]
2013	United Service Institute	*Perspectives of the Indo-Pacific Region*[32]
2013	Indian Council of World Affairs	*Geopolitics of the Indo-Pacific Region*[33]
2014	Observer Research Foundation	*Sea Change: Evolving Maritime Geopolitics in the Indo-Pacific Region*[34]
2014	Observer Research Foundation	*Regional integration in the Indo-Pacific*
2014	Institute of Peace and Conflict Studies	*India, Australia and Indo-Pacific: Regional Interpretations*
2014	Observer Research Foundation	*Evolving Security Architecture in the Indo-Pacific*
2015	National Maritime Foundation	*Maritime Dynamics in the Eastern Indian Ocean Region and the Western Pacific Ocean Region*[35]
2015	National Maritime Foundation	*India and China: Constructing Peaceful and Stable Maritime Order in the Indo-Pacific*[36]
2015	Observer Research Foundation	*Towards an Indo-Pacific Partnership: Reconnecting India and New Zealand*
2015	United Service Institution	*The Indo-Pacific Region: Security Dynamics and Challenges*[37]
2016	United Service Institution	*Strategic Balance in the Indo-Pacific Region*

Contd.

Contd.

2017	Observer Research Foundation	*Indo-Pacific Region: Converging India-Japan interests*
2017	Indian Council for Research on International Economic Relations	*Changing Security Dynamic in the Indo-Pacific*
2017	Vivekananda International Foundation	*Trilateral India-Japan-USA Dialogue – The Indo-Pacific*
2018	Institute for Defence Studies and Analyses	*Strategic Stability in the Indo-Pacific*

What became apparent in Indian discussions around government was that a perceived 'Indo-Pacific Great Game' between India and China was felt, as a Chinese push westwards across the Indo-Pacific, which was seen as encircling India, was met by counteracting, in effect balancing, Indian moves eastwards across the Indo-Pacific.[38]

Into government

In retrospect, what has become clear is that with regard to government use of the term 'Indo-Pacific' a geoeconomic focus under the Congress-led government of Manmohan Singh has given way to a more geopolitical China-concerned focus under the BJP-led government of Narendra Modi.[39]

Singh administration (2011–14)

The first appearance of 'Indo-Pacific' in Indian official terminology was in December 2011, when Nirupama Rao, India's ambassador to the US, argued that 'continuance of economic growth and prosperity […] is in many ways linked to the Indo-Pacific region'.[40] Within the Ministry for External Affairs, in February 2012, the then Foreign Secretary Ranjan Mathai noted a shift of terminology away from the Asia-Pacific; where 'as some here have begun to call it, the Indo-Pacific,' and in which 'while our Look East Policy began with a strong economic emphasis and content, we now have growing strategic and security engagement in the region'.[41] The same month, the Defence Minister A. K. Antony stressed 'the relevance of the Indian Ocean-Pacific or the Indo-Pacific combine' in Great Power relationships that India was involved in.[42] By July 2012, the Minister of External Affairs, Salman Khurshid, was pointing out that 'beyond ASEAN we are actually looking at the Indo Pacific now'.[43]

The Prime Minister Manmohan Singh deployed the term for the first time in December 2012 at the India-ASEAN Commemorative Summit: 'our future is inter-linked and a stable, secure and prosperous Indo-Pacific region is crucial for our own progress and prosperity'.[44]

The following year Indo-Pacific official usage became even more noticeable. In February 2013, Rao argued that 'the term "Indo-Pacific" which is increasingly defining the cultural, economic, political and security continuum that straddles the Indian and the Pacific Ocean regions [is] fast becoming a geo-strategic construct to comprehend the common opportunities, the intersecting maritime and security interests, and challenges'.[45] The following month, the Secretary (East) Sanjay Singh in his Welcoming Address to the Indian Council of World Affairs (ICWA) conference *Geopolitics of the Indo-Pacific Region* noted how 'since the last couple of years, the term "Indo-Pacific" is being used increasingly during discussions amongst policy makers, strategic thinkers and think tanks' because quite simple the term '"Indo-Pacific" has come to reflect contemporary realities'.[46]

At that ICWA venue, Khurshid also lent official impetus to this deployment of Indo-Pacific frames of reference, '"India-Pacific" could be looked upon as a natural corollary of the country's modern version of "Look East Policy"'.[47] In 'an exciting era in this region where the Indian and Pacific Oceans meet,' Khurshid advocated seapower:

Maritime supremacy is the hallmark of a great power. [...] India's future lies in its ability to harness the power of the Ocean – the Indian Ocean and the extended 'Indian-Pacific' Ocean region.[48]

Two months later in June, Khurshid was talking of 'a common future that has to be secured not just within the new security and economic future of Asia Pacific but also the Indo-Pacific' and with the need for India to 'build partnerships across the Indo-Pacific'.[49] One such partnership was with Japan. Khurshid invoked how Shinzo Abe 'had eloquently spoken of the confluence of the two seas which gave rise to the term "Indo-Pacific" that is commonly used by strategic thinkers today'.[50] Similarly, the Prime Minister Manmohan Singh in his trip to Japan invoked Shinzo Abe's earlier maritime formula, 'Abe's inspiring and visionary address to the Indian Parliament in August 2007, when he spoke of "the confluence of the two seas" – the Pacific and the Indian Oceans – which has defined the new framework for our bilateral relationship [in] the Indo-Pacific region.'[51]

Modi administration (2014–18)

The installation of a new BJP-led coalition headed by Narendra Modi brought a renewed push into the Indian Ocean, initiation of an *Act East* policy, further presence established in the South Pacific and specific Indo-Pacific anchoring for strengthened bilateral and trilateral security cooperation with France, Indonesia, Vietnam, Japan, Australia and the US, with China in mind.[52] Hence ministers arguing that 'in the wider Indo-Pacific region ... we have covered new ground extending our outreach'.[53] For the Foreign Secretary, Subrahmanyam Jaishankar, this outreach was 'a profound shift in India's geo-political outlook towards the world to its East [...] the transformation of the Asia-Pacific to the Indo-Pacific' in which India's 'leapfrogging capabilities' beckoned a role as 'a net security provider in the Indo-Pacific'.[54]

Modi has led from the top, arguing that from a maritime perspective, 'with a 7,500-kilometer long coast line, India has a natural and immediate interest in the developments in the Indo-Pacific region'.[55] The economic rise of India was rendering the previous reference point of the Asia-Pacific obsolete, 'people now speak of the Indo-Pacific. It is now the focus of the world economic dynamism'.[56] Consequently, in his speech at the East Asia Summit (EAS), whose membership spans countries from the Indian Ocean, South China Sea and Pacific Ocean, Modi noted:

> Since my government entered office 18 months ago, no region has seen greater engagement from India than the Asia Pacific and the Indian Ocean Region. This reflects a long standing national consensus in India on the importance of this region for India.[57]

Modi's note of a national consensus over the importance of the Indo-Pacific area was accurate and significant as was his labeling of the Indian Ocean and Asia-Pacific (that is, the Pacific Ocean) as one region. Modi's decision to attend the Shangri-la Dialogue in June 2018 included his Keynote Address which highlighted 'India's own engagement in the Indo-Pacific region'.

India's relations with France have been strengthening for over three decades in the Indian Ocean, but French President Emmanuel Macron's visit to India in March 2018 witnessed Modi anchoring their deepening strategic relationship into a wider Indo-Pacific framework. This included setting up a new bilateral dialogue on East Asia and agreeing on a Reciprocal Logistics Support agreement that will enable mutual use of each other's military facilities in the Indo-Pacific.

Modi was explicit on India's maritime role in his Joint Strategic Vision statement with Macron that 'India occupies a central position in the Indo-Pacific'.[58]

Modi set India–Indonesian relations in an Indo-Pacific (explicitly maritime and implicitly China) setting during the visit to India by the Indonesian leader in December 2016. The Indian leader affirmed 'Indonesia is one of India's most valued partners in our Act East Policy', and welcomed 'our convergences to act as a force of peace, prosperity and stability in the Indo-Pacific region'.[59] The return visit by Modi in May 2018 brought their joint Shared Vision of India–Indonesia Maritime Cooperation in the Indo-Pacific. With regard to the South China Sea, the link waters between the Indian and the Pacific Oceans, and the scene for Chinese claims over most of its waters, Modi's caution at the Raisina Dialogue forum in January 2017 was a careful warning that 'we believe that respecting Freedom of Navigation and adhering to international norms is essential for peace and economic growth in the larger and inter-linked marine geography of the Indo-Pacific'.[60] With China's assertiveness in the South China Sea in mind, Modi's explanation in March 2018 for increased defence links with Vietnam was that 'to enhance our maritime relations [...] we will jointly work for an open, independent and prosperous Indo-Pacific region where sovereignty and international laws are respected and where differences are resolved through talks'.[61]

Indian links with Japan were embedded in an Indo-Pacific context by Modi. In 2015, the joint *India and Japan Vision 2025* that Modi signed with the Japanese leader Shinzo Abe was subtitled as working together in 'the Indo-Pacific region'.[62] In 2016, Modi outlined both the geoeconomics ('we have agreed to cooperate closely to promote connectivity, infrastructure and capacity-building in the regions that occupy the inter-linked waters of the Indo-Pacific') and geopolitics ('the successful Malabar naval exercise has underscored the convergence in our strategic interests in the broad expanse of the waters of the Indo-Pacific') in an Indo-Pacific maritime fashion.[63]

Indian links with Australia were also firmly anchored as being 'Partners in the Pacific' in the *Joint Statement* signed by Modi and the Australian Prime Minister John Turnbull in April 2017.[64] It was no coincidence that the visit of John Key, the New Zealand Prime Minister, to India in October 2016 saw the Indo-Pacific deliberately used as an organizing framework for strategic cooperation:

The two Prime Ministers underlined the fact that India and New Zealand are both maritime nations with a strong interest in the Asia-Pacific and

Indo-Pacific regions being stable and prosperous, including by ensuring the safety and security of sea lanes and freedom of navigation.[65]

The key thing is the identification of the Indo-Pacific as a *region* that they were both members of, the strong maritime focus of their envisaged roles in that region, and the focus on the issue of freedom of navigation which was implicitly aimed at any future Chinese restrictions in the South China Sea.

Further east, the summit meetings held with South Pacific island leaders was given a firm maritime Indo-Pacific underpinning by Modi:

> The centre of gravity of global opportunities and challenges are shifting to the Pacific and Indian Ocean Region. The fortunes of nations in and around the two oceans are inter-linked. For this reason, the tides that bear hopes and bring challenges to the shores in India and the Pacific Islands are the same. That is why some call the region the Indo-Pacific Region.[66]

Modi's outreach to the South Pacific was welcomed by Nirupama Rao; it 'conjoins Indian interests and concerns in both the Indian and Pacific Oceans, providing ballast to the term "Indo-Pacific"'.[67]

Finally, the noticeable security cooperation now developing between India and the US not only involves tangible naval cooperation in both Indian and Pacific Ocean waters, it also involves common regional perspectives, indicated in the *Joint Strategic Vision for the Asia-Pacific and Indian Ocean Region* agreed upon by President Obama and Prime Minister Modi in January 2015. In his summit meeting with President Trump in June 2017, Modi maintained this 'logic of our strategic relationship' working together across 'the large maritime space of the Indo-Pacific' in 'ensuring that sea lanes, critical lines of trade and energy, remain secure and open to all'.[68]

Further down the government chain, other officials too deployed the Indo-Pacific language. A significant development was its explicit adoption by the Ministry of Defence. Modi's Defence Minister, Manohar Parrikar, was certain at the 2016 Shangri-la Dialogue about the geopolitical and geoeconomic significance of the 'Indo-Pacific region', a region that 'is now aptly and increasingly referred to by the strategic community as the Indo-Pacific'.[69] All in all, *Indo-Pacific* was mentioned five times by Parrikar, *Asia-Pacific* but once.

The geoeconomics of the Indo-Pacific, and with it responding to China's Maritime Silk Road (MSR) initiative going across the South China Sea and the Indian Ocean, were in play in April 2015, when Nirmala Sitharaman, the Minister of Commerce and Industry, signed the *Action Agenda for the*

India–Japan Investment and Trade Promotion and Indo-Pacific Economic Integration with her Japanese counterpart, Yoichi Miyazawa. This represented India's readiness to involve itself with Japan's Free and Open Indo-Pacific Strategy (FOIPS) initiative designed to strengthen infrastructure links across the Indo-Pacific, and which was seen as a more desirable scheme for India than the Chinese MSR initiative that both the Singh and Modi governments had avoided participating in. Less contentious economic mechanisms are represented by India's support for the setting up of a Regional Comprehensive Economic Partnership (RCEP), negotiation for which started in 2012, and which India's ambassador to Singapore, Jawed Ashraf, considered 'brings all major regional economies into a single arrangement, which can anchor integration and prosperity in the Indo-Pacific region'.[70] Significantly though it involves Pacific Asia countries like Japan and China, it does not involve the US.

Pranab Mukherjee also continued to pursue Indo-Pacific pathways as President. He portrayed the India–Indonesia naval cooperation as aimed at 'the security of the Indo-Pacific'.[71] In a pointed definition, Mukherjee argued that through 'sharing common values of democracy, freedom and rule of law' India and Japan were 'uniquely placed' to pursue economic and security cooperation 'in the Indo-Pacific region'.[72] China was an unstated background consideration in both these settings.

A significant type of new voice was from Ram Madhav, the General Secretary of the BJP. In 2015, he stepped into foreign policy utterances with his assertion:

> Today the global power axis has shifted from Pacific-Atlantic region to Indo-Pacific region. India is the third-largest and fastest growing economy in this region. We are an important counter-balancing power in this region too. We look at the great oceans as filled with great opportunities.[73]

This structural shift necessitated a change of terminology – 'the region, hitherto called Asia-Pacific, should now be renamed Indo-Pacific' – for while the term 'Asia-Pacific' reflected the rise of Japan and the Pacific Rim, the term 'Indo-Pacific' reflected the rise of India and the Indian Ocean in geopolitical and geoeconomic terms.[74] He welcomed as 'a pleasant departure PM uses phrase "Indo-Pacific" in place of "Asia-Pacific"' at the Raisina Dialogue in January 2017.[75] A degree of China-constraint was evident in his proposal of India as a counter-balance in the region, and like Modi he emphasized maritime underpinnings: 'today it is the Indo-Pacific region that has emerged as the new global power house. Our futures are invariably linked to the Indo-Pacific sea lanes'.[76]

India has a vision of Indo-Pacific economic cooperation, as presented by the Minister of State for External Affairs, Vijay Singh, in December 2017. In looking at the past he noted that 'our historical maritime trade flourished through the Malacca Straits across the Indo Pacific region' before going on to argue that 'in the context of current geo-political realities [...] let us unite to reconstruct the same trade connections today with other countries in the Indo-Pacific region'.[77]

However, the current geopolitical reality involves India's response to the MSR initiative pushed by Beijing since 2013, a maritime route going across the South China Sea and the Indian Ocean. Here it is significant that India continues to avoid participation in China's MSR initiative, thus refusing to send any representative to the Belt and Road Forum held in Beijing in early May 2017. Instead, India has mooted its own schemes for the Indian Ocean like *Mausam* and the *Cotton Route*. India has also moved to Indo-Pacific economic cooperation with Japan. This was first indicated in April 2015, when Nirmala Sitharaman signed the *Action Agenda for the India-Japan Investment and Trade Promotion and Indo-Pacific Economic Integration* with Yoichi Miyazawa. Indian support for an Africa–Asia Growth Corridor (AAGC), going from East Africa to Japan, was further signaled in the *Vision Document* drafted by the Delhi-based think tank Research and Information System (RIS), in conjunction with the ERIA from Singapore and the IDE-JETRO from Tokyo, and formally put forward by Modi at the African Development Bank meeting in late May 2017.

Looking forward: New directions

On 26 January 2018, Narendra Modi asserted that 'the Indo-Pacific region will be indispensable to India's future'.[78] Matters for observers to look out for in Indo-Pacific developments include India

1. Rearranging the internal structure of the Ministry of External Affairs to join together its Look South and Look East policies.
2. Gaining membership of the Asia-Pacific Economic Community (APEC).
3. Concluding negotiations for setting up the Regional Comprehensive Economic Partnership (RCEP).
4. Strengthening the Bay of Bengal (BIMSTEC) mechanism and pursuing its infrastructure projects overland to Thailand.
5. Strengthening the Ganga–Mekong Cooperation (GMC) mechanism.

6. Strengthening the Forum for India and Pacific Island Countries (FIPIC) mechanism.

7. Upgrading the officials-level India–Australia–Japan (IAJ) trilateral into a minister-level format like the India–Japan–US (IJUS) trilateral.

8. Establishing an India–Australia–US (IAUS) trilateral.

9. Moving to ministerial-level involvement in the Quadrilateral Alliance with Japan, Australia and the US, including naval exercises.

10. Blocking China's participation in the Indian Ocean Naval Symposium (IONS).

11. Furthering Indian strategic interest in the RIC (Russia–India–China) Consultation on Asia-Pacific Affairs (CAPA) mechanism.

12. Deciding whether or not to join in China's Maritime Silk Road initiative.

13. Actively synergizing with Japan's Free and Open Indo-Pacific initiative.

14. Actively synergizing with the US' Indo-Pacific Economic Corridor initiative.

15. Keeping China out of the MILAN exercises.

16. Building up the tri-service Andaman and Nicobar Island Command into an explicit Far Eastern Command, for operations further eastwards.

17. Developing bilateral naval exercises with Australia in the Pacific Ocean, as well as the initial ones started in the Indian Ocean in 2015 and 2017.

18. Considering whether to hold trilateral MALABAR exercises with the US and Japan in the South China Sea.

19. Considering whether or not to conduct joint naval operations with Vietnam in the South China Sea.

20. Making further use of Cam Ranh Bay as a focus point for India naval deployments in bigger strength in the South China Sea.

21. Making use of French military facilities in the Indian Ocean and Pacific under their Reciprocal Logistics Support agreement.

Matters 4–20 are unsurprisingly all explicitly or implicitly China-related. Admittedly there is some potential common ground in the Indo-Pacific with China over piracy threats and sea lane security.[79] However, the competitive dynamics seem more apparent, and with it the need for India to balance as well as to economically engage China in the Indo-Pacific. The suggestion in this chapter is that it will probably so continue, with regional friction more likely than cooperation. Stephen Waltz's 'balance of threat' logic, especially its drivers of *geographic proximity* and *perceived offensive intentions*, will continue to shape India's responses to China in the Indo-Pacific.

Looking ahead, how is research on the Indo-Pacific discourse evolving, what is the likely research agenda around the Indo-Pacific? Certainly, research needs to be done on clarifying exactly what maritime spaces (in the Indian and Pacific Oceans) the term 'Indo-Pacific' geographically covers, or at least what it means for India. This raises the question of establishing what actually constitutes a meaningful coherent strategic area. Research will continue on the nature of the Indo-Pacific concept. In other words, how far is it a geopolitical framework for analysis driven by competitive power politics of the realism strand of International Relations (IR) theory, and how far is it a geoeconomic framework for analysis incorporating cooperative interdependence theory? The answer in reality is that it covers both aspects.

The Indo-Pacific also sheds light on India's continuing development. As a process feeding into government, research can fruitfully look at the role of think tanks and their Track 1.5 events in shaping wider strategic discourse and government in India. Research may fruitfully be pursued on how far the Indo-Pacific is giving India an alternative to its previous restricted South Asian horizons. Partly this is with regard to nation identity, and calls for a greater maritime consciousness within India, as propounded vigorously by the National Maritime Formation. Research can be pursued on how far Indian is thinking of itself as less of a land power in South Asia and more of a maritime power in the Indo-Pacific. The role of organization and bureaucracy in Indian foreign policymaking can be pursued in terms of government structures, particularly at the Ministry of External Affairs being matched or perhaps not matched up with Indo-Pacific rationales.

Finally, although the term 'Indo-Pacific' may need further clarification, the pace of its acceptance in Indian strategic discourse and government formulations means that wider research directions will be from running other theoretical models through an Indo-Pacific lens. Models that can fruitfully be tested through the Indo-Pacific setting include balance of power (be it Mearsheimer's 'offensive realism' or Waltz's 'defensive/structural realism'), balance of threat, power transition, liberalism, interdependence and regionalism (identity formation and institutional mechanisms) and constructivism theories. Both geopolitics ('position' as location) and geoeconomics can be run through the Indo-Pacific setting, as indeed can critical geopolitics ('position' as aspirations, hopes and fears). Before getting drowned in such, at times competing, research paradigms, the researcher can of course be reminded of the approach recommended by Sil and Katzenstein, namely 'analytical eclecticism', since all the above theories and models have some application on the Indo-Pacific.

Notes

1   Subrahmanyam Jaishankar, 'Foreign Secretary's Keynote Address at the Inaugural Session of Second IORA Meeting of Experts for Maritime Safety & Security', 7 November 2017. Available at http://mea.gov.in/Speeches-Statements.htm?dtl/29095/.

2   G. Vijayachandra Naidu, '"Indo-Pacific" as a New Template of Analysis,' *Indian Foreign Affairs Journal*, 9, No. 2 (2014): 102–07. Also Saloni Sahil, 'India and the Emerging Indo-Pacific Strategic Space,' *Strategic Analysis Paper* (Future Directions), March 2013; Chietigi Bajpaee, 'Embedding India in Asia: Reaffirming the Indo-Pacific Concept', *Journal of Defence Studies*, 8, No. 4 (2014): 83–110; Priya Chacko, 'The Rise of the Indo-Pacific: Understanding Ideational Change and Continuity in India's Foreign Policy,' *Australian Journal of International Affairs*, 68, No. 4 (2014): 433–52; Jojin John, 'India Looks Beyond its Near Seas to Enhance its Interests in the Indo-Pacific,' *Strategic Vision*, 4, No. 22 (2015): 4–7; Deepa Ollapally, 'Understanding Indian Policy Dilemmas in the Indo-Pacific,' *Maritime Affairs*, 12, No. 1 (2016): 1–12; Gopal Suri, 'Case for a Regional Maritime Security Construct for the Indo-Pacific,' Occasional Paper (Vivekananda International Foundation), January 2016; Nyantara Shaunik, 'Conceptions of Security in the Regional Economic Cooperation Paradigm: The Curious Case of the Indo-Pacific,' *Jindal Journal of International Affairs*, 4, No. 1 (2016): 85–101.

3   For example, Gautam Mukhopadhaya, 'The Indo-Pacific Potential,' *The Hindu*, 13 December 2016; G. Parthasarathy, 'Revisiting Strategy in the Indo-Pacific', *The Hindu*. 20 September 2017; Sachin Chaturvedi, 'India-Asean Ties Hold the Key to Indo-Pacific Stability', *Hindustan Times*, 25 January 2018.

4   Sureesh Mehta, 'The Indo-Pacific Imperative,' in *Geopolitics of the Indo-Pacific*, edited by Pradeep Kaushiva and Abhijit Singh, 1–3 (New Delhi: KW Publishers Pvt. Ltd/ National Maritime Foundation, 2014). Also Saroj Bishoyi, 'Geostrategic Imperative of the Indo-Pacific Region,' *Journal of Defence Studies*, 10, No. 1 (2016): 89–102.

5   Jawed Ashref, 'Economic Links Integral to India's Act East Policy,' *Straits Times*, 27 July 2017.

6   Nirupama Rao, 'America's "Asian Pivot": The View from India,' Lecture (Brown University), 5 February 2013. Also Vijayachandra Naidu, 'What Does Indo-Pacific Mean to India?', ICWA Guest Column, 1 August 2014, p. 2.

7   Raghavendra Mishra, 'India in the Indo-Pacific: Maritime Stakes and Challenges', in *Indo-Pacific Region: Political and Strategic Prospects*, edited by Rajiv Bhatia and Vijay Sakhuja, 138–63 (New Delhi: ICWA, 2014); Abhijit Singh, 'Rebalancing India's Maritime Posture in the Indo-Pacific', *The Diplomat*, 5 September 2014.

8   Nitin Gokhale, 'From Look East to Engage East: How India's Own Pivot Will Change

Discourse in Indo-Pacific Region,' Article (Vivekananda International Foundation), 12 March 2013. Subhash Kapila, 'India's Strategic Pivot to the Indo Pacific', Paper (South Asia Analysis Group), No. 5831, 27 November 2014; Harsh Pant, 'Pivot to the Indo-Pacific', *The Hindu*, 12 April 2017.

9   Balaji Chandramohan, 'India's Strategic Outreach in the Indo-Pacific Region,' *Science, Technology and Security Forum*, 20 January 2017. Accessed on 15 December 2017. Available at http://stsfor.org/content/indias-strategic-outreach-indo-pacific-region.

10   Surbhi Moudgil, 'Geostrategic Convergence of India's Act East Policy and Indo-Pacific Strategies,' Article (CLAWS), 1675, December 2016.

11   Pankaj Jha, 'India as an Indo-Pacific Power,' Article (Centre for Indian Studies, Ho Chi Minh National Academy of Politics), 5 October 2016.

12   Pranab Mukherjee, 'Speech', 11 January 2014. Accessed on 15 December 2017. Available at http://pranabmukherjee.nic.in/sp110114.html.

13   Dinakaramohan Gnanagurunathan, 'India-Australia in the Indo-Pacific: A Blossoming Partnership,' *Viewpoints* (ICWA), 21 December 2012.

14   Ramanand Garge, 'India-Japan Strategic Partnership: The Evolving Synergy in the Indo-Pacific,' Articles (Vivekananda International Foundation), 23 March 2016; Sourabh Gupta, 'Abe and Modi Attempt to Bridge the Indo-Pacific,' *East Asia Forum*, 5 January 2016.

15   *Deccan Herald*, 'Modi, Macron to Shape India-France Cooperation in Indo-Pacific', 6 March 2018.

16   Shreya Upadhyay 'The Indo-Pacific and the Indo-US Relations: Geopolitics of Cooperation,' Issue Brief (IPCS), 562, November 2014.

17   'Inaugural U.S.-India-Japan Trilateral Ministerial Dialogue', Press Release, 30 September 2015. Accessed on 15 December 2017. Available at http://www.mea.gov.in/press-releases.htm?dtl/25868/. See also Hemant Singh and Karl Inderfurth, 'An Indo-Pacific Triangle of Consequence,' Issue Brief, 1, No. 2 (20 December 2011).

18   Titli Basu, 'India's Approach towards Indo-Pacific Triangularity,' *IDSA News*, 27 May 2016.

19   Ministry of External Affairs, 'India-Australia-Japan-U.S. Consultations on Indo-Pacific', Press Release, 12 November 2017. Available at http://www.mea.gov.in/press-releases. htm?dtl/29110/. Also Abhijnan Rei, 'Reclaiming the Indo-Pacific: A Political-military Strategy for Quad 2.0', Occasional Papers (ORF), 27 March 2018.

20   Nitin Pai, 'India and the Indo-Pacific Balance,' in *Indo-Pacific Maritime Security: Challenges and Cooperation*, edited by David Brewster, 84–87 (Acton: National Security College, 2016).

21   Abhijit Singh, 'India as Maritime Security Partner in the Indo-Pacific,' in *Asian Strategic Review 2015*, edited by S. D. Muni and Vivek Chadha, 145–65 (Delhi: IDSA, 2015).

22   Government of India, 'Visit of Indian Warship to Port Majuro, Marshall Islands,' Press Information Bureau, 13 August 2016. Accessed on 15 December 2017. Available at http://pib.nic.in/newsite/PrintRelease.aspx?relid=148884.

23   Ramanand Garge, 'MALABAR-2015 – Emerging Collective Defence in the Indo-Pacific,' *Australian Journal of Maritime and Ocean Affairs*, 7, No. 4 (2015): 252–55.

24   Government of India, *Indian Maritime Doctrine*, 65–67 (New Delhi: Integrated Headquarters, Ministry of Defence, 2004).

25   Premvir Das, 'Maritime Violence in the Indian Ocean,' 13 October 2006, in *Indo-Japan*

Dialogue on Ocean Security, 108–32, 111, 115 (Tokyo: Ocean Policy Research Foundation, 2006). See also Premvir Das, 'India's Maritime Interests in the Indo-Pacific,' *Seminar*, 6, No. 70 (June 2015). Available at http://www.india-seminar.com/semframe.html; Premvir Das, 'India's Indo-Pacific Challenges,' *Business Standard*, 1 April 2017.

26 Gurpreet Khurana, 'Security of Sea Lines: Prospects for India-Japan Cooperation,' *Strategic Analysis*, 31, No. 1 (2007): 139–53; Khurana, 'China's maritime Strategy: Implications for the Indo-Pacific Region,' in *The Rise of China*, edited by Ved Malik and Jorg Schultz, 155–81 (New Delhi, Pentagon Press, 2008). See also Gurpreet Khurana, 'The Indo-Pacific Concept: Retrospective and Prospect,' Issue Brief (National Maritime Foundation), 2 February 2017.

27 Arun Prakash, 'Assuming Leadership,' *Force*, December 2009. Accessed on 15 December 2017. Available at http://forceindia.net/FORCEINDIAOLDISSUE/arunprakash15. aspx.

28 Arun Prakash, 'Rise of the East: The Maritime Dimension,' *Maritime Affairs*, 7, No. 2 (2011): 1–13. Also Arun Prakash, 'Maritime Security: An Indo-Pacific Perspective,' *Defence Watch* (March 2012): 9–14.

29 Shyam Saran, 'Mapping the Indo-Pacific,' *Indian Express*, 29 October 2011.

30 'Indo-Pacific is the New Geopolitical Reality,' Press Release (Institute for Defence Studies and Analyses), 1 November 2012. See also Dinakaramohan Gnanagurunathan (ICWA), 'India and the Idea of the "Indo-Pacific",' *East Asia Forum*, 20 October 2012; Priya Chacko, 'India and the Indo-Pacific: An Emerging Regional Vision,' *IPGRC Policy Brief*, November 2012.

31 Conference papers collected in Kaushiva and Singh (eds), *Geopolitics of the Indo-Pacific*.

32 Seminar papers collected in Sandeep Dewan (ed.), *Perspectives of the Indo-Pacific Region: Aspirations, Challenges and Strategy* (New Delhi: United Service Institute/Vij Books, 2014).

33 Conference papers collected in Rajiv Bhatia and Vijay Sakhuja (eds), *Indo-Pacific Region: Political and Strategic Prospects* (New Delhi: ICWA, 2014).

34 Conference papers collected in David Michel and Ricky Passarelli (eds), *Sea Change: Evolving Maritime Geopolitics in the Indo-Pacific Region* (Washington: Stimson Center, 2014).

35 Seminar papers collected in Vijay Sakhuja and Kapil Narula (eds), *Maritime Dynamics in the Indo-Pacific* (Delhi: National Maritime Foundation, 2016).

36 Conference papers collected in Gurpreet Khurana and Antara Singh (eds), *India and China: Constructing Peaceful and Stable Maritime Order in the Indo-Pacific* (New Delhi: National Maritime Foundation, 2016).

37 Papers collected in Sharad Tewari and Roshan Khanijo (eds), *The Indo-Pacific Region: Security Dynamics and Challenges* (New Delhi: Vij Books, 2016).

38 Ranjit Rai, 'India and China: New Great Game in the Indo-Pacific Ocean Region,' *Defence and Security Alert*, 3, No. 12 (2012): 47–50; Kamal Davar, 'The Indo-Pacific Great Game Unfolds,' *Hindustan Times*, 23 January 2014; Bawa Singh, 'New Geopolitical Great Game of Indo-Pacific: Challenges and Options for India,' *Modern Diplomacy*, 22 May 2016.

39 Priya Chacko, 'India and the Indo-Pacific from Singh to Modi: Geopolitical and Geoeconomic Entanglements,' in *New Regional Geopolitics in the Indo-Pacific: Drivers, Dynamics and Consequences*, 43–59 (London: Routledge, 2016).

40   Nirupama Rao, 'Address by Ambassador Nirupama Rao at UC-Berkeley,' India and the Asia-Pacific: Expanding engagement, 5 December 2011. Accessed on 15 December 2017. Avaiable at https://www.indianembassy.org/archives_details.php?nid=1690.

41   Ranjan Mathai, 'Building on Convergences: Deepening India-U.S. Strategic Partnership,' 6 February 2012, in *India's Foreign Relations-2012: Documents*, edited by Atvar Bhasin, 1509 (New Delhi: Ministry of External Affairs, 2012).

42   Arackaparambil Antony, 'Address,' Annual Maritime Power Conference, 27 February 2012. Accessed on 15 December 2017. Available at http://pib.nic.in/newsite/erelcontent.aspx?relid=80543.

43   Salman Khurshid, 'Interview ("India Eyes Stronger Ties with S-E Asia"),' *Straits Times*, 5 July 2013.

44   Manmohan Singh, 'PM's Opening Statement at Plenary Session of India-ASEAN Commemorative Summit,' 20 December 2012, in *India's Foreign Relations-2012: Documents*, edited by Atvar Bhasin, 457. See also Indrani Bagchi, 'Indo-Pacific Finds Pride of Place in Asean Lexicon,' *Times of India*, 20 December 2012.

45   Nirupama Rao, 'America's "Asian Pivot": The View from India,' 5 February 2013. Accessed on 15 December 2017. Available at http://www.indianembassy.org/prdetail2097.

46   Sanjay Singh, 'Valedictory Address,' Geopolitics of the Indo-Pacific Region conference, ICWA, 22 March 2013, in *India's Foreign Relations-2013: Documents*, edited by Atvar Bhasin, 291, 294 (New Delhi: Ministry of External Affairs, 2013). Also Sanjay Singh, 'Indo-Pacific – a Construct for Peace and Stability,' *Indian Foreign Affairs Journal*, 9, No. 2 (2014): 96–101.

47   Salman Khurshid, 'Keynote Address', in *Indo-Pacific Region: Political and Strategic Prospects*, edited by Rajiv Bhatia and Vijay Sakhuja, ix–xii, xi (New Delhi: ICWA, 2014). Also Saloni Sahil, 'India and the Emerging Indo-Pacific Strategic Space,' *Strategic Analysis Paper* (Future Directions), March 2013.

48   Khurshid, 'Keynote Address', xi.

49   Salman Khurshid, 'Speech of External Affairs Minister at the launch of ASEAN India Centre', 21 June 2013, in *India's Foreign Relations-2013: Documents*, 295, 298

50   Salman Khurshid, 'External Affairs Minister's speech at Rikkyo University, Tokyo', 26 March 2013, in *India's Foreign Relations-2013: Documents*, 1176

51   Manmohan Singh, 'Prime Minister's Address to Japan-India Association', 28 May 2013, in *India's Foreign Relations-2013: Documents*, 1182.

52   Rakesh Sood, 'Strategic Networking in the Indo-Pacific,' *The Hindu*, 12 September 2014; Subhash Kapila, 'India's Strategic Pivot to the Indo Pacific,' Paper (South Asia Analysis Group), 5831, 27 November 2014; Patrick M. Cronin and Darshana Baruah, 'The Modi Doctrine for the Indo-Pacific Maritime Region,' *The Diplomat*, 2 December 2014; C. Raja Mohan, 'Modi's Indo-Pacific,' *Indian Express*, 21 November 2015; Kunal Mukherjee, 'Security Challenges Faced by the Modi Administration in the Indo-Pacific Region,' *Journal of Comparative Asian Development*, 15, No. 1 (2016): 156–78.

53   Vijay Singh, 'Speech' (Gateway of India Dialogue), 14 June 2016. Accessed on 15 December 2017. Available at http://www.mea.gov.in/Speeches-Statements.htm?dtl/26910/.

54   Subrahmanyam Jaishankar, 'India, ASEAN and Changing Geopolitics,' 11 July 2017. Accessed on 15 December 2017. Available at http://www.mea.gov.in/Speeches-Statements.htm?dtl/28609/.

55 Narendra Modi, 'Interview,' *Wall Street Journal*, 26 May 2016. Accessed on 15 December 2017. Available at http://blogs.wsj.com/indiarealtime/2016/05/26/read-an-edited-transcript-of-the-wall-street-journals-interview-with-indian-prime-minister-narendra-modi/.

56 Narendra Modi, 'Prime Minister's Address to the Joint Session of the Australian Parliament,' 18 November 2015. Accessed on 15 December 2017. Available at http://www.mea.gov.in/Speeches-Statements.htm?dtl/24269/. See also 'India, Australia and the Indo-Pacific Matrix,' *Deccan Chronicle*, 20 December 2014.

57 Narendra Modi, 'Remarks by Prime Minister at the 10th East Asia Summit,' 22 November 2015. Accessed on 15 December 2017. Available at http://www.mea.gov.in/Speeches-Statements.htm?dtl/26053/. Also Sreeram Chaulia, 'Out of APEC, India Eyes Indo-Pacific Influence,' *Today*, 13 November 2014.

58 'Joint Strategic Vision of India-France Cooperation in the Indian Ocean Region', 10 March 2018. Accessed on 11 March 2018. Available at http://www.mea.gov.in/bilateral-documents.htm?dtl/29598/.

59 Narendra Modi, 'Press Statement,' 12 December 2016. Available at https://www.mea.gov.in/Speeches-Statements.htm?dtl/27803/. Also Gautam Mukhopadhaya, 'The Indo-Pacific Potential,' *The Hindu*, 13 December 2016.

60 Narendra Modi, 'Inaugural Address by Prime Minister at Second Raisina Dialogue,' 17 January 2107. Accessed on 15 December 2017. Available at https://www.mea.gov.in/Speeches-Statements.htm?dtl/27948/.

61 Narendra Modi, 'Statement by PM at Joint Press Meet with Vietnamese President', 3 March 2018. Accessed on 4 March 2018. Available at https://www.narendramodi.in/prime-minister-narendra-modi-vietnamese-president-tran-dai-quang-at-a-joint-press-statement-539179.

62 Bhaskar Roy, 'India and Japan Affirm Security of Indo-Pacific Region,' Paper (South Asia Analysis Group), 6052, 4 January 2016. Also Dhruva Jaishankar, 'India and Japan: Emerging Indo-Pacific Security Partnership,' *RSIS Commentary*, 130, 30 May 2016.

63 Narendra Modi, 'Media Statement, by Prime Minister during His Visit to Japan,' 11 November 2016. Accessed on 15 December 2017. Available at https://www.mea.gov.in/Speeches-Statements.htm?dtl/27595/.

64 'India-Australia Joint Statement,' 10 April 2017. Accessed on 15 December 2017. Available at http://www.mea.gov.in/bilateral-documents.htm?dtl/28367/.

65 'India-New Zealand Joint Statement,' 26 October 2016. Accessed on 15 December 2017. Available at https://mea.gov.in/bilateral-documents.htm?dtl/27535/.

66 Narendra Modi, 'Opening Remarks by Prime Minister at Summit of Forum for India Pacific Island Countries,' 21 August 2015. Accessed on 15 December 2017. Available at http/www.mea.gov.in/Speeches-Statements.htm?dtl/25746/.

67 Nirupama Rao, 'New, Strong and Clear Outreach,' *The Hindu*, 4 March 2016. Also Aniket Bhavthankar, 'India Broadens Strategic Canvas, Establishes Role in Indo-Pacific,' *SPS Insight*, 6 June 2016.

68 Narendra Modi, 'For the U.S. and India, a Convergence of Interests and Values,' *Wall Street Journal*, 27 June 2017.

69 Manohar Parrikar, 'Speech' (Shangri-La Dialogue), 4 June 2016. Accessed on 15 December 2017. Available at http://pib.nic.in/newsite/PrintRelease.aspx?relid=145975. See also Raja Mohan, 'Sailing into the Indo-Pacific,' *Indian Express*, 7 June 2016.

70   Ashref, 'Economic Links Integral to India's Act East Policy.'
71   Pranab Mukherjee, 'Speech' (Banquet in honour of the President of Indonesia), 12 December 2016. Accessed on 15 December 2017. Available at http://presidentofindia. nic.in/speeches-detail.htm?578.
72   Pranab Mukherjee, 'President of India's Message on the Eve of National Day of Japan,' Press Release, 22 December 2015. Accessed on 15 December 2017. Available at http:// presidentofindia.nic.in/press-release-detail.htm?1968.
73   Ram Madhav, 'Singapore and India – Civilizational Bonding to Strategic Partnership,' 22 May 2015. Accessed on 15 December 2017. Available at http://www.rammadhav. in/articles/singapore-india-civilizational-bonding-to-strategic-partnership/.
74   Ram Madhav, 'Emerging Challenges in the Indo-Pacific Region,' Article (India Foundation), 23 March 2017. Accessed on 15 December 2017. Available at http:// www.indiafoundation.in/articles-and-papers/emerging-challenges-in-the-indo-pacific-region.html.
75   Ram Madhav, 'In a Pleasant Departure PM Uses Phrase "Indo-Pacific" in Place of Asia-Pacific', Twitter, 17 January 2017. Accessed on 15 December 2017. Available at https://twitter.com/rammadhavbjp/status/821344454481055745.
76   Ram Madhav, 'The Advent of BRICS Era', 11 June 2017. Accessed on 15 December 2017. Available at http://www.rammadhav.in/speeches/brics2017-the-advent-of-brics-era/.
77   Vijay Singh, 'Address' (India-ASEAN Connectivity Summit), 11 December 2017. Accessed on 15 December 2017. Available at http://www.mea.gov.in/Speeches-Statements.htm?dtl/.
78   Narendra Modi, 'Shared Values, Common Destiny', *New Straits Times*, 26 January 2018.
79   Antara Singh, 'India, China and the US: Strategic Convergence in the Indo-Pacific,' *Journal of the Indian Ocean region*, 12, No. 2 (2016); 161–76.

11

India and Nuclear Deterrence

Rajesh Basrur

Nuclear deterrence has been a formal component of India's defence strategy for the past two decades. The public debate, as well as the specialist literature on the subject, has been, unexceptionably and predominantly, concerned with two questions: First, what are the requirements of deterrence or, if put in another way, how much is enough? And second, how can a stable strategic environment be best maintained under the shadow of nuclear weapons? Not much scholarly effort has been devoted to historically rooted theoretical analysis that might clarify some of the difficult problems facing Indian deterrence strategy. This chapter will attempt to do so.

The Indian experience has been uneven with regard to these questions. First, notwithstanding the adoption of a doctrine of 'minimum credible deterrence,' it is not at all clear what 'minimum' means, and critics have argued that the Indian arsenal has gone well beyond the requirements of a minimal deterrent. Second, Indian policymakers have been deeply troubled about how to make an adequate response to the problems of stability emanating primarily from Islamabad, but also from Beijing. Below, I assess the Indian strategy's attempts to respond to these two fundamental questions. I do so under the assumption that a theoretically informed analysis helps us understand better the foundations of policy. From the standpoint of international relations (IR) theory, my analysis draws extensively from the classical and neoclassical realist approaches. With respect to the first question, which is about the sufficiency of capability, neoclassical realists – at least in their original avatar, for they have become more diverse now – would identify the source of the problem as the domestic roots of suboptimal policy responses to systemic incentives, that is, the failure of policymakers to respond cost-effectively to the requirements of a specific external environment in which the state finds itself.[1] I will show how the understanding of 'minimum' deterrence in India is riddled with inconsistencies arising from a lack of clarity about just what a minimum deterrence doctrine is. These contradictions are driven by a conventional pre-nuclear interpretation of nuclear reality that persists in spite of a mass of evidence to the contrary.[2] Here, the neoclassical realist approach more or less merges with the constructivist view because the problem centres on a structure of thought that constrains thinking and produces a suboptimal result. As I will show, Indian deterrence strategy lacks coherence because it carries two contradictory ways of thinking: one that is minimalist and one that is maximalist.

The second question calls for a more nuanced analysis: India's early inability to anticipate an unstable relationship with Pakistan can be partly explained from the neoclassical realist position – India's political elite failed to understand that, under certain conditions, instability is inherent in a nuclear-strategic relationship. But the problem goes deeper since it does not make a difference to outcomes even if it *is* understood. If one state in a nuclear rivalry is revisionist, stability is very hard to achieve as the revisionist state may be in a position to exploit its deterrence capability to apply pressure on the other. This is precisely what has happened to India: Pakistan has been able to employ a strategy that is 'asymmetric,' that is, one which involves backing terrorist groups to target India and thereby force the latter to the negotiating table. This is the intellectual domain of classical Cold War nuclear strategizing that, in terms of IR theory, falls within the classical realist paradigm, where the focus is not only on the constancy of conflict in the international system, but on the ways diplomacy and strategy are exercised by states to maximize gain.[3] In policy terms, this places India in a deeply problematic situation that confounds solutions since war is not an option. Moreover, the source of Pakistani revisionism is domestic politics: the state is unstable and lacks legitimacy, so that the main source of national solidarity lies in unifying against the 'other,' which is India. So New Delhi has little control over Pakistan's revisionism.

In the case of China, the problem is more complex. Neither India nor China is a revisionist state in the way that Pakistan is, which makes the relationship more stable. Yet, for two reasons, it carries a degree of sustained tension that could conceivably bring greater instability. First, a characteristic feature of the Sino-Indian relationship has long been a security dilemma – where the defensive measures taken by a security-seeking state are regarded as potentially or actually offensive by the other, which produces tensions between them.[4] In this particular case, the tension has grown considerably as a result of typical balance-of-power politics that reflect the realist paradigm, both in its classical form and in its later neorealist version.[5]

A greater measure of complexity comes from what might be called a 'cascading' security dilemma, that is, China's response to the security dilemma stemming from its competitive relationship with the United States intensifies the security dilemma for India, which sees China's military strengthening efforts (aimed primarily at the US) as threatening. But China, while not a revisionist state, is not fully a status quo state either. Rather, given its internal vulnerabilities arising from the challenges to its authoritarian system, China can be viewed as intentionally sustaining a degree of tension with India (and others) in order to mobilize nationalist public opinion for domestic political support. This makes it something less than a pure security-seeking state and to a significant degree an *insecurity-generating state* that prefers to foster an unstable equilibrium with India. With respect to both the Pakistani and Chinese cases, the security dilemma is conducive to stabilization, but the evidence shows that they are not purely security seeking states, which makes stabilization truly problematic for India.

In the next section, I critique India's nuclear doctrine and strategy and show its internal contradictions with respect to the question of sufficiency. In the section that follows, I examine the reasons why India has been unable to attain stable strategic relationships with Pakistan and China.

Contradictions in India's minimalism

Indian writings on minimum deterrence display a singular lack of close attention to the basic question asked above, that is, what exactly are the requirements of minimum deterrence and what are the central principles around which a minimalist strategy should be built? But first let us obtain a clear sense of what might be the basis of a minimalist doctrine. The seminal Cold War era debate between the maximalist ideas of Albert Wohlstetter, an American thinker, and the minimalist response of Patrick Blackett, a British academician, sets the two approaches against each other in their essence.[6]

The chief differences between them on specific criteria and the practical implications that follow from their views are outlined below.

Surprise attack

Wohlstetter was deeply influenced by Pearl Harbor, on which his wife Roberta had written a major study. The entire edifice of his carefully structured views about deterrence rested on his concern about the risk of a surprise nuclear attack. He rejected the opinion of observers on both sides of the Atlantic (specifically referring to Blackett as well as others) that deterrence is 'automatic' once two adversaries have nuclear weapons. In his view, a nuclear Pearl Harbor was possible because (1) an adversary might judge that, notwithstanding the high costs associated with a first strike, the cost of attacking first would be lower than the cost of not doing so; and because (2) the target state might suffer from intelligence failure, thus making it vulnerable to a surprise strike. The authoritarian Soviet system, in his view, had the advantage of secrecy compared to the open and democratic American one.[7] Blackett, on the other hand, downplayed the risk of a potential surprise attack. He believed that the scope for such an attack would be significantly reduced by the numerous signals that would inevitably appear during the course of preparations for what would have to be a very large-scale attack in order to minimize the adversary's capacity to retaliate. The Soviet Union, he asserted, could not be confident that American intelligence would have no inkling of such preparations, for instance, the actions of civil defence authorities preparing to defend against a counterattack.[8]

The scale of damage required to deter

Wohlstetter believed that the Soviet Union, which had survived twenty million deaths in the Second World War, would be willing to absorb high levels of damage in a nuclear conflict, particularly if its leaders were confident of limiting damage to less than this number.[9] It followed that the Soviet Union could only be deterred by the prospect of catastrophic damage. Blackett's rejoinder asserted that Russia had a history of defending against attack rather than aggression and that 'any country which has experienced the horror of losing twenty million people in one war is very unlikely to take any avoidable risk of it happening again'.[10] In his view, the Soviet Union – and states generally – could be deterred by much lower levels of damage than those envisaged as necessary by Wohlstetter.

Second-strike capability

Taken together, the possibility of a nuclear bolt from the blue and his belief in the Soviet Union's high tolerance of damage led Wohlstetter to assert that 'to deter an attack means being able to strike back in spite of it. It means, in other words, a capability to strike second'.[11] A second-strike capability, he held, involved the ability to survive a first attack, to 'make and communicate the decision to retaliate', and to 'reach and destroy enemy targets after penetrating enemy defences'.[12] And, of course, the damage inflicted would have to be of great magnitude if deterrence was to be ensured. Blackett retorted that a state contemplating aggression could not afford to assume that it could knock out all enemy forces in a first strike and that, given the massive destructive power of atomic weapons, there would always be the risk of millions of fatalities arising from a relatively small counter-strike.[13] Since he believed that the Soviet Union did not have a high tolerance of casualties, he held that deterrence was already in place.

The problem of imbalance

A key implication arising from the debate relates to the question of balance. Wohlstetter's belief that an effective second-strike capability meant the capacity to inflict large-scale damage on an adversary led inevitably to the preference for an advantage in the balance of nuclear forces. If the forces were equal in capability, the side striking first would have the capacity to inflict greater damage. This would, by inference, apply even if the United States strengthened its forces by reducing their vulnerability since the adversary could do the same. Indeed, Wohlstetter specifically argued that 'an effective system of retaliation must meet changing demands placed upon it by the aggressor' and that this inevitably meant the need to bear high costs.[14] Consequently, small forces would be unable to deter large ones effectively. Blackett, because he believed the damage requirement for deterrence was not very large, averred that an attacker five times stronger than the defender would still be deterred since the cost imposed on the former by the latter's retaliation would remain unacceptably high.[15] It followed that 'no country could make use of even a substantial degree of nuclear superiority by staging a first strike without incurring a high probability of very heavy destruction'.[16]

The debate has an important bearing on how states determine their nuclear doctrines and postures. The practical implications of the two arguments diverge considerably for decision-makers seeking optimal allocation of resources. The contrasting 'models' may also be labelled 'assured destruction' and 'minimum deterrence' models respectively. These are, of course, ideal types, but they do clearly approximate the divergent doctrines and postures adopted by the United States and the Soviet Union/Russia on one hand and by China and India on the other. The Wohlstetter model presses in the direction of maximalism, the Blackett model in the direction of minimalism. The two models shape proclivities with respect to force acquisitions, postures, the degree of arms competition, and approaches to arms control and disarmament.

There is no consistent enunciation of a Blackett-type model in the Indian discourse. Even the most minimalist of Indian experts on nuclear deterrence, K. Sundarji, who asserted that India must not make the mistake of the United States' 'obscene amassing of unusable weapons',[17] regularly based his arguments about sufficiency on Wohlstetter's concepts like 'vulnerability' and 'survivability', which are the primary drivers of force expansion.[18] Similarly, a strongly minimalist outline of deterrence doctrine enunciated by Minister for External Affairs Jaswant Singh in a press interview in November 1999, wherein he expressly rejected Cold War nuclear doctrine, simultaneously stressed the importance of 'credibility' based on 'survivable' forces in an unintended expression of Wohlstetter's doctrinal tenets.[19] The contradiction was even more glaring in the Draft Nuclear Doctrine released by the National Security Advisory Board in August 1999. The document was a mishmash of minimalist and maximalist precepts with recommendations ranging from non-deployment of weapons systems to a triad of delivery systems resting on credibility, effectiveness and survivability.[20] These inconsistencies continue to be widely reflected in more recent writings, which are replete with Wohlstetterian language and unfettered by any effort to interrogate their utility in the light of actual historical experience drawn from the working of deterrence. It is ironic that Indian strategic experts rarely refer to Blackett's thinking despite his close links to the Indian policy establishment. He was a personal friend of Nehru, wrote an influential report on the organization of India's defence apparatus, and his views on atomic weapons, including his advocacy of 'the reduction of nuclear weapons to the absolute minimum',[21] were well known.[22]

More importantly, the history of nuclear confrontation clearly shows that power balances – so central to Wohlstetter's thinking – are of no consequence in determining nuclear crises' outcomes. Three Cold War crises provide evidence of this. In 1961, when the Berlin Crisis occurred, Soviet warheads, numbering 2,492, constituted just 11.21 per cent of the US total of 22,229 warheads. Again, in the Cuban Missile Crisis of 1962, the proportion was only marginally larger: Soviet warheads numbered 3,346 and were 13.10 per cent of the American total of 25,540 warheads.[23] Similarly, during the 1969 Sino-Soviet border conflict, China possessed just 50 warheads, which amounted to a mere 0.47 per cent of the Soviet total of 10,671 warheads.[24] In none of the crises did the 'balance' of nuclear or even conventional capability have any impact on the outcome. The evidence clearly shows that nuclear weapons upend the notion of balance of power, held so dear by practitioners and scholars of nuclear strategy, and backs Blackett's view of how deterrence works. However, no effort has been made by those who study and write on deterrence to draw from the lessons of history. This, of course, is a general malaise and not confined to the Indian strategic community.

The net result of the absence of a coherent doctrine has been that components of Indian nuclear strategy have drifted in different directions. Two distinctly divergent trajectories are visible. On the one hand, key aspects of early minimalism remain in place. Notwithstanding India's refusal to sign the Comprehensive Test Ban Treaty (CTBT) and some criticisms about the reliability of Indian warheads, there is no interest in further testing. India also retains the non-deployed or 'recessed' posture of its weapons systems. There is no indication that India (in contrast with Pakistan) is pushing hard to increase the quantity of its warheads. India still supports universal nuclear disarmament, though perhaps with less optimistic enthusiasm than before.

In contrast – and fuelled by the refrain that 'second-strike capability' and 'survivability' are the essential requirements for 'credible' deterrence – India is developing a wide range of weapons systems: a triad of delivery platforms, a wide range of missiles, including missiles with ranges exceeding 5,000 kilometres (and possibly 10,000 kilometres), multiple warhead missiles, manoeuvrable warheads and hypersonic cruise missiles.[25] It is not clear how cost-effective these systems are for the deterrence of nuclear adversaries.

What explains the prevalence of these contradictory pulls in different directions? The continuation of key components of minimalism since the 1990s seems to represent a low-cost/low-risk option – there is no pressure for deployment since deterrence clearly has been at work, notably in India–Pakistan crises, from the early 1990s, beginning well before the overt declaration of nuclear status by the two countries.[26] More importantly, why has research and development on weapons systems taken on a life of its own and departed from the minimalist stance? The reasons include the technological imperative, which propels competitive development of weapons systems, the bureaucratic interests of missile producers and the failure of civilian policymakers to fully understand weapons systems and their roles, which stems from their peculiar notion that weapons are not their 'territory' (except where costs are concerned).[27] But, above all, the acceptability of a discourse that has no basis in fact, but nevertheless captivates strategists worldwide, reflects an intellectual reality: the 'nuclear revolution' remains, in a sense, a non-revolution.[28] Nuclear strategy is still dominated by a conventional 'thought style' – a persistent habit that has resisted the nuclear revolution with considerable success.[29] With respect to Indian strategic thinking, the conventional thought style is particularly deeply embedded because the basic vocabulary is drawn almost entirely from Wohlstetterian writings reflecting the dominant discourse of the Cold War.

Stability

In the present context, the term 'strategic stability' is about the degree to which a nuclear rivalry exists in a stable state. Traditionally, this has meant crisis stability (the absence of incentives to use nuclear weapons first) and arms race stability (the absence of incentives for arms racing). But strategic stability can be seen in a more nuanced way. First, while stability tends to be equated with equilibrium, it is useful to distinguish between a stable and an unstable equilibrium.[30] An unstable equilibrium (the instability may vary in degree) such as a détente between nuclear rivals is subject to rapid change (which occurred during the Cold War after the Soviet invasion of Afghanistan), whereas a stable equilibrium is highly unlikely to be upset. In essence, the degree of stability is political. India's relationship with its adversaries have been different in this respect. With Pakistan, the relationship has been very unstable; with China, we find elements of comparatively greater stability, but the degree of stability has been decreasing and there are portents of greater instability.

The key factor determining the degree of stability between rivals is the extent to which a state is willing to adhere to the status quo or wants to alter it. Between India's two nuclear adversaries, Pakistan is strongly revisionist and, because of its constant efforts to alter the status quo on Kashmir, the India–Pakistan relationship has been dogged by instability. Over time, India's inability to retain the status quo and the costs imposed by Pakistani strategy have in turn made it a revisionist state, or at least a dissatisfied state seeking to reinforce a status quo which it is finding increasingly difficult to defend. In effect, over time, costly instability has itself become the status quo that India seeks to revise. India's main problem is how to alter the current unstable status quo or, put in another way, how to revert to the status quo ante, in a controlled way that evades the risk of nuclear conflict. This has been a vexing problem that Indian leaders have been hard put to tackle satisfactorily since its central source is Pakistani domestic politics. Lacking internal legitimacy, the 'hybrid' Pakistani state – a system designed formally as a 'democracy' but in practice dominated by the military – depends on its adversarial relationship with India to keep its elites in power and the polity glued together.[31]

With respect to China, though there are more positive elements to the relationship – notably a substantial trade and investment relationship – there are two sources of instability that have grown significantly in the post-Cold War years. First, there is a security dilemma arising from the efforts of each to defend its strategic interests and the perception in both states that the other is hostile. Here, it is a matter of two security-seeking states unable to build trust between them. Second, from the Indian standpoint, China is not entirely a security-seeking state since it has shown signs of generating tension for domestic political reasons: reasons that are not the consequence of the bilateral relationship. Rather, China appears to have an interest in keeping its border dispute with India simmering in order to mobilize domestic support – or offset domestic political opposition – in an environment characterized by domestic political uncertainty and potential threats to the current regime. Together, the two sources of India–China instability portend a possible nuclear rivalry that could assume significant proportions. India's capacity to respond effectively to this troubling relationship is limited because of its relative weakness, because China's attention is primarily directed towards the United States, and (analogous to the Pakistan relationship) because of the domestic roots of Chinese policy.

In both cases, the key to understanding instability is the 'stability–instability paradox', under which stability at the nuclear level (incentives not to fight) is offset by instability at lower levels. In its original form, the paradox meant that when states are restrained by the fearsome destructive power of nuclear weapons from crossing the nuclear threshold, sub-nuclear instability can exist because conventional war is possible.[32] In a more recent formulation, instability is located at the *subconventional* level since nuclear-armed states find it prudent not to fight conventional wars either.[33] The difference between the Pakistani and Chinese cases is that China's aims are restricted to generating limited non-violent frictions, whereas Pakistan's aims involve the use of potentially unlimited violence by third parties (non-state actors) against the Indian state. The latter strategy has greater potential to unleash nuclear conflict and is therefore more unstable.

Pakistan: High-level instability

The advent of nuclear weapons in South Asia activated the stability–instability paradox as one side of the India–Pakistan relationship was a revisionist state. While India had not given up its claim to all of the divided territory of Kashmir, it was fundamentally status quo-ist because it was content to leave the division unchanged as a de facto dividing line. In contrast, Pakistan was deeply discontented, even more so after Bangladesh was separated from it by war with India in 1971. Further, in 1984, the Indian Army occupied the Siachen Glacier, a no-man's land that had been left undefined by an agreement to formalize the Line of Control (LoC) which separated the armed forces of the two countries in Kashmir. Islamabad then exploited its nuclear shield, which it had acquired in the mid-1980s, and put India under pressure by backing terrorist groups like Jaish-i-Muhammad and Lashkar-i-Taiba, whose *jihadi* fighters took advantage of domestic turbulence in Indian-held Kashmir to perpetrate violent attacks on Indian civilian and military targets.[34] Tension grew as *jihadi* strikes escalated during the 1990s.

Indian political leaders assumed that the formal declaration of nuclear weapons status by the two countries in 1998 had in effect frozen the Kashmir dispute because they believed that Pakistan would no longer be in a position to go to war against a nuclear India.[35] They were in for a rude surprise when, in the spring of 1999, Pakistani troops disguised as militants occupied the frosty heights of the Kargil region in Kashmir on the Indian side of the LoC. The fighting that ensued between May and July 1999 was similar to the 1969 Sino-Soviet border conflict in that combat was limited to the LoC region and did not involve major offensive operations that could have triggered an all-out conventional war with the attendant risk of nuclear use.[36] The lesson drawn by Indian policymakers from Kargil was that nuclear weapons did not rule out war altogether between India and Pakistan – an imperfect conclusion that still leaves unclear what exactly is meant by 'limited war'.

The Kargil adventure proved to be costly for Pakistan, but the setback did not alter mindsets in Islamabad. On the contrary, the strategy of cross-border terrorism – low-cost and deniable – remained in place. As an Indian government-appointed committee noted, Pakistan's 'proxy war' strategy was reinforced by the possession of nuclear weapons.[37] The revisionist state had the advantage since India was unable to resort to conventional war against a nuclear Pakistan.

Indian policymakers struggled to develop a response that might enable them to break out of their strategic shackles. With political engagement unworkable, they looked for ways in which they might project military force against an obdurate Pakistan. The possibilities listed included hot pursuit of terrorists into Pakistani territory, limited strikes, special operations missions against terrorist camps in Pakistan and an inchoate conception of 'limited war'. India's Defence Minister, George Fernandes, claimed that Kargil had shown that Indian forces 'can fight and win a limited war, at a time and place chosen by the aggressor' and that war 'has not been made obsolete by nuclear weapons'.[38] Once again, Indian thinking was muddled. The real lesson was that unleashing war under the nuclear shadow is too risky to contemplate – a lesson Pakistan learned well since Kargil brought its leaders widespread opprobrium and no real gain. But Indian thinking erred in concluding that since Kargil had revealed that limited war is possible between nuclear rivals, *they* could choose to launch limited war against Pakistan.

This they discovered very soon was an illusion. In December 2001, after a series of spectacular *jihadi* attacks culminating in an assault on India's parliament, the Indian government threatened war and engaged in a massive military mobilization for it.[39] But Pakistan reacted with a similar mobilization and, in the end, the 10-month confrontation between the two states yielded nothing for New Delhi but a limited and temporary commitment on the part of Pakistani leaders not to support *jihadi*s targeting India. Once again, the wrong lesson was drawn: that the problem lay not in the unviability of a strategy of limited war, but in India's slow mobilization and the lack of a surprise element that could have given Indian forces an advantage.

The Indian Army turned accordingly to crafting a new blitzkrieg-style strategy that would enable light and fast-moving forces to slice bits of territory from Pakistani control for the purpose of bargaining – a strategy that was called 'Cold Start'.[40] Conversations with Indian military officers at the time revealed no clear conception of what India could expect as a strategic response from Pakistan. That response was to bolster the Pakistani deterrent by introducing nuclear weapons at the tactical level. The Nasr short-range missile, a 60-kilometre-range tactical nuclear-armed missile, was tested in 2013 in reaction to Cold Start.[41] India has produced no clear response to this shortening of the nuclear fuse.

In September 2016, Prime Minister Narendra Modi's government informed the public that Indian forces had crossed into Pakistan and conducted a series of 'surgical strikes' against terrorist camps.[42] However, this was not a new tactic: the previous government of Manmohan Singh had done this already in 2011, though without publicizing it.[43] The effect of 'surgical strikes' does not appear to have been significant. It is too early to gauge the impact of the 2016 strikes, but we do know that after the 2011 strikes, fatalities in the Indian state of Jammu and Kashmir remained high. The number of deaths resulting from such incidents numbered 167 in 2011, 99 in 2012, 135 in 2013, 185 in 2014 and 164 in 2015.[44]

The end result is that Indian policy has been confounded by the nuclear trap it finds itself in. Perhaps the one strategy that has not been seriously attempted is to respond to Pakistan's 'asymmetric' strategy of pressurizing India at the subconventional level by means of a 'symmetric' strategy of doing the same. This is obviously constrained by the risk of the Pakistani state becoming seriously destabilized and falling prey to its internally rampant religious extremists, notably the Taliban. A window of opportunity could nevertheless be available – India has the option of extending material support to nationalists in the province of Balochistan, where a low-level insurgency has been ongoing since decades. Modi has hinted at the possibility by verbally declaring his support for the 'people of restive Balochistan'.[45] It remains to be seen whether this option will be opened up in the future.

Thus far, none of India's responses to Pakistan's use of cross-border terrorism – from engagement to the threat of limited war – has worked and the lessons drawn from each effort have only brought new frustrations. But this is a dilemma very much inherent to a situation when nuclear-armed states are at daggers drawn – even though the revisionist state may not succeed in altering the status quo, it is hard to stop it from trying. The one time when there was significant forward movement – when India's Manmohan Singh and Pakistan's Pervez Musharraf came to an understanding in 2004–06 that lowered tensions and expanded the cross-LoC movement of people and goods – did not last long as Musharraf's personal political star descended and the interests of those opposed to an entente (the Pakistani military and its *jihadi* proxies) ensured that the moves failed.

China

In contrast with the volatility of the India–Pakistan relationship, India has been able to enjoy greater stability in its relations with China.[46] The India–China relationship carries many of the characteristics of nuclear rivalries. There is an old pre-nuclear rivalry between the two countries. They have a long-standing border dispute that stretches over 4,000 kilometres. The dispute produced a short but intense war in 1962, followed by crises in 1967 and 1986–87. The fallout was a balance-of-power politics that kept tensions alive, with China building close relations with Pakistan and India leaning on the Soviet Union until the end of the Cold War. Their common elements, such as Buddhism and the colonial experience, have not formed any sort of bond between them.

There are important sources of tension between India and China that appear to be rising and have the potential to generate conflict. First, the tussle over their long border remains alive and troubling. The problem is compounded by the lack of a stable dividing line between Indian and Chinese troops. The so-called 'Line of Actual Control' (LAC) has not been formally demarcated. This has resulted in periodic low-level frictions, with each side claiming that the other has occupied slices of its territory. Given the rising frequency of such apparently minor incidents, the environment has deteriorated considerably and the spectre of armed conflict is ever present.[47]

Second, domestic political uncertainties have the potential to aggravate tensions. For China, the Tibetan border with India is its weak underbelly. While India officially recognizes Chinese sovereignty over Tibet, Chinese anxieties are compounded by tensions relating to Tibet. Tibet's spiritual leader, the Dalai Lama, who is based in India, is unquestionably the fountainhead of a movement that asserts Tibet's separate identity, which is viewed with great anxiety in Beijing. Tibetan separatism has strengthened over the last several years and has been characterized by episodes of violence. In 2008, with the Beijing Olympics approaching, violence broke out in Tibet and elsewhere, while Chinese embassies in more than a dozen countries were attacked by protestors. From 2011, a large number of incidents of self-immolation by Tibetans, including Buddhist monks and nuns, set Beijing on edge. In combination with other sources of domestic unrest, this had an unsettling effect at a juncture when the transition to a new leadership under Xi Jinping was yet to be consolidated. Beijing's consequent shift to a tough line on several territorial disputes was evident. On the Indian side, the coalition government of Manmohan Singh, constantly under challenge both from the opposition and from coalition partners, was buffeted by a slowing economy and a host of political difficulties. Prime Minister Singh, though conscious of China's sensitivities, sought to adopt a tough approach and was keen not to be seen as backing down on the border issue. Singh still tried to avoid irritating China, which, for instance, caused him to suspend trilateral naval exercises with Japan and the United States. But Modi has been less inclined to pay heed to how China might react and has revived the trilateral exercises.

Third, the end of the Cold War marked the beginnings of a transition in the global power structure, which had its repercussions on southern Asia. The power equations that emerged saw India and China on opposite sides. Between 2005 and 2008, the United States pushed for and secured a nuclear agreement that allowed the Nuclear Suppliers Group (NSG) to permit trade in civilian nuclear materials with India.[48] Though China was a party to the deal, it was a reluctant one. From Beijing's point of view, it symbolized a strategic India–US partnership that was aimed at containing China and preventing it from attaining its rightful place in the sun. From India's perspective, this was a useful hedging strategy that offset both the loss of its Soviet card and China's continuing support for Pakistan. Geopolitically, the rise of China, and to a lesser extent, India, meant that an overlap of their widening strategic horizons was inevitable. China began to expand its presence among India's neighbours, raising concerns about a 'string of pearls' or potential bases in Pakistan, Sri Lanka, Bangladesh and Myanmar.[49] India responded by building strategic partnerships with the US, Singapore, Japan and Vietnam, among others.[50] China's strategic activities – propelled by its maritime interests – inevitably turned to the Indian Ocean, while Indian naval vessels began to make regular trips to the South and East China Seas and exercise with regional navies. India also became involved in oil exploration off Vietnam in waters claimed by China.

The rise of China has also induced India to bolster its border defences, augment its conventional forces, and engage in a vigorous nuclear weapons build-up. India's defence expenditure has risen substantially. Indian military spending, which stood at US$13.95 billion in 1998, rose to a hefty US$42.95 billion in 2015, with India topping the list of global arms importers for the period 2010–14.[51] The response is clearly to the security dilemma posed by the rise of Chinese military power. Yet the irony is that China is engaged in an active military build-up in response to an entirely different threat perception: that emanating from the US. Thus, the Indian security dilemma with respect to China is inseparable from the Chinese one vis-à-vis the US. In short we have a cascading security dilemma that links the China–US rivalry to the India–China one. On its own, India would not be considered a serious threat in Beijing – the economies and consequently the military spending of the two sides are hugely disparate. India's GDP in 2014 was only US$2.04 trillion compared to China's US$10.4 trillion Similarly, India's defence expenditure in 2015 was US$47.9 billion, against China's US$145.8 billion.[52] But as India draws closer to the US and Japan, there is gradually emerging a new pattern of power distribution where the combination of the three makes India an emerging component of the Chinese security dilemma.[53] The prospect of growing tension arising from the complex security dilemma environment is thus quite significant despite mitigating factors.

The plus side of the India–China relationship – in contrast with the India–Pakistan one – is notable. First, they have built a growing economic relationship. Trade has grown rapidly in the post-Cold War era from US$188 million in 1992 to US$81 billion in 2015 (though recently there has been a slight downturn in dollar terms, reflecting shifts in exchange rates).[54] Chinese investment in India has risen massively since mid-2016: in June–August 2016 alone, Chinese foreign direct investment in India was US$2.3 billion, exceeding the total for the entire period from April 2000 to March 2016.[55] On the political–military side, the two countries have in place a number of avenues of cooperation, for example, multilateral forums like BRICS (Brazil, Russia, India, China, South Africa), the Shanghai Cooperation Organization, the ASEAN Defence Ministers' Meeting Plus and the Asian Infrastructure Investment Bank. Bilaterally, they have regular border talks, periodic (if small-scale) military exercises, and, most importantly, not a shot has been fired on their contentious border over the past half-century. This gives their relationship a substantial degree of stability. To the extent that both exhibit this willingness to engage with each other, and because neither side is a revisionist state, there is a significant degree of stability between them.

On the question of status quo versus revisionist orientation, from the standpoint of system-wide politics, *both* India and China are revisionist states in the sense that both are rising powers (with China much ahead) and both seek accommodation and higher status within the system. Bilaterally, however, China is something of a status quo power that appears to be unwilling to acknowledge – and in some ways tries even to resist – India's rise. Two symptoms of this are readily evident. First, China has blocked India's pathway to membership of the Nuclear Suppliers Group (NSG) despite having earlier (2008) acceded to a change in the NSG's rules allowing its members to trade in nuclear materials and technology with India.[56] Having allowed India into the nuclear trading system, China is now apparently intent on keeping it on the back foot by preventing it from obtaining a place in the non-proliferation regime. Since the issue is viewed as vital to national interests, Indian opinion has been much exercised by the Chinese policy and this has raised the tension between them. In a sense, on this issue, China has shown itself to be status quo ante in orientation.

Second, on the main border issue, there is evidence that Beijing has deliberately raised tension along the disputed border. As noted earlier, the LAC has been at the centre of periodic friction as troops from the two states have repeatedly confronted each other there. While it may be coincidental, observers note that a major confrontation occurred at precisely the time when President Xi Jinping was on a formal visit to India in September 2014.[57] More importantly, Chinese policymakers have explicitly turned aside Indian proposals to negotiate a formal demarcation of the LAC.[58] In 2015, a senior Chinese official claimed a resolution of the LAC would be a 'stumbling block' to the larger issue of an

agreement on the disputed border.[59] The Chinese are said to have objected to
a resolution on the ground that it could affect their positions on the border
negotiations, but Modi's explicit assurance that any agreement on the LAC
would be 'without prejudice to our position on the boundary question' has
not brought a response from China.[60] The Chinese stand displays obliquely a
preference for not resolving the LAC problem, which has been the chief source
of tension on the ground between the two states.

Finally, the Chinese initiative to build the China–Pakistan Economic Corridor
(CPEC) has tread on Indian toes. The CPEC, a multi-billion dollar project that
is part of China's larger Belt and Road Initiative, runs through the portion of
Kashmir held by Pakistan and claimed by India. China has long avoided taking
a position on the Kashmir dispute, but the CPEC is clearly a commitment
that ignores Indian objections. Modi formally placed India's objection before
Xi in September 2016, but to no avail.[61] Though the Chinese have previously
constructed roads in the area, the CPEC plan makes their commitment a long-
term one. China can no longer claim to be impartial on the issue.

In sum, while China is in some sense a status quo state in its bilateral
relationship with India, this does not mean it is inclined to resolve their
differences. The NSG, LAC and CPEC issues, taken together, imply a
direction that is quite the opposite – a policy framework designed to keep
tensions with India simmering even as the two states cooperate in numerous
ways. The LAC friction, in particular, carries the seeds of armed conflict
of the kind that occurred on the disputed Sino-Soviet border in 1969.[62]
The backdrop to the 1969 conflict was domestic turmoil in China and the
ruling elite's use of external conflict to bolster its domestic position. China's
current leadership is less susceptible to internal attack – Xi has clearly gained
control over the party and the state. Yet the vulnerabilities remain as China's
economy has slowed down, while domestic dissatisfaction with the system in
place has brought substantial, though fragmented, protests that have grown
significantly in number.[63] Not surprisingly, Xi's domestic authoritarianism
has been accompanied by a tougher stance toward China's adversaries abroad
from Japan to Southeast Asia to India.

The picture that emerges with regard to India's difficulties in ensuring
strategic stability with Pakistan and China is that, while the prospects of nuclear
conflict appear remote, both relationships are dogged by uncertainties that still
leave space for conventional conflict and consequent nuclear risk. In the Pakistan
case, repeated crises and a high degree of tension have been constant after

1998 as Islamabad had sought to leverage its nuclear capability to pressurize India at the risk of seriously destabilizing the relationship between the nuclear adversaries. In the China case, the pot has been kept simmering rather than boiling by Beijing, which means the level of instability appears manageable. Both Pakistan and China are what one might call 'modified greedy states', that is, states that are neither defensively oriented and purely security-seeking nor bent on expansion (Pakistan would not see attaining Kashmir as expansion, but as recovering lost territory). Rather they are states that want to alter the status quo for their own primarily domestic purposes. As long as they want to do so, India will have to be reactive in fending them off and trying to press for stability as best it can.

Conclusion

The above analysis lends itself to two conclusions. First, the confusion surrounding India's answer to the question of 'how much is enough' is primarily due to internal problems. The threatening environment plausibly calls for a response and the content of that response is internally determined. But Indian policymakers and most strategists have failed to come to grips with the requirements of minimum deterrence, which has created an internal schism between the minimalist and maximalist components of nuclear strategy. This is clearly the consequence of a conventional thought style that is firmly embedded in the Indian mind. From a theoretical perspective, it represents a typical case of suboptimal response to systemic incentives of the kind neoclassical realists have illuminated. The problem, then, is one that lies within the realm of national policy and is not, in this sense, externally caused.

Second, in its relationships with both strategic adversaries, India faces elements of the security dilemma, which makes stabilization feasible through joint efforts such as confidence building measures and border talks. The chief source of instability is that both adversaries do not have a strong interest in stability: Pakistan is intensely revisionist, while China is not deeply committed to stabilization for domestic political reasons. For India, this means that the sources of its difficulty with regard to stability lie outside – in the domestic interests of its adversaries – and that its own efforts are not likely to yield positive results unless they change their preferences.

Taken together, both types of problems have domestic roots. From the standpoint of theory, undesirable outcomes arise in the first case from within

India, while in the second, they arise from without. In short, there are two domestic sources of difficulty, but we require separate theoretical frameworks – neoclassical realism and classical realism respectively – to understand them fully.

Notes

1   Steven E. Lobell, Norrin M. Ripsman and Jeffrey W. Taliaferro, eds, *Neoclassical Realism, the State, and Foreign Policy* (Cambridge: Cambridge University Press, 2009); Brian Rathbun, 'A Rose by Any Other Name: Neoclassical Realism as the Logical and Necessary Extension of Structural Realism', *Security Studies*, 17, No. 2 (April 2008): 294–321; Gideon Rose, 'Neoclassical Realism and Theories of Foreign Policy', *World Politics*, 51, No. 1 (October 1998): 144–77.

2   Rajesh Basrur, 'Nuclear Deterrence: The Wohlstetter-Blackett Debate Re-visited', Working Paper, S. Rajaratnam School of International Studies, Nanyang Technological University, Singapore, 15 April 2014. Available at https://www.rsis.edu.sg/wp-content/uploads/rsis-pubs/WP271.pdf.

3`   The classical realist paradigm is best represented by Hans J. Morgenthau, *Politics among Nations: The Struggle for Power and Peace*, Fifth Edition, Revised (New York: Alfred A. Knopf, 1978).

4   Charles L. Glaser, 'The Security Dilemma Revisited', *World Politics* 50, No. 1 (October 1997): 171–201; Robert Jervis, 'Cooperation under the Security Dilemma', *World Politics* 30, No. 2 (January 1978): 167–214.

5   On neorealism, see Kenneth N. Waltz, *Theory of International Politics* (Reading, MA: Addison-Wesley, 1979) and John J. Mearsheimer, *The Tragedy of Great Power Politics* (New York: W. W. Norton, 2001).

6   Albert Wohlstetter, *The Delicate Balance of Terror*, revised, Document No. P-1472, Santa Monica, CA: RAND, December 1958. I refer to this document rather than to the slightly abbreviated and more well-known journal version published with the same title the following year. See Albert Wohlstetter, 'The Delicate Balance of Terror', *Foreign Affairs*, 37, No. 2 (January 1959): 211–34; P. M. S. Blackett, 'Critique of Some Contemporary Defence Thinking', *Encounter* (April 1961): 9–17.

7   Wohlstetter, *Delicate Balance of Terror*, 8.

8   Blackett, 'Critique of Some Contemporary Defence Thinking', 11–12.

9   Wohlstetter, *Delicate Balance of Terror*, 16.

10   Blackett, 'Critique of Some Contemporary Defence Thinking', 12.

11   Wohlstetter, *Delicate Balance of Terror*, 3.

12   Ibid., 7.

13   Blackett, 'Critique of Some Contemporary Defence Thinking', 10–11.

14   Albert Wohlstetter, 'Nuclear Sharing: NATO and the N+1 Country', *Foreign Affairs* 39, No. 3 (April 1961): 364.

15   Blackett, 'Critique of Some Contemporary Defence Thinking', 11.

16   Ibid., 12.

17   K. Sundarji, *Blind Men of Hindoostan: Indo-Pak Nuclear War*, 150 (New Delhi: UBS Publishers' Distributors, 1993).

18 K. Sundarji, 'Nuclear Deterrence: Doctrine for India – I', *Trishul*, December 1992, 10–13.

19 *The Hindu*, 'India Not to Engage in A Nuclear Arms Race: Jaswant' (Interview), 29 November 1999, 14.

20 Government of India, Ministry of External Affairs, *Draft Report of National Security Advisory Board on Indian Nuclear Doctrine*, 17 August 1999.

21 C. K. Karunakaran, 'Atoms and Man', *SainikSamachar*, 17 July 1960. Archives of the Royal Society, London, doc. no. PB/8/27/ H53-56.

22 Rajesh Basrur, 'Deterrence, Second Strike and Credibility: Revisiting India's Nuclear Strategy Debate', Institute of Peace and Conflict Studies, New Delhi, July 2014. Accessed on 11 December 2016. Available at http://www.ipcs.org/pdf_file/issue/IB255-RajeshBasrur-IndiaNuclear.pdf.

23 Robert S. Norris and Hans M. Kristensen, 'Global Nuclear Inventories, 1945–2013', *Bulletin of the Atomic Scientists*, 69, No. 5 (2013): 78, Figure 2.

24 Norris and Kristensen, 'Global Nuclear Inventories, 1945–2013'.

25 Hans M. Kristensen and Robert S. Norris, 'Indian Nuclear Forces, 2015', *Bulletin of the Atomic Scientists*, 71, No. 5 (2015): 77–83.

26 Sumit Ganguly and Devin T. Hagerty, *Fearful Symmetry: India-Pakistan Crises in the Shadow of Nuclear Weapons* (New Delhi: Oxford University Press, 2006).

27 For a brief discussion on the forces propelling the expansion of India's nuclear arsenal, see Rajesh Basrur and Jaganath Sankaran, 'India's Slow and Unstoppable Move to MIRV', in *The Lure & Pitfalls of MIRVs: From the First to the Second Nuclear Age*, edited by Michael Krepon, Travis Wheeler and Shane Mason (Henry L. Stimson Center: Washington, DC, 2016).

28 On the nuclear revolution, including the intellectual difficulties associated with it, see Robert Jervis, *The Meaning of the Nuclear Revolution* (Ithaca: Cornell University Press, 1989).

29 On 'thought styles', see Barry O'Neill, *Honor, Symbols, and War* (Ann Arbor, MI: University of Michigan Press, 2002).

30 On stable and unstable equilibria, see Robert Gilpin, *War and Change in World Politics*, 91 (New York: Cambridge University Press, 1981).

31 Rita Chowdhari Tremblay and Julian Schofield, 'Institutional Causes of the India-Pakistan Rivalry', in *The India-Pakistan Conflict: An Enduring Rivalry*, edited by T. V. Paul (Cambridge: Cambridge University Press, 2005).

32 Glen Snyder, 'The Balance of Power and the Balance of Terror', in *The Balance of Power*, edited by Paul Seabury (San Francisco: Chandler, 1965).

33 Michael Krepon and Chris Gagné, eds, *The Stability-Instability Paradox: Nuclear Weapons and Brinkmanship in South Asia* (Henry L. Stimson Center: Washington, DC, June 2001).

34 Peter Chalk, 'Pakistan's Role in the Kashmir Insurgency', *Jane's Intelligence Review*, 1 September 2001, reproduced on the web site of the RAND Corporation. Accessed on 14 February, 2003. Available at http://www.rand.org/hot/op-eds/090101JIR.html.

35 Sabina Inderjit, 'Advani Tells Pakistan to Roll Back Its Anti-India Policy', *Times of India*, 19 May 1998, 7.

36 On the Kargil conflict, see D. Suba Chandran, *Limited War: Revisiting Kargil in the*

Indo-Pak Conflict (New Delhi: India Research Press, 2005) and Peter R. Lavoy, ed., *Asymmetric Warfare and in South Asia: The Causes and Consequences of the Kargil Conflict* (Cambridge: Cambridge University Press, 2009).

37   *From Surprise to Reckoning: The Kargil Review Committee Report*, 197–99 (New Delhi: Sage, 2000).

38   C. Raja Mohan, 'Fernandes Unveils 'Limited War' Doctrine', *Hindu*, 25 January 2000. Accessed on 13 February 2017. Available at http://www.thehindu.com/2000/01/25/stories/01250001.htm.

39   Michael R. Kraig and Sumit Ganguly, 'The 2001-2002 Indo-Pakistani Crisis: Exposing the Limits of Coercive Diplomacy', *Security Studies*, 14, No. 2 (2005): 290–324; V. K. Sood and Pravin Sawhney, *Operation Parakram: The War Unfinished* (New Delhi, Thousand Oaks & London: Sage, 2003).

40   Walter C. Ladwig III, 'A Cold Start for Hot Wars? The Indian Army's New Limited War Doctrine', *International Security*, 32, No. 3 (Winter 2007/08) Vipin Narang and Walter C. Ladwig III, 'Taking 'Cold Start' out of the Freezer?' *Hindu*, 11 January 2017. Accessed on 11 January 2017. Available at http://www.thehindu.com/opinion/lead/Taking-%E2%80%98Cold-Start%E2%80%99-out-of-the-freezer/article17019025.ece.

41   Zachary Keck, 'Pakistan Wants "Battlefield" Nukes to Use against Indian Troops', *National Interest*, 6 February 2015. Accessed on 13 February 2017. Available at http://nationalinterest.org/blog/the-buzz/pakistan-wants-battlefield-nukes-use-against-indian-troops-12200.

42   Rahul Kanwal, 'Inside Story of India's Daring Surgical Strikes against Pakistan', *Mail Today*, 8 October 2016. Accessed on 13 February 2017. Available at http://indiatoday.intoday.in/story/inside-story-of-indian-armys-daring-surgical-strikes-against-pakistan/1/783055.html.

43   Vijaita Singh and Josy Joseph, 'Operation Ginger: Tit-for-tat across the Line of Control', *The Hindu*, 9 October 2016. Accessed on 9 October 2016. Available at http://www.thehindu.com/news/national/operation-ginger-titfortat-across-the-line-of-control/article9202758.ece.

44   Government of India, Ministry of Home Affairs, *Annual Report 2015-16*, 5.

45   Shubhajit Roy and Anand Mishra, 'Narendra Modi's Independence Day Speech: PM Throws down Balochistan Gauntlet', *Indian Express*, 16 August 2016. Accessed on 16 August 2016. Available at http://indianexpress.com/article/india/india-news-india/pm-narendra-modi-balochistan-independence-day-congress-pakistan-salman-khurshid-2977554.

46   David Brewster, 'Beyond the "String of Pearls": Is There Really a Sino-Indian Security Dilemma in the Indian Ocean?' *Journal of the Indian Ocean Region*, 10, No. 2 (2014): 133–49; John Garver, 'The Security Dilemma in Sino-Indian Relations,' *India Review*, 1, No. 4 (October 2002): 1–38; Jonathan Holslag, 'The Persistent Military Security Dilemma between China and India,' *Journal of Strategic Studies*, 32, No. 6 (December 2009): 811–40; Mohan Malik, China and India: Great Power Rivals (Boulder, Co: First Forum Press, 2011).

47   Daniel S. Markey, *Armed Confrontation between China and India: Contingency Planning Memorandum No. 27*, Council on Foreign Relations, New York, November 2015. Accessed on 13 February 2017. Available at http://www.cfr.org/china/armed-confrontation-between-china-india/p37228.

48   Harsh V. Pant, *The US-India Nuclear Pact: Policy, Process and Great Power Politics* (Oxford: Oxford University Press, 2011).

49   Christopher J. Pehrson, 'String of Pearls: Meeting the Challenge of China's Rising Power across the Asian Littoral', Strategic Studies Institute, US Army War College, Carlisle, PA, July 2006. Accessed on 14 February 2017. Available at http://www. strategicstudiesinstitute.army.mil/pdffiles/PUB721.pdf.

50   'India and Asia-Pacific Security', *Asia-Pacific Regional Security Assessment 2016*, International Institute of Strategic Studies, London, 2016.

51   For 1998 spending, see International Institute of Strategic Studies, *The Military Balance, 2000-01*, 299 (Oxford: Oxford University Press, 2000) (constant 1999 prices); for 2015 spending, see International Institute of Strategic Studies, *The Military Balance, 2016*, 486 (Oxford: Oxford University Press, 2016) (current prices); and for import ranking, see Stockholm International Peace Research Institute, *SIPRI Yearbook 2015* (Oxford: Oxford University Press, 2015).

52   GDP comparison data are taken from the World Bank website: http://data.worldbank. org/indicator/NY.GDP.MKTP.CD. Military expenditure comparisons are from International Institute of Strategic Studies, *Military Balance 2016* (Oxford: Oxford University Press, 2016).

53   Ashley J. Tellis, *India as A Leading Power*, Carnegie Endowment for International Peace, Washington, DC, April 2016. Accessed on 14 February 2017. Available at http:// carnegieendowment.org/files/CP_268_Tellis_India_final1.pdf.

54   International Monetary Fund, *Direction of Trade Statistics* (Washington, DC: International Monetary Fund, n.d. [2016]). Accessed on 13 February 2017. Available at http://data.imf.org/regular.aspx?key=61013712.

55   Keshav Sunkara, 'Chinese Investment in India Shoots to US$2.3 billion in Past 3 Months against US$1.35 billion in 2000-2016,' VCCircle.com, 30 August 2016. Accessed on 13 February 2017. Available at http://www.vccircle.com/news/economy/2016/08/30/ chinese-investment-india-shoots-23-bn-past-3-months-against-135-bn-2000–16.

56   *Indian Express*, 'India's NSG Membership Can't be Farewell Gift: China to US', 16 January 2017. Accessed on 16 January, 2017. Available at http://indianexpress.com/ article/world/indias-nsg-membership-cant-be-farewell-gift-china-to-us-4476997/.

57   Niharika Mandhana, 'China's President Talks Trade in India as Troops Face Off at Border', *Wall Street Journal*, 18 September 2014. Accessed on 14 February 2017. Available at https://www.wsj.com/articles/chinas-president-xi-jinping-arrives-in-delhi-as-troops-face-off-at-india-china-border-1410968062.

58   Gardiner Harris, 'India Takes Tough Stance with China on Kashmir', *New York Times*, 18 September 2014. Accessed on 14 September 2017. Available at https://mobile.nytimes. com/2014/09/19/world/asia/modi-pushes-xi-to-resolve-border-issue-in-kashmir.html.

59   Ananth Krishnan, 'One Step Forward, Two Steps Back', *India Today*, 11 June 2015. Accessed on 11 June 2015. Available at http://indiatoday.intoday.in/story/china-india-lac-modi-visit-xi-jinping-border-dispute/1/443886.html.

60   Srinath Raghavan, 'Modi Speaks India's Mind Clearly in China', *NDTV*, 15 May 2015. Accessed on 14 September 2017. Available at http://www.ndtv.com/opinion/modi-speaks-indias-mind-clearly-in-china-763393.

61   *Indian Express*, 'PM Modi Raises India's concern over CPEC Which Runs through PoK', 4 September 2016. Accessed on 14 February 2017. Available at http://indianexpress.

com/article/india/india-news-india/prime-minister-narendra-modi-raises-indias-concern-over-cpec-which-runs-through-pok-3013260/.

62 Thomas W. Robinson, 'The Sino-Soviet Border Conflict of 1969: New Evidence Three Decades Later', in *Chinese Warfighting: The PLA Experience since 1949*, edited by Mark A. Ryan, David Michael Finkelstein and Michael A. McDevitt (Armonk, NY: M. E. Sharpe, 2003).

63 Hudson Lockett, 'China: Strikes and Protest Nos. Jump 20%,' *Financial Times*, 14 July 2016. Accessed on 14 February 2017. Available at https://www.ft.com/content/56afb47c-23fd-3bcd-a19f-bddab6a27883.

12

India and Its Diaspora

Latha Varadarajan

In January 2016, the United Nations Department of Economic and Social Affairs (UN DESA) published its annual report on migration trends. There were several striking results from the survey that had been conducted, including the fact that the number of international migrants had increased by over 40 per cent just in the new millennium, reaching an all-time high of 224 million.[1] However, the fact that was highlighted in Indian media outlets was a different one – according to the DESA report, India had become the country with the largest diaspora population in the world.[2] Serendipitously, or so it seemed, the report's findings were released around the time of the *Pravasi Bharatiya Divas* celebrations organized by the Indian government. The annual event, inaugurated in 2003, has been touted by successive administrations as the Indian state's acknowledgement of not just the 'contributions of Overseas Indians to India's development', but also the critical importance of this constituency to India's position on the global stage. In that sense, insofar as the Indian state was concerned, the results of the UN survey only served to underscore the correctness of its stance towards its overseas population. This stance – premised on highlighting the Indian state's appreciation of the role of the diaspora as well the necessity to further develop that role – has been a relatively novel one in the history of postcolonial India.

While the existence of a migrant population is not a recent development in Indian history, it was not until almost the end of the twentieth century that this group became a focus of the Indian state's policymaking apparatus, marking a distinct shift from the immediate post-independence era. The goal of this chapter is to explain the logic and nature of this shift, and to interrogate its potential implications. To do so, the chapter is divided into three parts. The first section provides a short history of the waves of colonial and postcolonial migration from India, laying out the fundamental problems underlying the usage of the umbrella category of the 'Indian diaspora'. The second lays out the history of the Indian state's relationship with this group, drawing out the stark contrast between the immediate post-independence foreign policy agenda and the one that emerged towards the last decade of the twentieth century. In parsing out this history, the chapter makes the argument that the valorization of the Indian diaspora by the Indian state can only be understood in the context of changes in the global capitalist economy, manifested in the turn towards neoliberal restructuring. In that sense, the role of the Indian diaspora in the foreign policy agenda of the Indian ruling class is both less and more than it seems. The chapter concludes with a brief discussion of the possible future trends in this relationship.

The making of a diaspora

When India became independent in 1947, there were nearly four million 'Overseas Indians' spread across various parts of the British Empire.[3] With roots generally traced to the colonial migration that began in the early decades of the nineteenth century, groups of emigrants were discursively constituted as a community variously described as 'Indians abroad' and 'Overseas Indians' through a series of political struggles that took place both in settler colonies as well as within India itself. Despite what a prominent sociologist had once described as a 'lack of migratory instincts', a significant number of people from the subcontinent had migrated initially as part of the indentured labour forces that were demanded by British capital, followed later by small groups of voluntary migrants who helped create South Asian diasporic enclaves in regions ranging from East Africa to Southeast Asia.[4] At various points in the late nineteenth and early twentieth century, the colonial state cast itself in the role of the 'protector' of the various diaspora communities, occasionally even taking cudgels on their behalf in other dominions as well as in the British parliament. However, with the emergence of a nationalist consciousness among Indian political elites in the early twentieth century, there was a distinct shift in the nature of this relationship. Beginning with attempts to pressure the British Indian government to ban recruitment of unskilled labour, and appoint commissions to investigate charges of abuse against plantation and mill owners, nationalist involvement in causes pertaining to overseas 'Indian' communities soon took on distinct political overtones. This was in part due to different problems faced by the voluntary middle-class migrants: namely problems of political disenfranchisement and systematized racial inequality.

By establishing a common cause with overseas Indians, the Indian nationalist movement initially articulated its demand for 'equality within the Empire', a demand that was already being made by settlers from India in East African colonies such as Tanganyika. However, by the early decades of the twentieth century, it had become obvious not just to the settler communities but also to the leaders of the Indian nationalist movement that these demands would never be met within the framework of the British Empire, despite its patina of political liberalism.[5] It was at this juncture that the Indian nationalist movement began to move away from its own moderate past. Making a direct connection between the problems faced by migrant communities and British rule, nationalist leaders further claimed that the reason why 'Indians abroad' faced institutionalized discrimination was that India was a colonized nation and could not respond to the needs of her people. This was the sole reason why other countries could enact discriminatory legislative acts against Indians abroad with impunity. The contrast that was usually drawn was with China. Some Indian nationalists argued that although China was not necessarily regarded as a great power prior to Japanese occupation, the Chinese government could still afford to look after the interests of its citizens because of its independence. By this logic, it was only by gaining political independence that the Indian state could begin to protect the interests of the Indian nation in all its territorially dispersed glory.

The connections made between India's status as a subject nation and the mistreatment of overseas Indian communities suggested that the emergence of an independent Indian state would ensure a closer relationship between India and 'Overseas Indians,' wherein the former would actively intercede to protect the interests of the latter. However, the actions of the newly independent Indian state ran counter to these expectations. In the next section, we will return to the question of why this was so. For now, it suffices to note that these earlier waves of migration created the groups that in contemporary political discourse are generally categorized as 'Persons of Indian Origin' (PIO).

The second major wave of migration from India took place largely in the post-independence era, more than a century after the commencement of the first. What distinguished it from the earlier period were a number of factors. For one, the migrants who left India in the period starting in the late-1960s began their journey as citizens of an independent Indian state. As such, the citizenship rights accrued by the migrants and the duties of the Indian state towards them were qualitatively different. Beyond that, the migrations occurred primarily in two directions, and the direction largely coinciding with the skill-level of the migrating populations – the West (predominantly the United States) which drew a steady stream of highly skilled professionals, and the petroleum-rich Gulf states which became the destination for 'non-skilled' and 'semi-skilled' labourers. Apart from the skill-level, there were many differences between the two groups.

While the migration of one group was seen as a 'drain' of national resources and a matter of concern, the Indian government actually encouraged the migration to the Gulf, seeing it as a means to stem growing levels of unemployment, particularly in some states of India. While the professional migrants to the West had the choice of giving up their Indian citizenship to acquire the citizenship of their host countries (a choice that was exercised by a growing number), the migrants to the Gulf worked without that option. While the migrants to the West were accompanied (or gradually followed) by many among their immediate families, the Gulf migrants were primarily male labourers who were generally separated from their families while they served the duration of their contract. The new post-independence wave of migration created first-generation emigrant communities that continued to be linked through close familial ties to India. It is these communities that are generally referred to as 'Non-Resident Indians' (NRIs) in popular discourse, despite the fact that a significant number amongst them do not legally fall into this category, having given up their Indian citizenship.

At one level, the binary division of the PIO and the NRI appears to encapsulate the existing differences among the various groups that constitute the Indian diaspora. However, a closer look reveals a different picture. A 'PIO' could be a fourth generation emigrant, a descendant of indentured labourers whose connection to India is at best tenuous and symbolic; or this PIO could be a first generation emigrant who has close familial ties to India. An 'NRI' could refer to an IT professional working in the European Union (EU), a doctor practsing in the United States, a contract labourer working in the construction industry in Qatar, or a teacher in Muscat. It is hard to conceptualize what exactly it is that would unify these very different social groups, to the extent that they could be seen as a single constituency for the purpose of crafting a foreign policy agenda.

Trying to think of the diaspora in terms of its location does not necessarily help overcome that problem. Take, for instance, the United States, which is presently home to the largest Indian emigrant community. The roughly 2.2 million individuals said to constitute the Indian diaspora can be broadly divided into NRIs and PIOs. But that is merely the tip of the iceberg. For once we start breaking the headline figure down, it becomes obvious that this diaspora consists of a wide range of populations differentiated by numerous factors: newly arrived students and descendants of the first Sikh migrants to North America in the early twentieth century, highly skilled professionals who migrated from India and motel owners who were forced to leave East Africa in the 1970s, entrepreneurs and restaurant workers, IT professionals from Andhra Pradesh and cab-drivers from Punjab. Thus, to talk even of the 'Indian-American diaspora' as a unified actor becomes a problematic proposition. In this context, it becomes clear that the question of whether the 'Indian diaspora' as a whole has played a role in shaping India's foreign policy or has been a central concern for state policymakers is one that cannot be answered in any meaningful way. Rather, we need to re-frame our query to ask whether specific sections of the diaspora have played such a role, and, if so, when and under what conditions. In the next section, we turn to this question.

The making and re-making of a nation-state

As laid out in the previous section, the connections made by leaders of the anti-colonial nationalist movement between the plight of the 'Overseas Indians' and the colonized status of India led to the general expectation that a focus on the Indian diaspora would be a crucial component of independent India's foreign policy. However, that did not come to pass. And in fact, until almost four decades later, the Indian state's official stance towards its diasporic populations remained one that could be best described as benign neglect. To understand why this is so, it is essential to follow the trajectory of Indian nationalism and state building in the context of the developments of capitalism on a global scale.[6] Given space constraints, in this section, I will provide a snapshot of two moments that encapsulate what are arguably the two major shifts in both the nature of Indian nationalism and the post-Second World War global capitalist economy.

In September 1957, Prime Minister Jawaharlal Nehru declared in the Indian parliament that his government had successfully resolved the question of 'Indians abroad'. While acknowledging that people of Indian origin were facing discrimination in different parts of the world, the Prime Minister framed the Indian government's post-independence policy in terms of a choice that had to be made by the 'Indians abroad' themselves. Indians abroad, the Prime Minister asserted, were at a crossroads. They could choose to claim Indian citizenship, thus officially becoming a part of the independent Indian nation-state. In that case, while the Indian state would accept its duties towards them and strive to protect their interests through the means of traditional diplomacy, they could not expect anything other than 'favourable alien treatment' outside of Indian territory. As for those who chose to accept 'the nationality of the country they live in', the Indian state wished them well and in that spirit, exhorted them to comport themselves in their new countries as true citizens, and not exploitative agents. [7] At one level, the Prime Minister's declaration took no one by surprise for it was the clearest yet articulation of a policy that Nehru's government had been following since independence in 1947. However, within the broader setting of the anti-colonial nationalist struggle that had led to India's independence, this declaration did seem to mark a dramatic turnaround. So, why did the post-independence Indian state go against expectations and distance itself from the Indian diaspora? The answer, I have argued, lies in both the nature of the anti-colonial struggle that gave meaning to Indian nationalism, as well as the kind of state that came into being after independence. This state, often categorized as 'Nehruvian', was one that emphasized the importance of state sovereignty, particularly in the realm of domestic economic policy. Such a state was both necessary and possible because of two reasons: one, the success of Indian bourgeoisie (the capitalist class, as it were) in shaping the contours of the nationalist movement in its final stages; and two, the broader acceptance of Keynesianism and the Bretton Woods system at the global level, that supported state-sponsored developmental initiatives. But these conditions had an effect beyond just setting the stage for particular economic policies.

By the time India was on the verge of attaining independence, the leadership of the Indian national movement had come to see the movement as something larger than a struggle for purely national freedom. India's freedom was but a part of the larger process of anti-colonial struggles taking place around the world. Given this emphasis, it was not surprising that one of the main foci of Nehru's government was the building of an alliance among the newly independent states of Asia and Africa. Nehru argued that notwithstanding the differences in specific foreign policy goals, the formerly colonized states had a common interest in ensuring true economic development and, more importantly, the complete end of the colonial system of rule. To that extent, the foreign policy of the independent Indian state was predicated on the principle of supporting the sovereign right of other newly independent state to decide who their citizens were, and to take the steps they considered necessary to end the exploitative legacy of colonialism.

Some scholars have argued that this 'ideological rubric' emphasizing the respect for territorial sovereignty led the Indian state to simply ignore the plight of the Indians abroad after independence. For them, this was a blunder, and constituted a 'missed opportunity' since the Indian diaspora could have been a valuable political and economic resource.[8] However, the point is not so much that the Indian government ignored the plight of the Indian diaspora. In fact, time and again, it entered into long-drawn negotiations with the host states to arrive at some kind of settlement on their plight. But it is undeniable that the role of the Indian diaspora is shaping the foreign policy agenda of the Indian state was virtually non-existent in the early decades of independence. The reason for this had less to do with losing sight of the potential of the diaspora, and more with a particular understanding of the very meaning of the independent Indian state. 'India', defenders of the Nehruvian foreign policy agenda argued, stood for certain principles – to fight against colonization, to challenge all forms of exploitative socio-economic relations and to uphold the right of each country (especially the poorer ones) to nationalize state institutions during these battles. In that context, the foreign policy of the Indian government could not be shaped by anything other than commitment to these values, even if it meant marginalizing the interests of certain emigrant communities.

For instance, though the Indian government declared its willingness to offer repatriation benefits to those Indians who returned from Burma (the country that, apart from Ceylon, had the largest concentration of Indian emigrants at the moment of independence), it did not consider itself obligated to make demands on behalf of the shopkeepers and landowners of Indian origin who were being affected by policies of nationalization. The argument that the Indian state made was that the nationalization policies were being applied without discrimination, and that the PIO had no grounds to object to this either as Burmese citizens or as Indian nationals.[9] To be good Burmese citizens, the onus was on the PIO to ensure that they 'associated themselves as closely as possible with the interests' of the Burmese people, and not become an 'exploiting agency there', which in this case required the acceptance of the Burmese government's nationalization policies. If they chose instead to give up Burmese citizenship and accept Indian citizenship, then as Indian nationals, 'all they could claim abroad [was] favourable alien treatment', which in turn meant that they could not expect the Indian state to take special steps to safeguard their properties.

Over the ensuing decades, as the plight of Indian emigrant communities not just in neighbouring Asian countries, but also in East Asia (particularly Kenya and Uganda) deteriorated, the question of the Indian state's obligations to its emigrant communities was raised constantly in parliamentary debates. However, this did not alter the broader contours of the state's foreign policy agenda. In fact, if anything, what altered was the perception of Indian emigrant communities as victims needing the assistance of the Indian state, particularly in the context of the rising militancy in Punjab in the 1980s, and the presumed involvement of the Sikh diaspora in fermenting the movement for an independent Khalistan. Given this situation, it is not surprising that despite occasional moments when the Indian government made formal protests on behalf of its emigrant communities (such as in the aftermath of the Fijian coup of 1987), the Indian government's official policy remained more or less unchanged. It was only in the 1990s that the issue of the diaspora came to the forefront once more.

In 1991, in the thick of a major economic crisis, the Congress-led Indian government of P. V. Narasimha Rao presented a budget that has been regarded as one of the most important and controversial in post-independence history. At the heart of the controversy was not just the fact that the government proposed a major economic restructuring (earlier Indian governments in the late-1960s and the 1980s had already instituted their versions of structural adjustment), but that it did so through a rhetorical disavowal of the Nehruvian framework that had dominated the political landscape. To preserve the 'economic independence' of the country, to 'restore the health of the economy', and to remain competitive in a rapidly changing global environment, the government claimed that India needed to choose a 'different path'. As part of this new path, the budget included policies that made possible the greater involvement of NRIs in the Indian economy by offering them greater incentives and opening up new sectors for potential investment.[10] While the claims made about the NRIs and their connection to India were hotly contested in the Indian parliament as well as in the media, what cannot be denied is that the embrace of neoliberal economic restructuring by the government also marked the official re-entry of the diaspora as important actors in public and political discourse.

Over the course of the 1990s, the question of the Indian state's relationship to the diaspora – formerly treated as more or less settled – once again came to the forefront of policy debates. Developments within diasporic communities, particularly in the United States, served to facilitate this process. Chief among them was the creation of the 'Global Organization of People of Indian Origin' (GOPIO) in 1989 and the establishment of the 'India Caucus' within the US Congress in 1993. While the former served to provide a semblance of coherence to the interests of a variegated community, the latter suggested the potential for at least a section amongst the Indian diaspora to be conscious political actors in their adopted homeland. GOPIO members, for instance, kept alive the question of institutional recognition of the special place of the diaspora by proposing the idea of a 'Person of Indian Origin' card in their meetings with Indian government representatives in the mid-1990s. Within the Unites States, politically active lobbyists of Indian origin became de facto spokespersons for the new BJP-led Indian government, particularly in the aftermath of the nuclear tests of 1998. The support of these groups in mitigating the post-tests economic sanctions imposed by the United States, along with their enthusiastic response to the 'Resurgent India' bonds issued by the Indian government in the immediate aftermath of the nuclear tests as a measure to withstand the sanctions, was cited as an important indication of the continued commitment of the diaspora to the homeland. It was a commitment that according to the Indian government needed to be officially recognized in the new millennium.

In August 2000, the BJP government announced the setting up of a 'High Level Committee on the Indian Diaspora' that would be given carte blanche to engage with all sections of the Indian diaspora and recommend to the government a 'broad but flexible policy framework' to facilitate the involvement of the diaspora in India's development while making it possible for the Indian government to be more receptive to their needs. After meeting with representatives of various diaspora groups and carefully perusing the policies adopted by other countries towards their diasporas, the High Level Committee presented its final report to the Indian government in December 2001. Among its recommendations was the institution of a PIO card scheme that would institute a visa-free regime for people of Indian origin, the establishment of *Pravasi Bharatiya Samman* awards that would recognize the achievements and contributions of Indians Abroad and the celebration of the *Pravasi Bharatiya Divas* (Day of the Indians Abroad) that would highlight 'the pride of the motherland' in the successes of 'her children abroad', who now numbered over 20 million.

The first such celebration was hosted by the Indian government on 9 January 2003, a date heavy with symbolism since it marked the anniversary of Mahatma Gandhi's return to India after his sojourn in South Africa. Gandhi's return, the speakers at the inaugural *Pravasi Bharatiya Divas* were quick to point out, marked a new stage in the Indian journey towards independence. While the diaspora's 'return' to India remained more figurative, the Indian government made no secret of its hope of a new chapter in what it acknowledged had been a somewhat limited relationship. To facilitate the start of this new chapter, the government announced several institutional initiatives, the most important among which was the establishment of a Ministry of Non-Resident Indian Affairs (created in 2004, the Ministry was almost immediately renamed the Ministry of Overseas Indian Affairs) and the passage of new legislation that would for the first time in post-independence history extend limited citizenship rights to certain sections amongst the diaspora.

Over the past decade, the Ministry of Overseas Indian Affairs, which positioned itself as a 'services ministry', interpreted its stated goal of building a partnership with the Indian diaspora through a variety of programmes including the continued hosting of the *Pravasi Bharatiya Divas* (now an annual celebration), the provision of specific policy measures to facilitate investments from overseas Indian communities, the management of emigration and engagement with Indian missions abroad to create institutional links with younger members of the Indian diaspora through schemes such as 'Know India' and 'Study India'.[11] Its self-identified constituency consists of the categories of the Indian diaspora already discussed (PIO, NRI) as well as the newly created 'Overseas Citizens of India' (OCI). Passed by the Indian parliament in August 2005, the amendment of the Citizenship Act (1955) allows certain sections of the diaspora to acquire specific types of citizenship rights.[12] While couched in language familiar to many other diasporas around the world, the OCI scheme does not confer any political rights – it is, in that sense, not similar to the idea of dual citizenship – but rather enables eligible members of the diaspora to acquire a life-long visa for visiting India (as against the PIO card that allows a 15-year visa), and have parity with NRIs on all 'facilities available to them in economic, financial and educational fields, except in matters relating to the acquisition of agricultural or plantation properties'.

The goal of these measures is at one level quite obvious – in the new millennium, the Indian state has been very committed to the institutional recognition of its relationship to the Indian diaspora, or at least specific sections of the diaspora. Given the dominant policy posture since independence, how do we account for this turnaround? There have been two major explanations of this phenomenon from scholars and political commentators alike, with both focusing on the novelty of the post-1991 reform period. The first of these highlights the long-overdue recognition of the economic potential of the diaspora by the Indian state as the engine spurring these new policy initiatives, while the second (reflecting in many ways the official state rhetoric) emphasizes the 'coming of age' of both India and the Indian diaspora on the global stage. Elements of both explanations deserve to be taken seriously. According to the World Bank, India has over the past few years been the top recipient of officially recorded remittances, with the estimated amount for 2013 expected to top $71 billion, nearly $10 billion ahead of the next recipient, China. However, these figures do not necessarily constitute a causal explanation for the Indian state's changed diaspora policies. Approximately a third of that comes from the Gulf state migrants who have been consistently remitting earnings to the Indian economy since the 1980s and have not actually been the main targets of the new diaspora initiatives. In addition, as economists have pointed out, the increased remittance flows have been connected to specific economic incentives and circumstances, including the recent depreciation of the Indian rupee relative to the US dollar. Furthermore, in terms of foreign direct investment (FDI), the Indian diaspora – unlike its Chinese counterpart – has hardly been a significant factor in the past decade. The point here is not to deny the economic potential of the Indian diaspora or an economic rationale for the evolution of the Indian state's diaspora policies. However, this rationale cannot and should not be reduced to merely a question of remittances or FDI. A more nuanced understanding of the shift in India's diaspora policies needs to engage with the aforementioned 'coming of age' of both India and the diaspora.

The restructuring of the Indian economy was presented by supporters of neoliberalism as an overcoming of the 'self-doubts' that characterized the Nehruvian era, and the expression of 'self-confidence' in the ability to 'compete in the global economy'. This rhetoric, of course, hid the actual social processes at work at both national and global levels. In terms of the global economic climate, Keynesianism, which had enabled policies like nationalization, investment in the public sector and protection of domestic industries (all essential features of the Nehruvian state), had become delegitimized. Domestically, the storied Indian capitalist class that had played a significant role in the nationalist movement and prevailed in the immediate post-independence era had been forced to cede its leadership to a faction that favoured privatization. Thus, in embracing the structural reforms, the task facing the Indian state was two-fold: one, to dismantle any remnants of the Nehruvian state; and two, to present this not as a failure, but rather a progressive step in the right direction. From this perspective the official re-entry of the Indian diaspora – emblematic of India's global success – onto the main stage of Indian politics makes sense. In other words, while the symbolic value of the diaspora to the Indian state's larger foreign policy goals seems undeniable, the question of how critical a role various sections of the diaspora play in helping shape those goals is one that is still far from settled.

Conclusion

On 28 September 2014, a 19,000 strong crowd comprising predominantly of Indian-Americans gathered in the storied Madison Square gardens in New York City. They were there to cheer on a man who less than a decade ago had been banned from travelling to the US for his role in the 2002 Gujarat massacre. Striding into the centre-stage now as the newly elected Prime Minister of India, Narendra Modi thanked the audience for the 'kind of love [that] has not been given to any Indian leader ever'. This validation by overseas Indians, he said, was a loan that he would repay by 'forming the India of [their] dreams', by making it easier for the cheering crowds and their extended community to return to India and bring their talents back to the homeland.

Despite the fact that the Ministry of Overseas Indian Affairs – opened with much fanfare in the new millennium – has now been folded into the venerable Ministry of External Affairs, the Modi government has continued the practice of wooing sections of the diaspora, extending the celebrations of the *Pravasi Bharatiya Divas* celebrations to various parts of the world, and holding out the promise of 'immense opportunities' for those who wish to return. However, it is worth noting that those who are being wooed are members of the diaspora that could bring in investments in fields ranging from manufacturing and infrastructure development to education and health. The language being used by policymakers these days is not the old one of trying to attract much-needed FDI, but rather one of channeling 'Diaspora Direct Investment' (DDI). In a slight variation of an old theme, Indian policymakers have highlighted the focus on the diaspora as an extension of rational economic planning – diaspora members already are involved in funneling vast amounts as remittances back into the country, they have familial ties and as such by extension, they have a greater stake in the cause of Indian development. Regardless of whether the Shangri-La of DDI will ever be attained, it is worth reiterating two main aspects of the 'new' policy orientation: once again, while couched in the language of facilitating the role of the diaspora at large, the actual focus is on those who have the ability to invest in manufacturing, technology or finance, by definition a very narrow stratum of entrepreneurs; and, more importantly, this orientation rests on the notion that furthering the agenda of economic deregulation and privatization is the only way forward. In that sense, the figure of the 'NRI/PIO' serves a function that goes well beyond any particular focus on the diaspora itself.

What about members of the Indian diaspora? Is it not possible that well-organized sections within the broader constituency can have a greater impact on shaping the foreign policy agenda of the Indian state? It can definitely be argued that there are certain groups that seem to have close connections with the Indian ruling elite. Take, for instance, the fact that a recently established organization like the innocuous sounding Indian American Community Foundation (IACF) (described often as an umbrella grouping of three hundred US-based organizations) could host a 'private' and supposedly 'apolitical' rally in one of the most expensive venues in New York city at the cost of approximately $3.5 million, featuring the current Prime Minister of India. While this does seem to indicate the possibility of overseas lobby groups, I would argue that their ability to influence the policy agenda of the Indian state rests not so much on their connections to state actors, but rather their class positions within a global capitalist economy. In the sense that if the demands of these groups went against the neoliberal agenda, their ability to command the hearing of the Indian ruling elite would be fairly limited. As Devesh Kapur has argued in a somewhat different context about the power of the Indian-American lobby, their role remains 'facilitative, rather than causal'.[13] And if that remains the case for what is unarguably the most visible and well-organized section of the Indian diaspora, one can only come to the conclusion that even the 'facilitative' role of other sections of the diasporic population remains highly circumscribed. Thus, notwithstanding the fact that the Indian diaspora today constitutes the largest migrant population in the world and that its economic ties to the homeland remain unsurpassed in terms of remittances, its role in the shaping of Indian foreign policy is limited at best. But this very limitation makes the study of the peculiar position of the Indian diaspora a critical subject for scholars and policymakers alike.

Notes

1   United Nations Department of Economic and Social Affairs (UN DESA), 'International Migration Report, 2015'. Accessed on 12 March 2017. Available at http://www.un.org/en/development/desa/population/migration/publications/migrationreport/docs/MigrationReport2015.pdf.

2   It should be noted that the number given by the UN DESA report puts the Indian

diaspora population at around 16 million. This is quite different from that given by the Indian Ministry of External Affairs, which claims that the population of 'Overseas Indians' (divided into the two categories of 'Non Resident Indians' and 'Persons of Indian Origin') is around 30 million. See http://mea.gov.in/images/attach/NRIs-and-PIOs_1. pdf. Accessed on 12 March 2017.

3   These included the following: [A] Colonies of the Indian system: Ceylon, Malaya; [B] Colonies of the Pacific Ocean: Fiji, New Caledonia; [C] Colonies of the South Indian Ocean: The Union of South Africa and East Africa in general, Mauritius, Reunion; [D] Colonies of the West Indian system: Foreign – St. Croix, Guadeloupe, Martinique, Cayenne, Surinam; British – Demarara (British Guyana), Trinidad, Jamaica, Grenada, St. Vincent, St. Lucia, St. Kitts, Nevis. Apart from this, considerable numbers of Indian settlers in British Columbia (Canada), California, Mexico, Cuba, Brazil, Gibraltar, Hong Kong, and New Zealand. For a detailed account, see Lanka Sundaram, *Indians Overseas: A Study in Economic Sociology*, 4 (Madras: G.A. Natesan and Co., 1933).

4   Ibid.

5   This became patently obvious with the policy proclamations such as the 'Devonshire Declaration' of 1923, in which the British government used the pretext of protecting 'native African interests' to undermine any efforts by non-white settlers to improve their lot. For further analysis on the Indian nationalist reaction to these colonial policies, see M. C. Lall, *India's Missed Opportunity: India's Relationship with the Non-Resident Indians* (London: Ashgate, 2001).

6   For an elaboration of this argument, see Latha Varadarajan, *The Domestic Abroad: Diasporas in International Relations* (New York: Oxford University Press, 2010).

7   Jawaharlal Nehru, *Lok Sabha Debates*, Vol. VI, 2 September 1957.

8   See, for instance, Lall, *India's Missed Opportunity*.

9   W. S. Desai, *India and Burma* (Bombay: Orient Longmans Ltd, 1954).

10   For details of the budget as well as the general framing of the crisis, see Manmohan Singh, 'General Budget 1991–91', *Lok Sabha Debates*, 24 July 1991.

11   Press Release, Ministry of External Affairs, Government of India, 18 August 2000.

12   'OCI' status according to the amendment is available to all persons of Indian origin who were or were eligible to become Indian citizens on 26 January 1950, except anyone who is or had been a citizen of Pakistan or Bangladesh or any other country specified by the Government of India by a notification in the Official Gazette.

13   Devesh Kapur, *Diaspora, Development and Democracy*, 200 (Princeton, NJ: Princeton University Press, 2010).

Bibliography

Abraham, Itty. 2014. *How India Became Territorial: Foreign Policy, Diaspora, Geopolitics.* Stanford: Stanford University Press.

Acharya, Alka. 1996. 'Prelude to Sino-Indian War: Aspects of the Decision-Making Process during 1959–62.' *China Report* (October–December). New Delhi: Sage Publications.

Acharya, Amitav. 2004. 'How Ideas Spread: Whose Norms Matter? Norm Localization and Institutional Change in Asian Regionalism.' *International Organisation* 58(2): 239–275.

———. 2009. 'Multilateralism, Sovereignty and Normative Change in World Politics.' In *Multilateralism Under Challenge?* edited by Edward Newman, Ramesh Thakur and John Tirman, 95–118. United Nations University Press.

Adler, E. 1997. 'Seizing the Middle Ground: Constructivism in World Politics.' *European Journal of International Relations* 3(3): 319–363.

Adler, E. and V. Pouliot. 2011. 'International Practices.' *International Theory* 3(1): 4.

Agarwal, Nipun. 2007. 'Why Multilateralism Can't Exist: Is The WTO Mandate Wrong?' Accessed on 28 July 2016. Available at http://papers.ssrn.com/sol3/papers.cfm?abstract_id=957765.

Aghion, Philippe, Pol Antràs and Elhanan Helpman. 2004. 'Negotiating Free Trade.' NBER Working Paper 10721. Cambridge: National Bureau of Economic Research.

Alagappa, M. 1998. 'India: Modified Structuralism.' In *Asian Security Practice: Material and Ideational Influences,* edited by M. Alagappa. Stanford: Stanford University Press.

Alamgir, J. 2009. *India's Open-Economy Policy: Globalism, Rivalry, Continuity.* New York and London: Routledge.

Alden, Chris and Marco Antonio Vieira. 2005. 'The New Diplomacy of the South: South Africa, Brazil, India and Trilateralism.' *Third World Quarterly* 26(7): 1077–1095.

Alexander, Jeffrey C. 2004. 'Toward a Theory of Cultural Trauma.' In *Cultural Trauma and Collective Identity,* edited by Alexander, Jeffrey C., Ron Eyerman, Bernhard Giesen, Neil Smelser, Piotr Sztompka and Björn Wittrock. University of California Press.

Allison, Graham T. and Philip Zelikow. 1999. *Essence of a Decision: Explaining the Cuban Missile Crisis*. US: Pearson.

Alter, J. S. 1997. 'A Therapy to Live by: Public Health, the Self and Nationalism in the Practice of a North Indian Yoga Society.' *Medical Anthropology* 17(4): 314.

Aneja, Urvashi. 2014. 'India, R2P and Humanitarian Assistance.' *Global Responsibility to Protect* 6: 227–245.

Appadorai, A and M. S. Rajan. 1985. *India's Foreign Policy and Relations*. New Delhi: South Asian Publishers.

Appadorai, Arjun. 1981. 'Non-Alignment: Some Important Issues.' *International Studies* 20(1 and 2): 3–11.

ASEAN. 2017. 'Overview of ASEAN-India Dialogue Relations.' Accessed on 15 April 2018. Available at http://www.asean.org/asean/externalrelations/india/item/overview-of-asean-india-dialogue-relations.

Ashref, Jawed. 2017. 'Economic Links Integral to India's Act East Policy.' *Straits Times*, 27 July.

Asirvatham, E. 1955. 'How Sound Is India's Foreign Policy?' *The Indian Journal of Political Science* 16(4): 383.

Averre, Derek and Lance Davies. 2015. 'Russia, Humanitarian Intervention and the Responsibility to Kosovo and the Challenge of Humanitarian Intervention: Selective Indignation.' *Collective* (6): 799–817. Available at DOI:10.1177/0309132510362603.

Bachrach, P. and M. S. Baratz. 1962. 'Two Faces of Power.' *The American Political Science Review* 56(4): 947–952.

Bajpaee, Chietigi. 2014. 'Embedding India in Asia: Reaffirming the IndoPacific Concept.' *Journal of Defence Studies* 8(4): 83–110.

Bajpai, K. 2002. 'Indian Strategic Culture.' In *South Asia in 2020: Future Strategic Balances and Alliances*, M. R. Chambers, 250–280. Carlisle: Strategic Studies Institute.

———. 2003. 'Indian Conceptions of Order and Justice: Nehruvian, Gandhian, Hindutva, and Neo-Liberal.' In *Order and Justice in International Relations*, edited by Rosemary Foot, John Gaddis and Andrew Hurrell. Oxford UK: Oxford University Press.

———. 2005a. 'International Studies in India: Bringing Theory (Back) Home.' In *International Relations in India: Theorizing the Region and Nation*, edited by K. Bajpai and S. Mallavarapu, 27–28. New Delhi: OrientBlackswan.

———. 2005b. 'Introduction.' In *International Relations in India: Theorising the Region and the Nation*, edited by K. Bajpai and S. Mallavarapu, 4. New Delhi: Orient BlackSwan.

———. 2014. 'Indian Grand Strategy: Six Schools of Thought.' In *India's Grand Strategy: History, Theory, Cases*, edited by K. Bajpai, S. Basit and V. Krishnappa, 113–150. New Delhi: Routledge.

———. 2015. 'Five Approaches to the Study of Indian Foreign Policy.' In *The Oxford*

Handbook of Indian Foreign Policy, edited by David M. Malone, C. Raja Mohan and Srinath Raghavan. Oxford University Press.

———. 2017. 'Narendra Modi's Pakistan and China Policy: Assertive Bi-lateral Diplomacy, Active Coalition Diplomacy.' *International Affairs* 93: 1. Available at https://www.chathamhouse.org/sites/files/chathamhouse/publications/ia/INTA 93_1_05_Bajpai.pdf.

Bajpai, Kanti and Harsh V. Pant (eds). 2013. *India's Foreign Policy: A Reader*. Oxford: Oxford University Press.

Baldwin, D. A. 1979. 'Power Analysis and World Politics.' *World Politics* 31(2): 163.

———. 2013. 'Power and International Relations.' In *Handbook of International Relations*, edited by W. Carlsnaes, T. Risse and B. A. Simmons, 276. Thousand Oaks, CA: Sage Publications.

Bandyopadhyaya, J. 1970. *The Making of India's Foreign Policy: Determinants, Institutions, Processes and Personalities*, 4. New Delhi: Allied Publishers.

Baral, Jaya Krishna. 1978. *The Pentagon and the Making of US Foreign Policy: A Case Study of Vietnam, 1960–1968*, 8–15. New Delhi: Radiant Publishers.

Baralou, Judy. 2005. *Trauma and Transitional Justice in Divided Societies*. The United States Institute of Peace.

Barnett, M. N. and M. Finnemore. 1999. 'The Politics, Power, and Pathologies of International Organizations.' *International Organization* 53(04): 699–732.

Barnett, Michael and Raymond Duvall. 2005. 'Power in International Politics.' *International Organization* 59(1): 39–77.

Barroso, Jose Manuel. 2010. 'Asian Giants Can Imbibe Europe's Values.' *Times of India*, 24 January. Accessed on 30 September 2016. Available at http://timesofindia. indiatimes.com/home/sunday-times/all-that-matters/Asiangiants-can-imbibe-Europes-values/articleshow/5493466.cms.

Barry, Ellen and Salman Masood. 2016. 'India Claims "Surgical Strikes" Across Line of Control in Kashmir.' *New York Times*, September.

Baru, Sanjaya. 2009. 'The Influence of Business and Media on Indian Foreign Policy.' *India Review* 8(3): 266–285. London: Routledge.

Basedau, Matthias and Patrick Köllner. 2007. 'Area Studies, Comparative Area Studies, and the Study of Politics: Context, Substance, and Methodological Challenges.' *Zeitschrift für Vergleichende Politikwissenschaft* 1(1): 105–124.

Basrur, Rajesh and Jaganath Sankaran. 2016. 'India's Slow and Unstoppable Move to MIRV.' In *The Lure and Pitfalls of MIRVs: From the First to the Second Nuclear Age*, edited by Michael Krepon, Travis Wheeler and Shane Mason. Washington, DC: Henry L. Stimson Center.

Basrur, Rajesh. 2014a. 'Deterrence, Second Strike and Credibility: Revisiting India's Nuclear Strategy Debate.' July. New Delhi: Institute of Peace and Conflict Studies. Accessed on 11 December 2016. Available at http://www.ipcs.org/pdf_file/issue/ IB255RajeshBasrur-IndiaNuclear.pdf.

————. 15 April 2014b. 'Nuclear Deterrence: The Wohlstetter-Blackett Debate Re-visited.' Working Paper. S. Rajaratnam School of International Studies, Nanyang Technological University, Singapore. Accessed on 15 April 2014. Available at https://www.rsis.edu.sg/wp-content/uploads/rsis-pubs/WP271.pdf.

Bass, Gary J. 2015. 'The Indian Way of Humanitarian Intervention.' *The Yale Journal of International Law* 40 : 227–294.

Basu, Titli. 2016. 'India's Approach towards Indo-Pacific Triangularity.' IDSA News, 27 May.

BBC. 2006. 'Bush Arrives to India Protests.' 1 March. Available at http://news.bbc. co.uk/1/hi/world/south_asia/4761956.stm. New Delhi: Ministry of External Affairs, GoI.

————. 2015. 'The links between UK and India.' 12 November. Available at http://www.bbc.com/news/uk34767180.

Behera, Navnita Chadha. 2007. 'Re-Imagining IR in India.' *International Relations of the Asia Pacific* 7(3): 341–368.

Bellamy, Alex and Tim Dunne. 2016. *The Oxford Handbook of the Responsibility to Protect.* Oxford: Oxford University Press.

Bellamy, Alex J. 2015. 'The Responsibility to Protect Turns Ten.' Ethics and International Affairs 29.2 (June): 166–167.

Benner, Jeffrey. 1984. *Structure of Decision: The Indian Foreign Policy Bureaucracy*, 3–5. New Delhi: South Asia Publishers.

Benton, Lauren. 2010. *A Search for Sovereignty: Law and Geography in European Empires, 1400–1900.* New York: Cambridge University Press.

Berenskoetter, F. 2007. 'Friends, There Are No Friends? An Intimate Reframing of the International.' *Millennium* 35(3): 647–676.

Berman, Sheri. 2001. 'Review: Ideas, Norms, and Culture in Political Analysis.' *Comparative Politics* 33(2): (January): 231–250.

Bhagavan, M. 2012. *The Peacemakers: India and the Quest for One World.* New Delhi: HarperCollins.

Bhagavan, Manu. 2010. 'A New Hope: India, the United Nations and the Making of the Universal Declaration of Human Rights.' *Modern Asian Studies* 44(2): 311–347.

————. 2013. *India and the Quest for One World: The Peacemakers.* New York: Palgrave.

Bhagwati, Jagdish. 1992. 'Regionalism versus Multilateralism.' *The World Economy* 15(15): 535–556.

————. 1996. 'Preferential Trading Areas and Multilateralism: Strategies, Friends or Foes?' In *The Economics of Preferential Trade Agreements*, edited by Jagdish Bhagwati. AEI Press.

Bhambhri, Chandra Prakash. 2006. 'Non-Alignment in the Changing Context of Twenty-First Century.' *India Quarterly* 62(3): 95–109.

Bharatiya Janata Party. 2014. 'Election Manifesto 2014.' Accessed on 2 July 2014. Available at http://bjpelectionmanifesto.com/pdf/manifesto2014.pdf.

Biermann, Frank, Philipp Pattberg, Harro Van Asselt and Fariborz Zelli. 2009. 'The

Fragmentation of Global Governance Architectures: A Framework of Analysis.' *Global Environmental Politics* 9(4): 14–40.

Bishoyi, Saroj. 2016. 'Geostrategic Imperative of the Indo-Pacific Region.' *Journal of Defence Studies* 10(1): 89–102.

Biswas, S. 2001. '"Nuclear Apartheid" as Political Position: Race as a Postcolonial Resource?' *Alternatives: Global, Local, Political* 26(4): 485–522.

———. 2014. '"Nuclear Apartheid" as Political Position: Race as a Postcolonial Resource?' In *Nuclear Desire: Power and the Postcolonial Nuclear Order*, edited by S. Biswas. Minneapolis and London: University of Minnesota Press.

Bjorkdahl, Annika. 1998. 'Norms in International Relations – Some Conceptual and Methodological Reflections.' *Cambridge Review of International Affairs* 15(1): 9–15.

Blackett, P. M. S. 1961. 'Critique of Some Contemporary Defence Thinking.' *Encounter* 16(4) (April): 9–17.

Blarel, N. 2012. 'India's Soft Power: From Potential to Reality?' *IDEAS Reports – Special Reports*, edited by N. Kitchen. London: SR010, LSE IDEAS, London School of Economics.

Blarel, Nicolas. 2015. *The Evolution of India's Israel Policy: Continuity, Change, and Compromise since 1922*. New Delhi: Oxford University Press.

———. 2017. 'Inside Out? Assessing the Domestic Determinants of India's External Behaviour.' In *Theorizing Indian Foreign Policy*, edited by Mischa Handsel, Melissa Levaillant and Raphaelle Khan. London: Routledge.

Bloomfield, Alan. 2015. 'India and the Libyan Crisis: Flirting with the Responsibility to Protect, Retreating to the Sovereignty Norm.' *Contemporary Security Policy* 36(1): 44.

———. 2016. *India and the Responsibility to Protect*. Farnham, Ashgate Publishing, Ltd.

Boraine, Alexander. 2006. 'L. Transitional Justice: A Holistic Interpretation.' *Journal of International Affairs* 60(1): 17–28.

Bose, Sugata and Ayesha Jalal. 2011. *Modern South Asia: History, Culture, Political Economy*. Third edition. New York: Routledge.

Boulden, Jane. 2001. *Peace Enforcement: The United Nations Experience in Congo, Somalia, and Bosnia*. Westport, CT: Praeger.

BRICS. 2012. 'Summit Delhi Declaration.' Accessed on 10 October 2015. Available at https://www.brics2017.org/English/AboutBRICS/DOPS/201701/t20170114_1117.html.

Brobst, Peter John. 2005. 'The Future of the Great Game: Sir Olaf Caroe, India's Independence, and the Defense of Asia.' *Middle Eastern Studies* 41(6): 1013–1015.

Brog, Mooli. 2003. 'Victims and Victors: Holocaust and Military Commemoration in Israel Collective Memory.' *Israel Studies* 8(3) (Fall): pp. 65–99.

Brooks, Roy L. (ed.). 1999. *Critical America: When Sorry Isn't Enough: The Controversy over Apologies and Reparations for Human Injustice*. NYU Press.

Bull, Hedley. 2002. *The Anarchical Society: A Study of Order in World Politics*. London: Palgrave Macmillan.

Carranza, M. E. 2016. *India–Pakistan Nuclear Diplomacy: Constructivism and the Prospects for Nuclear Arms Control and Disarmament in South Asia*. Rowman & Littlefield.

Carrapatoso, Astrid and Mareike Well. 2016. 'REDD+ Finance: Policy Making in the Context of Fragmented Institutions.' *Climate Policy*. August. Accessed on 10 January 2017. Available at DOI:10.1080/14693062.2016.1202096.

Carter, D. B. and H. E. Goemans. 2011. 'The Making of the Territorial Order: New Borders and Emergence of Interstate Conflict.' *International Organizations* 65(2): 275–309.

Chacko, P. 2011. 'The Search for a Scientific Temper: Nuclear Technology and the Ambivalence of India's Postcolonial Modernity.' *Review of International Studies* 37(01).

———. 2012. *Indian Foreign Policy: The Politics of Postcolonial Identity from 1947 to 2004*. London and New York: Routledge.

———. 2014a. 'A New "Special Relationship"? Power Transitions, Ontological Security, and India–US Relations.' *International Studies Perspectives* 15(3): 329–346.

———. 2014b. 'The Rise of the Indo-Pacific: Understanding Ideational Change and Continuity in India's Foreign Policy.' *Australian Journal of International Affairs* 68(4): 433–452.

———. 2016. 'Foreign Policy, Ideas and State-building: India and the Politics of International Intervention.' *Journal of International Relations and Development*. Available at DOI:10.1057/jird.2016.15.

Chacko, P. and A. E. Davis. 2017. 'The Natural/Neglected Relationship: Liberalism, Identity and India–Australia Relations.' *The Pacific Review* 30(1): 26–50;

Chacko, P. and Jayasuriya. 2017. 'A Capitalising Foreign Policy: Regulatory Geographies and Transnationalised State Projects.' *European Journal of International Relations*.

Chakravarti, R. 1963. 'India in World Affairs.' *The Indian Journal of Political Science* 24(4): 355–367.

Chalk, Peter. 2001. 'Pakistan's Role in the Kashmir Insurgency.' *Jane's Intelligence Review*, 1 September. Reproduced on the web site of the RAND Corporation. Accessed on 14 February 2003. Available at http://www.rand.org/hot/op-eds/090101JIR.html.

Chandramohan, Balaji. 2017. 'India's Strategic Outreach in the Indo-Pacific Region.' *Science, Technology and Security Forum*, 20 January. Available at http://stsfor.org/content/indias-strategic-outreach-indo-pacific-region.

Chatterjee Miller, Manjari. 2013. *Wronged by Empire: Post-Imperial. Ideology and Foreign Policy in India and China*. Stanford, CA: Stanford University.

Chatterjee, S. 2005. 'Ethnic Conflicts in South Asia: A Constructivist Reading.' *South Asian Survey* 12(1): 75–89.

Chaulia, Sreeram. 2016. *Modi Doctrine: The Foreign Policy of India's Prime Minister*. New Delhi: Bloomsbury.

Chawla, Shalini. 2000. 'NATO's Response to the Kosovo Crisis.' *Strategic Analysis* 24(6): 1143–1153.

Chenoy, K. M. and A. M. Chenoy. 2007. 'India's Foreign Policy Shifts and the Calculus of Power.' *Economic and Political Weekly* 42(35): 35–53.

Cherian, John. 2011. 'Libya in the Crosshairs.' *Frontline* 28(8) (April): 9–22. Available at http://www.frontline.in/navigation/?type=static&page=archiveSearch&aid=20110422280800400&ais=08&avol=28.

Chhibber, P. and R. Verma. 2014. 'The BJP's 2014 "Modi Wave": An Ideological Consolidation of the Right.' *Economic and Political Weekly* XLIX(39): 53–55.

Chiriyankandath, James. 2004. 'Realigning India: Indian Foreign Policy after the Cold War.' *Round Table: The Commonwealth Journal of International Affairs* 93(374) (April).

Chitalkar, Poorvi and David M. Malone. 2016. 'India and Global Governance.' In *The Oxford Handbook of Indian Foreign Policy*, edited by David M. Malone, C. Raja Mohan and Srinath Raghavan, 581–595. New Delhi: Oxford University Press.

Choedon, Yeshi. 2007. 'India and the Current Concerns of UN Peacekeeping: Issues and Prospects.' *India Quarterly* 63(2): 150–84.

Chowdhari Tremblay, Rita and Julian Schofield. 2005. 'Institutional Causes of the India-Pakistan Rivalry.' In *The India-Pakistan Conflict: An Enduring Rivalry*, edited by T. V. Paul, 227–237. Cambridge: Cambridge University Press.

Christie, Kenneth. 2000. *The South African Truth Commission*. London: MacMillan.

Clarke, M. 1989. 'The Foreign Policy System: A Framework from Analysis.' In *Understanding Foreign Policy: The Foreign Policy Systems Approach*, edited by M. Clarke and B. White, 27–59. Cheltenham: Edward Elgar.

Cohen, S. P. 2000. 'India Rising.' *The Wilson Quarterly* 24(3): 32–53;

———. 2001. *India: Emerging Power*. Washington, D.C.: Brookings Institution Press.

Cohen, Stephen P. and Sunil Dasgupta. 2010. *Arming Without Aiming: India's Military Modernization*. The Brookings Institution.

Cox, Robert W. (ed.). 1997. *The New Realism: Perspectives on Multilateralism and World Order*. St. Martin's Press/United Nations University Press.

———. 1996. 'Multilateralism and World Order.' In *Approaches to World Order*, edited by Robert W. Cox and Timothy Sinclair, 494–523. Cambridge: Cambridge University Press.

Cronin, Patrick M. and Darshana Baruah. 2014. 'The Modi Doctrine for the Indo-Pacific Maritime Region.' *The Diplomat*, 2 December.

Daddow, Oliver. 2009. '"Tony's War"? Blair, Kosovo and the Interventionist Impulse in British Foreign Policy.' *International Affairs* 85(3): 547–560.

Dahl, R. A. 1957. 'The Concept of Power.' *Systems Research and Behavioral Science* 2(3): 202–203.

Danish Institute for International Studies. 2010. *Danish Foreign Policy Yearbook 2010*, 113–35. Copenhagen: Danish Institute for International Studies.

Das, Premvir. 2006. 'Maritime Violence in the Indian Ocean.' 13 October. In *Indo-Japan Dialogue on Ocean Security*, 108–132. Tokyo: Ocean Policy Research Foundation.

———. 2015. 'India's Maritime Interests in the IndoPacific.' *Seminar* 670(June). Available at http://www.india-seminar.com/semframe.html.

———. 2017. 'India's Indo-Pacific Challenges.' *Business Standard*, 1 April.

Das, R. 2010. 'State, Identity and Representations of Nuclear (In)Securities in India and Pakistan.' *Journal of Asian and African Studies* 45(2).

———. 2012. 'The United States–India Nuclear Relations after 9/11: Alternative Discourses.' *Asian Journal of Political Science* 20(1): 86–107.

———. 2015. 'A Post-colonial Analysis of India–United States Nuclear Security: Orientalism, Discourse, and Identity in International Relations.' *Journal of Asian and African Studies*. Available at DOI: 0021909615609940.

Davis, A. E. 2015. 'A Shared History?: Postcolonial Identity and India-Australia Relations, 1947–1954.' *Pacific Affairs* 88(4): 849–869.

Devdutt. 1962. 'Non-Alignment and India.' *The Indian Journal of Political Science* 23(1/4): 380–397.

Dhowan, Admiral Robin K. 2014. 'Defence and Security Alert.' 6(3) (December): 6–11.

Dixit, J. N. 2003. *The Making of India's Foreign Policy: Raja Ram Mohun Roy to Yashwant Sinha*, 5–12. India: Allied Publishers.

———. J. N. 2005. 'India's Approach to Multilateralism.' In *United Nations: Multilateralism and International Security*, edited by C. Uday Bhaskar, K. Santhanam, Uttam K. Sinha and Tasneem Meenai. Shipra Publications.

Dorschner, John and Thomas Sherlock. 2007. 'The Role of History in Shaping Collective Identities in India and Pakistan.' In *Teaching the Violent Past: History Education and Reconciliation*, edited by Elizabeth A. Cole. Lanham: Rowman & Littlefield.

Doty, R. L. 1993. 'Foreign Policy as Social Construction: A Post-Positivist Analysis of U.S. Counterinsurgency Policy in the Philippines.' *International Studies Quarterly* 37: 298.

Dougherty, Mark J. 2001. 'Stalin's Gulag Prisoners and Prevalence of Post-traumatic Stress Disorder.' *Journal of Loss and Trauma* 6: 1–19.

Doyle, Michael. 2003. 'Kant, Liberal Legacies and Foreign Affairs.' *Philosophy and Public Affairs* 12(3) (Summer): 207–210.

Eck, Diana. 2012. *India: A Sacred Geography*. New York: Three Rivers Press.

Economic Times. 2005. 'BJP Raises Din over Manmohan's Colonial Musings.' 14 July. Accessed on 15 April 2018. Available at http://articles.economictimes.indiatimes.com/2005-07-14/news/27491491_1_prime-minister-freedom-strugglefreedom-fighters.

———. 2006. 'Indo-US Ties Not at the Cost of Other Nations.' September. Accessed on 10 December 2012. Available at http://economictimes.indiatimes.

com/news/politics-and-nation/indo-us-ties-not-at-the-costof-other-nations/
articleshow/1983638.cms.

Epstein, C. 2012. 'Stop Telling Us How to Behave: Socialization or Infantilization?'
International Studies Perspectives 13(2): 135–145

Fidler, D. P. and S. Ganguly. 2010. 'India and Eastphalia.' *Indiana Journal of Global Legal
Studies* 17(1): 147–164.

Financial Express. 2017. 'India, Sri Lanka Likely to Finalise ETCA by the Year End.'
17 May 17.

Finnemore, M. 1996. *National Interests in International Society.* Ithaca: Cornell
University Press.

———. 2009. 'Legitimacy, Hypocrisy, and the Social Structure of Unipolarity: Why
Being a Unipole Isn't All It's Cracked Up to Be.' *World Politics* 61(1): 58–85.

Firstpost. 2013. 'A Sorry Apology: David Cameron at Jallianwala Bagh.' Accessed on 15
April 2018. Available at http://www.firstpost.com/politics/a-sorry-apology-david-
cameron-at-jallianwala-bagh-632541.html.

Frey, K. 2006. *India's Nuclear Bomb and National Security.* London and New York:
Routledge.

Gaddis, John Lewis. 2005. *Strategies of Containment: A Critical Appraisal of American
National Security Policy during the Cold War.* Oxford: Oxford University Press.

Ganguly, Anirban, Vijay Chauthaiwale and Uttam Kumar Sinha (eds). 2016. *The Modi
Doctrine: New Paradigms in India's Foreign Policy.* New Delhi: Wisdom Tree.

Ganguly, Sumit and Devin T. Hagerty. 2006. *Fearful Symmetry: India-Pakistan Crises n
the Shadow of Nuclear Weapons.* New Delhi: Oxford University Press.

Ganguly, Sumit and Manjeet S. Pardesi. 2009. 'Explaining Sixty Years of India's Foreign
Policy.' *India Review* 8(1): 4–19.

Ganguly, Sumit and William R. Thompson. 2017. *Ascending India and Its State Capacity:
Extraction, Violence, and Legitimacy.* New Haven: Yale University Press.

Ganguly, Sumit. 1995. 'Wars Without End: the Indo-Pakistani Conflict.' *Annals of the
American Academy of Political and Social Science* 541(Small Wars): 175.

———. 2003–04. 'India's Foreign Policy Grows Up.' *World Policy Journal* 20(4)
(Winter).

———. November 2010. 'Structure and Agency in the Making of Indian Foreign
Policy.' ISAS Working Paper 116. ISAS.

———. 2011. 'A Pointless Abstention.' *The Diplomat*, 23 April. Available at http://
thediplomat.com/2011/03/a-pointless-abstention/.

———. 2016. 'India and the Responsibility to Protect.' *International Relations* 30(3):
364.

———. 2017. 'Has Modi Truly Changed India's Foreign Policy?' *The Washington
Quarterly* 40(2): 131–143.

Gardiner, Harris. 'India Takes Tough Stance with China on Kashmir.' *New York Times*, 18 September. Accessed on 14 September 2017. Available at https://mobile. nytimes.com/2014/09/19/world/asia/modi-pushes-xi-to-resolve-border-issue-inkashmir.html.

Garge, Ramanand. 2015. 'MALABAR-2015 – Emerging Collective Defence in the Indo-Pacific.' *Australian Journal of Maritime and Ocean Affairs* 7(4): 252–255.

———. 2016. 'India-Japan Strategic Partnership: The Evolving Synergy in the Indo-Pacific.' *Australian Journal of Maritime and Ocean Affairs* 8(3): 257–266.

Garver, John W. 2001. *Protracted Contest: Sino–Indian Rivalry in the Twentieth Century*. Washington: University of Washington Press.

Gehring, Thomas and Benjamin Faude,. 2014. 'A Theory of Emerging Order Within Institutional Complexes: How Composition among Regulatory International Institutions Leads to Institutional Adaptation and Division of Labor.' *Review of International Organizations* 9: 471–498.

Gilpin, Robert. 1981. *War and Change in World Politics*, 91. New York: Cambridge University Press.

Glaser, Charles L. 1997. 'The Security Dilemma Revisited.' *World Politics* 50(1) (October): 171–201.

Goh, Evelyn. 2006. 'Understanding Hedging in Asia-Pacific Security.' *PacNet* 43 (31 August). Accessed on 6 February 2011. Available at http://www.stratad.net/ downloads/PacNet%2043.pdf.

Gokhale, Nitin. 2013. 'From Look East to Engage East: How India's Own Pivot Will Change Discourse in Indo-Pacific Region.' Vivekananda International Foundation, 12 March.

Goldberg, Jeffrey. 2016. 'World Chaos and World Order: Conversations with Henry Kissinger.' *The Atlantic*, 10 November. Available at https://www.theatlantic.com/ international/archive/2016/11/kissinger-order-and-chaos/506876/. 460–480. Tokyo

Goswami, Manu. 2004. *Producing India*. Chicago: University of Chicago Press.

Gottlob, Michael. 2007. 'Changing Concepts of Identity in the Indian Textbook Controversy.' *Internationale Schulbuchforschung* 29(4): 341–353.

Government of India. 1999. *Draft Report of National Security Advisory Board on Indian Nuclear Doctrine*. 17 August. New Delhi: Ministry of External Affairs.

———. 2012. *Annual Report 2011–12*. New Delhi: Ministry of Defence, GoI.

———. 2015. 'Inaugural U.S.-India-Japan Trilateral Ministerial Dialogue.' Press release. 30 September. Accessed on 15 April 2018. Available at http://www.mea. gov.in/press-releases.htm?dtl/25868. New Delhi: Ministry of External Affairs, GoI.

———. 2016a. *Annual Report 2015–2016*, 5. New Delhi: Ministry of Home Affairs, GoI.

———. 2016b. 'India-New Zealand Joint Statement.' 26 October. Available at https:// mea.gov.in/bilateral-documents.htm?dtl/27535/. New Delhi: Ministry of External Affairs, GoI.

————. 2016c. 'Speech by Minister of State for External Affairs at the Gateway of India Dialogue'. 14 June. Available at http://www.mea.gov.in/Speeches-Statements. htm?dtl/26910/.

————. 2016d. 'Visit of Indian Warship to Port Majuro, Marshall Islands.' *Press Information Bureau*, 13 August. Available at http://pib.nic.in/newsite/PrintRelease. aspx?relid=148884.

————. 2017. 'Joint Statement – United States and India: Prosperity through Partnership.' Accessed on 15 April 2018. Available at http://www.mea. gov.in/bilateraldocuments.htm?dtl/28560/Joint+Statement++United+ States+and+India+Prosperity+Through+Partnership. New Delhi: Ministry of External Affairs, GoI.

Green, Bridget. 1992. 'The Non-aligned Movement in Perspective.' Sheffield Papers in International Studies, 10. Sheffield: University of Sheffield.

Groom, A. J. R. 2009. 'Multilateralism as a Way of Life in Europe.' In *Multilateralism under Challenge? Power, International Order and Structural Change*, edited by Edward Newman, Ramesh Thakur and John Tirman, 460–80. Tokyo: United Nations University Press.

Guha, R. 2008. 'Will India Become A Superpower?' *Outlook*, 30 June.

————. 2007. *India after Gandhi: The History of the World's Largest Democracy*, 168–169. London: Macmillan.

Guichard, Sylvie. 2013. 'The Indian Nation and Selective Amnesia: Representing Conflicts and Violence in Indian History Textbooks.' *Nations and Nationalism* 19(1): 68–86.

Gujral, I. K. 2011. *Matters of Discretion: An Autobiography*. New Delhi: Replika Press.

Gupta, Amita. 2007. 'Schooling in India.' In *Going to School in South Asia*, edited by Amita Gupta, 66–111. London: Greenwood Press.

Gupta, Arvind. 2011. 'Mind the R2P.' *Indian Express*, 22 April. Available at http://indianexpress.com/article/opinion/columns/mind-the-r2p/.

Gupta, M. G. 1987. *Rajiv Gandhi's Foreign Policy: A Study in continuity and Change*, 30–55. Agra: M G Publishers.

Gupta, Sourabh. 2016. 'Abe and Modi Attempt to Bridge the Indo-Pacific.' East Asia Forum, 5 January.

Hagerty, Devin T. 1991. 'India's Regional Security Doctrine.' *Asian Survey* 31(4): 351–363. New York.

Halbwachs, Maurice. 1992. *On Collective Memory*. Translated by Lewis A. Coser. Chicago, IL: University of Chicago Press.

Hall, I. 2012. 'India's New Public Diplomacy: Soft Power and the Limits of Government Action.' *Asian Survey* 52(6): 1089–1110.

————. 2013. 'Tilting at Windmills? The Indian Debate on Responsibility to Protect after UNSC 1973.' *Global Responsibility to Protect* 5(1): 93.

————. 2015. "'Mephistopheles in a Saville Row Suit": V. K. Krishna Menon and the West.' In *Radicals and Reactionaries in Twentieth Century International Thought*, edited by Ian Hall, 191–216. New York: Palgrave.

————. 2017. 'Narendra Modi and India's Normative Power.' *International Affairs* 93(1): 113–131.

Halperin, Morton H., Priscilla Clapp and Arnold Kanter. 2006. *Bureaucratic Politics and Foreign Policy*, 25–62. Washington DC: Brookings Institution Press.

————. 2015. 'Indian Foreign Policy and International Humanitarian Norms: A Role-Theoretical Analysis.' *Asian Politics and Policy* 7(1): 79–104.

Harder, A. 2016. 'When Nehru Refused American Bait on a Permanent Seat for India at the UN.' *The Wire*. Available at https://thewire.in/58802/when-nehru-refused-american-bait-on-a-permanent-seat-for-india-at-the-un/.

Harshe, Rajen. 1990. 'India's Non-Alignment: An Attempt at Conceptual Reconstruction.' *Economic and Political Weekly* 25(7/8): 399–400.

Harvey, Mary R. 1996. 'An Ecological View of Psychological Trauma and Trauma Recovery.' *Journal of Traumatic Stress* 9(1): 3–23.

Hashimoto, Akiko. 2008. 'Review: The Politics of Regret.' *Social Forces* 87(1): 603–604.

He, Kai. 2006. 'Does ASEAN Matter? International Relations Theories, Institutional Realism, and ASEAN.' *Asian Security* 2(3): 189–214.

He, Kai and Huiyun Feng. 2008. 'If Not Soft Balancing, Then What? Reconsidering Soft Balancing and U.S. Policy toward China.' *Security Studies* 17(2): 363–395.

Hedrick, Brian K. 2009. *India's Strategic Defense Transformation: Expanding Global Relationships*, 11–12, 42. Strategic Studies Institute.

Herman, Judith Lewis. 1992. *Trauma and Recovery*. New York: Basic Books.

Hindustan Times. 2016. 'All You Need to Know about BIMSTEC, the Huddle of Bay of Bengal Nations.' 14 October. Accessed on 10 December 2016. Available at http://www.hindustantimes.com/india-news/all-you-need-to-knowabout-bimstec-the-huddle-of-bay-of-bengal-nations/story-vaZIQ2o6Mwh5Yj3Ki1rzsI.html.

————. 2016. 'Foreign Policy, Good Governance.' 16 August. Available at http://www.hindustantimes.com/indianews/from-foreign-policy-to-good-governance-top-10-quotes-from-pm-modi-s-town-hall-event/storydkfPG5NKdieaFnWRvG2NRO.html.

Hirsch, Max. 2016. *Airport Urbanism: Infrastructure and Mobility in Asia*. Minneapolis: University of Minnesota Press.

Hirsch, Michal Ben-Josef. 2009. 'And the Truth Shall Make You Free: The International Norm of Truthseeking.' PhD dissertation, Massachusetts Institute of Technology.

Hirschi, Christian and Thomas Widmer. 2010. 'Policy Change and Policy Stasis: Comparing Swiss Foreign Policy towards South Africa (1968-94) and Iraq (1990-91).' *Policy Studies Journal* 38(3): 537–563.

Hochstetler, Kathryn Ann. 2012. 'The G-77, BASIC, and Global Climate Governance: A New Era in Multilateral Environmental Negotiations.' *Revista Brasileira De Politica Internacional* 55: 53–69.

Hofferberth, M. and C. Weber. 2015. 'Lost in Translation: A Critique of Constructivist Norm Research.' *Journal of International Relations and Development* 18(1): 75–103.

Holsti, K. J. 1970. 'National Role Conceptions in the Study of Foreign Policy.' *International Studies Quarterly* 14(3): 233–309

Hopf, T. 1998. 'The Promise of Constructivism in International Relations Theory.' *International Security* 23(1): 183.

Hopf, Ted. 2009. 'Identity Relations and the Sino-Soviet Split.' In *Measuring Identity*, edited by Rawi Abdelal, Yoshiko M. Herrera, Alastair Iain Johnston and Rose McDermott. Cambridge University Press.

Hudson, Philip. 2012. 'Julia Gillard will elevate India to the highest priority for Australia.' *The Australian*, 17 October.

Hudson, Valerie. 2005. 'Foreign Policy Analysis: Actor Specific Theory and the Ground of International Relations.' *Foreign Policy Analysis* 1(1) (March): 1–30.

Huotari, Mikko and Jürgen Rüland. 2014. 'Context, Concepts and Comparison in Southeast Asian Studies – Introduction to the Special Issue.' *Pacific Affairs* 87(3): 415–440.

Ikenberry, G. J. 2011. *Liberal Leviathan: The Origins, Crisis, and Transformation of the American World Order*. Princeton: Princeton University Press;

Ikenberry, G. J. and C. A. Kupchan, 1990. 'Socialization and Hegemonic Power.' *International Organization* 44(3): 293–315.

Ikenberry, G. J., M. Mastanduno and W. C. Wohlforth, 2009. 'Unipolarity, State Behavior, and Systemic Consequences.' *World Politics* 61(1): 3.

Inderjit, Sabina. 1998. 'Advani Tells Pakistan to Roll Back Its Anti-India Policy.' *Times of India*, 19 May.

India Today. 2014. 'CBSE Schools to Use Only NCERT Books: Minister of State School Education.' 19 May. Available at http://indiatoday.intoday.in/education/story/cbse-schools-to-use-ncert-only/1/362572.html.

———. 2016. 'Philippines Hails India's Support India's South China Sea Support as Modi Heads to China.' 1 September.

Indian Express. 2016a. 'India Can't Go to War with Pakistan till "Anti-national" Arvind Kejriwal Is CM: Subramanian Swamy.' 5 October. Accessed on 2 February 2017. Available at http://indianexpress.com/article/india/india-newsindia/india-cant-go-to-war-with-pakistan-while-anti-national-arvind-kejriwal-is-cm-subramanian-swamy3066703/.

———. 2016b. 'PM Modi Raises India's Concern over CPEC Which Runs through PoK.' 4 September. Accessed on 14 February 2017. Available at http://indianexpress.com/article/india/india-news-india/prime-minister-narendra-modi-raises-indiasconcern-over-cpec-which-runs-through-pok-3013260/.

———. 2016c. 'Vietnam Top Leaders Hail India's Position on Disputed South China Sea.' 3 September.

———. 2017. 'India's NSG Membership Can't Be Farewell Gift: China to US.' 16

January. Accessed on 16 January 2017. Available at http://indianexpress.com/article/world/indias-nsg-membership-cant-be-farewell-gift-china-to-us-4476997/.

Indira Gandhi. 1972. 'India and the World.' *Foreign Affairs* 51: 68.

International Institute of Strategic Studies. 2000. *The Military Balance, 2000–01*, 299. Oxford: Oxford University Press.

———. 2016a. 'India and Asia-Pacific Security,' 21–38. Asia-Pacific Regional Security Assessment. London: International Institute of Strategic Studies.

———. 2016b. *The Military Balance, 2016*, 486. Oxford: Oxford University Press.

International Monetary Fund. 2016. Direction of Trade Statistics. Washington, DC: International Monetary Fund. Accessed on 13 February 2017. Available at http://data.imf.org/regular.aspx?key=61013712.

Iqbal, Shahid. 2015. 'Trade Deficit with China Swells to $6.2bn.' *Dawn*, 16 August.

Jackson, P.T. and D. H. Nexon. 2004. 'Constructivist Realism or Realist Constructivism?' *International Studies Review* 6(2): 337–341.

Jackson, Patrick T. and Daniel H Nexon. 2002. 'Whence Causal Mechanisms? A Comment on Legro.' *Dialogue, International Organization* 1: 82.

Jackson, Robert and Georg Sorensen. 2010. *Introduction to International Relations: Theories and Approaches*. Oxford: Oxford University Press.

Jaffrelot, C. 1996. *The Hindu Nationalist Movement and Indian Politics: 1925 to 1990s*. C Hurst & Co Publishers Ltd.

———. 2015. 'What "Gujarat Model"?—Growth without Development—and with Socio-Political Polarisation.' *South Asia: Journal of South Asian Studies* 38(4): 835.

Jaganathan, Madan Mohan and Gerrit Kurtz. 2014. 'Singing the Tune of Sovereignty?' *Conflict, Security and Development* 14(4): 461.

Jain, Rajendra K. 2011. 'From Idealism to Pragmatism: India and Asian Regional Integration.' *Japanese Journal of Political Science* 12(2): 213–231.

Jaishankar, Dhruva. 2011. 'India's Acute Abstinence Syndrome.' *Polaris*. 19 March, Available at http://polaris.nationalinterest.in/2011/03/19/acute-abstinence syndrome/.

———. 2016. 'India and Japan: Emerging Indo-Pacific Security Partnership.' *RSIS Commentary* 130 (30 May).

Jaishankar, S. 2015a. 'IISS Fullerton Lecture by Dr. S. Jaishankar, Foreign Secretary in Singapore.' 20 July. New Delhi: Ministry of External Affairs, Government of India. Accessed on 2 February 2017. Available at http://mea.gov.in/SpeechesStatements.htm?dtl/25493/IISS_Fullerton_Lecture_by_Foreign_Secretary_in_Singapore.

———. 2015b. 'India, the United States and China.' IISS Fullerton Lecture, 20 July.

———. 2016. 'Indian Foreign Secretary Subrahmanyam Jaishankar's Remarks.' Carnegie India, 6 April. Accessed on 2 February 2017. Available at: http://carnegieindia.org/2016/04/06/indian-foreign-secretary-subrahmanyam-jaishankar-sremarks/iwq7.

Jalal, Ayesha. 1994. *The Sole Spokesman: Jinnah, the Muslim League and the Demand for Pakistan*. Cambridge University Press.

Jenkins, Rob. 2003. 'India's States and the Making of Foreign Economic Policy: The Limits of the Constituent Diplomacy Paradigm.' *Journal of Federalism* 33(4): 63–81.

Jepperson, R., A. Wendt and P. Katzenstein. 1996. 'Norms, Identity and Culture in National Security.' In *The Culture of National Security*, edited by Peter Katzenstein. New York: Columbia University Press.

Jervis, Robert. 1978. 'Cooperation under the Security Dilemma.' *World Politics* 30(2) (January): 167–214.

———. 1989. *The Meaning of the Nuclear Revolution*. Ithaca: Cornell University Press.

Jessop, B. 2010. 'Cultural Political Economy and Critical Policy Studies.' *Critical Policy Studies* 3(3–4): 341.

———. 2011. 'Constituting Another Foucault Effect: Foucault on States and Statecraft.' In *Governmentality: Current Issues and Future Challenges*, edited by U. Bröckling, S. Krasmann and T. Lemke, 65, 67–68. New York and London: Routledge.

Jetley, Nancy. 1979. *India-China Relations (1947–1977): A Study of Parliaments Role in the Making of Foreign Policy*. New Delhi: Radiant Publishers.

Jha, Pankaj. 2016. 'India as an Indo-Pacific Power.' Centre for Indian Studies, Ho Chi Minh National Academy of Politics, 5 October.

Jha, Prem Shankar. 2011. 'Does the West Have a Death Wish?' *Tehelka* 8(13) (2 April). Available at http://www.tehelka.com/2011/04/does-the-west-have-a-death-wish/.

John, Jojin. 2015. 'India Looks Beyond Its Near Seas to Enhance Its Interests in the Indo-Pacific.' *Strategic Vision* 4(22): 4–7.

Johnston, A. I. 2008. *Social States: China in International Institutions, 1980–2000*. Princeton: Princeton University Press.

Joshi, Manoj. 2011. 'Dodgy Stand on Libya Crisis.' *India Today*, 24 March. Available at http://indiatoday.intoday.in/story/dodgy-stand-on-libya-crisis/1/133200.html.

Joshi, V. 2016. *India's Long Road: The Search for Prosperity*, 217–328. Gurgaon: Penguin Allen Lane.

Jürgen, Rüland. 2012. 'The Rise of "Diminished Multilateralism:" East Asian and European Forum Shopping in Global Governance.' *Asia Europe Journal* 9(2–4): 255–270.

Kagan, Robert. 2017. 'The Twilight of the Liberal World Order.' 24 January. Brookings Institution. Available at https://www.brookings.edu/research/the-twilight-of-the-liberal-world-order/.

Kalyanaraman, S. 2014. 'Nehru's Advocacy of Internationalism and Indian Foreign Policy.' In *India's Grand Strategy: History, Theory, Cases*, edited by Kanti Bajpai, Saira Basit and V. Krishnappa, 153. New Delhi: Routledge.

Kanwal, Rahul. 2016. 'Inside Story of India's Daring Surgical Strikes against Pakistan.' *Mail Today*, 8 October. Accessed on 13 February 2017. Available at http://

indiatoday.intoday.in/story/inside-story-of-indian-armys-daring-surgical-strikes-againstpakistan/1/783055.html.

Kapoor, Harish. 1987. 'Indian Foreign Policy under Rajiv Gandhi.' *The Roundtable: Commonwealth Journal of International Affairs* 304: 469–480.

Kapur, Ashok. 1972. 'Indo-Soviet Treaty and the Emerging Asian Balance.' *Asian Survey* 12(6): 464.

Kapur, Devesh. 2009. 'Public Opinion and Indian Foreign Policy.' *India Review* 8(3): 286–315. London: Routledge.

———. 2010. *Diaspora, Development and Democracy*, 200. Princeton, NJ: Princeton University Press.

Karnad, B. 2002. *Nuclear Weapons and Indian Security: The Realist Foundations of Strategy*, 166. New Delhi: Macmillan, 2002.

———. 2014. 'An Elephant with a Small "Footprint": The Realist Roots of India's Strategic Thought and Policies.' In *India's Grand Strategy: History, Theory, Cases*, edited by Kanti Bajpai, Saira Basit and V. Krishnappa, 200. New Delhi: Routledge.

———. 2015. *Why India Is Not a Great Power (Yet)*. New Delhi: Oxford University Press.

Karunakaran, C. K. 1960. 'Atoms and Man.' *Sainik Samachar*, 17 July. Archives of the Royal Society, London, doc. no. PB/8/27/ H53-56.

Katzenstein, P. J., R. O. Keohane and S. D. Krasner. 1998. 'International Organization and the Study of World Politics.' *International Organization* 52(04): 645–685

Katzenstein, Peter and Sil, Rudra. 2008. 'Eclectic Theorizing in the Study and Practice of International Relations.' In *The Oxford Handbook of International Relations*, edited by Christian Reus-Smit and Duncan Snidal, 109–130. Oxford: Oxford University Press.

Katzenstein, Peter. 2007. 'Regionalism Reconsidered.' *Journal of East Asian Studies* 7: 395–412.

Kavic, Lorne J. 1962. *India's Quest for Security: Defence Policies, 1947–1965*, 21. Berkeley: University of California Press.

Kayaoglu, Turan. 2010. 'Westphalian Eurocentrism in International Relations Theory.' *International Studies Review* 12(2): 193–217.

Keck, Zachary. 2015. 'Pakistan Wants "Battlefield" Nukes to Use against Indian Troops.' *National Interest*, 6 February. Accessed on 13 February 2017. Available at http://nationalinterest.org/blog/the-buzz/pakistan-wants-battlefield-nukes-use-againstindian-troops-12200.

Keohane, R. O. and J. S. Nye, 1977. *Power and Interdependence: World Politics in Transition*. Boston: Little, Brown.

Keohane, Robert. O. 1984. *After Hegemony: Cooperation and Discord in World Politics*. Princeton: Princeton University Press.

———. 1988. 'International Institutions: Two Approaches.' *International Studies Quarterly* 32(4): 379–396.

———. 1990. 'Multilateralism: An Agenda for Research.' *International Journal* 45(4): 731–764.

———. 2000. 'The Contingent Legitimacy of Multilateralism.' GARNET Working Paper, No.9.

Khan, R. 1968. 'Crisis of National Interest in India.' *Economic and Political Weekly* 3(26/28): 1097.

Khilnani, S., R. Kumar, P. B. Mehta, P. Menon, N. Nilekani, S. Raghavan, S. Saran and S. Varadarajan. 2012. *Nonalignment 2.0: A Foreign and Strategic Policy for India in the Twenty First Century.* Centre for Policy Research. Available at http://www.cprindia.org/research/reports/nonalignment-20-foreign-and-strategic-policy-india-twenty-first-century.

Khurana, Gurpreet S. 2 February 2017. 'The Indo-Pacific concept: Retrospective and Prospect.' *Issue Brief*. National Maritime Foundation.

———. 2007. 'Security of Sea Lines: Prospects for India-Japan Cooperation.' *Strategic Analysis* 31(1): 139–53;

———. 2008. 'China's Maritime Strategy: Implications for the Indo-Pacific Region.' In *The Rise of China*, edited by Ved Malik and Jorg Schultz, 155–181. New Delhi: Pentagon Press.

Khurshid, Salman. 2013. Speech of External Affairs Minister at the launch of ASEAN India Centre in New Delhi, 21 June 2013.

———. 2014. 'Keynote Address.' In *Geopolitics*, edited by Rajiv Bhatia and Vijay Sakhuja. New Delhi: Vij Book and Indian Council of World Affairs.

Kirpal, P. N. 1945. 'Speculation on the International Relations of a Free and United India in the Post-War World.' *The Indian Journal of Political Science* 7(1/2): 398–99.

Kligler-Vilenchik, Neta, Yariv Tsfati and Oren Meyers. 2014. 'Setting the Collective Memory Agenda: Examining Mainstream Media Influence on Individuals' Perceptions of the Past.' *Memory Studies* 7(4): 484–499.

Kohli, A. 2004. *State-Directed Development: Political Power and Industrialization in the Global Periphery.* Cambridge: Cambridge University Press.

Kraig, Michael R. and Sumit Ganguly. 2005. 'The 2001-2002 Indo-Pakistani Crisis: Exposing the Limits of Coercive Diplomacy.' *Security Studies* 14(2): 290–324.

Krasner, S. D. 1976. 'State Power and the Structure of International Trade.' *World Politics* 28(3): 317–347.

———. 1982. 'Structural Causes and Regime Consequences: Regimes as Intervening Variables.' *International Organization* 36(2): 185–205.

———. 1991. 'Global Communications and National Power: Life on the Pareto Frontier.' *World Politics* 43(3): 336–366.

Kratochwil, Friedrich. 1993. 'Norms Versus Numbers: Multilateralism and the Rationalist and Reflexivist Approaches to Institutions.' In *Multilateralism Matters: The Theory and Praxis of an Institutional Form*, edited John Gerard Ruggie, 443–474. Columbia University Press.

Krepon, Michael and Chris Gagné (eds). June 2001. *The Stability-Instability Paradox: Nuclear Weapons and Brinkmanship in South Asia*. Washington, DC: Henry L. Stimson Center.

Krishna, S. 1999. *Postcolonial Insecurities: India, Sri Lanka, and the Question of Nationhood*. Minneapolis and London: University of Minnesota Press.

Krishna, Sankaran. 1994. 'Cartographic Anxiety: Mapping the Body Politic in India.' *Alternatives* 19: 507–521.

Krishnan, Ananth. 2015. 'One Step Forward, Two Steps Back.' *India Today*, 11 June. Accessed on 11 June 2015. Available at http://indiatoday.intoday.in/story/china-india-lac-modi-visit-xi-jinping-border-dispute/1/443886.html.

Kristensen, Hans M. and Robert S. Norris. 2015. 'Indian Nuclear Forces, 2015.' *Bulletin of the Atomic Scientists* 71(5): 77–83.

Kubalkova, Vendulka. 2015. 'Soviet "New Thinking" and the End of the Cold War: Five Explanations.' In *Foreign Policy in a Constructed World*, edited by Vendulka Kubalkova. New York: Rpoutledge.

Kuik, Cheng-Chwee. 2008. 'The Essence of Hedging: Malaysia and Singapore's Response to a Rising China.' *Contemporary Southeast Asia* 30(2): 159–185.

Kumar, Rajiv. 2016a. *Modi and His Challenges*. New Delhi: Bloomsbury.

———. 2016b. 'Role of Business in India's Foreign Policy.' *India Review* 15(1): 98–111.

Kurowska, Xymena. 2014. 'Multipolarity as Resistance to Liberal Norms: Russia's Position on Responsibility to Protect.' *Conflict, Security and Development* 14(4): 489–508.

Ladwig III, Walter C. 2007–08. 'A Cold Start for Hot Wars? The Indian Army's New Limited War Doctrine.' *International Security* 32(3) (Winter): 158–190;

Laffey, M. 2000. 'Locating Identity: Performativity, Foreign Policy and State Action.' *Review of International Studies* 26.

Lake, David A. 1999. 'Global Governance. A Relational Contracting Approach.' In *Globalization and Governance*, edited by A. Prakash and J. A. Hart, 31–53. London and New York: Routledge.

Lal, D. 1967a. 'Indian Foreign Policy, 1947–64.' Part 1. *Economic and Political Weekly* 2(19): 881.

———. 1967b. 'Indian Foreign Policy, 1947-64.' Part 2. *Economic and Political Weekly* 2(20): 936.

Lall, M. C. 2001. *India's Missed Opportunity: India's Relationship with the Non-Resident Indians*. London: Ashgate.

Lang, Jack. 2011. *Report of the Special Advisor to the Secretary General on Legal Issues Related to Piracy off the Coast of Somalia*. New York: United Nations.

Lavoy, Peter R. (ed.). 2009. *Asymmetric Warfare and in South Asia: The Causes and Consequences of the Kargil Conflict*. Cambridge: Cambridge University Press.

Lee, J. 2010. 'Unrealised Potential: India's "Soft Power" Ambition in Asia.' *Foreign Policy Analysis* 4.

Lee, Su-Mi. 2014. 'Understanding the Yalta Axioms and Riga Axioms through the Belief Systems of the Advocacy Coalition Framework.' *Foreign Policy Analysis Journal* 1–21.

Legro, Jeffrey W. 2000. 'The Transformation of Policy Ideas.' *American Journal of Political Science* 44(3) (July): 419–432.

Legro, Jeffrey. 2005. *Rethinking the World: Great Power Strategies and International Order*. Ithaca, NY: Cornell University Press.

Levy, Daniel and Natan Sznaider. 2002. 'The Holocaust and the Formation of Cosmopolitan Memory.' *European Journal of Social Theory* 5(1): 87–106.

Lobell, Steven E., Norrin M. Ripsman and Jeffrey W. Taliaferro (eds). 2009. *Neoclassical Realism, the State, and Foreign Policy*. Cambridge: Cambridge University Press.

Lockett, Hudson. 2016. 'China: Strikes and Protest Nos. Jump 20%.' *Financial Times*, 14 July. Accessed on 14 February 2017. Available at https://www.ft.com/content/56afb47c-23fd-3bcd-a19f-bddab6a27883.

Lukes, S. 1974. *Power: A Radical View*. London: Macmillan.

Lutz, Ellen and Kathryn Sikkink. 2001. 'The Justice Cascade: The Evolution and Impact of Foreign Human Rights Trials in Latin America.' *Chicago Journal of International Law* 2(1): 1–34.

Madhav, R. 2015. 'Singapore and India – Civilizational Bonding to Strategic Partnership.' Speech at Round Table on Singapore – India Relations.

———. 2016. 'A Different Leader.' *Indian Express*, 30 September. Accessed on 2 February 2017. Available at: http://indianexpress.com/article/opinion/columns/surgical-strikes-india-pkaistan-uri-attack-pathankot-attacknarendra-modi-nawaz-sharif-3056843.

———. 2017. 'The Advent of BRICS Era.' 11 June. Available at http://www.rammadhav.in/speeches/brics2017-the-advent-of-brics-era/.

Mahbubani, Kishore. 2014. 'Two Shades of Immunity.' *The Indian Express*, 12 January. Available at http://indianexpress.com/article/opinion/columns/two-shades-of-immunity/.

Maitra, S. N. 1967. 'A New Look at Foreign Policy.' *Economic and Political Weekly* 2(17): 793

Malik, J. Mohan. 2011. *China and India: Great Power Rivals*. Boulder, CO: FirstForumPress.

Malik, P. 2014. *India's Nuclear Debate: Exceptionalism and the Bomb*. Routledge.

Mallavarapu, S. 2005. 'Introduction.' In *International Relations in India: Bringing Theory Back Home*, edited by K. Bajpai and S Mallavarapu. New Delhi: Orient BlackSwan.

———. 2015. 'Theorizing India's Foreign Relations.' In *The Oxford Handbook of Indian Foreign Policy*, edited by David M. Malone, C. Raja Mohan and Srinath Raghavan, 35–48. Oxford: Oxford University Press.

Malone, David M. 2011a. *Does the Elephant Dance? Contemporary Indian Foreign Policy*, 249–273. New York: Oxford University Press.

———. 2011b. 'Soft Power in Indian Foreign Policy.' *Economic and Political Weekly* 46(36): 35–39.

Malone, David, C. Raja Mohan and Srinath Raghavan (eds). 2015. *The Oxford Handbook of Indian Foreign Policy*. Oxford: Oxford University Press.

Mandhana, Niharika. 2014. 'China's President Talks Trade in India as Troops Face Off at Border.' *Wall Street Journal*, 18 September. Accessed on 14 February 2017. Available at https://www.wsj.com/articles/chinas-president-xi-jinping-arrives-in-delhi-astroops-face-off-at-india-china-border-1410968062.

Manela, Erez. 2007. *The Wilsonian Moment: Self-Determination and the International Origins of Anticolonial Nationalism*. Oxford: Oxford University Press.

Mani, V. S. 2004. 'An Indian Perspective on the Evolution of International Law on the Treshhold of the Third Millennium.' In *Asian Yearbook of International Law*, edited by B. S. Chimni, Masahiro Miyoshi and Surya Subedi, Volume 9, 31–77. Martinus Nijhoff Publishers.

Mankekar, D. R. 1968. *The Guilty Men of 1962*. Bombay: Penguin Books.

Mansingh, Surjit. 1984. *India's Search for Power: Indira Gandhi's Foreign Policy, 1966–82*. New Delhi: Sage Publishers.

Markey, D. 2009. 'Developing India's Foreign Policy "Software".' *Asia Policy* 8(July): 73–96.

———. 2014. 'Reorienting U.S. Pakistan Strategy: From Af-Pak to Asia.' Council on Foreign Relations, Special Report no. 68.

———. 2015. 'Armed Confrontation between China and India: Contingency Planning Memorandum No. 27.' Council on Foreign Relations, New York, November. Accessed on 13 February 2017. Available at http://www.cfr.org/china/armed-confrontationbetween-china-india/p37228.

Martin, L. M. 1992. 'Interests, Power, and Multilateralism.' *International Organization* 46(4): 765–792.

Mathur, R. 2015. 'Sly Civility and the Paradox of Equality/Inequality in the Nuclear Order: A Post-colonial Critique.' *Critical Studies on Security* 4(1): 57–72.

Maxwell, Neville. 1970. *India's China War*. Bombay: Random House Publications.

Mazumdar, Arijit. 2014. *Indian Foreign Policy in Transition*. London: Routledge.

McCormack, Tara. 2010. 'The Responsibility to Protect and the End of the Western Century.' *Journal of Intervention and Statebuilding* 4(1): 69–82.

McGarr, Paul Michael. 2014. '"Quiet Americans in India": The CIA and the Politics of Intelligence in Cold War South Asia.' *Diplomatic History* 38(5): 1046–1082.

Mearsheimer, John J. 2001. *The Tragedy of Great Power Politics*. New York: W. W. Norton.

Mehlinger, Howard D. 1985. 'International Textbook Revision: Examples from the United States.' *Internationale Schulbuchforschung* 7: 287–298.

Mehrotra, Santosh K. 1990. *India and the Soviet Union: Trade and Technology Transfer*, 66–68. Cambridge: Cambridge University Press.

Mehta, P. B. 2006. 'Five Balancing Acts.' *Seminar* 560. Available at http://www. indiaseminar.com/2006/560/560%20pratap%20bhanu%20mehta.htm.

———. 2009. 'Still under Nehru's Shadow? The Absence of Foreign Policy Frameworks in India.' *India Review* 8(3): 209–233.

Mehta, Sureesh. 2014. 'The Indo-Pacific Imperative.' In *Geopolitics of the Indo-Pacific*, edited by Pradeep Kaushiva and Abhijit Singh, 1–3. New Delhi: KW Publishers Pvt. Ltd/National Maritime Foundation.

Meilstrup, Per. 2010. 'The Runaway Summit: The Background Story of the Danish Presidency of COP15.' UN Climate Change Conference.

Menon, S. 2011a. 'India and the Global Scene: Prem Bhatia Memorial Lecture.' 11 August. National Maritime Foundation. Accessed on 30 January 2012. Available at http://maritimeindia.org/article/india-and-global-scene.

———. 2011b. "India Will Be a Different Power.' *Outlook*, 8 December. Accessed on 2 February 2011. Available at http://www.outlookindia.com/article.aspx?279270.

Menon, Shivshankar. 2016. *Choices: Inside the Making of India's Foreign Policy*. New Delhi: Penguin Random House.

Michael, Arndt. 2013a. *India's Foreign Policy and Regional Multilateralism*. Basingstoke and London: Palgrave Macmillan.

———. 2013b. 'Sovereignty vs. Security: SAARC and Its Role in the Regional Security Architecture in South Asia.' *Harvard Asia Quarterly* 15(2): 37–45

———. 2015. 'Competing Regionalism in South Asia and Neighbouring Regions under Narendra Modi: New Leadership, Old Problems.' *Stosunki Międzynarodowe – International Relations* 51(4): 179–197.

Miller, Manjari Chatterjee and Kate Sullivan de Estrada. 2017. 'Pragmatism in Indian Foreign Policy: How Ideas Constrain Modi.' *International Affairs* 93(1): 27–49.

Miller, Manjari Chatterjee. 2013. *Wronged By Empire: Post-Imperial Ideology and Foreign Policy in India and China*. Stanford University Press.

Mitchell, David. 2007. 'Determining Indian Foreign Policy: An Examination of Prime Ministerial Leadership Styles.' *India Review* 6(4): 251–287. London: Routledge.

Modi, Narendra. 2017. 'For the U.S. and India, a Convergence of Interests and Values.' *Wall Street Journal*, 27 June.

Moe, T. M. 2005. 'Power and Political Institutions.' *Perspectives on Politics* 3(2): 215–233.

Mohan, C. R. 2000. 'Fernandes Unveils "Limited War" Doctrine.' *Hindu*, 25 January. Accessed on 13 February 2017. Available at http://www.thehindu.com/2000/01/25/ stories/01250001.htm.

———. 2003. *Crossing the Rubicon: The Shaping of India's New Foreign Policy*, 7. New Delhi: Penguin.

———. 2004. *Crossing the Rubicon: The Shaping of India's New Foreign Policy*. Palgrave.

————. 2006. 'India and the Balance of Power.' *Foreign Affairs* 85(4): 17–32.

————. 13 July 2009. 'The Making of Indian Foreign Policy: The Role of Scholarship and Public Opinion.' ISAS Working Paper Number 73. Singapore: Institute for South Asian Studies, National University of Singapore.

————. 2011a. 'India's Bridge to the Pacific.' *Indian Express*, 25 January.

————. 2011b. 'India, Libya and the Principle of Non-Intervention.' *ISAS Insights*, 122, 13 April. Available at https://www.isas.nus.edu.sg/ISAS%20Reports/ISAS%20 Insights%20122%20-%20Email%20%20India,%20Libya%20and%20the%20 Princple%20of%20Non-Intervention.pdf.

————. 2012. *Samudra Manthan: Sino-Indian Rivalry in the Indo-Pacific*. Oxford University Press.

————. 2015a. 'Modi's Indo-Pacific.' *Indian Express*, 21 November.

————. 2015b. *Modi's World: Expanding India's Sphere of Influence*. New Delhi: HarperCollins.

Mohan, Raja. 2016. 'Sailing into the Indo-Pacific.' *Indian Express*, 7 June.

Moravcsik, A. 1997. 'Taking Preferences Seriously: A Liberal Theory of International Politics.' *International Organization* 51(4): 524.

Morgenthau, H. 1947. *Scientific Man vs. Power Politics*, 6. London: Latimer House.

————. 1978. *Politics among Nations: The Struggle for Power and Peace*. Fifth edition, revised. New York: Alfred A. Knopf.

————. 2005. *Politics among Nations: The Struggle for Power and Peace*. Seventh edition, 23–26. US: McGraw Hill.

Moudgil, Surbhi. December 2016. 'Geostrategic Convergence of India's Act East Policy and Indo-Pacific Strategies.' CLAWS, 1675.

Mukherjee, Kunal. 2016. 'Security Challenges Faced by the Modi Administration in the Indo-Pacific Region.' *Journal of Comparative Asian Development* 15(1).

Mukherjee, Pranab. 2014. 'Speech.' 11 January. Available at http://presidentofindia.nic.in/sp110114.html.

————. 2016. 'Speech'. Banquet in honour of the President of Indonesia, 12 December. Available at http://presidentofindia.nic.in/speeches-detail.htm?578.

Mukherjee, Rohan and David M. Malone. 2011. 'From High Ground to High Table: The Evolution of Indian Multilateralism.' *Global Governance: A Review of Multilateralism and International Organizations* 17(3) (July-September): 311–329.

Mukherjee, Rudranghsu. 1990. 'Satan Let Loose upon Earth: The Kanpur Massacres in India in the Revolt of 1857.' *Past and Present* 128(August): 92–116.

Mukherjee, T. B. 1949. 'India's Foreign Policy.' *The Indian Journal of Political Science* 10(1/2): 47.

Mukhopadhaya, Gautam. 2017. 'The Indo-Pacific Potential.' *The Hindu*, 13 December.

Mullen, R. D. and S. Ganguly. 2012. 'The Rise of India's Soft Power.' Foreign Policy, 8 May.

Muni, Sukh D. and Anuradha Muni. 1984. *Regional Co-operation in South Asia*. New Delhi: National Publishing House.

Muppidi, H. 1999. 'Postcoloniality and the Production of International Insecurity: The Persistent Puzzle of U.S. Indian Relations.' In *Cultures of Insecurity: States, Communities and the Production of Danger*, edited by Jutta Weldes et al. Minneapolis: University of Minnesota Press, 1999.

Naidu, 2012. G. V. C. 'What Does Indo-Pacific Mean to India?' ICWA Guest Column, 1 August.

Naik, J. P. 1962. *The Role of the Government of India in Education*. New Delhi: Ministry of Education, Government of India.

Nambiar, Satish. 2000. 'India: An Uneasy Precedent.' In *Kosovo and the Challenge of Humanitarian Intervention: Selective Indignation, Collective Action, and International Citizenship*, edited by Albrecht Schnabel and Ramesh Thakur, 260–290. Tokyo: United Nations University Press.

Nandy, A. 1973. 'The Making and Unmaking of Political Cultures in India.' *Daedalus* 102(1): 119.

Narang, Vipin and Paul Staniland. 2014. 'Institutions and Worldviews in Indian Foreign Security Policy.' *India Review* 11(2): 76–94. New Delhi.

Narang, Vipin and Walter C. Ladwig III. 2017. 'Taking "Cold Start" out of the Freezer?' *The Hindu*, 11 January. Accessed on 11 January 2016. Available at http://www.thehindu.com/opinion/lead/Taking-%E2%80%98ColdStart%E2%80%99-out-of-the-freezer/article17019025.ece.

Narayanan, K. R. 1972. 'Towards a New Equilibrium in Asia.' *Economic and Political Weekly* 7(5/7): 221.

Narlikar, A. 2006. 'Peculiar Chauvinism or Strategic Calculation: Explaining the Negotiation Strategy of a Rising India.' *International Affairs* 82(1): 59–76, 77–94.

———. 2007. 'All That Glitters Is Not Gold: India's Rise to Power.' *Third World Quarterly* 28(5): 983–996.

———. 2013. 'India and the World Trade Organization.' In *India's Foreign Policy: A Reader*, edited by Kanti Bajpai and Harsh V. Pant, 415–437. Oxford: Oxford University Press.

Nayar, B. R. and T. V. Paul. 2003. *India in the World Order: Searching for Major-Power Status*, 3. Cambridge: Cambridge University Press.

Nayyar, Deepak (ed.). 2002. *Governing Globalization*. Oxford: Oxford University Press.

NCERT. 2011. *Leading the Change: 50 Years of NCERT*. Accessed on 15 April 2018. Available at http://www.ncert.nic.in/oth_anoun/leading_the_change.pdf.

———. 2014. Themes in Indian History, Part III. New Delhi.

Nehru, Jawaharlal. 1946. 'Inter-Asian Relations.' *India Quarterly* 2(4): 323–327.

———. 2 September 1957. Lok Sabha Debates, Volume VI. New Delhi: Lok Sabha Secretariat.

————. 1963. 'Changing India.' *Foreign Affairs* 41(3) (April): 457.

Newman, Edward, Ramesh Thakur and John Tirman (eds). 2009. 'Introduction' and 'Conclusion.' In *Multilateralism Under Challenge? Power, International Order and Structural Change*, edited by Edward Newman, Ramesh Thakur and John Tirman, 1–18, 531–540. United Nations University Press. Accessed on 18 October 2016. Available at https://collections.unu.edu/eserv/UNU:2470/pdf9280811290.pdf.

Niemann, H. and H. Schillinger. 2017. 'Contestation "All the Way Down"? The Grammar of Contestation in Norm Research.' *Review of International Studies* 43(1): 29–49.

Nizamani, H. K. 2001. *The Roots of Rhetoric: Politics of Nuclear Weapons in India and Pakistan*. New Delhi: India Research Press.

Norris, Robert S. and Hans M. Kristensen. 2013. 'Global Nuclear Inventories, 1945–2013.' *Bulletin of the Atomic Scientists* 69(5): 75–81.

Nye, J. S. 1990. 'Soft Power.' *Foreign Policy* 80: 153–171.

————. 2004. *Soft Power: The Means to Success in World Politics*. New York: PublicAffairs.

O'Donnell, Frank and Harsh V. Pant. 2015. 'Managing Indian Defence Policy: The Missing Grand Strategy Connection.' *Orbis* 59(2): 199–214.

O'Neill, Barry. 2002. *Honor, Symbols, and War*. Ann Arbor, MI: University of Michigan Press.

O'Rourke, Catherine. 2011. 'Transitioning to What? Transitional Justice and Gendered Citizenship in Chile and Colombia.' In *Gender in Transitional Justice*, edited by Susanne Buckley-Zistel and Ruth Stanley, 136–160. UK: Palgrave Macmillan.

Obe, Mitsuru and Niharika Mandhana. 2014. 'India and Japan Pursue Closer Ties to Counter China.' *Wall Street Journal*, 1 September.

Ofer, Dalia. 2013. 'We Israelis Remember, But How?: The Memory of the Holocaust and the Israeli Experiences.' *Israel Studies* 18(2) (Summer): 70–85.

Ogden, C. 2012. 'A Lasting Legacy: The BJP-led National Democratic Alliance and India's Politics.' *Journal of Contemporary Asia* 42(1): 22–38.

————. 2013. 'Tracing the Pakistan-Terrorism Nexus in Indian Security Perspectives: From 1947 to 26/11,' *India Quarterly: A Journal of International Affairs* 69(1): 35–50. New Delhi: ICWA, Sage Publishers.

————. 2014a. *Hindu Nationalism and the Evolution of Contemporary Indian Security: Portents of Power*. New Delhi: Oxford, 2014.

————. 2014b. *Indian Foreign Policy*. London: Polity Press.

Ollapally, D. 2005. 'Foreign Policy and Identity Politics: Realist versus Culturalist Lessons.' In *International Relations in India: Theorising the Region and the Nation*, edited by K. Bajpai, and S. Mallavarapu, 131. New Delhi: Orient BlackSwan.

————. 2016. 'Understanding Indian Policy Dilemmas in the Indo-Pacific.' *Maritime Affairs* 12(1): 1–12.

Onuf, N. 1989. *World of Our Making: Rules and Rule in Social Theory and International Relations*. Columbia: University of South Carolina Press.

Ornelas, Emanuel. 2005. 'Feasible Multilateralism and the Effects of Regionalism.' 25 April. Accessed on 28 March 2017. Available at https://ssrn.com/abstract=385704.

Padmanabhan, A. 2001. "Self-reliance Has Different Meanings for India's Polity.' Rediff, 20 August. Accessed on 8 February 2017. Available at: http://www.rediff.com/money/2001/aug/20man.htm.

Padukone, Neil. 2014. *Beyond South Asia: India's Strategic Evolution and the Reintegration of the Subcontinent.* New Delhi: Bloomsbury.

Pai, Nitin. 2016. 'India and the Indo-Pacific Balance.' In *Indo-Pacific Maritime Security: Challenges and Cooperation,* edited by David Brewster, 84–87. Acton: National Security College.

Paliwal, Avinash. 2017. *My Enemy's Enemy – India in Afghanistan from the Soviet Invasion to the US Withdrawal.* New York: Oxford University Press.

Panda, Ankit. 2014. 'Modi Reaches Out to SAARC Leaders Ahead of Swearing-In as Prime Minister.' *The Diplomat,* 22 May. Accessed on 24 May 2014. Available at http://thediplomat.com/2014/05/modi-reaches-out-to-saarc-leadersahead-of-swearing-in-as-prime-minister.

Panda, Pramoda Kumar. 2004. *Making of India's Foreign Policy: Prime Ministers and Wars,* 20. New Delhi: Raj Publications.

Pant, Harsh V. (ed.). 2009a. *Indian Foreign Policy in a Unipolar World.* London: Routledge.

———. 2009b. 'India in the Indian Ocean: Growing Mismatch between Ambitions and Capabilities.' *Pacific Affairs* 82(2): 279–297.

———. 2009c. 'A Rising India's Search for a Foreign Policy.' *Orbis* 53(2): 250–264.

———. 2011a. 'Libya Exposes New Faultlines in Indian Foreign Policy.' *ISN Insights,* 21 April.

———. 2011b. *The US-India Nuclear Pact: Policy, Process and Great Power Politics.* Oxford: Oxford University Press.

———. 2013. 'China Rises, India Ponders: India's "Look East" Policy Gathers Momentum.' Australia India Institute, 13. Available at http://www.aii.unimelb.edu.au/sites/default/files/China%20Rises,%20India%20Ponders.pdf.

———. 2014. 'Modi's Unexpected Boost to India-US Relations.' *The Washington Quarterly* 37(3) (Fall): 93–112.

———. 2016a. *Indian Foreign Policy – An Overview.* New Delhi: Orient BlackSwan.

———. 2016b. 'Is India Developing a Strategy for Power?' *The Washington Quarterly* 38(4) (Winter): 99–113.

———. 2017. 'Pivot to the Indo-Pacific.' *The Hindu,* 12 April.

Pant, Harsh V. and Yogesh Joshi. 2017. 'Indo-US Relations under Modi: The Strategic Logic Underlying the Embrace.' *International Affairs* 93(1) (January): 133–146.

Pant, Manoj and Amit Sadhukaran. 2008. 'Does Regionalism Hinder Multilateralism: A Case Study of India.' Discussion Paper 09-03. New Delhi: Centre for International Trade and Development, SIS, JNU.

Pape, Robert A. 2005. 'Soft Balancing against the United States.' *International Security* 30(1): 7–45.

Paranjpe, A. 2013. *India's Strategic Culture: The Making of National Security Policy*, 2013. 3–10. New Delhi: Routledge.

Parrikar, Manohar. 2016. 'Speech.' Shangri-La Dialogue, 4 June. Accessed on 15 April 2018. Available at http://pib.nic.in/newsite/PrintRelease.aspx?relid=145975.

Patnaik, J. K. 2005. 'International Political Economy and Regime Analysis: A Developing-Country Perspective.' In *International Relations in India: Theorizing the Region and Nation*, edited by K. Bajpai and S. Mallavarapu, 50. New Delhi: OrientBlackswan.

Paul, T. V. 2005. *The India-Pakistan Conflict: An Enduring Rivalry*. Cambridge: Cambridge University Press.

Pehrson, Christopher J. July 2006. 'String of Pearls: Meeting the Challenge of China's Rising Power across the Asian Littoral.' Carlisle, PA: Strategic Studies Institute, US Army War College. Accessed on 14 February 2017. Available at http://www.strategicstudiesinstitute.army.mil/pdffiles/PUB721.pdf.

Pennebaker, James. 2013. 'Introduction.' In *Collective Memory of Political Events*, edited by J.W. Pennebaker, D. Paez and B. Rim. Psychology Press.

Perkovich, G. 1999. *India's Nuclear Bomb: The Impact on Global Proliferation*. Los Angeles: University of California Press.

———. 2003. 'The Measure of India: What Makes Greatness?' *Seminar* 529. Available at http://www.indiaseminar.com/2003/529/529%20george%20perkovich.htm.

Pierce, Jonathan J. 2011. 'Coalition Stability and Belief Change: Advocacy Coalitions in the U.S. Foreign Policy and the Creation of Israel, 1922–44.' *Policy Studies Journal* 39(3): 411–434.

Podeh, Elie. 2000. 'History and Memory in the Israeli Education System.' *History and Memory* 12(1): 65–100.

Prabhakar, P. 1963. 'A Re-Examination of India's Foreign Policy.' *The Indian Journal of Political Science* 24(4): 373.

Prakash, Arun. 2009. 'Assuming leadership.' *Force*, December. Accessed on 15 April 2018. Available at http://forceindia.net/FORCEINDIAOLDISSUE/arunprakash15.aspx.

Prakash, B. S. 2005. 'Strengthening and Restructuring Multilateral Institutions: A Perspective.' In *United Nations: Multilateralism and International Security*, edited by C. Uday Bhaskar, K. Santhanam, Uttam K. Sinha and Tasneem Meenai, 442–456. IDSA: Shipra.

Puri, Hardeep Singh. 2016. *Perilous Interventions: The Security Council and the Politics of Chaos*. New Delhi: HarperCollins.

Purushothaman, U. 2010. 'Shifting Perceptions of Power: Soft Power and India's Foreign Policy.' *Journal of Peace Studies* 17(2/3).

Quiros, Laura. 2010. 'Trauma, Recovery and Growth: Positive Psychological Perspectives of Posttraumatic Stress.' *Journal of Teaching in Social Work* 30(1): 118–121.

Raghavan, S. 2010. *War and Peace in Modern India*. Ranikhet: Permanent Black.

Raghavan, Srinath. 2015. 'Modi Speaks India's Mind Clearly in China.' NDTV, 15 May. Accessed on 14 September 2017. Available at http://www.ndtv.com/opinion/modi-speaks-indias-mind-clearly-in-china-763393.

Rajagopalan, R. 2005. 'Neorealist Theory and the India-Pakistan Conflict.' In *International Relations in India: Theorising the Region and the Nation*, edited by K. Bajpai, and S. Mallavarapu, 142–72. New Delhi: Orient BlackSwan.

Rajan, M. S. 1968. 'India and World Politics in the Post-Nehru Era.' *International Journal* 24(1): 155.

———. (ed.). 1997. *International and Area Studies in India*. New Delhi: Lancer.

Ralph, Jason and Adrian Gallagher. 2015. 'Legitimacy Faultlines in International Society: The Responsibility to Protect and Prosecute after Libya.' *Review of International Studies* 41(3): 553–573.

Raman, Sunil. 2016. 'The Strategic Importance of the Andaman and Nicobar Islands.' *The Diplomat*, 3 January.

Rana, A. P. 1969. 'The Intellectual Dimensions of India's Nonalignment.' *The Journal of Asian Studies* 28(2): 299–300.

Rao, Nirupama. 2013. 'America's "Asian Pivot": The View from India.' Lecture at Brown University, 5 February.

Rathbun, Brian. 2008. 'A Rose by Any Other Name: Neoclassical Realism as the Logical and Necessary Extension of Structural Realism.' *Security Studies* 17(2) (April): 294–321

Rediff.com. 2005. Text of Manmohan Singh's Speech, Oxford, UK, 12 July. Available at http://www.rediff.com/news/2005/jul/12spec.htm

———. 2013. 'British PM Regrets "Deeply Shameful" Colonial Indian Massacre.' 20 February. Available at http://www.reuters.com/article/us-britain-india-amritsar-idUSBRE91J0AA20130220.

———. 2015. 'PM Approves Deal to Buy Eight Chinese Submarines.' 2 April.

Robinson, Thomas W. 2003. 'The Sino-Soviet Border Conflict of 1969: New Evidence Three Decades Later.' In *Chinese Warfighting: The PLA Experience since 1949*, edited by Mark A. Ryan, David Michael Finkelstein and Michael A. McDevitt. Armonk, NY: M. E. Sharpe.

Roht-Arriaza, Naomi. 2006. 'The New Landscape of Transition Justice.' In *Transitional Justice in the Twenty-First Century: Beyond Truth Versus Justice*, edited by Naomi Roht-Arriaza and Javier Mariezcurrena. Cambridge, UK: Cambridge University Press.

Rose, Gideon. 1998. 'Neoclassical Realism and Theories of Foreign Policy.' *World Politics* 51(1) (October): 144–177.

Rosenau, James N. 1997. 'The Person, the Household, the Community and the Globe: Notes for a Theory of Multilateralism in a Turbulent World.' In *The New Realism: Perspectives on Multilateralism and World Order*, edited by Robert W. Cox. St. Martin's Press/United Nations University Press.

Rotberg, Robert I. and Dennis Thompson (eds). 2010. *Truth v. Justice: The Morality of Truth Commissions: The Morality of Truth Commissions*. Princeton University Press.

Rothberg, Daniel. 2015. 'Trauma, Memory, Holocaust.' In *Memory: A History*, edited by Dmitri Nikulin. Oxford University Press.

Roy, Shubhajit and Anand Mishra. 2016. 'Narendra Modi's Independence Day Speech: PM Throws down Balochistan Gauntlet.' *Indian Express*, 16 August. Accessed on 16 August 2016. Available at http://indianexpress.com/article/india/india-newsindia/pm-narendra-modi-balochistan-independence-day-congress-pakistan-salman-khurshid-2977554/.

Ruggie, J. G. 1982. 'International Regimes, Transactions, and Change: Embedded Liberalism in the Postwar Economic Order.' *International Organization* 36(2): 379–415.

———. 1993. 'Multilateralism: The Anatomy of an Institution.' In *Multilateralism Matters: The Theory and Praxis of an Institutional Form*, edited by John Gerard Ruggie, 3–36. Columbia University Press.

———. 1998. 'What Makes the World Hang Together? Neo-utilitarianism and the Social Constructivist Challenge." *International Organization* 52(4): 855–885.

Sabatier, Paul A. (ed.). 2007. *Theories of the Policy Process*. US: Westview Press.

Sabatier, Paul and Hank Jenkins-Smith (eds.). 1994. *Policy Change and Learning: An Advocacy Coalition Approach*. Boulder, CO: Westview.

Sáez, Lawrence. 2012. *The South Asian Association for Regional Cooperation (SAARC): An Emerging Collaboration Architecture*. Abingdon, Oxon: Routledge.

Sagar, R. 2009. 'State of Mind: What Kind of Power Will India Become?' *International Affairs* 85(4): 801–816.

———. 2014. '"Jiski Lathi, Uski Bhains": The Hindu Nationalist View of International Politics.' In *India's Grand Strategy: History, Theory, Cases*, edited by Kanti Bajpai, Saira Basit and V. Krishnappa, 234–257. New Delhi: Routledge.

———. 2015. 'Before Midnight: Views on International Relations, 1857-1947.' In *The Oxford Handbook of Indian Foreign Policy*, edited by David M. Malone, C. Raja Mohan and Srinath Raghavan. Oxford, UK: Oxford University Press.

Sagar, Rahul and Ankit Panda. 2015. 'Pledges and Pious Wishes: The Constituent Assembly Debates and the Myth of a "Nehruvian" Consensus.' *India Review* 14 (2): 203–220.

Saran, Shyam. 2011. 'Mapping the Indo-Pacific.' *Indian Express*, 29 October.

———. 2017. *How India Sees the World: Kautilya to the 21st Century*. New Delhi: Juggernaut Books.

Sarkar, N. K. 1967. 'Indian Foreign Policy and Economic Development.' *Economic and Political Weekly* 2(38): 1741–1742.

Sasikumar, K. 2017. 'Branding India: Constructing a Reputation for Responsibility in the Nuclear Order.' Place Branding and Public Diplomacy. Available at DOI: 10.1057/s41254016-0038-2.

Sayantan. Gupta, 2009. 'Changing Faces of International Trade: Multilateralism to Regionalism.' *Journal of International Commercial Law and Technology* 3(4): 260–273.

Schaffer, Teresita C. and Howard B. Schaffer. 2016. *India at the Global High Table: The Quest for Regional Primacy and Strategic Autonomy.* Washington, DC: Brookings.

Scott, D. 2009. 'India's "Extended Neighborhood" Concept: Power Projection for a Rising Power.' *India Review* 8(2): 107–143.

———. 2017. 'The Rise of India: UK Perspectives.' *International Affairs* 93(1): 165–188.

Sengupta, Sandeep. 2013. 'Defending "Differentiation": India's Foreign Policy on Climate Change from Rio to Copenhagen.' In *India's Foreign Policy: A Reader*, edited by Kanti Bajpai and Harsh V. Pant, 389–414. Oxford: Oxford University Press.

Shaikh, M. U. 2016. '100% FDI in Retail is "Anti-national": RSS Affiliate Group Hits out at Narendra Modi Government.' India.com, 20 June. Accessed on 30 June 2016. Available at http://www.india.com/news/india/100-fdi-in-retail-is-antinational-rss-affiliate-group-hits-out-at-narendra-modi-government-1274002/.

Shaunik, Nyantara. 2016. 'Conceptions of Security in the Regional Economic Cooperation Paradigm: The Curious Case of the Indo-Pacific.' *Jindal Journal of International Affairs* 4(1): 85–101.

Shih, C. 1988. 'National Role Conception as Foreign Policy Motivation: The Psychocultural Bases of Chinese Diplomacy.' *Political Psychology* 9(4): 599–631.

Shrivastava, B. K. and Manmohan Agarwal. 2003. 'Politics of Intervention and the Bosnia-Herzegovina Conflict.' *International Studies* 40(1): 69–84.

Shukla, A. 2016. 'Army Mute as BJP Election Posters Feature Soldier, Surgical Strikes.' *The Wire*, 9 October. Accessed on 2 February 2017. Available at: https://thewire.in/71973/army-silent-surgical-strikes-bjp-election-posters/.

Siddharth. Mallavarapu, 2009. 'Development of International Relations Theory in India: Traditions, Contemporary Perspectives and Trajectories.' *International Studies* 46 (1 and 2): 165–183.

Sidhu, W. P. S., P. B Mehta and B. Jones. 2013. *Shaping the Emerging World: India and the Multilateral Order.* Washington, D.C.: Brookings Institution Press;

Sigal, John and M. Weinfeld. 1989. *Trauma and Rebirth: Intergenerational Effects of the Holocaust.* Praeger.

Sikri, Rajiv. 2013. *Challenge and Strategy: Rethinking India's Foreign Policy.* New Delhi: Sage India.

Singer, D. J., S. Bremerand and J. Stuckey. 1972. 'Capability Distribution, Uncertainty, and Major Power War, 1820-1965.' In *Peace, War, and Numbers*, edited by B. Russett, 19–48. Beverly Hills: Sage publications.

Singer, James N. (ed.). 1969. *Linkage Politics: Essays on the Convergence of National and International Systems*, 113–126. New York: Free Press.

Singh, Abhijit. 2014. 'Rebalancing India's Maritime Posture in the Indo-Pacific.' *The Diplomat*, 5 September.

————. 2105. 'India as Maritime Security Partner in the Indo-Pacific.' In *Asian Strategic Review*, edited by S. D. Muni and Vivek Chadha, 145–165. New Delhi: IDSA.

Singh, Hemant and Karl Inderfurth. 2011. 'An Indo-Pacific Triangle of Consequence.' *Issue Brief*, 1(2) (20 December).

Singh, Jaswant. 1999. *Defending India*. New Delhi: Macmillan India.

Singh, Manmohan. 1991. 'General Budget 1991-91.' Lok Sabha Debates, 24 July.

————. 1996. 'Speech of Shri Manmohan Singh, Minister of Finance Introducing the Budget for the Year 1996–97.' New Delhi: Ministry of Finance. Accessed on 2 February 2017. Available at http://mof.gov.in/press_room/fm_speech/bs4.htm.

————. 2009. 'Prime Minister's Address.' 15th Non-Aligned Movement Summit, Sharm ElSheikh, Egypt, 15 July. Accessed on 4 October 2013. Available at http://www. satp.org/satporgtp/countries/india/document/papers/primeministersaddress_al ignedmovement_summitEgypt.htm.

Singh, S. 2013. *India in South Asia: Domestic Identity Politics and Foreign Policy from Nehru to the BJP*. London and New York: Routledge.

————. 2014. 'From a Sub-Continental Power to an Asia-Pacific Player: India's Changing Identity.' *India Review* 13(3): 187–211.

Singh, Siddharth. 2013. 'The Manmohan Doctrine.' *Live Mint*, 19 November. Available at http://www.livemint.com/Opinion/1P5ZiAwokDqqPjAZRA0EyI/ The-Manmohan-doctrine.html.

Singh, Vijaita and Josy Joseph. 2016. 'Operation Ginger: Tit-for-tat across the Line of Control.' *The Hindu*, 9 October. Accessed on 9 October 2016. Available at http:// www.thehindu.com/news/national/operation-ginger-titfortat-across-the-line- ofcontrol/article9202758.ece.

Sinha, A. and J. P. Dorschner. 2010. 'India: Rising Power or a Mere Revolution of Rising Expectations?' *Polity* 42(1): 74–99.

Sisson, Richard and Leo E. Rose. 1990. *War and Secession: Pakistan, India and the Creation of Bangladesh*, 134–153. California: University of California Press.

Skinner, Julia. 2009. 'Recovery from Trauma: A Look into the Process of Healing from Sexual Assault.' *Journal of Loss and Trauma* 14: 170–180.

Smith, Anthony D. 1986. *The Ethnic Origins of Nations*. Oxford, UK: Basil Blackwell.

————. 1996. 'Memory and Modernity.' *Nations and Nationalism* 2(3): 371–388.

Smith, Chris. 1994. *India's Ad Hoc Arsenal: Direction or Drift in Defence Policy?* 42. Oxford: Oxford University Press.

Smith, Jeff M. 2012. 'Forgotten War in the Himalayas.' *Yale Global*, 14 September.

Snyder, Glen. 1965. 'The Balance of Power and the Balance of Terror.' In *The Balance of Power*, edited by Paul Seabury, 194–201. San Francisco: Chandler.

Snyder, Richard C. and Glenn D Paige. 1958. 'The United States Decision to Resist Aggression in Korea: The Application of an Analytical Scheme.' *Administrative Science Quarterly* 3(3): 343–351.

Sood, Rakesh. 2014. 'Strategic Networking in the Indo-Pacific.' *The Hindu*. 12 September.

Sood, V. K. and Pravin Sawhney. 2003. *Operation Parakram: The War Unfinished*. New Delhi, Thousand Oaks and London: Sage Publications.

Sprout, H. and M. Sprout. 1956. 'Man-Milieu Relationship Hypotheses in the Context of International Politics.' Center of International Studies, Princeton University, Research Monograph.

Steele, B. J. 2007. *Ontological Security in International Relations*. London: Routledge.

Stevenson, H. 2011. 'India and International Norms of Climate Governance: A Constructivist Analysis of Normative Congruence Building.' *Review of International Studies* 37(3): 997–1019.

Stockholm International Peace Research Institute (SIPRI) Military Expenditure Database. Defense expenditure figures. Accessed on 15 April 2018. Available at https://www.sipri.org/databases/milex.

Stockholm International Peace Research Institute. 2015. *SIPRI Yearbook 2015*. Oxford: Oxford University Press.

Stuart. Elden. 2010. 'Land, Terrain, Territory.' *Progress in Human Geography* 34(6) (April): 799–817.

Suba Chandran, D. 2005. *Limited War: Revisiting Kargil in the Indo-Pak Conflict*. New Delhi: India Research Press.

Subrahmanyam, K. 1972. *Perspectives in Defence Planning*, 5–23. New Delhi: Abhinav Publications.

———. 1996. 'Indian Security: The Absence of Conceptual Evolution.' *India International Centre Quarterly* 23(1): 84.

Sullivan Estrada, Kate and Rajesh Basrur. 2017. *Rising India: Status and Power*. London: Routledge.

Sullivan, Kate (ed.). 2015. *Competing Visions of India in World Politics*. New York: Palgrave Macmillan.

Sundaram, Lanka. 1933. *Indians Overseas: A Study in Economic Sociology*, 4. Madras: G.A. Natesan and Co.

Sundarji, K. 1992. 'Nuclear Deterrence: Doctrine for India – I.' *Trishul* (December): 10–13.

———. 1993. *Blind Men of Hindoostan: Indo-Pak Nuclear War*, 150. New Delhi: UBS Publishers' Distributors.

Sunkara, Keshav. 2016. 'Chinese Investment in India Shoots to $2.3 Billion in Past 3 Months against $1.35 Billion in 2000–2016.' VCCircle.com, 30 August. Accessed on 13 February 2017. Available at http://www.vccircle.com/news/economy/2016/08/30/chineseinvestment-india-shoots-23-bn-past-3-months-against-135-bn-2000-16.

Suryanarayana, P. S. 2015. 'Neighbourliness in India-Sri Lanka Ties – Analysis.' *Eurasia Review*, 21 March.

Tanham, George K. 1992. *Indian Strategic Thought: An Interpretive Essay*. Santa Monica, CA: RAND.

Teitel, Ruti G. 2003. 'Transitional Justice Genealogy.' *Harvard Human Rights Journal* 16: 69–94.

Teitt, Sarah. 2016. 'Asia Pacific and South Asia.' In *The Oxford Handbook of the Responsibility to Protect*, edited by Alex Bellamy and Tim Dunne. Oxford: Oxford University Press.

Tellis, Ashley J. 2006. 'The Transforming U.S.-Indian Relationship and Its Significance for American Interests,' 1–2. Nonproliferation Policy Education Center, 16 October.

———. 2012. 'Can India Revive Nonalignment?' *Yale Global*, 28 August.

———. 2014. India-US Relations: The Rupture Is Certainly Real and Quite Tragic.' Rediff, 17 February. Availabe at http://carnegieendowment.org/2014/02/17/india-u.s.-relations-rupture-is-certainly-real-andquite-tragic/h185.

———. 2016 *India as a Leading Power*. Washington, DC: Carnegie Endowment for International Peace.

Thakur, Ramesh. 1997. 'India in the World: Neither Rich, Powerful, nor Principled.' *Foreign Affairs* 76(4): 1522.

———. 2006. *The United Nations, Peace and Security: From Collective Security to the Responsibility to Protect*. Cambridge: Cambridge University Press.

Tharoor, Shashi. 2003. 'Why America Still Needs the United Nations?' *Foreign Affairs*. Accessed on 4 April 2010. Available at http://www.foreignaffairs.com/articles/59184/shashi-tharoor/why-america-still-needs-theunited-nations.

———. 2008. 'India as a Soft Power.' *India International Centre Quarterly* 35(1): 32–45.

———. 2012. *Nehru: The Invention of India*. Arcade Publishing.

The Guardian. 2013. 'David Cameron Defends Lack of Apology for British Massacre at Amritsar.' 20 February. Available at http://www.theguardian.com/politics/2013/feb/20/david-cameron-amritsar-massacre-india.

The Hindu. 1999. 'India Not to Engage in a Nuclear Arms Race: Jaswant,' p. 14. Interview on 29 November.

———. 2015. 'Queen May Face Legal Challenge over Kohinoor.' 8 November. Available at http://www.thehindu.com/news/queen-may-face-legal-challenge-over-kohinoor/article7858454.ece.

———. 2016. 'The Margarita Mirror.' 13 September. Accessed on 10 January 2017. Available at http://www.thehindu.com/opinion/op-ed/The-Margarita-mirror/article14634932.ece.

The Independent. 2015. 'Colonial mindset harming British trade with India.' 26 October. Available at http://www.independent.co.uk/news/uk/home-news/uk-india-relations-colonial-mindset-harming-britishtrade-with-india-a6709881.html.

Thomas, Raju G. C. 1979. 'Nonalignment and Indian Security: Nehru's Rationale and Legacy.' *Journal of Strategic Studies* 2(2): 158.

Tony Blair. 1999. 'The Blair Doctrine.' Transcript of speech by Rt. Hon. Tony Blair. Chicago, 22 April.

U.S. Department of State. 'USAID and PL–480, 1961–1969.' Office of the Historian, U.S. Department of State. Available at https://history.state.gov/milestones/1961-1968/pl-480.

UNGA Resolution. 1946. 'Treatment of Indians in the Union of South Africa.' 8 December.

———. 2005. World Summit Outcome, A/60/L.1, 15 September, para. 138, 31. Available at http://responsibilitytoprotect.org/world%20summit%20outcome%20doc%202005(1).pdf.

———. 2009. 'Implementing the Responsibility to Protect.' Report of the Secretary-General, A/63/677, 12 January, para. 10(a), p. 7 and para. 10(b), 8. Available at http://responsibilitytoprotect.org/implementing%20the%20rtop.pdf.

United Nations. 2003. *A More Secure World: Our Shared Responsibility*. High-Level Panel on Threats, Challenges and Change.

———. 2015. *International Migration Report, 2015*. Accessed on 12 March 2017. Available at http://www.un.org/en/development/desa/population/migration/publications/migrationreport/docs/MigrationReport2015.pdf.

Upadhyay, Shreya. November 2014. 'The Indo-Pacific and the Indo-US Relations. Geopolitics of Cooperation.' *Issue Brief* (IPCS), 562. IPCS.

Vanaik, A. 2005. '1945 to 1989: The Realist Paradigm and Systemic Duality.' In *International Relations in India: Bringing Theory Back Home*, edited by Kanti Bajpai and Siddharth Mallavarapu, 413. New Delhi: Orient Longman.

Varadarajan, L. 2004. 'Constructivism, Identity and Neoliberal (In)Security.' *Review of International Studies* 30(3): 319–341

———. 2010. *The Domestic Abroad: Diasporas in International Relations*. New York: Oxford University Press.

Vertzberger, Yascov Y. I. 1984. *Misperception in Foreign Policy Making: The Sino-Indian Conflict, 1959–1962*. Colorado: Westview Press.

Vijayachandra Naidu, G. 2014. '"Indo-Pacific" As a New Template of Analysis.' *Indian Foreign Affairs Journal* 9(2): 102–107.

Virk, Kudrat. 2013. 'India and the Responsibility to Protect: A Tale of Ambiguity.' *Global Responsibility to Protect* 5(1): 59, 82.

Vivekanandan, J. 2014. 'Strategy, Legitimacy and the Imperium.' In *India's Grand Strategy: History, Theory, Cases*, edited by Kanti Bajpai, Saira Basit, V. Krishnappa, 79. New Delhi: Routledge.

Wagner, C. 2005. 'From Hard Power to Soft Power? Ideas, Interaction, Institutions, and Images in India's South Asia Policy.' Working Paper No. 26. Heidelberg Papers in South Asian and Comparative Politics.

Wall Street Journal. 2015. 'Should Britain Pay Reparations to India?' 24 July. Available at http://blogs.wsj.com/indiarealtime/2015/07/24/should-britain-pay-reparations-to-india-shashi-tharoor-saysyes-narendra-modi-praises-him-what-do-you-think/.

———. 2016. 'Read an Edited Transcript of The Wall Street Journal's Interview With Indian Prime Minister Narendra Modi.' Interview on 26 May. Available at http://blogs.wsj.com/indiarealtime/2016/05/26/read-an-edited-transcript-of-the-wall.

Waltz, Kenneth N. 1979. *Theory of International Politics*. Reading, MA: Addison-Wesley.

———. 2000. 'Structural Realism after the Cold War.' *International Security* 25(1): 8–9

———. 2010. *Theory of International Politics*. Illinois: Waveland Press.

Wang, Zheng. 2008. 'National Humiliation, History Education, and the Politics of Historical Memory: Patriotic Education Campaign in China.' *International Studies Quarterly* 52(4): 783–806.

Weldes, J. 1998. 'Bureaucratic Politics: A Critical Constructivist Assessment.' *Mershon International Studies Review* 42(2): 216–225.

———. 1999. *Constructing National Interests: The United States and the Cuban Missile Crisis*. Minneapolis and London: University of Minnesota Press.

Weldes, J. et al. (eds). 1999. *Cultures of Insecurity: States, Communities and the Production of Danger*. Minneapolis: University of Minnesota Press.

Wendt, A. 1992. 'Anarchy Is What States Make of It: The Social Construction of Power Politics.' *International Organization* 46(2): 391–425.

———. 1999. *Social Theory of International Politics*. Cambridge: Cambridge University Press.

Wendt, Alexander E. 1987. 'The Agent-Structure Problem in International Relations Theory.' *International Organization* 41(3) (Summer edition): 338. USA: MIT Press.

Wertsch, James. 2002. *Voices of Collective Remembering*. Cambridge University Press.

Wheeler, Nicholas J. 2000. *Saving Strangers: Humanitarian Intervention in International Society*. Oxford: Oxford University Press.

Widmaier, W. W. 2005. 'The Democratic Peace is What States Make of It: A Constructivist Analysis of the US-Indian "Near-Miss" in the 1971 South Asian Crisis.' *European Journal of International Relations* 11(3): 431–455.

Wiener, A. 2014. *A Theory of Contestation*. Berlin: Springer.

Winters, L. Alan. 1996. 'Regionalism versus Multilateralism.' Policy Research Working Paper No. 1687. Washington, DC: World Bank.

Wohlforth, W. C. 1993. *The Elusive Balance: Power and Perceptions during the Cold War*. Ithaca: Cornell University Press.

Wohlstetter, Albert. December 1958. 'The Delicate Balance of Terror.' Revised. Document No. P-1472. Santa Monica, CA: RAND.

———. 1959. 'The Delicate Balance of Terror.' *Foreign Affairs* 37(2) (January): 211–234.

———. 1961. 'Nuclear Sharing: NATO and the N+1 Country.' *Foreign Affairs* 39(3) (April): 355–387, 364.

Wong, Erebus, Lau Kin Chi, Sit Tsui and Wen Tiejun. 2017. 'One Belt, One Road: China's Strategy for a New Global Financial Order.' *Monthly Review* 68(8). Available at https://monthlyreview.org/2017/01/01/one-belt-one-road/.

World Bank.'World Bank Group Historical Chronology.' World Bank Archives. Accessed on 15 April 2018. Available at http://web.worldbank.org/WBSITE/EXTERNAL/ EXTABOUTUS/EXTARCHIVES/0,contentMDK:20035657~menuPK:56 307~pagePK:36726~piPK:437378~theSitePK:29506,00.html.

———. Military spending and GDP data. Accessed on 15 April 2018. Available at http://data.worldbank.org/.

Wright, Quincy. 1956. 'Is Discussion Intervention?' *The American Journal of International Law* 50(1): 102–110.

Xuetong, Yan, 2011. 'From a Unipolar to a Bipolar World System: The Future of the Global Power Dynamic.' *The Global Times*, 30 December.

Zadek, Simon. 2007. 'Collaborative Governance: The New Multilateralism for the 21st Century.' Accessed on 4 April 2016. Available at http://www.zadek.net/ collaborative-governance.

Zamindar, Vazira Fazila-Yacoobali. 2007. *The Long Partition and the Making of Modern South Asia: Refugees, Boundaries, Histories.* New York: Columbia University Press.

Zürn, Michael and Benjamin Faude. 2013. 'On Fragmentation, Differentiation, and Coordination.' *Global Environmental Politics* 13(3): 119–130.

Contributors

Itty Abraham is head of the Department of Southeast Asian Studies at the National University of Singapore. His most recent book is *How India Became Territorial: Foreign Policy, Diaspora, Geopolitics* (Stanford University Press, 2014).

Rajesh Basrur is a professor of international relations and coordinator of the South Asia Programme at the S. Rajaratnam School of International Studies (RSIS), Nanyang Technological University, Singapore. His work focuses on South Asian security, global nuclear politics and international relations theory. Hs recent books include (with Kate Sullivan De Estrada) *Rising India: Status and Power* (Routledge, 2017), *South Asia's Cold War* (Routledge, 2008) and *Minimum Deterrence and India's Nuclear Security* (Stanford University Press, 2006). He is currently preparing a book manuscript on the domestic politics of India's foreign and security policies.

Priya Chacko is a senior lecturer in International Politics in the Department of Politics and International Studies at the University of Adelaide, Australia. She is the author of *Indian Foreign Policy: The Politics of Postcolonial Identity from 1947 to 2004* (Routledge, 2012) and the editor of *New Regional Geopolitics in the Indo-Pacific* (Routledge, 2016). She has also published numerous articles in journals such as *Modern Asian Studies, European Journal of International Relations and Journal of Contemporary Asia* and *Journal of International Relations and Development*.

Ian Hall is a professor of international relations and the acting director of the Griffith Asia Institute at Griffith University, Brisbane, Australia. He is the editor of *The Engagement of India: Strategies and Responses* (Georgetown University Press, 2014). His articles on Indian foreign and security policy have been published in various journals, including *Asian Survey, International Affairs* and *Nonproliferation Review*. He is currently working on an Australian Research Council funded project on Indian international thought since 1964.

Arndt Michael is a senior lecturer in the Department of Political Science, University of Freiburg, Germany. He teaches classes on international relations theory, India's foreign and security policy and emerging regional powers. He is the author of the multi-award winning book *India's Foreign Policy and Regional Multilateralism* (Palgrave Macmillan, 2013), co-editor of *Indien Verstehen* (Springer, 2016) and has published extensively on India's foreign policy, regional cooperation in South Asia and India in Africa in journals such as *Harvard Asia Quarterly*, *India Quarterly* and *India Review*.

Manjari Chatterjee Miller is an associate professor of international relations at the Pardee School of Global Studies at Boston University, USA. Miller works on ideas, security and foreign policy in international relations with a focus on South and East Asia. She specializes in the foreign policy of rising powers India and China. She is the author of *Wronged by Empire: Post-imperial Ideology and Foreign Policy in India and China* (Stanford University Press, 2013). In addition to academic journals, Miller has published in policy and media outlets including *Foreign Affairs*, the *New York Times*, *The Diplomat*, *The Hindu* and the *Christian Science Monitor*. She is currently working on her second book on historical and contemporary rising powers.

Rohan Mukherjee is an assistant professor of political science at Yale-NUS College, Singapore. His research focuses on rising powers and their impact on regional and international security. His writings on India's national security and foreign policy have appeared in journals such as *Survival*, *Global Governance*, *International Affairs* and *International Journal* as well as in edited volumes by Stanford University Press, Brookings Press and Oxford University Press.

Avinash Paliwal is a lecturer in diplomacy and public policy at the School of Oriental and African Studies (SOAS), University of London, UK. Specializing in the strategic affairs of South Asia and Afghanistan, he holds a doctorate in international relations from King's College London and an economics degree from the University of Delhi, India. Prior to joining academia he worked as a journalist and foreign affairs analyst in New Delhi.

Harsh V. Pant is Director of Research at Observer Research Foundation, New Delhi, and Professor of International Relations at King's College London. He is also a non-resident fellow with the Wadhwani Chair in US–India Policy Studies at the Center for Strategic and International Studies, Washington, DC. His current research is focused on Asian security issues. His most recent books include *Indian Nuclear Policy* (Oxford University Press, 2018), *The US Pivot and Indian Foreign Policy* (Palgrave Macmillan, 2016), *Handbook* *of Indian Defence Policy* (Routledge, 2016) and *The US–India Nuclear Pact: Policy, Process and Great Power Politics* (Oxford University Press, 2011). Pant is a columnist for the *Diplomat* and writes regularly for various media outlets including the *Japan Times*, the *Wall Street Journal*, the *National* (UAE) and the *Indian Express*.

David Scott is a consultant, analyst and writer (www.d-scott.com/ publications) on Indo-Pacific international relations, with specific studies on the appearance of the term 'Indo-Pacific' in American, Australian and Indian strategic discourse. Having retired from teaching at Brunel University, UK, in 2015, he currently lectures at the NATO Defense College in Rome, Italy, and the Baltic Defence College in Tallinn, Estonia.

Julie M. Super is a political science PhD student at George Mason University's Schar School of Policy and Government, with a focus on comparative politics and international relations. She holds a master's degree in conflict, security and development from the Department of War Studies at King's College London and a bachelor's degree in history from Truman State University, USA.

Latha Varadarajan is a professor of political science and the director of the International Security and Conflict Resolution programme at San Diego State University, USA. She is the author of *The Domestic Abroad: Diasporas in International Relations* (Oxford University Press, 2010) and *Imperialism Past and Present* (with Emanuele Saccarelli, Oxford University Press, 2015). Her articles on transnationalism, nationalism and imperialism have been published in journals including *The European Journal of International Relations*, *International Relations*, *New Political Science* and *Review of International Studies*.

Index

Index

293

Menon, Shivshankar 10, 58
migrants, Sikh 241
MILAN naval exercises 197
military cooperations 2, 156
Minow, Martha 74
Misra 115
Mitchell, David 117
Miyazawa, Yoichi 205–206
Modi, Narendra 1, 6, 49, 59–60, 67, 70,
127, 140, 145, 153–154, 158; Doctrine
of 4, for India First 106; meeting
Trump 144
Möller, Miriam 186–187
Morgenthau, H. 35, 51
Muddipi, Himadeep 52
Mughal Empire 70, 78
Mukherjee, Pranab 57, 205
Mukti Bahini movement 115
multifaceted memory 72
multilateral interventionism 54
multilateralism 9, 39, 52–53, 149–154,
156–158, 160–166; global 152–157;
India and 164–166; regional 157–164
Muppidi, H. 52, 54
Musharraf, Pervez 226
Muslim invaders 89
Myanmar 101, 159, 197, 228

Nandy, Ashis 37
Naoroji, Dadabhai 70, 93
Narang, Vipin 114
Narasimha Rao, P.V. 6, 244; Doctrine
of 106
Narayanan, K.R. 31
Narlikar, A. 154
Nasser of Egypt 85–86
National Council for Educational
Research and Training (NCERT) 76,
78–79
National Curriculum Framework
(NCF) 76

National Democratic Alliance (NDA)
54, 158
national: geobody 86, 88, 90, 100, 102;
geography 89, 92–93; identity 71–73,
76, 79, 138; security 3, 9, 31, 35–36,
86, 89
National Maritime Foundation (NMF)
198–199
National Security Advisory Board in
August, Draft Nuclear Doctrine of
220
nationalization 243, 247; of geography
88, 91
nation-state, re-making of 241–248
NATO intervention 174. *See also under*
Serbia
Nayyar, Deepak 161–162
Nazism 72
NDA government 58, 127; security
policy of 116
Nehru, Jawaharlal 30, 32, 34–36,
69–70, 85, 88, 106, 117, 128–132,
178, 241–242; foreign policy of 243;
government of 242;
Nehruvianism 69, 71, 86, 242, 247
Nepal 10, 90, 139, 158–159
Neutral Nations Repatriation
Commission in Korea 153
New Development Bank 156
New Zealand 197, 203
Newman, Edward 163
Nizamani, Haider 53
Non-Aligned Movement (NAM) 37,
129–135, 149, 152–53, 160, 165, 179;
summit 157
Nonalignment 2.0 11, 127, 137–140
non-alignment 3–4, 7, 11, 27, 30, 35–38,
58–59, 127–133, 136–138, 144–145,
152–153; idealism of 69; Nehru-
inspired policy of 150
non-proliferation 135